SUCCESSFUL DEER HUNTING

by SAM FADALA

DBI BOOKS, INC., NORTHFIELD, ILL.

STAFF

EDITOR
Robert S. L. Anderson

ASSISTANT TO THE EDITOR
Lilo Anderson

PHOTOGRAPHY
Nancy Fadala

COVER PHOTOGRAPHY
John Hanusin

PRODUCTION MANAGER
Pamela J. Johnson

PUBLISHER
Sheldon L. Factor

DEDICATION

This book is for John Doyle and Jim and Seymour Levy, great deer hunters and teachers, and for my friend, the late Eddie Stockwell, holder of the world record desert whitetail.

ISBN 0-910676-64-X   Library of Congress Catalog Card #83-072342

About Our Inside Covers

Over 40 years ago, a young, visionary engineer named Joyce Hornady quietly decided to get into the bullet-making business. Today, the Hornady Pacific lineup of bullets, reloading presses and Frontier ammunition has a following among knowledgeable shooters and hunters that's second to none.

Our inside front cover features Hornady bullets, the product that eventually brought Joyce Hornady his well-deserved fame and recognition. Available in calibers ranging from 17 to 45, the Hornady line of bullets for reloaders is indeed extensive. It suffices to say that hunters worldwide have used the Hornady product to take everything from prairie dogs to pachyderms—it's that simple. One of the most popular hunting bullets ever produced for the hunter who rolls his own is the Hornady Interlock, available in all popular hunting calibers and weights. (A sectional drawing of a Hornady bullet, complete with the Interlock feature, can be seen on our inside front cover.) What makes the Interlock design so valuable to hunters is the fact that the bullet jacket features an integral core-gripping ring that prevents core/jacket separation. This, and other Hornady Bullet construction features, all add up to maximum hunting-bullet performance. Some hunters used to say you couldn't "buy" that sort of performance. So much for the old days.

Our inside back cover features a selection of Frontier cartridges, a line of handgun and rifle ammunition that's built a solid following with shooters and hunters alike. In the old days, Frontier ammo was packaged in black-and-orange boxes and sold for prices that were downright easy to afford. Today, Frontier ammo sports distinctive red, white and black packaging, is still competitively priced, and the performance is even better. How? The answer lies in the fact that Frontier cartridges are loaded for reliability with Hornady bullets.

It must also be said that the Frontier line of ammo has developed a "cult following" among those hunters and shooters who demand top accuracy from factory ammo.

CONTENTS

CONTENTS

You Are the Deer Hunter

YOU are the deer hunter. You are the man or woman who works the coverts for whitetails, who walks the ridges in search of the mule deer, who finds and harvests the game and gets the meat back from the field. And you are good at it. I have seen you time and again. They talk about "The American Hunter." I'll tell you about the American hunter. He's a hell of a good shot. He knows his deer firearms inside and out. He's in better physical condition than the average guy on the street. He does not "hunt to get away from it all." He hunts because he loves to hunt. He does not litter the landscape with trash, this "average" hunter.

And this is his book. The book is not meant to toss information down from "on high." It is meant to share information. The deer hunter will agree with some of the ideas in this book, and he will disagree with others or he will have a better way. That is as it should be. I would not want him to agree all the time. I'm still learning about deer and deer hunting. I will be until my deer hunting days are over. No one knows all about deer hunting.

I have had uncommon good luck in the deer fields over the past 30 years because I have recognized the superior skills of many of my hunting partners. I have tried to learn from my betters. And this book is a compilation of information taught to me by many and now passed on to the reader for him to use, disregard or improve upon. We talk about deer hunting in three major ways in this book. We talk about finding out where the deer are and we talk about finding the deer after we have located his habitat. And we also talk about harvesting that deer after we have found him.

And there are the smaller points shuffled in among the major ones like individual cards in a deck. These are the game care tips, tips on what to wear and a few safety suggestions. We hope that you, the deer hunter, find our book to be truly your book. I use the term "we" instead of "I" in this case, because this book belongs to those hunters who took time to show me a better path. And now good luck and more than luck, good hunting, for hunting is much more than luck alone. It is a combination of many skills and the successful deer hunter is the one who combines those skills into one purposeful goal, the clean harvesting and careful use of this fantastic renewable resource, the deer of our land.

chapter 1
The Most Popular Big Game

THE UBIQUITOUS DEER is almost everywhere on the North American continent. On the low desert, deer tracks mark the meandering washes of dry sand. In the deep forest, the deer makes a successful home. Deep swamps of the South are often dwelling places for deer. And along the heavily vegetated coastline of Alaska, a deer can be found walking over the same grounds frequented by the mighty grizzly bear. The desert mountains hold deer, and the cultivated fields of the flatlands secret its kind too. Ubiquitous—our deer is the most popular big game animal on this continent.

America, and I am including Mexico and Canada in this general term, has been a stronghold for the deer and the deer hunter for centuries. The deer was important in the distant past, and it is still important on our continent today. Trying to assign a number to deer or to deer hunters is difficult at best. There are 26 million souls who annually go forth with hunting in mind, and a large number of this throng hunts for deer.

Each state has its own unique deer population, of course, but we can say in general that the deer is doing quite well for itself wherever it lives. Hunting is not allowed wholesale. Hunting for deer is a matter of the law, and the law is a matter of tags. Only so many tags are issued yearly, and these are allowed only on the basis of sound game management. We are not only limited by the number of licenses allowed for deer hunting, but also by the time of the year we may hunt. And yet, in many areas, one permit per hunter is not enough. The deer themselves may require more harvesting than what would otherwise be normal. Therefore, when the layman sees a great many permits allowed for deer, he immediately suggests that hunters are going to "wipe out" the race. No way. Hunters are not going to reduce the standing annual numbers of deer as long as there continue to be laws established by governing bodies who understand the biology of the animal.

The deer, in fact, is so widespread and so healthy in its continuance that we find some states virtually loaded with that game animal, not to mention the hunters who pursue them. Many hunters jokingly say that Pennsylvania represents the fourth largest standing "army" in the world if we consider the hunting licenses sold in that state alone. It's no joke. Following China, Russia and the United States, there is the state of Pennsylvania, with hunters so strong in numbers that they do, indeed, represent the fourth largest standing army in the world!

And yet the deer thrives. The deer lives on because it is a renewable resource. It is a crop. When totally unhunted, the normal cycle for a deer herd is boom and bust. Many studies have been made to relate this truth. The preservationist has little understanding of such events as the Kaibab die-off, where the huge deer herd destroyed its own habitat and perished by the thousands. Such die-offs seem impossible because sentiment has taken the place of science.

I had a chance to witness a die-off. I was a resident of Arizona, where I grew up in the 1950s, and I lived fairly close to the well-known Chiricahua Mountains of the southern part of that state. The deer were thick! It was wonderful. We could drive out on almost any evening and see them eating along the roadsides. All of us became angry when the game department suggested there was something wrong with this situation. Why, they went so far as to suggest a doe hunt. We were incensed.

Hunters have always felt that they were the only cause of deer mortality. Why they have felt this way is hard to say, but it is true. When the game department wanted to issue a couple hundred doe tags for our area, we cried out against this idea. "All the deer will be wiped out." That was the logic. Well, a lot of the deer were wiped out. But hunters had little or nothing to do with it.

Unfortunately, the game department did get its few hundred doe tags issued. That was a political mistake. They should have used their time and resources printing up pamphlets which explained that a deer crash was in the making, and these should have been given out instead of doe tags. When the mighty Chiricahua herd did fall, of course hunters cried out that the doe tags caused it.

I remember the change. Where I had seen deer eating by the side of the road, even in midday toward the end, there were no deer now. Even as a youth I should have reasoned that the intelligent whitetail of the Southwest,

Frederick Remington, the famous artist, did this work in honor of Jim Bridger, the well-known beaver trapper of the Far West of 19th century America. Modern hunters have continued a tradition of harvesting deer to the table.

(Left) John Fadala poses with a nice buck taken on the side of a mountain in high desert terrain. Deer hunting can be an important part of learning the ways of the outdoors.

a game animal praised as smartest of all North American game by Jack O'Connor, would not be standing in broad daylight chewing weeds by the side of the road if things were right. They had never done that before. Why were they doing it now? But reason did not enter into the picture. Sentiment did. We loved seeing the deer everywhere, like mayflies after a hatch. But the deer were starving to death.

The few deer cropped by the hunt made no difference at all to the whole picture. Soon, the crash came. But we still did not believe what we were told. Why, if the deer had truly perished, were their bodies not lying about everywhere? Finally, a few dogs were brought into the area. The hounds had no trouble in locating carcass after carcass. The deer did not die along the roads and trails. They died in the thicker places. And while we could not locate the bodies, the dogs could and did.

A very fine booklet was prepared by an Arizona game

This particular field held a single herd of deer numbering 49 head. That, of itself, is neither here nor there. However, similar herds of deer were seen up and down the road. In fact, author and son counted 110 head of deer within a 1-mile distance. The ranchers in the area were adamant about holding hunting of these deer to a minimum because they wanted to retain the herds in high numbers.

This is a perfect example of a deer crash in the making. Note the browse in the foreground, ample it would seem to support large herds of deer. However, in checking into the field, there were many plants which had been chewed back almost to destruction. The deer in this area may be seen feeding at all times of the day and night. The 110 count mentioned above was taken during the noon hour.

biologist on the subject of the crash. In fact, two very prominent biologists collaborated and shared information to complete the writing. The booklet is called *"Boom and Bust, The Story of the Chiricahua Whitetail Deer."* It is written by Jerry Day and Steve Gallizioli. Hunters should read such material. The truly expert deer hunter should know as much about his favorite game as he can digest.

The October 1967 booklet concludes, "Hunter and non-hunter alike must be aware of and accept the necessity for keeping deer herds within the range carrying capacity. They should also understand that frequently the only way this can be accomplished is by shooting does as well as bucks. History has demonstrated that nothing else works." (p. 12) However, in spite of the information which scientists have studied and the data these scientists have provided for us, even hunters prefer the myths to the facts.

The life of the deer is not a very long one. It is susceptible to many pitfalls. It is quite true that hunters can help in the important task of keeping a deer herd within the proper numbers for a given area. However, hunters are by far *not* the major factor in the lowering of deer numbers. In fact, motor vehicles take more deer annually than hunters take. Considering the value of a deer for meat and so much more, it seems a shame that this is true, but true it is.

Gene Lyons, in his article, "Politics in the Woods," *Harper's* magazine, July 1978, says that, "More deer by far are killed by automobiles than by all the hunters in

Kenn Oberrecht of Coos Bay, Oregon, with a small buck. Hunting deer can take a person into areas of small human population where the outdoors becomes a very meaningful experience.

Christendom.'' (p. 38) This is true. The statement has been proved. And yet hunters do not understand game management principles any better than non-hunters or anti-hunters understand these principles. When a game department tries to keep the deer herd in check by allowing a larger harvest, it is the hunter's cry which goes up first and loudest. Hunters, you see, still think of themselves as the only force in deer harvesting.

A general rule of thumb allows for a herd harvest of 40 percent annually in the areas where I live. That is to say that if 40 percent of the herd is taken each and every year by whatever means, then the deer herd number will remain about the same, for the sheer force of procreation will replace that 40 percent loss. Since the 40 percent includes all forms of deer population decrease, to mean winter kill, disease and even accident, then the hunter cannot be allowed to crop 40 percent of a deer herd each year. The game department must decide first how many deer will drop to ''natural causes,'' and then allow the hunter to take up the slack.

The hunter should be aware of ''deer facts'' if he is going to understand the fine points of his hunt. In fact, he'll be a better hunter for knowing more about his game, including its life cycle. The ranks of the hunter grow ever wider, and this is why we have offered our book. Successful deer hunting is more than bagging a buck, much more, and while our aim, certainly, is to help hunters claim a fair share of the deer harvest, we hope to do much more. We hope to arm him with facts that will uplift the entire sport for him.

Nature is a tough old dame. Every winter 80 percent of the rabbits will perish, and not by the hand of the hunter. The quail chicks that happen to be born in a rainy season will die in large numbers. Drought will claim its toll. Disease will collect its number. And yet, the deer herds of America have remained strong enough to be harvested annually with no ill effect to total numbers.

They will continue to do so as long as we leave habitat. If we want to reduce deer numbers, the best way to do so is to pave the deer range with asphalt. Then man will have accomplished a complete harvest. At this point, the hunter, even when armed with the best tools of the harvest, will never reduce the deer herds of America to dangerously low levels as long as he is obliged to operate within the rules and framework set down for him by the game managers of each state.

In fact, the number one cause of wildlife demise in our country is not from hunting, not even from automobiles or general pollution, but from the raising of vegetables. I am friend to the farmer, and he is certainly of utmost importance in our culture. However, we have to admit that the clearing of the land for crops has taken away much wildlife domain. When I fly east from my home state of Wyoming, I leave behind the vast herds of antelope and find instead vast ''herds'' of wheat. That is as it should be and must be. America has to be fed. But we also have to understand what is going on around

Deer hunting is much more than the harvest of game. This setting is one example of the outdoor environment waiting the hunter of deer.

A couple bucks hang in camp ready for skinning and care. The author took his with one shot from a .54-caliber muzzle-loading rifle.

Author with a buck taken at only 10 paces, jumped at only 5 paces. The buck was bedded on a high ridge with only its antlers and part of its head showing and it was sighted with the aid of the binocular. Buck was taken with a .54 muzzleloader.

us, and as deer hunters we need to be aware of the facts—the truth. When DDT was invented, it was to save vegetables and no one even considered that the long-range effect could be harmful for the egg of an eagle.

This is our world. And we each view it from the individuality of our own eyes. The deer hunt, for me, is a harvest, not a kill. The clearing of the land, in my eyes, was needed for our people. Hopefully, with a more stable population, we need not clear away too much habitat again. We will have enough growing land to feed our population.

Time and again, I hear arguments which suggest that anyone who eats meat has no right to malign the hunter who takes a deer with a swift bullet. And this allows for the vegetarian to claim himself blameless because he eats no meat. But thousands of animals must die for his vegetables to grow and millions of acres of land which once were homes for wild animals are now fields for vegetables. So, each of us must understand that we are a part of a cycle and our presence on the planet will mean that something else is deprived of a spot.

If we keep it all in reasonable check, with the emphasis on *reasonable,* the entire process becomes a smoother flowing one. In some cases, we hunters can act to harvest the way the farmer does, on an annual basis, taking some of the renewable resource, not too much of it, not too little.

American deer hunting today remains an important harvest. Millions of dollars in meat value are cropped from the numerous herds of deer our land holds in trust for us. But more important than the dollar value is the hunt itself, for there can be no price tag placed upon the joys of taking to the field and procuring a little venison on your own, "making meat," as they used to say in the West of early America.

Successful deer hunting does not always mean bagging a buck, but it sure is nice to come home with the meat some of the time. Hopefully, this book will help the hunter in that endeavor. And with that we wish the reader happy hunting and good luck.

chapter 2

Bagging a Buck

I WANT TO talk about luck. In my opinion, luck or chance plays a roll in every deer harvest. However, I think it is very defeating to the hunter when he considers luck the *major* factor in bagging a buck. Again, I do believe in chance. Even when I have scouted hard, and I know where the deer are and I find them again right where I last saw them, I feel that luck played a minor role in the harvest. After all, had chance gone against me instead of in favor of me, the weather might have changed, and the herd might have had reason to move off. Or I may not have been able to reach the right spot because snow closed the road. So, luck is there, all right, and as they say, "luck is like health; you always have it." You can be in good health or you can be in bad health, but you have to be in some degree of health, and the same goes for luck; it can be good luck or bad luck, but it's there.

What I aim to do, however, is to reduce the luck factor in my own deer hunting so that chance no longer holds sway. I like to feel that my odds of getting a deer, if I follow a set of rules and principles, are excellent at all times, and that if I fail, that is bad luck, not bad hunting practice. I'd hate to toss hunting practice to the wind and rely on luck alone to fill my freezer. Therefore, I look at successful deer hunting as comprised of three major parts.

The three major parts are: First there must be deer in the area. Second, a hunter has to find the deer. Third,

the hunter must be able to harvest the deer once he has found it. I know this is simplification of the worst sort, but I think it is also a truth. Let me relate a hunt that brought these three principles into play.

I recall being dropped off in a hunting area I had never before seen in my life. The huge range was located 12, 4-wheel-drive miles from a major road, and our path to the ranch was actually awash for much of the way. We simply drove up this big cut in the earth with its soft sand base for miles and miles, finally leaving it to go cross-country for a distance and then onto a wagon road. I was surprised to find such remoteness and thrilled at the prospect of being able to hunt the place for the better part of a month.

In the main, the object of the chase was whitetail deer, not the big eastern or Virginia variety, but a smaller fellow, cousin to the larger kind. I had hunted near the area once before, but in the specific spot we had chosen, the deer had regressed in size, so we were told. I did not then, nor do I now, have the facts on this situation; however, we hunted a whitetail deer the natives of the area called a "cabrito." It was so darn tiny that I think a good-sized German shephard dog would outweigh some of the specimens we saw.

Asking about the cabrito, we were told that the deer was in fact the standard Sonoran whitetail, but that its size was diminished from overgrazing by the badly over-

bait and catching a single one is remote. The same goes for deer. If a huge area holds but a few deer, our mathematical odds of being in the same area as the deer, plus seeing that deer, grow small.

Therefore, one reason my hunt went well was the fact of deer numbers. There were enough to give good odds, not great odds, but good ones. But even that would not be sufficient in bagging a deer. What else was going for me?

I had asked the cowboys where they had seen deer. That sure is basic. But how many times will a deer hunter strike out without asking for help? There are two places to go for truly valuable advice as to "where the deer are." The first is the game department. The second is either ranchers/farmers or other hunters who may know the area. That is what I had done in this case. There were no statistics available on the area as far as deer were concerned; however, the cowboy-hunters had some ideas to share, and I listened to those ideas.

Armed with a general knowledge of where the deer

One of the very best means of locating good deer territory is to "ask the rancher." Ranchers and farmers may or may not be hunters, but in their daily course of activities they often see game and note its patterns. They also are well aware of crop damage and can often show a hunter to fields which are being used by deer as part of their diet.

This blacktail buck was taken in Wasco County, Oregon. Although the terrain is somewhat thickly vegetated, the hunter used a scope-sighted (variable) in a bolt-action rifle for his harvest, which supports the fact that a hunter should use what works for him best. The blacktail rack is not as large, on the average, as the mule deer rack; however, the blacktail deer is an impressive big game trophy.

populated herds. Again, I am reporting what I was told. I do not know for a fact that the cabrito was a diminished western whitetail or another type of deer altogether. But in asking around, we were directed to hunt another area where the deer were still large and healthy.

That is how I ended up in an area I had never set eyes on. My host could not stay with me, so I had the whole place to myself. And yet, ranging from my base camp, I was able to harvest my deer, seeing a number of bucks and selecting one that actually was large enough to "make the book," which was verified later by measurement.

I thought little of it, that hunt so very long ago, but in fact, how was success accomplished? Well, being a remote area, the deer were just thick and plenty stupid, right? In fact, the deer were not thick, and they were anything but stupid. The game was hunted by locals to some degree, though lack of ammo kept this activity at a minimum. The deer were their usual selves, damn wild and secretive as western whitetails are. I gave it little consideration until this book came to mind, but all of the principles of hunting deer were carefully adhered to or I feel my larder would have gone empty.

First, I was indeed in an area that had deer. Secondly, while the population was not terribly high, there were enough deer to give me a reasonable chance of seeing one. This is a very important factor. Deer population in terms numbers per acre, are not unlike fish numbers when it comes to being able to find a deer to catch a fish. We know that we can fish a pond down to a certain number of fish and then our mathematical chance of tossing in

were hanging around, I set out. Looking back, I know exactly how I bagged my buck even after passing up a number of other bucks I could have shot. I used many of the tips and tricks which will be explained in this book, and I had a good "shooting iron," carefully sighted in with my best handloads, plus I had practiced with the rifle so I could shoot it fairly well.

The three major elements of successful deer hunting were riding with me—I was in decent deer country, armed with a basic knowledge of my game, its habits and habitat. I used deliberate methods to locate my quarry, and I stalked within range while carrying tools that were proper for the hunt. Lucky? You bet I was lucky. I could have been laid up in camp with a case of Montezuma's revenge or a broken foot. But I wasn't. So I was lucky. All luck? Not on your life. Methods and good tools were a lot stronger "medicine" than luck on this hunt. It is amazing that the more we learn about our game and gear and the harder we work, the luckier we get.

Bill Fadala poses with his mule deer buck, a buck which was in the velvet in October. The buck was a stag, a term sometimes used by some hunters to describe a deer which has lost its testicles. The buck was hanging with a band of does and fawns, though its age was mature, not juvenile.

When to Hunt

Fall is the primary hunting season for deer in North America, although it is very difficult to put a specific set of dates on our hunting because each state has the right to set its own seasons. But generally speaking, we will find the deer seasons in our land open in October and November, for varying lengths of time depending upon the decisions of the individual game departments. There are seasons as short as a couple of days. There are seasons as long as a month, occasionally (rarely) even longer. But we want to hunt our deer, speaking in general terms, in the fall of the year because it is in good physical shape at that time, and also because a reduction of numbers in the fall is most desired. After all, the next season to arrive is winter, and winter kill is a major factor in deer herd reductions. Therefore, it is wise to crop before the winter sets in, thereby allowing for a better ratio of winter feed to game herd numbers. Quite often, a poor hunter harvest in the fall is reflected in a greater winter kill.

The fall is also a perfect time to hunt deer in terms of the antler condition of the buck. As we all know, the buck deer will not retain its bony antlers throughout the year, but will drop them and regrow them each season. The only time this is not true is in the case of physical problems, or a stag, which is a buck without testicles. When the buck suffers the loss of the testicles, shedding of the antlers will not occur. My son Bill's first mule deer was such a buck. The antlers were in velvet in mid-October. We took the buck to the rancher who had allowed us to hunt his grounds, and he stated that he had seen this condition one other time on his range. He had also seen it occur several times in domestic sheep, his theory being that the young sheep's testicles were accidentally damaged or removed when the mother sheep cleaned the young ram. The rancher told us he had witnessed this, and it was his opinion that the deer could have possibly been neutered in the same manner.

The cycle for antler development is not precisely the same all over the North American range. However, as hunters, our concern is only general, and we can generally say that a buck will drop its antlers after the rut. In other words, in late December and early January the buck's antlers will be lost. Note that this is not going to be the case for the Coues deer of the Southwest, for very often this deer is in the rut in January and even up until the month of February, and it is certainly carrying its antlers at this time. But in the main, especially for our eastern whitetail, the antlers will begin to fall off in very late December and into January. The buck will then go through the winter without its antlers. As to how the antlers are removed, there are many opinions. I have seen two things happen and can therefore speak to these without guesswork. I have seen a buck simply stretch its neck back and kick an antler right off its head using a hind foot, much as a dog scratches its head with its hind

In the spring a buck's antlers begin to grow back. Here we see a blacktail "button" buck with the buds of its new antlers just beginning to show and in the foreground a young forkhorn.

foot. I have also seen a buck scrape an antler off by rubbing it against a tree. This latter method was a scraping, by the way, and not a banging of the head and/or antlers against the tree.

So our buck has gone through the winter without its regal rack in place. In April, generally very late in the month, or even more likely in the month of May, antler growth begins again and the new bulb, for it looks like a bulb, shows itself right over the spot where the previous base was. The antlers grow rapidly. Precise triggering of antler growth is not known; however, we do know that the pituitary gland could be responsible for initial regrowth patterns. It is believed that the hormone testosterone has much to do with the process. The antler is of course soft and very much "alive." It is rather soft, not bony, and there is a supply of blood flowing within the growth itself.

Again we must be careful in our dates, for the process of antler regrowth varies with different geographical locales. However, since our interest is understanding deer as deer hunters, again we will allow ourselves to generalize. The antlers begin to branch out soon. A fork may appear in June if the antlers commenced a regrowth in May, and by July, the beam could be fully extended or almost so. In August, we will see a full-sized rack, but

remember, this rack will still be somewhat soft, still supplied with blood and still in "the velvet." The velvet is that mossy covering of the antler proper. Of course, this velvet will be stripped off, but we are getting ahead of our story. Certainly by mid-August, the rack will be complete in every way and will probably do little further growing. The buck will act as if its rack itches. This statement is made only from observation, but it does seem that the rack is annoying the buck, and it soon begins to scrape its antlers, mainly on bushes and small trees.

This action helps the velvet peel away. By middle-September, the rack will be bony. No further blood will flow in it, and it will be the solid structure with which the buck can now fight its own kind when the rut arrives. Therefore, from the hunter's point of view, October will find the buck, even the late bloomers, with a hardened bony rack. From a game management point of view, this factor does not constitute the number one reason for fall deer hunting, of course, but it is a factor nonetheless. The mule deer may show a different timing in antler shedding and regrowth, as does the whitetail deer of the Southwest. The hunter must always remember that deer are somewhat different according to different locales. The dedicated deer hunter will have to explore his own areas if he truly wants first-hand knowledge of "his" deer.

A buck in the velvet is a deer in a sensitive state. It will not be very aggressive at this time of the season, generally, and may in fact be somewhat shy in terms of dealing with other deer. Usually, the deer hunter will not encounter a buck in velvet during open season. However, this is not true of some bowhunts where an early season is possible.

A buck has used this sapling to rub the velvet off its antlers.

(Right)This buck is a prime example of what can go wrong with antler growth. Note that the deer's right antler is fairly normal, what would be called a small 4-pointer in the West. But the deer's left antler is badly deformed. In fact, we have only an eyeguard (scarcely any eyeguard on the right side) and a bit of main beam. Possibly, the antlers were injured when the buck was in velvet. Gene Thompson poses with his buck, taken at a distance of 30 yards.

Finally, deer seasons are not set solely on the basis of biological appropriateness nor antler development. There are many other factors. We must understand that game departments have to run as a business, and often manpower and funds may be limited. Therefore, some hunting seasons are set at a time most beneficial to the budget of the game professionals, budgets of both funds and of time. Furthermore, as we have hinted above, the minor migrational patterns of deer may be important to a certain game season. Also, we must consider historical reasons for season dates. Remember that the first American settlers had to take their game when it was most successfully handled. In other words, the meat would last longer in colder weather. Even if jerking or canning were part of the preservation methods, it was better to take the meat when it was not so warm and bacterial growth was slower. Farmers may have had to finish their fall work, too, before they could hunt, and this helped to set the deer

The deer is an interesting and challenging big game animal, and its habits can be strange from our point of view. Here, two big bucks have fought and their antlers have interlocked. The buck on the ground has died. After the standing buck was released with the aid of hunters, it retired to the trees in the background. However, when the hunters were removed by a couple hundred yards, the buck came back and "worried" the carcass of the dead buck with its antlers.

Since we are speaking of when we hunt deer, then our discussion of antler growth is accurate enough. There are always going to be arguments as to exact dates, of course, in this process of antler shedding and re-growth. Our interest in the matter stems from a desire to know and to understand our game better. In summary, then, the buck's life cycle includes a shedding of its antlers, the antlers sometimes being kicked off, sometimes being scraped off and often falling off on their own accord, for the antlers will indeed simply fall off when the time comes. Important to the serious deer hunter is the fact that there is a pattern, that the deer lives out its life cycle according to nature's plan, according to nature's dictates.

Therefore, our seasons historically occur in the fall, October or November, and very often into December. Several states which I studied had deer hunting into December, especially in specific game management units. This latter factor may have to do with migration in the case of the mule deer, for the deer of the high country may not be harvested in some specific instances unless a late hunt is allowed, a time when the herds may move downward from somewhat inaccessible areas to areas more likely reached by hunters, thereby allowing for some harvest where there might be no harvest at all. And we have to add, too, that the bowhunter often enjoys an earlier season for deer. In many areas, September marks the opening of the deer season for those who carry a bow into the field.

seasons for early America, season dates which have not been abandoned. Game departments must also consider other game animals when setting a deer season. They may or may not wish to have seasons coincide. For the sake of manpower, and where applicable, it could be wise to have a deer season during an elk season, when both are hunted in close proximity to each other. Or we may find a combination deer/antelope season out West.

Weather must also be considered when setting up a deer hunting season. In the fall, middle November for example, a tracking snow may fall, but the true winter has not yet arrived. Access by roads and trails will still be open in the fall, but not always in the winter. And in the fall, the hunter may be more welcomed than he would be earlier in the year when farmers and ranchers are taking care of important duties, such as roundup or harvesting. Weather dictates these often, and therefore the weather, indirectly, also dictates the deer season.

The Rut

There are many factors to consider concerning deer seasons, all right, and game departments must include them all when they are responsible for setting up a time block to hunt deer. Aside from the many factors mentioned above, there is also the rut. Now, one may consider it foolish to hunt deer before the rut. After all, the bucks may not have yet mated, and the does could be without

Note the well-placed lung shot just behind the right front foreleg. Marksmanship like this pays off at the dinner table.

pregnancy, thereby reducing the herd's numbers if bucks are taken prior to the rut. In fact, this is not quite the case, though it seems to have a logical foundation.

Deer are, in the first place, polygamous. One buck may service many does. In fact, the mating season may go all the better for some thinning of the bucks prior to full rut. But there are many seasons set in the rut, too. And as with so many other things, there is both good and bad associated with buck hunting during the rut. As for the good, these points are rather obvious. The bucks are moving much more than they were before the rut. They are at times less cautious now. Instead of being "bushed up" during the day, the bucks may roam through the entire daylight hours, a very important factor and obviously a plus for the deer hunter. If a buck is going to be called, lured or "rattled up," then the rut improves all of these methods.

As already stated, the rut may take place at different times of the year depending upon the locale. But we can be fairly sure that middle to late November means rut over much of the country. I have hunted in the rut only a few times, however, for I find one outstanding problem with this time of the deer's cycle—the meat. Having only taken three bucks in the rut, all of these on my annual out-of-state trips, I must not be overly confident that all deer meat is lessened in "sweetness" by the rut. but in the instances of those three bucks, each was much poorer in meat flavor than other bucks I have taken before the rut. My son brought home a buck from Idaho which had been taken in the rut, and it proved to be a fourth sample of meat far less appealing to us. The meat was still appreciated and certainly not disliked, but it was definitely less palatable than the pre-rut buck meat had been. A fifth instance came when an Arizona friend gave us some meat taken in the rut on a late bowhunt. Again the meat was less appealing to us than previous meat had been.

The only other factor concerning the rut which is not always a good one is weather. While some hunters prefer a snowy setting for their deer hunting, other hunters may not. Chances of bagging a buck are quite likely going to improve with the rut, all right, and with the snow, but there are many hunters who would rather work a little harder in good weather than wait for the rut in order to make their deer-harvesting task a bit more surefire. Now, we are certainly dealing with personal preference here, and I recognize that there are more good points about rut-hunting than bad points. Not only are hunter chances improved, but we must also consider that the taking of the bucks during the rut generally means that the does will have been bred already, so that original concern about cropping a buck before the rut and mating season is avoided, if indeed the factor is a real one in the first place.

Doe-Buck Hunts

Mostly tradition lies behind the buck-only deer season.

On the face of it, one would simply have to believe that the only way to crop a herd is to shoot bucks only. After all, as we have said, one buck may service many does so we can surely crop more bucks than does from a herd. Also, until medical history is made, there is no chance of any buck giving birth to young, so we want to keep the does and harvest the bucks. Without any game management knowledge, this is the logic used for the buck only hunt, and it is a widespread in belief.

In fact, the major problem facing deer managers is not doe hunting *vs.* buck hunting, but rather habitat and food, especially winter feed. While hunters seem to consider themselves the only factors in the taking of deer, in fact the human hunter plays a much smaller role than, perhaps, his ego has told him. It, of course, is up to game management professionals to determine whether an area is more suitable to buck-only hunting, either buck or doe, or, in fact, doe-only hunting. The latter may seem preposterous to many hunters, but there are doe-only seasons on occasion, especially where herd numbers simply must be thinned for the good of the entire deer population in the area.

We mention buck-doe hunting only to insure that our modern successful deer hunter understands that the buck-only hunt is not the only way to go, and in many cases is in fact the wrong way to go. Sentiment and a certain bravado among hunters keeps alive the tradition that suggests the taking of a doe is heresey. As Jack O'Connor stated in *The Big Game Animals of North America*, 1961, page 94:

> During the years of the buck law, the doe became a sacred animal to the American hunter, and his attitude toward the doe was about as rational as the attitude of a Hindu toward the sacred cow of India. The man who would shoot a doe (even legally) was in the same class as one who would rob widows and orphans or swindle his aged mother. I grew up in Arizona under the buck law and as a youngster was thoroughly indoctrinated. In my day I have shot a few fat does for meat, but in spite of the fact that they have all been perfectly legal, I have not enjoyed it and have always felt a nagging sense of guilt.

I very well understand the feelings that Jack O'Connor expressed, for I too grew up under the buck law, and though there is a second hunt, doe-only, no bucks allowed, near my home, I found myself partaking of the hunt as a means of securing additional meat, and never feeling quite right about it in spite of knowing better. In fact, contrary to the actual purposes of this specific second deer doe-only hunt, I found myself looking for the older doe only and in fact finding these older animals to harvest, a fact proved at the checking station when not only my does but those taken by family members were aged by the biologists as older animals. We took only the does lacking in color, slower-moving and in some cases lagging in the herd. This may all sound very gallant, but where thinning was the reason for the hunt, the taking of the old does was not in strict accord with what was best for the welfare of the entire herd.

We have touched upon a few general deer hunting precepts, luck factors, skill factors, times to hunt and times not to hunt, doe/buck laws, and the like. In the following chapter we are going to talk about this animal, the deer, its general nature, its specific nature, its abilities and qualities as a coveted and respected game animal. All the while we must bear in mind that we are talking about deer hunting, successful deer hunting, and our goals are not strictly those of biological know-how, but of knowing our quarry better so we can help in an annual harvest, a logical harvest and a necessary one.

This nice buck was brought down in the desert with a Remington 700 ADL.

chapter 3

What Kind of Deer Do We Have?

AMERICAN FORESTS, swamps, deserts, brushlands, flatlands and mountains (as well as just about any type of terrain in between), all make a home for the deer in its many varieties. For the sake of hunter interest, it is nice to know where the ecological niches lie, which type of deer lives where and how the animals have managed to thrive in a land which has grown so rapidly in only 200 years. Of special interest to the hunter, however, is the deer itself. What makes it tick? I suppose we could look at any game animal in the same light. The more we know of its ways, the better we can harvest the surplus stock which professional game biologists tell us must be taken in order to maintain the population in good health.

In this chapter, we will talk about the kinds of deer, from a hunter's point of view, in order to try to learn something of their habitat, and habits. Deer hunters who learn more about deer, it must follow, will be better deer hunters. Or, to paraphrase a familiar quotation: "Hunter, know thy game!" Generally, we are going to speak of the two major deer types in North America. These are the whitetail and the mule deer. Yes, there are many dozens of variations in each rank, and the blacktail is often considered a cross between the whitetail and the mule deer, but these two types make up the major split with significant differences between the two. All of the various species and subspecies are interesting to hunt. All are challenging, and each is a welcome addition to the food larder of the hunter.

The Whitetail Deer
(Odocoileus virginianus)

This is our most abundant deer, and there are many subspecies of its kind, variations on the theme, we might say. Aside from the major representative of the whitetail clan, *Odocoileus virginianus virginianus,* we also have the little Coues (pronounced "cows") deer of the Southwest, *Odocoileus virginianus couesi.* (Note the subspecies taxonomical attachment.) There is the Northern Woodland whitetail and the Northwestern whitetail. There is the Dakota whitetail and the Columbian whitetail; the Louisiana and Florida whitetail. The list goes on beyond half a hundred.

These deer are well-known for their shy secretive ways, cautious movements, and use of protective cover. If we could make a single statement of fact concerning the habitat differences between whitetails and mule deer, we might say that the former prefers the thicker regions while the latter enjoys the more open spaces. Roughly speaking, this is true, but woe to the hunter who lets this "fact" stifle his imagination, for he may fail to look for whitetail deer in the meadowlands and mule deer in the thickets. This failure could be a mistake in tactics. It is impossible to isolate all of the traits of any of the given deer types. I have seen whitetails of the eastern variety bedded in terrain that would give a mule deer agoraphobia. In contrast, I have seen mule deer holed up in thickets that would give a whitetail claustrophobia. All the same, it is not wrong to begin our discussion of the two major branches of the deer family by thinking of the whitetail as a lover of dense cover and the mule deer at home in the more open areas.

Where the Whitetail Lives

The whitetail deer is distributed over much of our country, all the way from central Canada (roughly) down into South America. It is easier to speak of areas where the whitetail does not live, rather than where it does live. We find no whitetail deer in the Arctic, very few in California and none down in Baja California, Mexico. There are very few in Utah. Nevada is hardly famous for whitetails either.

But it comes as a surprise to some hunters from the East to learn that there are very huntable numbers of whitetails in states such as Montana and Wyoming. We need not belabor this point. After all, the hunter has a fairly good idea concerning the type of deer he is going after. But is it not interesting to know that there are very probably more whitetails in North America today, in spite of increased human population, than there were when Columbus came to these shores? That is pertinent, for it speaks of the nature of this wild animal. I find it useful to think of the whitetail as highly adaptable to its home, for then I will not tend to pigeon-hole it too much. In other words, it does not surprise me that I jumped a whitetail buck near Spearfish, South Dakota that was living within sight of a major highway with houses in sight of its thickets.

Jack O'Connor (*The Big Game Animals of North America,* p. 94) relates the fact that in Pennsylvania in the year 1907 only 200 whitetails were reported taken by hunters. Look at the figures now. Today in Pennsylvania, the harvest is more like 100,000. In 1923 in that same state, O'Connor shows 6,452 legal bucks taken. Other states show similar figures. Here, fellow hunters, is a deer which adapted to change and flourished. And that says much for its personality, telling us bluntly that if we are to hunt its kind with success, we had best learn its ways as much as we can learn the ways of a wild animal.

Remember that it is our desire to talk of deer hunting as a deliberate process, a plan. Luck is always there; however, we like to think of Lady Luck as taking up the tail end of our hunting success story rather than being a leader in our harvests. When we consider the wide distribution of the whitetail deer, we should, as hunters, attribute this successful habitation to the deer's very nature. This will supply us with the respect that this game animal so richly deserves, and it will also tell us something else—there are a lot of whitetail deer in our land! In fact, in many areas, the harvest by hunters is *too low* in terms of keeping the whitetail in balance with its food supply. And yet, success ratios, even in areas well endowed with high whitetail numbers, can be very low for hunters. In spite of a plethora of deer in a given area, bagging a buck may be no cinch.

How Big Is the Whitetail?

Of course, with so many subspecies the whitetail varies quite a bit in size and weight. The little Florida Key

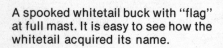
A spooked whitetail buck with "flag" at full mast. It is easy to see how the whitetail acquired its name.

WHITETAIL AND COUES DEER RANGE

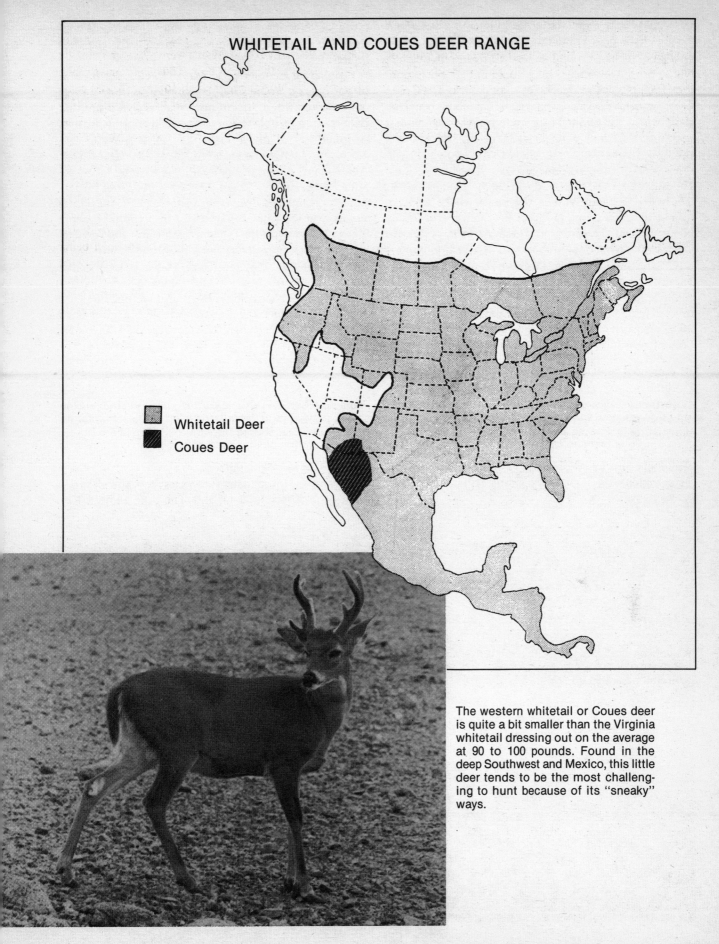

Whitetail Deer
Coues Deer

The western whitetail or Coues deer is quite a bit smaller than the Virginia whitetail dressing out on the average at 90 to 100 pounds. Found in the deep Southwest and Mexico, this little deer tends to be the most challenging to hunt because of its "sneaky" ways.

whitetail is only about 41 inches long with a tail about 7 inches in length. At the shoulder, this little fellow may only go 21 inches. I found no verified figures on weights, but a deer only 41 inches long would not go much more than 100 pounds *live weight* for a good buck. The Coues deer, another very small whitetail, will be about 60 inches long, with a tail about 11 inches long. At the shoulder, the Coues buck may stand about 35 inches. I have hunted the Coues extensively and believe that a good buck will dress (dressed weight, remember) at 90 to 100 pounds. He might go 130-140 pounds on the hoof, live weight. The larger Northern Woodland whitetail will be 95 inches long with a tail about 14 inches in length and a full 41 inches high at the shoulder. These are general figures.

So what? What does this mean to us? Well, as hunters it is interesting to note the weights of deer which we may harvest, so there is that factor, one of interest. For example, it is fascinating to note that a Maine whitetail dressed at 355 pounds. This buck hanging was 9½ feet long, measuring from the hind hoof to the tip of the beam. One must stop to consider that bull elk are annually

taken which weigh no more than this. Therefore, I consider the monster whitetails an intrigue for the deer hunter.

But there is another good reason to consider the size of our quarry. To be sure, the whitetail is more a lover of brush and wood than of open spaces, so it is not that important to be able to judge its size in contrast with its surroundings. This is important in the West, and wherever a hunter can see a great distance, east or west. All the same, it is very important to understand the whitetail's dimensions as a target. I have no proof, but I firmly believe most missed deer are overshot. That is, the hunter shoots over the animal. Part of this is no doubt the fact that with iron sights the face must come into good contact with the stock in order to gain the correct sight picture. An excited hunter may fail to bring his face down on the stock. Therefore, he is in fact taking a very "coarse bead," and he shoots high. But I also feel the hunter is looking for a much taller animal whether the deer be in the woods or mountains. I further feel that the hunter may shoot as if his target is taller than it is, instead of

Even the western whitetail (Coues deer) may at some times be taken in the brush. This mount by taxidermist John Doyle illustrates a typical bedding spot for a Coues deer, and one can see that he may have to take a shot in dense cover. The typical hunter will very often use his scope-sighted high velocity rifle in this terrain, and he will do well if he shoots through the holes in the brush. Brush-busting calibers are mostly theory.

holding down into the deer, realizing the buck for what it is, quite low to the ground.

Senses

The hunter already knows that a deer enjoys acute senses. However, it is very difficult for the hunter to put this knowledge into perspective. Just how good are the senses of our whitetail deer, for example? We know that at birth, the fawn is already equipped with certain gifts. It can hear very well from the first. Of course, the instinct to hide is also there, and if the hunter considers the fact that even the fawn has a sense for concealment, he will all the better appreciate the wonderful whitetail trait of "laying low and staying put." The fawn is quite possibly without much body scent of its own at first, so it gets by well from simply "hunkering down" when its mother acts in a nervous fashion. Later, that very same "hunkering down" is going to be a number one defense against being seen, by man or any other creature in the whitetail's domain.

The fawn can probably smell danger on the wind quite early in its life, but there have been observations which indicate that a fawn is not developed all that well in this department, and that it must increase its ability to smell danger as it matures. In fact, one may observe fawns trying to "sniff out" mother, while actually mistaking several deer for the dame before actually locating it by scent. But the fawn can run, and it does run quite soon. It also has an early urge to fight. Although wild fawns should never be captured by well-meaning humans who think the fawn's mother has abandoned it because the dame is not in sight, it is a fact that a fawn will often fight quite forcefully if picked up by a person. What does this have to do with "successful deer hunting?" After all, the latter is our goal. Well, it points up the nature of our deer. And the hunter betters his ability by understanding that nature better.

For example, we begin to understand the whitetail as a creature of immense gifts in the senses department. No, eyesight may not seem overly acute at first in the fawn, but it does develop soon into better than average, if we consider human eyesight an average from which to judge. We also see a deer of certain character. The whitetail is not a cowering and timid creature, really. It is watchful, not afraid in the human sense as far as we can judge. I mean, in observing whitetails myself I have often seen them flee at the first sound of intrusion. I have also seen them stomp the very life out of a snake. I observed this occurrence only once and that a couple decades ago, but I was lucky enough to be close. The deer attacked the snake, not the other way around. So the hunter should consider his whitetail quarry as not a fearful titmouse, but instead an astute observer, clever enough to seek safety by staying still without any movement whatever, fleeing for better cover, fighting if it must.

The hunter should observe his own dog. Learn from the dog just how keen animal senses are. See how the dog

can remain patiently in one spot listening to a sound for as long as it takes to identify it. That's a deer too. Human time has nothing to do with animal time. Deer don't wear watches. We impose time on them. The dog's hearing, we know, is remarkable when compared with our own, which is our only way to really compare, and so is the hearing of the deer. Fido can sniff out a hamburger if the meat is wrapped in three layers of plastic wrap. It is the nose of the deer which is perhaps the keenest organ of its warning system. If we had to list the deer's attributes in the area of senses, sniffing would be number one. The hunter has to know that. Hearing would be number two, and sight would be third. The senses of the deer are sharper than a double-edged razor blade, while ours are as dull as a knife blade that has been cutting sandpaper. Hunters have to also know this.

Even sight, which we rank third on our list of three, is quite proficient in the deer. The deer seems to pay little attention to an object which is motionless, however, though we certainly can't say that it does not observe the object. We don't really know for sure. But watch out when that object moves. The eye of the deer can pick up the flick of a gnat's wing, and it appears to us that the deer sees better than we do in dusky hours. One season my partner and I were taking turns on mini-drives for whitetails. I was on stand, as it were, and my partner was circling a hill. The hill had a well-used trail on it, and as my friend went around the other side of that hill, a buck was pushed out if its bed. The only problem was that by the time the buck was "spooked," shooting time had elapsed. My rifle was unloaded, and I was now on the move to intercept my friend who would be coming back around the hill. I should point out that by "hill" I refer to a large uprising in the earth, not a hillock.

The buck rounded the bend. I could hear it, but I could only make out a crude outline. It not only saw me, but took a leap over a blowdown that was a total tangle. I could not see it from where I was; I only saw a form take to the air, as it were. Then the buck made few quick turns in the trees and was gone. When I walked over and observed the spot, it was evident that the buck saw me quite clearly for what I was, because it turned abruptly and leaped off the trail. It was also evident that the buck could maneuver in this half-light just fine. It not only cleared the pile of branches, but it also zigzagged a trail among the trees. This sort of thing is hardly what we would call scientific observation, but along with other examples, I can assure the hunter that a deer can see just fine, and its "night vision" is quite probably better than our own.

These are the senses of the whitetail, then. It can smell us a long way off. We must watch the wind when we stalk or take a stand. It can hear any movement we made. We must move quietly, not at all, or in a manner which does not indicate "man." As for that, in many areas I have used "field position" to my favor, forgetting about being quiet. It was impossible to be quiet, and sneaking around trying to be still only created a very suspicious sound. It was as well to sound like a cow walking to water than a man sneaking. The deer can see well, too. It's equipped to allude the hunter.

Physical Abilities

The whitetail is supposed to be able to run at a speed of about 35mph. Others say 40mph. A friend tells me that a deer kept up with his car for about 50 yards with the car's speedometer indicating 45mph. Of course, these are not necessarily scientific statements, are they? A speedometer can be wrong, and so can calculations on a wild whitetail deer in its own natural setting. But deer can "move out," and this much we know. From a hunter's point of view, it is important to note that a whitetail buck can take off from a standing start and no doubt hit 30mph in a big hurry. That may seem a trifling bit of information, but it isn't. After all, it gives us an idea of the lead you need on a deer in order for good shot placement. Now, this lead is not to be confused with "time of flight" of the bullet. After all, that bullet will reach 50 or 100 yards, certainly fairly normal whitetail distances for shooting, in a split second. A lowly round ball fired from a muzzleloader can reach 100 yards in about two-tenths of a second.

However, time of flight for a bullet is not the only factor in leading running game. We must take into account the angles involved and human reflex factors. A running deer must be led, and the fast hunter can get out in front of the running deer with a good lead, hoping to put a bullet through an open space as the buck enters that space. This may require practice, all right, but it also requires something else—a respect for the speed of the whitetail deer. Even if 35mph is a top speed, given that the shot is but 50 yards away, the hunter should consider a clean swing of the rifle with the sights at least up front on the deer if not in front of the deer, and the rifle *going off* while the barrel is still swinging. In short, we do not swing, stop and shoot. We swing and shoot while the sight picture is up front on the target. I have made a few running shots on western whitetails which were 50 to 200 yards distant and more, and I know for a fact that lead made these shots possible, and I led because I believed in the speed capability of the whitetail buck. I doubt that it is of very much consequence, but the whitetail is credited with a leaping ability of 20 feet. Again, we get differences of opinion. I have read figures of 30 feet. But the hunter need not worry about the actual figures, only the fact that his whitetail can become airborne in an instant and cover some ground while actually off the ground. Finally, if the hunter happens to jump a buck and if that buck should, by chance, head toward water, the hunter better shoot before the animal reaches the water, for it could be illegal as well as poor sportsmanship to shoot a deer in the water, and besides, once in the water, the buck will swim off at a rather high rate of speed.

J. Wayne Fears poses with a fine whitetail buck taken with a Mowry muzzle-loading rifle. One can see the typical whitetail rack, with its main beam and then tines branching up from that main beam. Unlike the mule deer's rack, the tines will not often branch. (Photo courtesy of J. Wayne Fears)

Antlers

Perhaps it is unfortunate that bucks have antlers or while we are speculating we could turn it around and suggest that it would be more fortunate still if does and bucks wore racks. Game management could be easier in some areas if this were the case, and more difficult in others. But the rack of the whitetail buck is certainly a prize, and it is also a factor in hunting it. First, we can assume that the whitetail in most eastern areas will have shed its antlers pretty much as we outlined in Chapter 2. And we can further assume that the buck will be wearing its rack again when the fall season rolls around.

With the fall season comes the rut. Now is the time when the rack is used for fighting, and the hunting method of "rattling up a buck" is possible and successful in some areas. The general method of rattling will be discussed later. We only include the mention of the buck's antlers here as a part of understanding the the ways of the whitetail, for the rack and time of year do go hand in hand.

Glands

The glands located on the hind legs and feet of deer have nothing to do with hunting the deer really, but those metatarsal glands, tarsals and interdigitals each give off an odor which in fact leaves a trail. A human can't follow such a trail, but a dog certainly can. Where the use of dogs is legal, it will be these deer odors which point the way for the dogs. The glands on the feet, the interdigitals, seem to leave a specific scent, but we do not know for certain just how this benefits the deer. Perhaps there is a communication in it just for them.

For the hunter, the scent glands mean two things, and only one is important for most of us who do not hunt with dogs. The first is the fact that indeed while man will not be able to stick his nose to the ground and "trail" a deer by scent alone, many of us have at times smelled deer nearby. My friend John Kane, a Colorado professional bear hunter, has more than once stuck his nose in the air and taken a straight path to a thicket which has contained deer. He's done it too many times for it to be an accident and I have, in fact, been able to detect the pungent musk odor of the deer myself on occasion.

Second, during the rut I have seen a buck moving rapidly on a trail with its nose glued to the ground like a bloodhound. In fact, one time I saw a buck in the rut on such a sniffing expedition, and I was able to move into position on the trail so that when the buck passed me I was so close I could have reached it with a tossed rock. There was no deer season, and I began to make some odd sounds, odd for a human anyway, and the buck looked up, seemed to see me very plainly, and then as if I were no more threat than a hummingbird (which I really wasn't) the buck put its head back down on the trail and went on its solitary way. Was it following musk?

Illustrated here are the metatarsal gland of the whitetail and the antler conformation. Unlike the antlers of either the mulie and blacktail, the antlers of the whitetail consist of a *single* beam with individual tines or points emerging from that beam.

Or was it on the actual scent trail of a doe, musk not truly being a main odor? I do not know.

The metatarsal gland, which hunters are told to remove immediately upon field dressing the deer (in rut yes, otherwise leave it alone) is very large on the mule deer, "midsized" on the blacktail, and very small on the whitetail buck. I have sniffed these, and an odor is there. It is my fancy that on the couple bucks I have taken in rut, this gland had more odor, but I am sticking my neck out here and can't prove a word of it.

Color Phases

It is important for the deer hunter to know that a whitetail is brown to red-brown in summer and more of a gray in fall. The knowledge of this color phasing is very important to the hunter. The gray color for the fall/winter season is the ideal camouflage. Here is a vital factor for the hunter, because I have been with hunters who stopped and glassed or studied everything that was brown, while in fact the deer during that open season time were *gray*, not brown. Also, if the hunter recognizes the fact that he's looking for a gray super-camouflaged animal, then he has a chance to find it. If he's training his eye to see a brown furball walking around in the fall/winter, he's looking for something that isn't even there! And yet I myself *call* the deer brown. It is a matter, almost, of verbal reflex. Deer are supposed to be brown, doggone it, and I will often tell a fellow hunter, "Take a look at that brown patch by the log over there. I think it's a deer." And it darn well is a deer much of the time, but it sure isn't brown. That is just a slip of the tongue. So color of the whitetail plays a role all right, and the hunter has to train his eye and his mind to think gray, and to think camouflage.

Sounds

Some animals can be hunted because of the sounds they make. The wild turkey is a wonderful example, but so also are geese, ducks, coyotes, even antelope. But deer sounds are few. The fawn may bleat a bit, and the buck can snort loudly. When the latter occurs, it's usually because the buck has caught a snoot full of human scent (or maybe a mountain lion's scent). I have heard the snort a time or two but the deer was long gone before I could do anything about it. It is apparently only the buck that truly snorts, or so I have been taught all my life.

But there is another sound which can help us hunt whitetails. A deer can move as silently as the proverbial shadow, but deer can be very noisy, too. I have been on a riverbottom thicket when I heard a deer coming on a trail for several moments before the arrival of the animal. I once got a buck which I could hear coming—a western whitetail moving over rocky terrain. I could hear its hooves scattering rocks. Only a season before writing this I bagged a buck which I heard jumping through deep snow. It was leaping, and the leaps were pretty far apart, making a definite noise each time the buck landed in the

Hearing is an asset not always used to full potential by the deer hunter. On stand, for example, the hunter can cup his hands, ears tucked in by the fingers, and increase not only his ability to hear the approach of game, but also his ability to pinpoint the direction of sounds.

The Ways of the Whitetail

If a hunter knew what a whitetail buck did, not only per each given time of year, such as summer, fall or winter, but also as a daily routine, he would be armed with a knowledge that would help him immensely in fulfilling the title of this book, SUCCESSFUL DEER HUNTING. In fact, there are many things we can say about the whitetail in terms of its daily life-style and his annual cycle. Will all of these points be accurate? No, they will not be accurate for all places and for all deer because man always has a problem in judging animal behavior. Animals do not respond as humans respond to life, and yet we tend to judge animal movements and "habits" based upon our own emotions and ways.

Nonetheless, in our quest to remove deer hunting from the luck category more into the skill column, we need to know our quarry as best we can know it. The first thing we might want to know about the whitetail is that it is not quite as gregarious on a year-around basis as we may first think. Often, a whitetail family will be an older doe and her fawn or fawns—does of mature years often drop two young, not one. A yearling may be tagging along as

The little Coues buck of Arizona, parts of New Mexico and Sonora is one of the most interesting of the deer. Many hunters, including the late Jack O'Connor, felt that the Coues was the smartest game animal in North America. This buck is a smaller one, but is not that immature at all. In many areas, this head would be somewhat representative if many bucks were checked through a game department check station.

snow. It was like a shuffling sound.

Often, I have used my favorite method of increasing my hearing capacity by cupping my hands in behind my ears, in order to detect a sound and pinpoint it. The ears are tucked into the palms of the hands, and the hands are "aimed" toward sounds. This will be mentioned again. I think it is an important hunting tidbit, and the whitetail hunter on stand or even still-hunting should use it from time to time. It works. So, the deer's actual noises, that is sounds eminating from the body, are of little value to us. But the sounds a deer makes in its movements can help out a great deal at times if the hunter only faces the fact that while his hearing is certainly not as acute as the deer's, it's still a very important personal tool worthy of development.

The last thing I can say on sound is that due to the fact that we know the fawn will bleat from time to time, we can use this knowledge effectively in calling a deer in to us. I have called upwards of a dozen deer in an hour, but I must admit that in these instances I, personally, got no buck to come in. More on calling will be discussed later on. Calling is an important bit of knowledge for the hunter, and having called bucks in, I know it can be done.

This hunter approaches his whitetail buck, which was taken from heavily timbered or dense country, though in a western state. Whitetails inhabit territory where they have cover; however, it is not impossible to jump a whitetail in a grain field, and the Coues whitetail of the West can make a hideout from a small bush.

Knowing deer movement is very important to the hunter. This nice whitetail was caught early in the morning moving from bed to feeding area. Being on stand before dawn, being quiet and listening intently for the sounds of deer moving through dry fallen foliage paid off for these hunters.

well, maybe a couple yearlings from last year's family. In the fall of the year, we may see this little unit wandering about. A buck may not be with this group, and probably will not be in terms of a social order. As far as we can tell, the bucks may often be alone or in small buck groups at this time of the year. I have, in the fall, seen five to 10 bucks in a group. I have also seen whitetails which seemed to be a double family unit, two older does and several fawns and yearlings. At any rate, all of this means only one thing to a hunter. It means that before the rut the whitetail social life may be one of buck clans or single bucks, and it also means that if the hunter is inclined to harvest a doe where legal, he may prefer to look at that unit in terms of an older dame or two and the young, the older animal rendering the most in weight of meat.

The life cycle of the eastern whitetail will include a rather quiet summer life, somewhat slow in pace, totally different from the rut—in other words, calm and relaxed. The buck's antlers are tender, remember, and it's not inclined to boss too many other animals around, though in the pecking order there is no mistake that the buck is at the top of the ladder, pushing around not only those of its own kind, but also other animals. I have seen a

western whitetail buck bully a whiteface bull out of a pasture. But the important consideration is hunting season, fall to early winter months, and this is when the buck becomes increasingly more aggressive as the neck swells for the rut, a condition not totally understood.

Prior to the rut, the buck may be in a small buck group or on his own. One thing bothers me about trying to create an example of a buck's life on a daily basis, and that is the fact, and I think we can use that word, that the whitetail may indeed make *choices* each and every day, choices which are somewhat different from time to time and not always the same. I have found whitetails with my binoculars, and I have moved in close enough to watch them. It has often been quite a lesson for me. But we are forced to believe that the deer does in fact elect to do certain things at a given time. I have seen a deer in a thicket along a trail. The deer comes to a fork in the trail, stands there, and then moves to the left branch or the right branch of that trail. Was there not some decision-making force at work here?

The deer hunter should consider his whitetail buck to be a creature of habit, all right, but also of choice. The rut seems to change this to a degree when love blinds the bucks, and they tend to do what, in our eyes, seems foolish and certainly less cautious than the buck would have been before the time of the rut. The fighting, for example, is somewhat without actual benefit in our eyes. While the bucks are generally not badly injured in these battles, my friends and I have found a few whitetails which were indeed hurt after a struggle in the rut, and the locked antlers of some combatants has spelled death for both gladiators.

But let's look at the buck on a fall day. What does it do with itself? I wanted to establish that at least some of its behavior is based on *choice* because the hunter should not consider the whitetail totally chained by habit. A buck may rise in the early morning from a bed used only sparingly at night. It may, on the other hand, feed at night, walk around and not rest at all or very little during the night hours. Often, and in all parts of the country, I have seen whitetail deer feeding right off the highway in the dead of night while I was traveling. We all have. That's important to know. But let's get back to our morning buck. I have caught a whitetail buck in my binoculars, even in somewhat thicker terrain and in the meadowlands and pasturelands on an early morning and watched its movements.

Somewhat as we might do, the buck stretches, looks around, ears twitching and nose testing the wind, and then it moves a short distance from its bed, and takes a few bites at something. Maybe it's hungry and maybe it's not. If the buck fed all the night long, it's probably full. But it might nibble a little anyway. Its bed is left behind now, and bed it is. I have located whitetail beds which seemed well-used and somewhat permanent. In the instances I have observed, the buck may move into the sunlight for a while, and often will bed right down again with the sun on it. It probably watered last night, and I would not count on finding this whitetail at the watering hole in full light.

It may bed down most of the day. It has, in the fall, very little to do. If the buck is with companion bucks, they do not tend to make much of an interaction out of it, not until rut that is. In my opinion, it is this steady slow-motion life, with the buck occupying its bed much of the day, which makes it hard to hunt. Instead of moving around, the buck is down on the ground. It's already hard to see. After all, standing up, the buck is not tall, but bedded down it all but disappears if there is any kind of bush around. So, we have had a short feeding session, a half-hearted one, and some bedding time coming up.

If the buck is hungry, it may eat for a couple hours, however, and this is why our whitetail hunter should look at "edge," where open lands meet thicker brush, where food is often prominent. Our hunter should also spend time looking in these areas in the morning hours, for our buck *may* be putting on a feed at that time, standing up, not bedded down, and even moving a bit from bush to bush as it feeds. It is easier to see now than it will be after it beds down.

We have now two methods of hunting to use on our early-morning whitetail—we look for it by still-hunting the "edge," or we glass for it by moving slowly and looking into as many open areas as possible. After it beds down, we simply have to still-hunt it or construct a drive. These are discussed later. Right now, we are only trying to establish a life-style for our whitetail. What does the whitetail do and when does it do it? Those are the pertinent questions. For much of the day, then, the whitetail may be secretive, enjoying a sunny slope when there is sun to enjoy, and mostly doing nothing whatsoever. These traits make it hard to hunt, as we already admitted, but at least if we think of the deer as being up or down, in the sun or in the shade, feeding or bedded, we can decide how to approach our hunting tactics.

Later in the day, the buck is going to get up. I have mustered all of my patience and watched a bedded buck literally for hours. I have seen a single whitetail bedded for hours at a time, but in all cases I have personally observed, the buck rises for at least a moment or two from time to time. This, I think, is why we have arguments concerning the buck's feeding patterns. Hunters see a buck standing and feeding at 11 AM and feel that the deer are, after all, up feeding all day. Quite likely that buck was bedded down only a few moments before the hunter saw it. We also find deer droppings and urination spots in the earth or snow not far from the bed, but seldom smack in the bed. I did, however, find a deer bedded down, and I got that deer and then discovered that this particular animal was using its bedding grounds as its bathroom, for the immediate area was loaded with pellets, though no pellets were found directly in the bed itself, but perhaps no more than a foot away from the perimeter of the bed.

The most important point for the hunter to consider now is that by afternoon the whitetail may seek its supper. Certainly, it will that evening, and if we are lucky, it will get started early enough so that in later afternoon it is up and moving about, giving the observant hunter a little better chance of seeing it. I believe strongly in the early morning and late afternoon time blocks for deer hunting, both whitetails and the other two major classes as well, mule and blacktail. Armed with this very basic information, the hunter is going to still-hunt, perhaps, looking for all he's worth, in the early morning and late afternoon. Or he may be certain to take special care in observing from his stand, placing that stand where it seems that deer have been feeding.

Deer movement, then, is very important to the hunter's knowledge. I feel we can call early morning and later afternoon hours the best in terms of deer being on the go instead of being "bushed up." The rest of our hunting hours, in the main, are spent looking for a whitetail which is quite likely doing little to nothing, and that is a hard whitetail to find. To be sure, certain areas and conditions change these factors. A friend of mine who owns a farm in Pennsylvania finds that his deer tend to

rise and feed during the day quite a lot. Bad sign! The deer were feeding during daylight hours because they were not able to nourish themselves properly with less time looking for food. When deer stand around in plain sight all day, especially whitetail deer, often seeking food right off roads and not heading for the bush at the sight of man or dog, watch out. These could be deer in trouble.

We should also note that deer may have a longer daylight feeding and roaming pattern in very remote wilderness areas. In British Columbia, my family and I used to see whitetail deer in remote areas, and they would be up feeding. As to the balance between game populations and feed, we were told by biologists that the deer

(Above and right) This nice 8-point whitetail buck was taken in the heart of the Midwest farmland while feeding in this meadow early in the morning.

were in very good shape in the area and that the lack of any kind of pressure seemed to be the major reason for their daylight movement patterns.

On a larger scale, what about migration? In the clan of the whitetail, long migration is not in the cards. Yes, there have been proven cases of herds migrating 50 miles or so, but this is not the usual circumstance for whitetail deer. In fact, some experts feel that the whitetail lives its entire life cycle within a few square miles. There is also the feeling that the deer will return to various areas religiously, almost a homing tendency and a staking out of territorial rights. If so, the hunter may want to think of his better whitetail places in long-range terms, learning an area well and trying to take notice of whitetail concentrations. Some studies suggest that the whitetail is there,

right where you saw it last. The reason a hunter goes back and declares an area ''shot out'' is that he simply can't find what is so hard to find, a whitetail deer.

Bad Weather

My own feelings are to forget it when the wind is blowing badly or the rain is pouring down. But if I am more objective about the matter, I suppose that the reason I don't have much luck in rainy and windy weather is that I don't care to hunt very much in that type of weather. I consider deer hunting a very important function, a getting back to the land practice, though practiced on a limited basis, to be sure. I enjoy the deer seasons, and I like to hunt in decent weather more than in mud. Snow is fine. Rain and wind I can do without.

The Midwestern whitetail deer have left the background of heavy cover to feed. In the winter, or very late fall, the deer may forsake heavier thickets in order to search out plant life that is growing in the less dense areas.

My good friend, Spike Jorgensen, a dedicated and successful whitetail hunter as well as all-around big game hunter, *prefers* to hunt for big bucks when the wind or rain are prominent elements. Spike feels that he has found some very good bucks during these conditions because the deer tend to "head for cover." Instead of being scattered all over the terrain at will, the deer will seek sheltered areas when high wind or bad rain attack. Now the range in which a hunter has to spend his energy shrinks greatly. It makes sense. I have seen this without taking careful note of it. Though they were mule deer, I recently had an experience which backs up the idea my friend Spike has about hunting deer in the rain/wind. In fact, it was raining and had been for 2 days straight. I had limited time and decided, like it or not, to get out and tramp in the wet for what it was worth. I saw several bucks, and all were in ravines and somewhat "brushed up." In fact, they were all easy to approach and it was true—the total range in which I would normally seek a buck had shrunk down to only a few percent of its former size. The deer were now low, in the bottomlands, and in the brush along ravines. They were pinpointed!

This shrinking situation is even more evident for whitetail deer when hard winter sets in. It is estimated that the range is then cut down as much as 90 percent. In other words, the deer herd is now living upon only 10 percent of its former normal range. Talk about concentration, this is the time for it. I can't help but mention the writings of the famous outdoorsman, George W.

Sears, known as "Nessmuk." Out in the forests of the Northeast, Nessmuk ran across a virtual army of deer near the Muskegon. From what I can gather, the deer may have been getting ready to "yard up" at some time in the near future, though of course some other explanation could be more accurate than mine. Nessmuk said:

And again, on the morning of the sixth day out, I blundered on to such an aggregation of deer as a man sees but once in a lifetime. I had camped over night on low land, among heavy timber, but soon after striking camp, came to a place where the timber was scattering, and the land had a gentle rise to the westward. Scarcely had I left the low land behind, when a few deer got out of their beds and commenced lazily bounding away. They were soon joined by others; on the right flank, on the left, and ahead, they continued to rise and canter off leisurely, stopping at a distance of one or two hundred yards to look back. It struck me finally that I had started something rather unusual, and I began counting the deer in sight. It was useless to attempt it; their white flags were flying in front and on both flanks, as far as one could see, and new ones seemed constantly joining the procession. Among them were several very large bucks with superb antlers, and these seemed very little afraid of the small, quiet biped in leaf-colored rig. (pp. 84-85 of *Woodcraft*)

Biologists I spoke with felt that the number one reason for deer yarding up is not the food supply, though surely food is a factor, but actually the congretation is concentrated in the yard because the terrain offered more favorable winter conditions, perhaps less snow, perhaps more cover to keep a few pieces of ground somewhat more open. Yarding of whitetails is a very interesting situation and so is the movement which changing food supplies can bring. In the spring, new fresh green growth can attract a deer herd to a specific spot, which of course is of no consequence to the hunter, but is mentioned as a fact. The summer forage is changed somewhat from the spring feed pattern, and the fall/winter food situation again changes. We certainly know how plant life changes from season to season, and as hunters we enjoy the fall because the brush is less thick and the foilage somewhat dropped from the trees, offering more open sighting and shooting conditions. But we should also note that as we hunt in the fall we must look for areas which are still blessed with browse plants *in good condition.*

Elevations

To be sure, elevations can affect deer movement. A whitetail herd may move downward following very bad snows, for example. Also, the hunter should consider that the whitetail deer is prone, in many areas, to elevations which are not terribly lofty. As with all statements, there are exceptions, but where I hunt I find mule deer all the way up to timberline. I never see whitetail deer that high, not ever. However, in the Southwest I have seen the little Coues whitetail deer at 9,000 feet above sea level in central Arizona not far from Hannigan Meadow. Overall, however, the whitetail is a lover of thickets and places not quite so high as the tops of mountains.

Intelligence

Man has a very difficult time separating animal instinct from animal intelligence. Is a sea otter intelligent because it can crack open a shellfish by the use of a stone? Or is that instinct? Is a chimp intelligent because it throws a stick (as one would heave a spear) at a leopard? Or is the chimp doing what "comes naturally" for it? A water buffalo may wait on a trail and ambush a follower. Is that smart or instinct showing up? All the same, we try to rank animals according to intelligence. When we do this, I think the whitetail deer shows well. Call it instinct or brains, the fact is the whitetail is a keen observer, and it uses the terrain it lives in to its best advantage. In many areas, the whitetail harvest is terribly low in terms of percentage. For a hundred hunters in the field, maybe only 10 will take a deer, even though there are plenty of deer around. I don't want to get into long-winded arguments on which animal is the smartest as far as North American big game goes, but if I have a right to voice an opinion, I would say the whitetail deer and more specifically the Coues type of whitetail deer. I have not hunted every species of North American big game, but I have been among most of them, having lived from the Mexican border to Alaska and Canada, and though a big-country elk is often terribly hard to come by, the little whitetail deer, there, right under our noses, so to speak, evades us in our own backyards and very often makes

a monkey of our hunting ability, which pleases me personally and makes my deer chasing all the more enjoyable.

The New Whitetail Deer

While any sort of evolution is slow in coming, micro-evolution is not that slow to transform living creatures. A good example of this fact would be the moths of late 19th century, early 20th century London. The light-colored moths survived well in the days before the industrial revolution, but as the city buildings grew darker and darker with the soot deposits of industry, the moths fared poorly, standing out against the buildings and being eaten up by birds. However, the moths evolved and adapted to the problem by changing color, from light to dark. Once they became darker, they again were camouflaged, and the population was less vulnerable to birds.

Surely, deer have enjoyed some form of micro-evolution in the past 200 years of American sprawl. I doubt that the deer of the day is the same deer our first Americans hunted. For the hunter, this has meaning. The hunter of the day should consider his whitetail quarry a bit more sophisticated than it was in the past. I am not even talking about increased intelligence in terms of brain capacity. I'm speaking of the fawns learning caution from the dame. I believe that the whitetail deer of the moment is quite probably better equipped to avoid man than ever before. That is speculation on my part, but I don't think it is too farfetched. Only recently, I wrote an article on

The whitetail buck will often feed on "edge" terrain, just as a mule deer will. This whitetail buck will look for browse plants which grow in the edge type of area where sunlight reaches the ground. Note the typical whitetail tail, the brown top hairs and white underside.

hunting cottontail rabbits with a flintlock. The editor of a prominent magazine turned the article down. He said ". . . this form of hunting—stalking cottontail rabbits with a shotgun (much less a rifle) is almost impossible over much of the East, the Midwest and the South if dogs aren't available. Cottontails are so secretive nowadays, that it's almost impossible to get a shot unless the dog puts the animal out and brings it around." Well, if the cottontail rabbit has changed so much due to "pressure," surely the whitetail deer of the day must also be a super specimen.

The Mule Deer
(Odocoileus hemionus hemionus)

Teddy Roosevelt called him a Black-tail (sic) deer. In fact, through all my youth growing up in Arizona, the mule deer was called a blacktail by most hunters and non-hunters alike. The mule deer is noted as a deer of the West, and this is correct. Although we can't leave out the northlands of Canada, even here it is the western provinces which boast the mule deer. This is a big deer, and though not as plentiful nor as widespread as the number one whitetail, it is a very important game animal for many thousands of American sportsmen. The mule deer has also changed in terms of numbers and distribution. And this deer now thrives over much of its "original" range, in other words the areas it inhabited when the first white man set foot on the continent.

Where Does the Mule Deer Live?

The mule deer lives from as far north as Great Slave Lake, Northwest Territories, Canada, to as far south as Tiburon Island, Mexico. I have visited both of these areas in my travels, and to realize how different they are is to understand how adaptable the mule deer really is. We do not think of the mule deer as being the flexible and adaptable animal the whitetail is. However, its kind has certainly adapted to life over extremes in terrain and temperature.

Of special importance to the hunter is realizing that the mule deer can live in wide open spaces, *very* wide open spaces. Quite often, hunters from the East spend a great deal of time beating the brush for the mule deer instead of studying the more open parts of the range. If we have to make distinctions, just for the sake of trying to separate the whitetail from the mule deer in terms of where both live, we'd probably agree that the whitetail is more a creature of the thicker places where cover is rich and complete, while the mule deer is more a lover of the open areas. Of course we will get into trouble immediately if we try to chisel such general statements into a block of concrete, but as a rule of thumb this idea serves us well as hunters.

I do, however, know of many areas where the mule deer thrives in very thick cover. For example, there are places in central and northern Arizona where I have found good concentrations of mule deer in black timber.

Here is a typical mule deer rack, with its main beam and then the branching tines forming a Y-shape. White throat patch is typical, too. Note the eyeguards. Eyeguards on some mule deer bucks may be even smaller and less pronounced, or even missing altogether.

Not only was the timber closely growing together, one tree after another, but there was a reasonable amount of undergrowth. Generally, truly thick trees will not permit good ground cover because the treetops block out the sunlight necessary for plant growth. However, in these areas decent ground cover did exist, along with very heavy forests, and plenty of mule deer. For general purposes, however, we will go along with the idea that the whitetail is more at home in heavy cover, while the mule deer can successfully inhabit the lands which are less dense in vegetation.

How Many Are There?

There are a lot of mule deer. Exact numbers are impossible to even guesstimate; however, game department figures show large herds of mule deer over the West. Zane Grey fell in love with the Kaibab Plateau of Arizona

MULE AND BLACKTAIL DEER RANGE

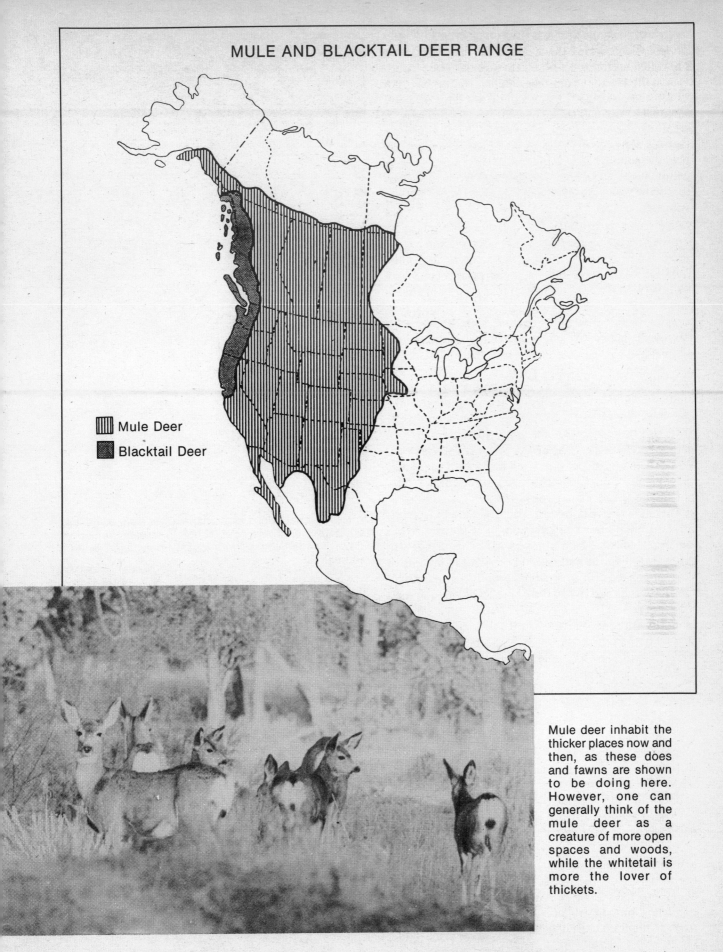

Mule Deer
Blacktail Deer

Mule deer inhabit the thicker places now and then, as these does and fawns are shown to be doing here. However, one can generally think of the mule deer as a creature of more open spaces and woods, while the whitetail is more the lover of thickets.

because of the mule deer and went on to write *30,000 on the Hoof*, concerning the area and the deer. That area is now famous for its die-off and though the deer perished back in the 1930s, the old-time numbers of deer have not yet returned because the deer still do not have the good range they once had there. In short, the food supply of old has not revived yet from the onslaught of mule deer overpopulation. Even in areas which we may not think of as holding supreme numbers of mule deer, we may be surprised. California, for example, is said to have well over 25 million mule deer, and some say this estimate is very low.

The numbers of mule deer are often misjudged by hunters, too, because the deer is often a rather quiet individual who stays to itself in the backcountry. In the West, where ranches can be 15,000 acres large and where national forests are huge, human beings will not always gain a true estimate of the actual number of mule deer roaming their habitat. For example, when people drive through the state of Wyoming, they remark at the number of antelope they see. It is common for out-of-staters and even residents to think that certainly the antelope is the number one game animal in Wyoming in terms of numbers. Not true! The mule deer outnumbers the antelope very handily. In fact, as this is written, the Wyoming resident need not apply for a special area permit for mule deer; however, he must for antelope. While the non-resident does need a special area permit, those areas are huge, covering vast portions of the state, not smaller game management units.

The mule deer can be managed quite nicely in terms of controlling hunter distribution. It is the winter kill which can damage herd numbers, and disease has also taken its toll on the mule deer in the West from time to time though the disease situation seems better today than it was a decade ago. When there are a lot of game animals inhabiting a specific locale, a disease if it does break out, is more easily transmitted than if the game population was scattered out and lower in numbers. Hence, when we have had superior mule deer numbers, such as in Colorado, and disease has struck, that disease has traveled faster than a prairie grass fire.

How many mule deer are there? Nobody knows. But there are quite a few. In Utah alone as many as 100,000 mule deer can be harvested in a single season. Utah has even shown higher rates of harvest. About half that many can come out of Nevada. Idaho probably has more than a half million mule deer in its forests and high desert country. In Colorado, harvests of 100,000 mule deer per year have been recorded. Other states have good mule deer populations, and in several states, Nebraska, Montana, South Dakota, even Colorado, the mule deer and whitetail seem to split the state, the mule deer taking the western half, the whitetail taking the eastern half. Texas may have as many as 3 million and even 4 million deer, most of them whitetails. But desert mule deer and Rocky Mountain mule deer inhabit parts of west Texas.

These mule deer does explore the water's edge and also take a drink from the cold mountain stream. Mule deer inhabit various ecological niches, from desert to high mountain.

We can't discount Canada or Mexico for mule deer, for the mule thrives in both countries in good numbers. The hunter of the mule deer has, then, a very large crop of this renewable hunting resource.

How Big Is the Mule Deer?

As a general rule, the average mule deer buck which is checked through a game department checking station will weigh a bit more than the average whitetail buck. As far as the largest individual samples go, the whitetail may be the winner. On the whole, however, the mule deer hunter will probably come home with a bit more meat in pure pounds weight. Is this because the secretive whitetail buck is harder to come by? It could be, for overall harvest ratios are higher for mule deer than for whitetails. Therefore, the larger whitetail bucks may in fact die primarily from old age and winter kill rather than being harvested by a hunter.

On the hoof, however, we can count on the mule deer weighing from 150 pounds for a mature buck to possibly 475 pounds. The spread is great, but so is the spread in any other species. If I had to make a statement concerning the weights of mule deer bucks, I believe that in most of the West the hunter who bags a buck dressing out (dressed weight, remember) at 150 to 160 pounds has a mature animal. In some areas, it is not totally uncommon for a buck to dress at 200 pounds and even more. A friend of mine shot a buck that dressed at 250 pounds, weighed, not guessed weight, and I have taken a few in the 180- to 200-pound range, dressed. In terms of length, the mature mule deer will go 55 to over 70 inches long, and it will stand from about 3 feet to 45 inches high at the shoulder.

Senses

As far as I can tell, and in accord with studies, there seems to be little difference between the actual acuteness of whitetail, blacktail and mule deer senses. However, as hunters I believe we should be careful how we rank the senses of the mule deer. In my own experience, I believe that I would give the mule deer about even ranking for eyesight and its sense of smell. In some locales, I am quite sure that eyesight ranks number one in the defense of the deer, at least where hunters of the two-legged variety are concerned. Often, I've seen a mule deer buck bedded on what is without question a vantage point in terms of vision. In watching these deer through a spotting scope or binoculars, it became evident that the animal was looking all the time, using its eyes to detect the presence of anything not to its liking. In my opinion, this fact is quite important to the mule deer hunter, for he must not stand silhouetted against the sky, carelessly booming over the hill. He should, I think, consider the fact that the mule deer is going to try to spot a problem with its eyes and then the hunter acts accordingly, using

field position to keep the balance in his favor as much as possible, so that when he does encounter the mule deer buck there is a chance for a fair and reasonable shot.

Physical Abilities

Once again, we are concerning ourselves with something which plays a role in hunting our deer, though it is a minor role when compared with other attributes of our quarry. However, we can fairly well put the mule deer in with the whitetail in abilities of running and leaping. We will once again find argument in exact figures; however, we can assume that a mule deer will be able to run at 35mph or so and jump 25-30 feet through the air. The mule deer is noted for its bounce, too. This is not of great importance to the hunter, but for one thing. A bouncing deer can offer a very interesting target, to be blunt about it. I have no doubt that some mule deer are missed because of this peculiar jump-jump-jump way of getting over the ground. However, in my experience I have found that the mule deer bounce is more associated with the smaller bucks, and not with the big boys. The big mule deer bucks I have seen, and I live near several herds in my area, simply run without the bounce.

Antlers

The mule deer's rack differs from that of the whitetail in that the tine normally rising from the beam closest to the skull branches into a "Y" configuration. Therefore, coupled with the top of the main beam and the branch formed by the tip of the main beam and the tine at that end, the rack often appears to have two "Y" branches. I have seen mule deer which had several tines coming off the main beam, all of which branch into the "Y," and I have seen mule deer which have no "Y" branches at

Getting close to a deer is difficult, but not impossible. The nose of the deer is its prime organ for sensing danger, and with the wind in the hunter's face and some reasonably quiet footing, plus little cover to hide the stalk, a hunter can close in on his quarry, even in the thick of the forest.

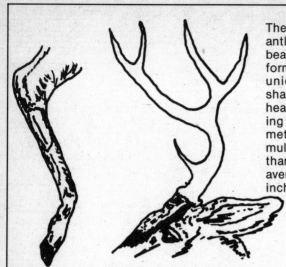

The mulie has bifurcated antlers—that is, the antler beams branch and rebranch forming forks. Also note the unique, dark horseshoe-shaped patch on the forehead which is a distinguishing feature of the mulie. The metatarsal gland on the mulie is considerably longer than that of the whitetail, averaging approximately 5 inches in length

The spike deer is not a sign of good herd condition, and yet we do find some spikes in fine condition, or what seems to be fine condition. This deer was passed up and not harvested, but it looks healthy. This buck would have to be judged by its teeth before comment on age is determined.

all, the rack truly looking very much like whitetail antlers—a main beam with tines coming up from that main beam. The latter are usually what is known out West as a three-pointer.

A yearling spike buck is no more a good sign in the western mule deer than it is in the whitetail deer. Spikes are quite often less biologically advanced deer and do not suggest sound conditions in the herd. Recently, I was in an area in which my son and I saw very large springtime herds of deer. Among these deer were many smaller animals which we thought were bucks. Having been in the area during the winter, we saw dozens of spike bucks, in fact, and it appeared that the mild winter had allowed most of these animals to live. We counted over 100 deer in two small pastures, saw deer feeding along the road at noonday, and in fact found obvious signs of over-population. Our talk with the rancher brought the response that ''we plan to let these deer grow into some big bucks.'' And in fact, they closed the ranch to all deer hunting for the coming seasons.

These facts are related to antlers in this respect—those many spike bucks were an indication of a problem. The rack of the deer does indicate a condition, and a yearling should be a two-pointer. In southern ranges, the condition of having spikes is more frequent than it is up north, however, and as with all attributes of wild animals, it is difficult to make broad sweeping statements. In the main, however, spike bucks do not indicate a good condition among deer—mule deer or whitetail or blacktail.

Antler growth is supposed to be associated with limestone in the soil, as well as many other minerals. In fact, the condition of the soil and consequent plant nutrition do mean much to antler development. But for the most part, it is the well-fed buck which grows not only in body size, but also rack size. Areas which have poor feed will not generally show a large number of big-antlered bucks. A good healthy buck will also shed its antlers soon after the rut. By the middle of January or certainly in the last

week of that month, the antlers will be off. Less vigorous animals maintain their antlers longer after the rut.

Color Phases

In summer, the pelage of the mule deer may be rather ruffled and not nearly as sleek as later in the year. About the only important thing for the hunter to bear in mind concerning mule deer color is that the lowland bucks, or bucks of the high desert for that matter, are often the ghost gray color which blends in with anything in those areas, especially the lighter colored vegetation. In the forest, the richer brown color, which is not a deep brown either, also blends well with the surroundings. Hunters who look for mule deer hoping to see a stand-out on the hillside, some strongly contrasting image, had best change their viewpoints immediately. The best bet is that rump patch, and mule deer's color does serve it admirably no matter where it lives. The mule deer is a camouflaged animal, almost as much as if it were able to blend its color with its background. In the desert, I have seen mule deer bucks which were bedded so much in the open, especially along sandy washes, that the vegetation surrounding the deer was actually covering only a small portion of the animal. In spite of this, the buck was almost invisible. Even after knowing right where the animal lay, I have looked away and then looked back to the deer, not finding it instantly. The mule deer blends, and that is the message important to mule deer hunters.

Sounds

The mule deer is a rather quiet fellow. Its sounds are few and of little general importance to the hunter. Again, we say that the mule deer can be called in with a deer call. The success of calling varies with the time of the year, the call and caller, concentration of deer and many other factors, of course. But mule deer have been called in to the hunter. As for the deer making a great deal of noise, the mule deer is just as quiet as its cousin the whitetail and on some occasions just as noisy. Listening for a coming deer is not without merit. And what we have said about sounds pertaining to whitetails can be mostly applied here.

These mule deer are thriving in a forested area. Mule deer are indeed thought of as creatures of more open spaces, but they certainly do inhabit forests and areas of heavy brush. These deer were not far from farmlands where they may have fed upon domestic plant life as well as natural plant life.

The Ways of the Mule Deer

Whitetails and mule deer are not alike in many of their daily movements and patterns, as well as annual movements and patterns. We might add that the apparent temperament, or personality, if we can use that term, of the mule deer is actually quite unlike that of the whitetail. At least I think so. I have hunted mule deer in several western states and at this stage of my hunting experience I'm branching out even more. I like deer. While others may find it more exciting to pursue different species of game, my deer hunts are filled with reward for me. Montana, South Dakota, Idaho, Utah, Arizona, Colorado, Nevada and Wyoming are some of the states I'll hunt on a somewhat regular basis, and my statements here are generalizations based upon hunting these areas. Remember, I said *generalizations*.

I find the mule deer to be a much more sedate animal than the whitetail. This may lead to some very wrong conclusions about the deer, but even the "new" mule deer, which we will discuss soon, tends to leave an area with less fanfare than its cousin with the big white flag. Upon jumping a whitetail buck, even the whitetails of the more open Southwest areas, the deer of my experience take out of their beds like aircraft from the deck of a carrier. They seldom stop to find out exactly what it was that spooked them either. The mule deer can certainly put on a disappearing act, too, but I'm not surprised when a buck slows down before going over the ridge, though the old-time notion that every single buck mule deer that jumps its bed is going to soon stop and stand, looking back at the intruder, is outdated now.

A whitetail buck can sit all day long. I have seen whitetails in lowland brush country which I spotted with my binoculars or by chance, the buck not seeing me. I have taken an hour or two out to watch these bucks. A few times, hunters have come by. When this happens, the buck often "hunkers down" and simply allows the hunter to walk right by. The mule deer can often do the same exact thing. This is why I urge mule deer hunters to look hard, preferably with optics, for in the usually more open mule deer range that bedded buck might be spotted and stalked.

I have seen the Coues deer, which is in my mind the most tricky of the bunch, actually sneak away from a hunter, and I mean sneak, down low to the ground, belly dragging like an overweight cougar. I do not hesitate to relate this fact because many other hunters have seen the same thing. As for the mule deer, I have never seen quite this much finesse in an escape plan. The mule is more likely to hang in tight if it has cover, and sometimes even when it does not have much cover, and then it breaks out. Where I have hunted, I find the mule deer to move on and away fairly much nonstop. Yes, a hunter is advised to walk over the ridge if a buck has just topped out, for the buck could be feeding right over that ridge. But a badly spooked mule deer is not likely to stop and hang around after only a hundred yards of running. If it does this, it probably has a stand of trees or other cover to jump into and stay put in.

I think of the mule deer as a bit more calm than its whitetail cousin. It can sneak out on a hunter, and it does. It can hear wonderfully, as we all know, and its powers of distinguishing scent are amazing. As we have said above, it sees well, certainly as well as we do from what I can detect, and it uses that calm manner to wait the hunter out and let him pass. If the hunter gets too close, the mule deer tries its escape.

There is no need to develop a life cycle discussion of our mule deer. The fawns are precocious, as are the whitetails. If there is a distinction, and I can't prove a word of this, I'd guess that the mule deer has a bit less escape instinct going for it than does the whitetail deer. I truly feel that a mere two-point whitetail buck has craft and guile imbued in it from its first moments of life. A two-point mule deer can often be a rather easy mark. But give the mule deer some time, and it seems to develop—and that is the key word here, develop—some pretty darn good avoidance tactics. Are these due to actual learning?

I would dare not say. But there is nothing in the zoology books to preclude a deer's instinctive ways from sharpening up with time and experience. I do know that I have scouted areas and seen some huge bucks, many of them, and I mean a few days before season. I further know that in that territory those big bucks are pretty hard to find when any indication of pressure is evident to them. In one locale, where I often hunt wild turkey, the rut shows many bucks of grand size, whereas in that same locale only 2 weeks earlier trying to find one of these bucks was quite a chore. No, migration was not the answer here at all, for this is a type of area where migration is very limited, plus a few days earlier all of the same deer sign, plus smaller deer were all over the same area. The big bucks were just laying low.

In the fall, bucks can be in buck groups. I have seen several bucks in a bunch. I suppose it is true that some of the truly older animals tend to lone it, but I have seen four or five big busters in a cluster, too. At the same time, a mule deer herd may have does and fawns, plus smaller bucks all together. As for the temperament of the mule deer, I think it is enough to tell hunters that this blocky,

While the antlers on the smaller bucks are quite hard to see, due to their lack of contrast with the brush behind them, we have a small buck herd of mule deer in the picture. The deer will spend its time in such herds for a part of the year, though there are some bucks which may keep to themselves more in the fall and early winter of the year, while in November they are in rut and will often be seen with does.

(Left) This small buck heads for cover. It was totally invisible to the author until it jumped its bed. In the experience of the author and others, it seems that some of the older bucks "hang tight" better than the younger ones, but such things are difficult to prove.

strong animal is slower-paced on a day to day basis, and perhaps even more sedentary than the patient whitetail.

As for its movements, we can talk of the mule deer as a migrating animal. In summer, its troops may well be in the high country, and I mean right up to timberline, 8,000 feet, 9,000 feet, 10,000 feet above sea level. But as the summer disappears, so will the bulk of the deer, not every deer, but a large number. By October, the mule deer has moved down a bit from its summer range, but it is not generally so low as to be found on the winter range. Cold weather seems to prompt a movement, for I have seen deer seemingly heading down when colder temperatures have set in without snow. If the hunter scouts mule deer in the summer, he should study the lower ranges in the fall, but not the bottomlands. Instead of looking where the forests fade away because of altitude, the hunter should study the "middle ground." I know this is very general, but it would be impossible to identify this territory for every patch of mule deer range that exists.

In the fall, vegetation patterns change, of course, and with that change the mule deer drops downward. Of course, we hunt our mule deer in the fall of the year for the most part, with some exceptions for certain archery hunts and a few black powder hunts which we could call very early fall. What are the deer doing on a fall day? In short, what would a daily routine be like? Nobody can pinpoint daily mule deer routines for all areas. But I think we can say a few general things which might be useful to the hunter. I have found a herd of mule deer in the morning and stayed with that herd all day. What does this suggest? It suggests that the deer did not go far in that given day. I have found a mule deer buck of obvious maturity in the morning and stayed with that buck all day long. That, too, suggests a modest daily movement where I have hunted and for my particular experiences.

My mule deer mentioned above were feeding in early morning in every case. The deer were somewhat scattered while feeding in those early hours. I mean that a herd of 15 might take up a width of 50 yards, even 75 yards or more on the hill, rather than all bunched up like a sounder of wild pigs. After feeding, these deer may take in a bit of sun by bedding, sometimes in very open spaces. But even then, seeing the deer took some true observation, not mere glancing, for the bedded deer blended in with the surrounding rock, plant and earth background like a white can on a snowbank. I have seen the mule deer stay down for a few hours without a move. Then one might rise, relieve itself, nibble a bush and then go back to its rest. I am most impressed that the mule deer seems to use whatever hunk of range comes to its fancy. In an area with ravines and stands of timber, I have seen the deer bed on an open grassy slope. I have also seen them disappear into the center of jackpines so close together that a man would have to push individual trees in a squeeze to get through.

As for watering holes and such areas, it seems to me that they are of value, but not as stands so much. In most of the locales where I found good mule deer hunting, the water holes seemed to be used in late afternoon more than at any other time of the day, but the evening and night-time hours saw the most use. However, I have found decent concentrations of deer within a short distance of well-used water holes. In one area, a place I had never hunted before, I checked for tracks at a water hole that I found. There were tracks which seemed to be quite fresh. I rubbed these out over an area a few yards wide and rechecked the next day. Fresh tracks were printed right over the muddy spot that I had rubbed clear of tracks the day before.

Late that afternoon, I spotted a couple of mule deer bucks heading for the water hole, though neither would make it to water before legal shooting light terminated. That was not important. What was important to me as a mule deer hunter was the fact that the ridges and draws surrounding the water hole held deer in good numbers. Whether they were there for the water or not, I can't say. I did end up getting a buck within 200 yards of that water hole, and more than that, I saw a good 50 deer in all surrounding that area, more deer than I saw when I moved away from the water hole. It seemed that the deer were bedded within ½-mile of the water. This was an early fall hunt, I should add, in Colorado country.

Enough on the ways of the mule deer for now. Our most important points concerning the personality of this deer pertain to the deer's ability to use sparse cover as a home, and to stay put in it. Its camouflage and stay-still ability serve it well, too. It feeds during the hours of darkness quite often but can be found up and stirring in the very early morning and late afternoon. Its drinking habits no doubt vary a great deal from place to place. We know that desert mule deer use water holes, mostly at night, and I believe that it is at least worthwhile to study an area around a watering site to see if there are deer bedded and feeding in that immediate locale.

Elevations

We have talked of mule deer and elevation a bit earlier. To summarize that, the deer live up in the higher elevations in summer and come down in the fall/winter. This situation is not as true of desert mule deer, of course, and I doubt that there is very much migrating going on among these lowland deer. I have seen mule deer right along the ocean near Libertad in Old Mexico, living in desert terrain which seems unable to support the life of a lizard let alone a deer, but some fine big bucks are taken along the desert associated with the ocean. I have seen mule deer amidst *saguaro* cacti and *cholla* cacti on the desert. I have seen mule deer in oak thickets. I have seen them, too, right at timberline. In fact, on an outing for sheep, we found mule deer sign actually slightly above timberline at about 10,000 feet above sea level elevations. But the hunter should think of the mule deer and elevation not in terms of habitat, but rather in terms of movement.

Now and then a female deer will have triplets as is the case here. Generally, however, a mature female deer will often have twins. Twins are not uncommon. The mule deer fawns are following single file in the trail of the doe, as often they do.

If he scouts in summer, then he should search out the lower portions of the summer range in the fall. And as the season progresses, if it is still open in early winter, then the hunter should look more to that winter range, the lower terrain. This is a matter of reading sign, to be sure, and a matter of scouting. But that is what proficient deer hunting is all about anyway, leaving luck at the starting gate and riding with careful planning and skill-building instead.

Intelligence

If there is any solid evidence to support the notion that a ratio between body mass and brain mass counts for something in true intelligence, then I suppose the whitetail deer, in the cases I have studied, might win over the mule deer. I have not checked on the size of the brain in the blacktail and cannot speak to that subject. I have, however, autopsied several whitetail and mule deer, and it has seemed to me that for the size of the cranium, the whitetail's brain was larger *by proportion* than that of the mule deer. Probably, this means little to nothing, but I toss it in for the reader to ruminate over.

I have suggested that the whitetail seems more wary from birth than the mule deer. I have also hastened to add that the mule deer seems to *learn* how to be wary. These are speculations. But it is not speculation when I say that I have seen mule deer give hunters the slip, including this hunter, in a very fashionable way. Furthermore, I think that the hunter who *consistently* brings in trophy-sized mule deer bucks has put in the scouting time and study in order to do so. The mule deer—is it smart? By what standards? It can certainly "out-instinct" us. As for the hunter who has gone out and bagged a big mule deer buck with no more problem than putting a rabbit in the freezer, I say to him "beware of early success." The next big buck may come a lot harder. The mule deer may not be as crafty as the whitetail, though here I go again applying human traits to deer by using the term "crafty," but I don't think the mule deer is a pushover. It does live in more open country, and therefore it can be generally easier to hunt than the whitetail.

The New Mule Deer

Today's mule deer has certainly advanced in micro-evolution. While I have still seen the mule deer make its escape with less enthusiasm and speed than the whitetail, the old idea that every buck is going to run 50 yards and then stop to look at the hunter for 5 full minutes is not true today. Some bucks will, yes. But the hunter who has heard that a mule deer buck is simply no challenge hasn't been hunting the same places I have been hunting for the past couple decades.

The Blacktail Deer
(Odocoileus hemionus columbianus)

Except for the *columbianus* part, the taxonomical name of this deer suggests the mule deer. This is all right, since the deer tends to resemble the mulie quite a bit. But I like to think of the blacktail deer as a cross between the mule deer and the whitetail. Scientifically, this may or may not be quite the case. When a whitetail and mule deer have been bred successfully, the resulting fawn(s) certainly look like blacktails. From the layman's point of view, however, the blacktail deer is very much a cross between the mule and whitetail. First, the ears are generally porportionally larger than the whitetail's ears, but smaller than the mule deer's, in between the two, we might say. The tail is not the rope of the mule deer, nor the flag of the whitetail. So it, too, is in between the whitetail and mule deer. The metatarsal gland is another in between feature, larger than the whitetail's, but smaller than the mule deer's. The rack is mostly mule deer. As for size, the deer varies and this feature does not suggest an in between circumstance.

The blacktail is indeed a superb game animal, but it is a creature of limited range and number and fewer hunters will pursue the blacktail than will take to the field for whitetail or mule deer, by far. Here is a deer of the Northwest. The range of the blacktail might be called that of northern California to coastal Alaska. It lives primarily along that coastal region, though it must not be thought of as a deer which actually dwells always within view of the ocean, for that is not the case. Oregon has a large

A blacktail doe exhibits the grace of this animal. The tail is clearly seen as smaller than a whitetail's tail and yet not at all like the mule deer's "rope." Because of the dense cover often associated with the blacktail deer, the hunter is often advised to use whitetail hunting tactics in his quest for a harvest. However, there are blacktail ranges which are much more open than the forested coastal area where this photo was taken.

The coastal blacktail deer can be thought of as a blend of whitetail and mule deer. The ears seem to be in between whitetail and mule deer in size, and the overall appearance of the animal also suggests a "cross" between the two major deer types. Matings between mule deer and whitetail produce fawns which are blacktail in appearance.

herd of blacktail deer. In fact, a hunter friend of mine said, when I asked him what he thought of blacktail numbers in his home state of Oregon, "Where I hunt we are up to our ears in blacktails." Washington has its fair share of blacktail deer and British Columbia does, too. Coastal Alaska also has blacktail deer in good numbers. When I left Alaska in 1970, a hunter could fill several blacktail tags. I cannot recall the exact number, but it seems to me it may have been as many as six in some areas.

As for total numbers, the deer has not been as carefully studied as the whitetail or mule deer and close figures are not, or at least were not available when I requested them. A rough figure suggests at least a million blacktail deer and some say there are more. But we still must consider the deer limited in range, for even though we are talking about vast stretches of land from California to Alaska, when compared with the range of the whitetail and even the mule deer, the blacktail is certainly not as widespread.

The size of the blacktail varies considerably. It is often called a Columbian blacktail along the coastal areas of California and in Oregon, and then a Sitka in British Columbia and Alaska, and the weights I heard of ranged from 150 pounds live weight for a buck to 300 pounds live weight for a buck. My personal experiences suggest the blacktail deer to be on the smaller side, and while larger than the Coues deer, not as large as the Rocky Mountain mule deer, on the average.

Its senses are deer-keen, and I would place it into the whitetail category here, relying heavily on the sense of smell and then on hearing and then on eyesight. The eyesight, as with our other deer, is good, and this deer can

The blacktail buck and doe clearly exhibit the cross features of whitetail/mule deer. The body of the buck shows a mule deer coloration with the forehead wearing the mule deer's dark patch. However, the tail is certainly not mule deer in appearance, nor are the ears as large as those of the mulie.

certainly detect movements with no trouble whatsoever. Its physical abilities are deer-strong. It is not noted for high-speed running and is said to be slower than either mule deer or whitetail with a top speed of 25mph or so, and its leaping ability is also less, so I am told, than mule or whitetail. However, where man is concerned the blacktail is plenty fleet of foot and can leap out of the way quicker than a rodeo clown avoids a brama bull.

The antlers of the blacktail are mule deer in configuration, the typical dichotomous, twice-branched rack with the "Y" tines. But the rack is smaller than the big mule deer antlers, even if they are shaped the same. Spikes seem more common among the blacktail than either whitetail or mule deer, and it appears that the spike buck is not quite so much a bad sign of range condition in the blacktail habitat. However, at the same time, in top rated terrain with good food in abundance, the blacktail rack is forked in the yearling and the spike is not common.

The glandular situation for the blacktail is in common with the other deer, and we will not delve into this aspect of the blacktail's physical attributes. Its color phases are in accord with the seasons, and though the coat may be a bit on the dark side in early fall, it becomes gray enough by the usual hunting season to give the deer an edge in the camouflage department. In sounds, these deer do make the typical sounds referred to earlier, and again we do not, as hunters, concern ourselves greatly with these noises. A blacktail deer can be called into the hunter, and in one account of Ishi, the last of the Yana Indians of the Northern California tribe from which he came, called up a buck for Dr. Pope and Mr. Young. That it was a blacktail buck I do not know for certain, but Ishi explained he had called other bucks and he was from blacktail deer country.

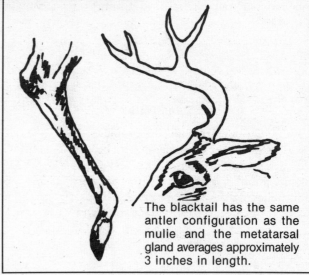

The blacktail has the same antler configuration as the mulie and the metatarsal gland averages approximately 3 inches in length.

The ways of the blacktail are somewhat whitetail in fashion. But there are also some differences. Here again we have a sedentary creature which can live in thick foilage and be happy about it. Therefore we call it whitetail-like in nature. But it often prefers to feed on open slopes, which is not so much a whitetail trait, I suppose, as a mule deer trait. When I was in Oregon I noticed a number of blacktail deer, and they very much seemed to follow the pattern of early morning and late afternoon feeding, and often these deer were indeed on open slopes. I would not leave my binoculars home if I hunted blacktails under these particular circumstances.

As for movement, there is a distinct difference between blacktail deer according to the area. Those deer which live in higher mountain elevations tend to migrate just like mule deer, not so much traveling hundreds of miles, but rather moving downward as the colder weather dictates, with its changing of the plant life of the area. So, some blacktail deer may live their lives out in fairly small ranges especially those on the coastal ranges where there are no severe weather changes, while other inland tribes migrate from higher meadows of summer down to the valleys in fall and winter.

As far as intelligence goes, we are again in a problem area if we try to give human-like traits to animals. However, I know of several hunters who are as fond of blacktail hunting as they are devotees of the whitetail or mule deer. One of my friends used to drive 400 miles one way to be in Sitka deer country. He always said that the major reason was meat. He knew where to hunt the deer, and he was assured of filling a few tags annually. However, I reminded this fellow that he had a whole moose cut up in his freezer, and I also suggested that I did not quite buy his meat story. He grinned and said, "Well, I sure do like to be down there in the blacktail country this time of year."

The blacktail is a challenge, to be sure, and a very worthy big game animal. In some locales it is taken from long-range, and the fellow with a 6mm Remington or .270 Winchester is well-equipped, and in other parts of his range the blacktail is snap-shooting fast, and a man with a fast-action rifle in any of the shorter-range calibers is well off. The hunter who has experienced the whitetail and the mule deer may be wise to seek out a blacktail to round out his hunting adventures.

Deer Tails

I wanted to separate this little topic from the body of information we are dwelling on here because the tails of our various deer do constitute a very important part of identification. And there are a few peculiarities that the hunter should always bear in mind. This short discussion is aimed toward a better understanding of deer tails in terms of the hunter's knowledge more than the interest of the naturalist.

The Whitetail Tail

Everyone knows that the whitetail's tail is its claim to fame. After all, the deer is even named for its tail. Brown on top and white on the bottom, the whitetail's tail is its flag, and is often called a flag. For the hunter, there are a couple of points to bear in mind. First, the swishing of the whitetail's tail, even though the brown surface will be visible at this time, can be picked up by the human eye at a great distance. The tail may exhibit a fringe of white at its borders, and I have spotted a whitetail buck based strictly on catching sight of a swishing movement in the brush across a meadow or on an opposite hillside. A hunter should bear in mind that the tail of the whitetail is a very important marker.

Furthermore, the "jumped" whitetail will generally raise its tail high as it runs off. I have seen a number of deer shot in the rear portion where the hunters have suggested that the attraction of the tail itself may have made that area a target. The whitetail hunter should certainly mark the big white flag of the deer when it jumps, but

he then has to put things into perspective and move his aiming point forward toward the frontal area of the deer. The whitetails of the East which I have seen seem to raise the tail and run with no specific movement of that tail, though specific regions may be different in this respect of tail movement. The Coues is the same way. Its abundant flag, and it does appear beautifully overlarge for its small body, is not necessarily waved in any particular direction and in fact may stay erect and still as the deer is running. When the deer stops running, the tail slowly falls back into place in the rest posture, not dropping instantly, but lowering like the swinging arm at a railroad crossing.

On the other hand, whitetail deer which I have seen in Wyoming and Montana and South Dakota have the same movement of the tail when the deer is in flight. That is the movement of a windshield washer blade, back and forth, back and forth. In my observation, this has been totally true of the whitetail deer we have jumped in Wyoming.

Also, it is very important for the hunter to know that the tail of the whitetail deer may drop downward immediately if that deer is hit anywhere by a bullet. This is not 100 percent true. But it is often the case. I have personally seen this occur very often. The shot is fired and instantly the tail, which is normally held erect, droops downward. That could indicate a hit. Of course, every hunter is obligated to go and look after every shot fired at a deer, no matter if it did seem to be a miss. But when the flag of the whitetail has dropped upon the shot being fired, then my suggestion is to look even longer and harder than usual, for that deer may be hit.

The Mule Deer Tail

The mule deer tail is a pitiful bit of rope compared with the bounteous and thickly haired flag of the whitetail deer. It is hairless on the inside surface and is typically white with a black tip. But there is one thing the mule deer hunter must mark with great care. While the mule deer tail is not much, it is valuable in helping the hunter spot his game. When that tail is used, like a small slow-moving propeller, to shoo away a fly, this movement combined with the narrowness of the tail allows a total view of the large rump patch of the mule deer. I would say that 90 percent of the bucks which my hunting partners and I have discovered at very long distances with the aid of binoculars and a spotting scope have been seen first because of the creamy-white rump patch. This patch is the most visible portion of the mule deer at long range and yes, even in the timber.

The Blacktail Tail

This tail is in between the whitetail and the mule deer in size, and it is usually not used as a flag. It is quite black on top and white underneath, hence comes the name for the deer. It is bushier and wider than the mulies' but pales when compared to that of the whitetail. When running this tail usually droops but is not held against the body

The white rump patch and "rope" tail of the mule deer is highly visible in this photograph. One can also see that the deer are very much at home in open terrain. However, once they are bedded, these deer will not be easy to see any longer due to their body coloration and sedentary ways.

as is the mulies'. But there is always movement patterns which can be spotted by the hunter, and the blacktail's tail can be the single appendage which gives it away as it feeds or stands in its habitat.

Eastern Count/Western Count

We should point out that often we'll have to speak of a 4-point buck or a 3-point buck, or whatever antler configuration we may be dealing with. Where I live, we use the western count. I don't like it as much as I like the eastern count, but I've used it so long it is automatic. In fact, we count only the main beam and the main points arching from it on *one side only*. And we leave the eyeguards out altogether in our survey. So, if a deer happened to have the usual, normal main beams, one for each side of course, and then three more tines growing up on each of the two main beams, plus the usual two eyeguards found on the whitetail and sometimes on the mule deer, out West that would be a 4-point buck. But back East the buck would be a 10-pointer. And if a western buck has uneven points, it may be called a 3x4, for example, meaning a beam plus two points on one side and a beam plus three points on the other side.

The other point we need to make is that a point is sometimes counted even when it's really no more than a nub sticking up. Some of my buddies claim if you can hang a ring on it, you have a point. If I went by that measure, I have taken bucks with 20 points or better easily. I like to think that a full inch of tine constitutes a point, and even then I have a hard time convincing myself that an inch of antler is a point.

These are, generally speaking, our deer in North America. If we were to study each and every individual variation on the theme, we would be looking at quite a number of whitetail types, certainly a few mule deer types and at least two to three blacktail types. But all of these deer have many things in common. They all inhabit interesting terrain and they are all interesting to hunt. Plus, they all yield a high value in meat. And all of these deer demand planned, step-by-step hunting methods if success is to be steady instead of now and then. Let's go forward and look at a few of the things we might do in order to put Lady Luck where she belongs, way behind Lady Skill and Madam Determination.

chapter 4

Scouting for Deer

WHAT BEGAN as a friendly meeting at the hunting club had turned into an argument. Most of the noise was coming from a white-haired man who had been calm until I mentioned scouting for deer. Then he went about as *loco* as a bull getting the hotshot treatment at the rodeo. "Scouting is a fool waste of time," he shouted, "and all you're doing is misleading these new hunters sitting here. Just 'cause you find a deer out there a couple weeks before the season, that's no indication that you'll see a deer in the same place later on!" The man was very serious about his argument against scouting. I knew this for certain when he stood up from his chair and threw the papers he was holding up into the air.

The hunting club had invited me to speak on the subject of deer hunting. At that point in time, I had managed to bag 14 whitetail deer that would qualify for the "Book" at the time they were taken. That I had not elected to enter the heads was my personal business, but all the bucks had been witnessed kills, so there was no argument as to their validity. Most of the heads were quite low in the record ranks anyway and would drop out within a couple years as the minimum score was raised; however, I had gotten the bucks because of hard hunting and mainly because I had hunted with partners who were far better outdoorsmen than I would ever be. They knew more about deer harvesting than I would ever know, and they had shown me the route to record heads. A big part of the success we all had came from the fact that we scouted our hunting areas ahead of the season.

Later, I learned that a number of other hunters felt that scouting for deer was fairly much a waste of time. I was surprised. They offered the following theories: (A) Whitetail deer change territory and do not frequent the same locales indefinitely; (B) Mule deer migrate, so if you find a herd in the summer, it won't be there in the fall. What can we say about these two ideas? First, I disagree almost entirely with the first. Yes, the eastern whitetail will move about and change its daily habits depending upon a number of things, such as vegetation alterations which are seasonal, different rainfall levels, which can bring on various changes in the growth of deer food, the rut, human activity in an area, and many more. On the other hand, there are many whitetail deer which die within a couple miles or less of their birthplace, too.

As for the Coues deer, the whitetail of the Southwest, it is not an animal of migration habits either. So, either way, it is certainly a good idea to scout for whitetail deer, be these deer living in upper New York State, Alabama or Arizona. As for the mule deer, yes it may migrate quite a distance. We do have to use a commonsense approach to scouting, and that approach includes scouting fairly close to the opening date for the season rather than months ahead of time. As an example, even though whitetail movements may not be as great as those of the mule deer, we scouted a whitetail haunt in South Dakota, and when we returned, 3 months later, the deer had

During a scouting venture, a most unlikely range of small dry hills proved to contain a large number of deer. Be the hunter in the East or the West, he should maintain an open mind about deer hunting and deer habitat. Sometimes that most unlikely looking spot will hold good deer numbers. Scouting means looking, looking not only into the likely areas, but also the unlikely areas.

(Left) Early scouting is often a boon to the hunter in spite of migrations which may occur between the scouting period and the actual hunt. This buck in velvet may not be in the same area when the hunting season arrives, but a hunter who has scouted has a good chance of going back to a spot where he has seen deer and in fact finding out where they have gone if they are no longer in the area.

moved down, in general, by several hundred feet in elevation. They darn well should have, too, for the snows were deep in the higher ranges where there had previously been no snow at all. Common sense dictates that we scout within a reasonably close time to the hunting season.

Even with mule deer, however, I have scouted in summer and found the deer in the general area in the fall. The deer will not migrate out of an area in a single day! A friend of mine in Idaho kept track of a mule deer herd, and after a few years of observation he concluded that the herd moved very slowly from summer to winter range. The bulk of the deer were, in fact, in what we would call the *lower summer range* by fall, and definitely not in the winter range, which was a parcel of land adjacent to cultivated fields at a lower elevation. To capsulize this, I believe that we should scout fairly closely to opening day, but I would still scout an area before I hunted it, if conditions permitted, even if I had to see that territory in summer or spring for that matter.

Reasons for Scouting

1. The first reason to scout, and this is about as obvious as a sonic boom on a quiet day, is to see if the area is home for deer. This is, of course, a matter of reading sign, of asking questions of game department personnel, ranchers or farmers, and of actually sighting deer. We

In scouting, we must have an open mind. While this terrain did not seem worthy of a real investigation, we scouted the area and did find deer browse in the background and much deer sign. Later, a whitetail buck was harvested not far from this location.

In this particular high desert terrain there seemed to be no appreciable movement of the deer herds. Bucks were found on the land year-round, and the hunter who located bucks prior to the season would be fairly well assured that the bucks would still be in the same general area when the season opened up.

have chapters yet to come on the topics of sign-reading and how to locate deer, so for now we will simply state that our scouting trip is designed to locate deer. That is our number one concern.

2. Our number two concern is the lay of the land. We want to learn the country, the habitat of our deer. No one is going to find out all there is to know about the particular deer family or herd from a scouting trip or two, but we can learn which way the roads go in and out of the area. We can also learn the type of terrain the country is made up of. The latter is very important for two major reasons: First, the type of landscape may dictate how we can hunt the locale, and second the structure of the land may also dictate the best tools of harvest, long-range, quick-action, and so forth. We will offer more on these later.

3. Having established that deer occupy the area, we can then set about looking for deer trails, water holes, areas which might constitute preferred feeding conditions, even deer beds, sunny slopes which the deer might be using in the hours of mid-morning, and more.

4. We also scout to save time. I have often been asked, "Why bother going into an area for scouting? Scout when

you get there during the hunting season. Then if you see a buck, you can harvest it instead of just looking at it." True, that aspect of scouting *vs.* hunting is quite right, but I really dislike using my precious hunting time *finding out* if there are deer in the area, where they are and what they might be doing. Obviously, the non-resident cannot be expected to drive several hundred miles in order to scout and then turn around in a few weeks and do it all over again. However, the resident can often do just that, for he usually does not have to drive several hundred miles to his deer areas. It takes time to scout, but I think the disappointment of going to a deer spot only to find out that the deer have left the area is even more of a disservice to the hunter.

5. Scouting's long-time values are often a reality for a hunter. I have scouted many areas which served me for several years' worth of hunting. In other words, if a hunter scouts an area and likes it, finds it a good place to harvest deer, then he can go back time and again, learning the place all the better each time he goes there. If the area is close enough, a bit of pre-season annual scouting is still a good idea, to be sure. Things can certainly change in a year. But it is highly unlikely that the entire area is going to undergo a total change in 12 months. So scouting often carries over year after year in most locales, the area

In this case, waiting at a deer trail paid off; however, it only presented us with a look at a doe. The trail showed a good deal of use, and quite probably bucks were taking the trail, but not necessarily during daylight hours. The trail wound along the edge of a river and stayed parallel with a fence for miles.

Scouting paid off in this area. Just prior to the hunting season, a scouting trip proved that the area was now being used for domestic sheep and the bulk of the deer had moved away to another locale.

The end result of scouting and learning a deer area can be a fine buck, as Wayne Fears displays here. Wayne often studies an area prior to the season, and he will go back ready to stay awhile, with pack and gear in tow. This buck was taken with a muzzleloader. (Photo courtesy J. Wayne Fears)

changing to be sure, but the hunter keeping "tabs" on it all the same and modifying his tactics to meet those changes.

6. We can learn of camping sites in an area by scouting. I cannot rate how important this is. If there is a lodge, and if the hunter has entered himself at the lodge prior to the season, fine, but quite often our American deer hunting has to do with some sort of camping, and this is true of all parts of the country. It is essential that we have a decent camp within modest distance of our hunting. A deer camp is not merely a shelter for hunters. Oftentimes, the camp makes or breaks the hunt. Scouting can turn up some fine camping situations.

7. Field experience is another important reason for scouting. Even if the hunter arrives early into his area and has only this time to scout, that time is still valuable to him. Part of hunting success lies in our ability to make our way outdoors, and making our way outdoors stems from planning and experience. The scouting trip can afford both an outdoor plan, just how we are going to negotiate the area, and that important experience at the same time.

8. Learning the capabilities and shortcomings of our equipment is another very important reason for scouting. I do not suggest that a hunter must carry all of the gear he will normally use on the hunt, but how much better is it to find out that a pair of hiking boots is all wrong

for the terrain *before* the season instead of during the season? This holds true for camping gear, compasses, maps, and all other manner of equipment as well. I once tried a new packframe prior to the hunt during one of my scouting sessions and found it to be totally unsatisfactory because I could find no way to get comfortable in that frame. When the hunting season arrived, the new frame had been given to a friend and it fit him perfectly.

9. Meeting people is another important reason for scouting. In one area, I met a rancher and we had a chance to exchange ideas not only on hunting but other topics. We found that we had a lot in common. It turned out that I hunted that ranch until our rancher friend passed away. Meanwhile, both of my sons and oldest daughter all harvested their first deer on that ranch. A meeting in the pre-season cemented a relationship that lasted the better part of a decade. There are a number of people to be met on a scouting trip, from gas station operators to farmers, ranchers and game department personnel.

10. The tenth reason which I offer in favor of scouting has to do with "scouting from a distance." After a hunter has done some scouting, he gets a pretty good idea of what he is looking for, and he can eventually do some scouting long distance, so to speak. Quite a number of times, I have purchased maps of an area which I could not pre-scout, but by studying those maps I at least knew something about the place before getting there. If a hunter

The scouting session is always of value. In this photo, we see some high "mesa" country. On top, the land is as flat as a silver dollar. Our scouting trip uncovered very few deer along the lower reaches of this country, but there were big bucks up on the mesa and bedded along the rimrocks.

Here, actually just at timberline, the mule deer was still found. In this terrain, which is mainly elk country, very few mule deer were located and sign was at a premium. However, there is no doubt that a hunter should scout this type of country. Some very large bucks were harvested just below the ridge in the photo.

will simply ask himself one question, I think he will have to agree that scouting has merit. This one question is, "What makes a guided hunt more successful than an unguided hunt in many instances?" I'm not suggesting here that a deer hunter must get a guide. I am only trying to make a point. And that point is this: The guide usually has a very good idea of where the deer are and when they will be there. How does he learn this? He scouts.

How to Scout

Since the very next chapter deals with sign-reading, there is no point in detailing that subject here. Let it suffice to say that we scout an area by pre-hunting it, *sans* firearm or bow and arrow. In other words, we do what we would normally do during the season. We look for deer, which usually begins with looking for the signs that deer leave in an area. Much of this is quite obvious, and it goes without saying that the hunter scouts by looking. He covers the legal area, and he studies the place for deer sign, for watering spots, trails, feed and so forth.

Another good way to scout is to employ a map. Maps can make a big difference in scouting and in future hunting. A map is designed to give us four basic pieces of information. These are: distances, directions, positions and identification of landmarks. All of these are very important to good deer hunting. Maps are not hard to read. Certainly, if we want to become highly sophisticated map readers who can deal with any type of map under almost any circumstance, then we need to school ourselves in the subject. But to use a map in a basic way,

Game department check stations can help a hunter discover more about a given area. He should take heed to what he hears in such a checking point, speaking not only to game department personnel but also with other hunters.

which is all we are interested in here, there are only a few points to take note of.

Map Design

In the northern hemisphere, a map is laid out with true North at the top of the page. So, the top of the map is North, which makes the bottom South, the righthand portion East and the lefthand portion West. With a simple compass and precious little map reading ability, the hunter can determine the four directions on his map. Once he has one solid piece of information, such as a prominent landmark, be that landmark a farm, a village, an airstrip or whatever, he can extrapolate a whole lot of further information.

Important Information Learned From a Hunting Map
1. *Legal boundaries*

It is certainly vital to know of legal boundaries. Out West, these are often referred to as game management units. However, East or West, the hunter has to understand his confines, where he may hunt and where he may not hunt.

2. *Property boundaries*

Aside from game units or areas, it is vital for the hunter to understand legal boundaries. If a hunter is allowed on a given farm, he must understand where he may go and where he may not go, and a map can help a great deal. In the West, I almost always present a good map of the area to a rancher when I am new in an area, and I ask him to quickly outline my boundaries. The owners of

private property certainly know what belongs to them and what does not belong to them. Only once was this not the case. On a huge ranch out West, the rancher admitted that he had actually never been to the specific part of the ranch I was to hunt and in fact he called his neighboring rancher and asked if it would be all right if I happened to trespass by accident. I was mightily impressed with the size of this spread.

The hunter also knows from maps which are public areas and which are not. There will generally be some feature in the landscape which will mark off U.S. Forest Service land from private, for example. While the western states generally have more of this type of public land, there are many instances where the hunter may pursue deer on public lands of the Midwest and East, too, and the topo map and a good compass will help keep that hunter oriented.

3. *Using a map during scouting trips*

The map is of great value for scouting trips. Everyone would admit that the map can show the roads in and out of an area. Along with this, the map can also reveal trails and four-wheel-drive paths, as it were. Old logging roads may show up, for example, or roads to mines or farms now abandoned. In short, the map shows us *access,* access into and out of our hunting area plus trails we may be interested in using. This information is also valuable in getting our game *out* of the area.

Another use of the map during a scouting run is actually noting interesting information on the map itself. When I was deeply involved in hunting trophy whitetails, I used to place a dot on the topographical map wherever I saw a big buck or picked up large shed antlers. I also updated the map, as it were, by adding or deleting information. Those maps ended up being a story of my hunting areas, and they paid off in big dividends, too. In fact, after several scouting runs, I was building up a sort of pattern for the whitetail deer in those areas. I noticed that specific parts of the country seemed to offer more buck sightings for me than did other parts of the country. Things change, and the maps which served me so well in my trophy hunting days would probably be of little service today. But for a long time they helped the cause of locating and keeping track of big bucks in big buck country.

4. *Finding feed areas*

A topo map can be used to make note of areas which contain deer food. As we admit, deer eat a huge variety of plants. But they may in fact prefer certain plants at certain times, and they may feed in specific areas more often than in other areas. I find it worthwhile to use my hunting maps in making note of specific locations where I see heavily browsed flora or in fact have often located feeding deer.

5. *Sharing learned information*

A good topo map can make a big difference in scouting and in future hunting.

The map is also used to share information with other hunters. I have, often, presented my maps to a fellow hunter who uses the same areas, and together we have helped each other learn more of the locales in question. My experiences may differ from his, his from mine. Combined, the experiences may be upgraded quite a bit.

6. *Experimentation*

This is my favorite use of the hunting map. During the scouting period, or at least prior to a hunt if it is an out-of-state affair which cannot be scouted, I use the map directly to aid me in getting into deer areas, often locating spots which may have been overlooked by the majority of outdoorsmen. In fact, one such area yielded a record class head for me and a record class head for my partner. We were studying maps one day when we noticed a place which had only one road going into it to a road which was in actuality a washout. The territory lay only a mile or so off of a major highway. However, it seemed to have all of the attributes of what we termed a "sleeper," a good hunting spot known to few.

First, elevation suggested that the place was just right for whitetail deer, being neither too low nor too high for them. By looking at the vegetation patterns, which topographical maps can depict, there may have been good deer food in the area, we surmised (before actually going into the location). There was water in the form of two prominent water holes according to the map. As it turned out, one of the water holes was a terrible trap for deer and in our scouting we found dead fawns in it. The deer could get down to the water, but the rocks were slippery

Having mapped out and scouted an area, a hunter at least has an idea of which way to begin his search for deer. Sometimes and in some areas the deer will have moved off from pre-scouting season to hunting season. However, a hunter can scout closer to the opening of the season in this case and be fairly sure of successfully applying the knowledge that he picked up prior to the season's opening. (Photo courtesy of J. Wayne Fears)

This deer was feeding in lowland grasses when it was startled and jumped the fence, shown here. It is a small buck, though the antlers are not visible because they blend with the brush background. Note that the ears are fairly flat on the head, indicating a buck even though the antlers are not visible here. This locale showed signs of deer feeding, and fresh tracks, or what appeared to be fresh tracks. Scouting the area during normal feeding hours worked in locating the buck.

and some of the deer would fall back into the waterhole and eventually drown. This condition was reported to the game officials and they repaired it with a cement landing—no more drowned deer.

The other water hole was a dandy. It was deep and seemed to be fed from a spring. In fact, in our scouting trips and during the hunting season, this water hole was always filled with good sweet water. Nearby, there was superb cover, and we found good deer food, well-used, all over the place, but especially in a few more specific areas. Our map reading had paid off. We not only got good bucks there, but we also took friends into the area who got good bucks. Unfortunately, the close proximity to the major highway finally took this spot out of contention for whitetail deer hunting because a development was erected nearby. But for a while we had some fine hunting based upon reading our maps with an experimental point of view.

I believe that there are many such places, and having located at least a half dozen such spots, know it is true. There are good deer hunting areas which are overlooked by hunters. Maps can help in the location of such areas. Therefore, I feel that map reading, as a scouting measure into country never before visited by the hunters, is worthwhile. Of course, some of these spots may surprise the hunter in two ways. First, the area may be as devoid of deer as the lack of use suggests. Second, while the spot may seem lightly used by deer hunters, this can be misleading. Opening day may find the area inundated after all.

7. *Finding camps*

The topo map is excellent in terms of locating good camping sites. In the first place, the map will generally show access to and from the camp. It will give an idea of the condition of the terrain—steep, flat, vegetated and so forth. It may show sources for water, such as streams in the area. It can also reveal land status, private or public. And on many maps, actual maintained camping sites are marked clearly.

8. *Safety*

There is also safety in using the map. One safety factor inherent in the map is that of "staying found." A hunter can use the map on scouting trips in conjunction with a compass in order to maintain his bearings. I have also used a topo map in country I have never before seen, and by making use of landmarks, have managed to get in and out with no trouble. Knowledge of an area in general can lead to a safer outing. One pre-season, my whole family and I were looking into an area which was quite remote. While we were scouting, a rainstorm developed and continued for 2 days. The road we had taken into the area was flooded. But our map showed another road which eventually took us out of the area and back to the main road.

Scouting and Hunting by Map

A hunter can, therefore, use the map to teach him how to look for deer in a given area. Being guided by the map, he may locate some superior deer habitat during scouting. Then he can turn to the map for help in his actual hunt. Where does a hunter begin in his map use, however? If I had never seen the area I was about to scout or hunt, I would begin by consulting the game regulations. Here again, we have a map, generally, and often with a legal description of hunting boundaries. But this map is going to lack detail in most cases. The hunter simply transfers the general information from the hunting map to his own personal map. That is step one, describing the actual area to be hunted.

The next step is checking the map key. The key will tell how to use the map, how to read it. This is not a map course, nor do we have information on all types of map information. Therefore, the key must be consulted. From the key, the hunter will learn how to interpret the markings on his individual map. He will be able to use the four basics we spoke of earlier, for he will see which direction to take, the position of his hunting camp, trails and byways, and the distances between all of these features. He will also be able to identify many important aspects of the area to include: hills, mountains, valleys, steepness of terrain, flatness of terrain, vegetation description, roads, trails, railroad tracks, power lines, canals, rivers, lakes, streams, building sites and so forth.

It certainly helps if the hunter knows what deer country looks like. For example, if he takes a road into an area by using a map, he should have an idea of what constitutes deer cover. Then he knows where to start scouting or hunting. But even if he does not know, he does know that this area is marked by the game department as having deer habitat! That is the key to all of this, for he has marked off legal hunting land, and from this, any ambitious hunter can then take it upon himself to study the area for deer sign. What to look for, in general?

I would say that we want to find a life support system for deer in a given locale. This life support system includes the following although these are not to be considered complete as a list: Food in the area; sign of the food being used (nipped off and cut back) by game; shelter/cover for game; water, space—isolation is not essential in most cases, but is this area so built up that deer would have a hard time surviving here?; and lack of competition, which must be explained. Lack of competition means this: Do the deer have sufficient area to avoid being shut out by human endeavors? For example, there are places which have been virtually fenced in so that deer will not damage crops. Such an area may have deer on the fringes, but not necessarily in the major portion of the area.

There is also competition from domestic animals. I have seen areas used heavily by sheep which held deer sign, but all the sign was old. The deer had moved off when the domestic sheep moved in. In other areas, heavy browse by cattle may preclude sufficient food for deer. In the West, there are areas which are wonderful for elk, but though some deer will inhabit the locale, and some darn good bucks at that in some places I have hunted, numbers of deer will not be high.

Deer Food and Deer Hunting

A deer of a mere live weight of 150 pounds may consume from 10 to 12 pounds of forage (browse) in a single day. Obviously, a prime daily mover of the deer is food. It not only requires the food for the reasons of survival, but the food hunt is also a "way of life" for the animal. In short, a deer spends a good bit of its allotted time chewing away on this or that, and the hunter can turn this fact into an advantage. In our quest to discuss *successful* deer hunting, we are obligated to look at the deer as a biological machine which must be fueled often. Of course, as hunters we also know that as the

Even in the desert, such as this location not far from Tucson, Arizona, one will often run into a water hole surrounded by heavy vegetation. This canyon held mule deer in its lower reaches and whitetail deer (Coues) in the upper end. A hunter's best preparation for such shooting is to take along a familiar firearm, an accurate one with which the hunter can place his shots well.

53

All along this area, where the forest left off and the open spaces presented themselves, lower browse bushes were evident and every bush encountered by the hunters showed signs of being used as food. Deer tracks in the immediate area of the browse suggested that at least some of the feeding was done by deer. While this type of country is best hunted on foot in the still-hunting tradition, with heavy use of binoculars, the wise hunter will pay special attention to the "edge" terrain.

for what it is, and then he must be able to determine whether or not the deer are using that food during the hunting season.

In spite of these drawbacks, knowledge of deer food and use of that knowledge has helped me bag a buck many times, so it is hardly a hopeless case, and knowing deer foods can be a significant part of the hunter's bag of tricks. There are a few basic suggestions that we can make in regard to using deer food recognition to aid us as hunters.

1. *Recognition*

A hunter must learn to recognize some of the major feed plants in his area. But the first thing he has to do is isolate those plants which are used as food by the deer *in his area during the deer season*. Deer food in one state or locale may not at all show up as deer food in another area. In addition, what a deer chews on July 1, may have very little to do with what it eats on November 1. In learning deer foods, then, the first point is to find out what the deer eat in the given, specific locale the hunter wishes to harvest his deer in. This means those plants which are used as staple food items during the hunting season.

One way to learn these facts is to snip off a small bit of those plants which appear in connection with deer sign. In short, if we go into an area and we find plenty of tracks, hopefully fresh tracks, amidst certain plants, and there is evidence that the plants are being eaten (cleanly nipped off in places), then we can snip a small sample of this plant and head for the game biologist or biology teacher with the sample. The expert can tell us not only what the plant is, but whether or not it is a prime deer food in that area during the fall of the year.

Another way to learn deer browse and feed in general is to observe on our own. If we see deer in the fall, especially during our scouting trips, we can take note of what feed is being used by the deer. While it is easy for me to give this advice now, I recall that I never actually took advantage of the above situation until only a decade ago. During my scouting treks for both whitetail and mule deer, I often saw deer feeding, saw the very bush that the deer was tugging on, and yet when the deer either left or was pushed off by me, I did not go over and study that plant to learn it. That is poor deer hunting for you.

There are not many books which show good clear photos of deer foods, but here again we can consult our local game biologist for advice. In my own area, the game department library had a few notes on deer foods, plus

quality and quantity of the food supply diminishes, so will the deer, not only in body size and condition, but even in the size of the rack.

The successful deer hunter thinks deer food when he scouts an area and when he hunts an area, be that East, West, North or South, and this applies to whitetail as well as mule deer and blacktail. Hunt them where they eat, we might say. There are two big problems, possibly three, which the hunter must face as he tries to apply deer food knowledge to hunting tactics. First, we have to concede that deer have such a tremendous variety of food it is almost safe to say that a deer eats the majority of the greenery in which it resides. Therefore, trying to pick out one ridge on which to hunt, or one valley, based on the type of vegetation that grows there is difficult at best. Second, our deer does not feed throughout the day in most places. So, if we do find a spot which we think is loaded with deer food, so what? The deer probably won't be up eating when we are out hunting anyway. We can add a third problem, which is the fact that although the deer do eat many of the browse plants, forbs and grasses in a given area, it does not consume all varieties of vegetation. So the hunter has to first be able to spot deer food a book which at least gave the names of prominent deer browse used by local herds during the fall. These are three suggestions which may help a hunter learn a little bit about deer foods, and we are going to list some major food plants here, too, as a starter for the hunter.

2. *Deer Food Plus Deer Sign*

We have already alluded to this, but after we gain an idea of what deer foods we are looking for, then we should try to combine deer food and deer sign. We will not always be able to tell when deer tracks are totally fresh in a given locale, but sometimes we can, and I urge the hunter to think about deer food as he still-hunts, checking likely plants. In a moment, we will talk about the value of combining good sign and obvious deer food. For now, let us concede that if we find plants which are being used by deer, then we at least have hope that we have located a deer herd's "supermarket." The plants may be clearly nipped off. In some situations, this condition is really quite easy to see. I have located plant life in both eastern and western settings which were nipped back markedly and very certainly used by animals. To say that these plants were eaten by deer, we need to combine some sign which shows that deer were in amongst the plants themselves. That is not always so difficult to do. Tracks can mean a lot. So can strands of deer hair caught by the bushes. So can obvious tracks of other animals. If there are cattle tracks all over the browse area and precious few deer tracks, we must conclude that the thinning of vegetation is being performed mostly by domestic stock. Deer have three lower incisors on each side of the midline. There are zero incisors above to match with these. The branches and stems of browse are nipped off fairly cleanly by this arrangement but can have a somewhat more shredded look at the tips than those plants nipped off by cattle.

3. *Using Deer Food to the Hunter's Advantage*

Knowing where the deer are feeding is no small bit of information for the hunter. Whether whitetail, mule deer or blacktail, there will be some feeding patterns established by the deer, generally an early morning, late afternoon, and a nighttime feeding pattern. The latter does us no particular good, but it certainly is good hunting practice to be on the feeding grounds early in the day and late in the day. Remember, the deer are up and moving as they feed, and they are far easier to see than they are when bedded. Even in the more thickly overgrown areas of the eastern whitetail, the hunter may find some very good "edge" feeding areas where a shot across a meadow is highly likely. In one such area, I found an old burn which was well-tracked and which had plenty of evidence of use by feeding deer. That evening I was on the spot and so were the deer. The bucks, only two of them at that time, came in later and were smaller than I was looking for, but I recall the instance because I told another hunter about it. The next day he bagged a buck in that same burn.

Here is a deer browsed manzanita bush.

No one method will ever work for a deer hunter all by itself, and in our discussion of deer foods, the object is to combine this knowledge with all the rest of our tactics, of course. But in the more open areas, a hunter is wise to glass out likely feeding grounds early and late in the day, and in the thicker regions he is wise to look for heavy feeding activity, especially in "edge" terrain, where open areas combine with thicker vegetation.

We must remember that the feeding patterns will change with the season, of course. In autumn, frost changes the status of vegetation, obviously, and with leaves falling off of some deer food plants, the deer may turn to a few more grasses. The hunter may wish to study areas which seem to be used by deer nipping away at patches of grass. Hardwood foliage may be more used, especially in mule deer locales. Shrub use will remain high. Among the mule deer, forbs may constitute as much as a quarter of the diet in the fall, for example. Forbs are weeds or herbs which are not true grasses, and we may see a deer with its head buried in what we see as 100 percent grass, when in fact, there are forbs in among those grasses, and these are the primary food target of the deer.

A blacktail buck feeding on thimbleweed.

A Few Deer Foods (Fall consumption)

1. Northern Forest (Upper northeast corner of U.S.A: the Lake States, Maine, New Hampshire, Massachusetts, Pennsylvania, New York, Wisconsin, Minnesota)

a. yew
b. apple fruit
c. hemlock
d. mountain ash
e. black ash
f. white cedar
g. maple
h. basswood
i. sumac
j. white ash

2. Central Forests (Alabama, Missouri, Arkansas, North Carolina [part], Ohio)

a. mountain laurel
b. acorns
c. maples
d. hazels
e. greenbriar
f. lowbush (Vaccinium)
g. blueberry
h. Christmas fern
i. grape
j. Antennaria

3. Southern Forest (Mississippi, Texas, Louisiana, etc.)

a. sumac
b. white oak
c. supplejack
d. grasses
e. sweetgum
f. black gum
g. horse sugar
h. sweet leaf
i. maple
j. flowering dogwood

4. Rocky Mountains (Colorado, Arizona, New Mexico, Wyoming, Idaho, Montana)

a. dogwood
b. choke cherry
c. old man's beard
d. juniper
e. Ceanothus
f. bearberry
g. buckbrush
h. fungi
i. grains
j. grass

The hunter, as already stated, must learn the deer foods for his hunting areas, of course. Where I hunt mule deer,

Winter feeding can often present a problem to the deer of our colder regions. These deer will feed heavily on sagebrush during the winter months, but will turn to browse plants later as the winter departs.

Examples of Trees Used for Browse

Mountain Ash

Hemlock

Flowering Dogwood

Blackgum

Juniper

White Oak

for example, I have come to recognize the buckbrush and mountain mahogany, Oregon grape, juniper and bur oak. In the Southwest, I have learned to recognize the false mesquite and other plants used by the Coues deer, a favorite deer of mine. Yes, the foods do vary widely, and deer foods in one area may not look like deer foods to a hunter who knows the deer food of his area. There is also availability to consider. Good rains in the spring can aid the growth of certain greens that might be somewhat stunted if the spring is dry, so there could be a specific deer food available and prominent right up to late fall due to a good wet spring. In one area, the whitetail deer were working heavily on acorns, but by November mountain maple was more important to the herd as a mainstay food and in winter balsam proved an important source of food to the herd. Algae, mushrooms, moss and grasses were consumed by those deer, too, depending upon availability and the time of year.

Deer do not prefer the same foods as other browse animals all of the time, either, nor will various deer types eat the same foods as preferences. The blacktail, for example, likes leafy foods and brushy foods, preferring mushrooms in some areas, but leaving grasses alone quite a bit of the time. These blacktail deer may eat lots of mushrooms and willow and lichens and acorns while leaving the grasses go. If a herd of mule deer were moved

into the same area occupied by these blacktails, the diets of the two deer would quite probably differ, though the plant life available would be the same.

Knowledge and recognition of deer foods is no panacea for the dedicated deer hunter, of course, but it is one more hunk of know-how that adds a link to the chain of successful deer hunting. Eating is more than sustenance to a deer, I feel, and I have watched deer go about the feeding process as if there were no tomorrow. In fact, I have managed some close-in stalks based upon the sole fact that the deer were so busy filling their bellies that they were not able to detect my approach.

Instead of relying on luck, then, our plan is to build our success on being able to find where the deer are. In short, when we scout we are looking for an area which offers an ecological niche suitable for deer. We finally decided upon that area based upon: permission to hunt the area in the first place; indication that the game department feels there are deer in huntable numbers in that specific area; our own scouting; information gathered from others—game rangers, forest service officials, residents of the area (try the local gas station), ranchers, farmers and hunters; and finally our own success in the area. All of these factors, every one of them, stem from scouting. In our scouting we can learn enough of the area to really give us a true yes or no as to whether or not we want to hunt there.

chapter 5
Reading Sign

READING SIGN is a very important part of deer hunting, as most of us would agree. We read sign during our scouting sessions to determine the presence or lack of deer in a given area. We read sign while we are hunting in order to help us locate a deer. Good, sound, logical sign-reading is, then, a vital part of the deer hunting effort, and one of the keys in opening the door to success. My only caution is that sign-reading should be accomplished with an open mind, and with the firm knowledge that we are not able to determine everything we would like to know from the impressions left behind by deer. In fact, I call the overdoing of sign-reading "Natty Bumppoism," the reference being to Natty Bumpo, the hero of Cooper's "Leatherstocking Tales." Natty could tell the color of an Indian headdress by checking out a moccasin track in the dust.

I have a friend who suffered badly from a case of "Natty Bumppoism." He was, in fact, a good hunter, but his expertise lay in his ability to cover country, to keep himself well-situated with good field position, and to scout ahead of season for top deer habitat. He was a good shot, too. But when this fellow came upon deer sign, he'd bend down and read it better than most of us can read a book. Or so he thought. From a mere deer track, he would relate when the deer made the impression in the ground, whether it was a buck or a doe, how big the rack was, how old the animal was and its social security number as well.

During one hunting trip, which included my friend who could read sign, one of our party harvested a very small buck. It was legal but that was all that could be said for it. We had listened to about 48 hours of Natty Bumppoism from my friend at that time, and I decided to try an experiment. Taking two hooves which were removed from the buck when it was dressed and hung, I put them in my pocket. When my friend and I were on the trail, as he answered the call of nature, I went to work making tracks. I pressed the hooves into the ground very neatly and then stopped suddenly.

My pal's attention was called to the tracks. "Hey," I baited him, "what do you think we have here?" He bent low and studied the tracks. His gaze was intent.

"Buck," he concluded. And he was right about that, I'd have to admit. "A big buck," he continued. *(Oops!)* "You can tell he's got a big rack because of the way the tracks print in the ground." My friend went on to describe the animal in great detail right down to its food preferences and opinions on the stockmarket. Suddenly, the tracks, of course, came to a halt. My friend looked all around. He even looked up in the tree with an embarrassed glance at me when he caught me looking intently at him. Then I pulled the hooves out of my pocket. No words were said. No words were necessary.

I relate the story because I think it is just as bad to think that we hunters can put all of our faith in the sign we read as it is to simply ignore all sign and charge for-

Deer tracks are an obviously useful part of sign-reading. The tracks can be "over-read" by hunters who draw untenable conclusions about the actual age of the track or size of the deer; however, tracks remain a basic source of sign-reading and an important part of the hunter's knowledge of an area.

J. Wayne Fears, guide and hunter, checks tracks in the snow and ice. Telling if such a track is fresh or old is linked primarily to when the snow fell and not to many other factors. (Photo courtesy J. Wayne Fears)

ward into the forest cognizant of nothing at all. Before going into sign-reading, then, it is my opinion that we can find out a great deal by the messages left behind by deer, but to get carried away with the process is defeating, not helpful. Some things we can indeed find out from sign, and a lot of things we cannot find out. Let's read sign. But let's be very careful about the conclusions we derive from this important deer hunting tactic.

Tracks

Perhaps the most obvious sign-reading clue is the deer track. Certainly, if there is a deer track printed in the earth, it must follow that at some time since the dawn of creation a deer trampled over that piece of earth. But do we learn much more than this from a track? I think so, but within limits. Given a particular hardness of soil, we can look at a track and try to determine how heavy a deer was by the actual impression (depth) of that track into the ground. As long as we are very careful about our conclusions, such guesswork is all right. If we are on a deer trail and there are some tracks imprinting ¼-inch into the soil and some tracks imprinting ½-inch into the soil, supposing the tracks were made at about the same time, we can figure that the deeper track was made by a bigger animal, *probably*.

One time I found a set of tracks that resembled those made by a bull elk, except they were deer tracks. It was an exciting find. However, the earth was damp and soft

there. I took a look at my own tracks and they appeared to have been made by the abominable snowman. On the other hand, I located a set of large tracks on some hard-pan soil in country seldom blessed by rain. The tracks were big and they were cut deeply into the ground. I had to kick the earth with the heel of my boot in order to make an impression. I had to go away feeling that those tracks were made by a larger animal.

How about sheer hoof size? I have seen hooves on doe deer, especially mule deer but also whitetail, which were simply grand in size. We like to think that a buck track is more rounded, while a doe track is more narrow and pointed. Generally, there is probably truth in this. But, again, I only suggest that we read such sign with an open mind, and just because a track is large and rounded does not *prove* that we have a buck ahead.

How old is a track? Unless there has been a brand new snow or very recent rain, I think the safest thing we can say about the age of a deer track is, "I don't know how old it is, but I'll make a general guess." In this way, we are not letting Natty Bumppoism rule us. We are using our common sense instead. There are, however, a few things we can look for in a deer imprint. The edges of a track will break down as the earth settles back into place after being disturbed. A very sharply imprinted track in rather soft soil may indeed be somewhat fresh. That same track with the edges collapsed may be older. One time I was hunting deer in a very remote area, and there was a beautiful set of tracks right by my tent. A couple weeks later that same set of tracks looked precisely as it had the week before.

If a track is loaded with twigs or sand which has blown into the track itself, this may indicate an older track, unless the wind has only recently kicked the twigs or sand into the track. If the wind has not been blowing for the past 12 hours, then it probably suggests that the twigs or sand was blown into the track more than 12 hours ago. When I am going to stay in an area, however, I certainly will set up a condition so that the deer track can mean more to me.

First, it is wise to clear off a likely spot, dusting it with a makeshift broom of sorts, a broom which can be constructed from a fallen tree branch for example. Along a trail, or at the edge of a field or meadow or at a likely watering spot, we clear a good place with our broom and then go back and check for tracks. Now we can say something about these tracks if we indeed find that our dusted areas are now showing deer sign. We can now say that these tracks are fresh ones and that deer are nearby. I think that such track sign is very worthwhile then. But to look at a set of tracks and read the date, hour and size of deer is more an impediment than a help, I think. Remember, the tracks left by the pioneers crossing the Oregon Trail can still be seen to this day! I have witnessed the deep impressions made by the wagons in what surely was mud, and one can even locate a few animal tracks in the same condition. If tracks can last 100 years, I think

we should be careful about our assessment of such sign as deer tracks when we are hunting.

If we find a set of tracks, what, as hunters, should we do about it? I think we can take a step-by-step approach to this question. First, we are happy because we know that at some time a deer has been on this spot, and it may follow that deer are still in the immediate area. Second, while we can't always determine the age of a track, we may have some indication that the track before us is not so terribly old, and then what? Third, I think, is to go ahead and see if the tracks will reveal more information. Generally, it is very difficult to follow deer tracks in the forest or anywhere else. But in the case of a trail, let's stay on the track for a while. This can't do us any harm, can it? We might end up next to a deer if we take a path used by a deer.

Fourth, if the land is soft from rain or if there is snow on the ground, then the hunter should by all means stay to the tracks for a while. Can a hunter actually "walk a deer down?" This may meet with guffaws by some, but I say yes, if we mean walk far enough to catch up to a deer. I have done it so many times, not only in the open country, but in the forest. A deer does not necessarily cover ground at high speed, and it is entirely possible for a hunter to catch up to a deer if the track is fairly fresh. The hunter may in fact come upon the deer right on its trail as the deer feeds along or heads slowly for a particular spot. It is very difficult for us to understand the actual motives of deer. I have followed a deer for hours,

Immediately following a rain, a deer print in the soft earth is clearly imprinted. The widespread appearance would lead many hunters to call this track that of a buck. It may be a track of a buck. However, the hoof may also splay out in such soft terrain and thereby make a track which appears quite wide.

While tracking is not always possible nor workable, tracks in fresh snow certainly are worthy of pursuit. (Photo courtesy J. Wayne Fears)

only to learn that the animal made a meandering trail in the snow, heading for only a spot it either knew of or perhaps randomly ended up at. I could see where it stopped from time to time. I could see where the deer nipped some food from a low bush or two. As for buck or doe, in some places where the clean snow was somewhat higher, I could see the marks made by the animal's reproductive organ where the latter made contact with the snow.

Staying on the tracks, I could see a urination pattern which had to be that of a buck, somewhat randomly printed in the snow instead of in a single spot. Conversely, I have seen a patch in the snow with a urination mark made obviously by a doe, her rump making the round mark in the snow and the urine concentrated in one spot only. And then, all of a sudden, there is the deer. In the sense of "walking the deer down," I suppose we have not. In the sense of "catching up to the deer," you bet your rifle the deer was caught up with. In a couple of instances I have jumped a buck, had it give me the slip, and then stayed on the fresh trail in the snow and, several hours later, caught up with the animal. So following deer tracks in fresh snow or soft earth after a new rain is hardly a fool's work. It makes sense. Thinking that a deer is going to be at the end of any track we hunters happen to run across, however, is more wishful thinking than anything else.

Trails

Is it not exciting to locate a trail upon which the handsome prints of deer hooves are printed? Of course it is, and the find is hardly without value. But, again, I do not think that we should use that trail, no matter how good it is, as our sole source of deer hunting just because it looks so good to us. Prudence rules again. I think the majority of tracks made on a trail are put there during the late hours of the afternoon and into the night. I have sat in observance of many deer trails over the past 30 years of deer hunting, and I have seen deer walking on those trails, too, but often I felt that my time would have been better spent by doing something else. I think deer mostly wander where the spirit moves them. But there are exceptions and times when trails can mean a lot.

If we are a part of a deer drive, then a trail is a worthwhile place to rest a bit and look a lot. Deer which are driven may very well take to a trail. If a trail leads to obviously well-used watering places or feeding areas, then that trail is worth watching. If we are going to set up a stand or a blind, it might as well be near a trail. As for a deer, however, using a trail as the sole means of access to a given area, I just do not believe it. Find a trail, then, and use that find to best advantage. Read the tracks on the trail. Follow the trail. While a deer may not use that trail at the very moment the hunter is observing it or on it, the trail may very well take a hunter into the right spot to find a buck.

This happened to me one time. I located a deer trail which had been heavily used. The trail was dusted, and

A deer trail blackened by droppings in an overbrowsed deer yard.

After a rain, these tracks stand out along a seldom-used road. It is worth taking a look and finding out where they lead. Scouting can often pay off in getting a hunter back into an area when the season opens, as it has here. (Photo courtesy J. Wayne Fears)

This winter browse has been chewed back considerably, and the work was accomplished by deer, for there were no cattle in the immediate area. Sagebrush varieties offer good winter range feed for deer and other animals, being high energy yielding and generally of good quantity.

This buck was bedded in rather high grass. Trying to find sign in such an area would be difficult without getting down close to the ground and deliberately looking for it. Hunters may pass up an area such as this due to the fact that sign is hard to see, but that sign could be there all the same.

the very next day fresh tracks were on it, tracks of varying sizes from small to large. However, in a couple days I never once saw a deer on that trail, though I did see deer above the trail and below it, walking in the brush as if there were no pathway within a mile of the spot. However, I finally took to the trail myself. It wound up through the forest and over a series of small hills and then into a brushy little valley. At the edge of that brushy valley I found deer beds and in the afternoon I located deer, several of them, including a buck which became mine.

So a trail has several uses. We can dust it to see if deer are in the area and using that trail. We can wait on a trail, especially in early morning and late afternoon. We can follow a trail to see where it leads us. A hunter should consider a deer trail a good find. And he should take advantage of this type of sign-reading, for trails are information holders, holders of sign, not only in tracks, but also sign of beds just off of main trails and feeding off of trails.

Beds and Food

Elsewhere, we mentioned deer food and beds. Both can be read as sign. Not to belabor the issues here, but we should state that deer beds are often located and are not that difficult to mark as deer beds, as opposed to bedding sites for other animals. Tracks, obviously, help in

deciding which animal may have used the bed. There also may be hairs caught in branches near the beds. A bedding area is a worthwhile find. What to do with it? I say use a bedding area as a starting point for a still-hunt. Also, there is nothing wrong with coming into the area in early morning. Probably, the deer will have risen if they were using the beds for any length of time in the night. Remember, deer may often be feeding at night, and the beds will get no use at that time. But they may use a bed at night briefly. One time we were engaged by a rancher to see if we could help him with a coyote problem. We failed, and the rancher ended up removing his sheep from the range, but as part of our investigation we studied the area at night, which was legal. Often, we found deer which were bedded, as well as many deer which were feeding, indicating that the deer were doing both in that area at night at that time, middle November.

We can also use deer beds for still-hunting by day. If the deer are going to use those beds, daylight hours will make a good time for a hunter to still-hunt the bedding grounds. This type of hunting will result in a jumped buck, hopefully, and the hunter will be obliged to stay on his toes, ready for a quick shot. The bed is just one more bit of information to put into our bag of data. By finding a deer bed or beds, we can then hope to judge the recentness of use and act accordingly. A deer bed does something else for the hunter. It tells him that his quarry is in the area, one of the most important pieces of information he can have. But the bedding area may be an old one. So, once again, we use prudence in our find. We, as hunters, consider the find important, but we do not use that information to the exclusion of other information and a variety of hunting tactics.

How about browse? We stated that one can see when browse has been used. If there seems to be recently nipped off browse plants, or "cut back" plants, with obvious feeding patterns, and if this sign is combined with deer tracks, then I think it reasonable to assume that deer are either using, or have used, that browse. Sometimes it is rather easy to detect the freshness of deer browse which is being eaten on. The stems are nipped off and the chewed area is fresh and clean, not too dark. I have taken my knife and cut off a small bit of browse right next to browse which has been obviously chewed on, comparing the freshness of both. One can sometimes see immediately that the chewed browse is freshly nipped off, or old sign. We add this sign-reading to our repertoire of hunting data, then.

Rubs and Scrapes

This sign must be interpreted along with the season of the year. In most cases, the rub may be made before the hunting season. A rub is the place which has been used by the buck to polish the antlers. We spoke of antler development and cycle, and now that data becomes useful to our hunting. If the buck used a specific area as a rub, that bit of information has two possible applications. If we are involved in an early season hunt, as some bow-hunting seasons are, then the buck might be at work in that very locale and hunting around the rub(s) is probably worthwhile. If the rub is found later in the year, we still have this value: a buck was there not that long ago. If the area supports deer which do not migrate or do not migrate far, as is the case with most whitetails and some blacktails, then we can still do some serious scouting in that specific spot. If the herd is migratory by nature, at least we have a starting point to work from, and we might wish to put on a good search, working down into what we can assume to be the lower end of the summer range.

To sit for great periods of time, then, at a rub is not always fruitful. To use the rub as a starting point, hunting the area, either the immediate locale or nearby, is worthwhile. The scrape is just that, an area upon the ground which has been "pawed clear." I use the inaccurate term pawed, because a hunter can get the correct image in his mind, a deer "pawing the ground" about like a bull will do. The scrape is cleared of vegetation in the process and becomes a bare spot. During the mating season (rut), the doe may in fact locate a buck's scrape and urinate in it. The buck may then discover this "lure" and follow up on the doe. But that is only of small consequence to us as hunters. I have seen a doe coming on a deer trail, and within a few moments to ½-hour, here comes a rutting buck, right on the trail. That is fine, but a scrape more

Guide and hunter, J. Wayne Fears, friend of the author, shows a location where a buck has polished its antlers. While we may not put total faith in such a spot, we are certainly wise to recognize the fact that a deer did make this sign and in our scouting chalk this place up as one to study seriously. (Photo courtesy J. Wayne Fears)

J. Wayne Fears checks the work of a whitetail buck. There is no guarantee that a buck is going to be in the immediate area because of this sign, but it is a starting point and the scouting hunter should use the information to its fullest value. (Photo courtesy J. Wayne Fears)

A water hole can sometimes lead a hunter to deer, especially in the drier climates where deer may depend upon a local watering station. This particular water hole was located in fairly arid terrain, and there was good deer sign in the country surrounding the water. When a hunter locates such a water hole, he is well off to investigate the nearby countryside for deer sign, especially bedding areas.

directly serves as a stand. A hunter who finds a fresh scrape with signs of urination in that scrape may be best off to take a stand near this spot and watch it for a while.

Since most of my own deer hunting does not coincide with the rut, my personal use of scrapes is limited. But I have observed scrapes in my study of deer and they are very interesting. The scrape itself is not very large. I do not know how to put an optimum size on a scrape, but I guess 6 inches wide and 18 inches long gives the hunter a ball park figure to work with. The buck scrapes the earth and urinates on the spot. There is nothing unusual in members of the animal world marking off such a place.

The scrape and the rub may be near each other, and even though the antlers of the deer are polished by the rut, the buck will often "spar" with a branch which is near a scrape. This leaves sign, and sign-reading is our interest of the moment. I caution the reader to remember that these scrapes are only made during the rut, so they are not the same as scent posts prepared by some other mammals. What, perhaps, is most useful to the hunter is the fact that a buck may have several scrapes in a given area. Therefore, the buck will use these scrapes during the rut as if it were on patrol. In the very process of looking for more scrapes, the hunter is actually doing something toward his harvesting of the buck, for he is up and about in the same territory most likely occupied by the buck.

Let us suppose, for example, that this specific sign is read by the hunter: A scrape is located. Then another scrape is located nearby. The scrapes are freshly cut into fairly dry earth, and it is obvious that they have been used as sites for deer, because we can see urination marks in the scrapes themselves. The branches near these scrapes are obviously damaged as if by antlers rubbing on them. We may find, too, the bushes within the immediate area chewed upon. All of this leads us to several worthwhile actions—stand hunting, still-hunting the immediate area or we may try "rattling up a buck" in this locale, too.

More on rattling later, but for now let's bear in mind that it is the fruit we have gathered by reading sign which is our current topic. By reading sign we may have located a specific area being used by a buck or bucks, and we can also apply a calling technique here, too. We may also use a deer call after we have tried other tactics, because the buck during rut is a very interesting fellow. I have called bucks in during the rut. What possibly could have been the reason for a buck, during the rut at that, coming to the "bleat" of a deer? I do not know. But the deer react according to their own interests. Again, we find a mule deer/whitetail difference here. The mule deer will respond less well to the rattling technique. Even in rut, I have never had a mule deer buck come charging to the fight because of clashing antlers, though I have seen two deer whacking heads together when a third mule deer buck suddenly shows up, interested, too.

For mule deer hunting, the scrape is less meaningful in this one hunter's opinion, than the scrape is for whitetail hunting. In my own mind, when I do hunt the rut for mule deer, as I will occasionally do (in Idaho, for example), I will not spend time looking for scrapes, but will spend my time more directly looking for deer, especially from vantage points with binoculars. I have seen mule deer scraping the earth, but have not, personally, been satisfied that scrapes are quite the same for mule deer and whitetail deer.

Water Holes and Waterways

When I was a young hunter, living in Arizona, I decided that one of the best ways to get a buck, whitetail or mule deer, would be to find a well-used watering spot and stick around it. Fortunately, I was too fidgety to sit around water holes all the time or I probably would have compiled a very unimpressive record of harvests. It took a while, but I came to realize that no matter how important the water hole might be to the deer, and no matter how many tracks I found around the water hole, the odds of a big buck coming in to that liquid while I was there in daylight hours were none too good. I always used the water holes for sign-reading, but changed my tactics from taking a stand around a water hole to using the water hole as a starting point for hunting.

Water holes and drinking areas, however, can mean a lot in the sign-reading department. On a couple of occasions, I have harvested bucks because I located a watering site and then studied all of the immediate area for beds and other deer sign. This proved more useful to me than trying to take a stand by a water hole. In South Dakota I found a small stream which served the same purpose. The stream was a wonderful place to read sign. Here was a chance to sweep an area clear and then check it in the morning for tracks. The whitetail deer were using a part of the stream which widened out into shallow pools for watering, and they must have been watering at night, for I never saw a deer near the water itself in my stay, but I soon learned where it was the deer were feeding and bedding, and I learned that by reading sign at a watering site.

Droppings

What about deer droppings, also known as pellets? Do they mean anything? I think so. Again, aging such pellets exactly is not possible, for they will dry out in accord with the humidity and conditions of the area, but I do not think it is wrong to say that we can tell a very old pellet from a fairly recent one. Remember, in some areas the grasses will hide such sign, and in some areas the pellets will last a long time, though I still contend that we can tell very old ones from new ones. I have, however, seen old pellets, or what I thought were old, which had been recently rained on or had been under a morning dew and they looked, I suspect, fresher than they were.

One point which needs to be made, I think, is that just because an area is not replete with pellets does not mean there are no deer around. I have already suggested that pellets can be lost in the grass, but I'd also like to say that a deer does not spend all of his time making waste where we are likely to find it. Being the free spirits that they are, deer seem to have no compunction against going wherever they so please, and this means the thickets and grassy draws as well as the more open places we might choose to walk in.

Fencelines can offer a little bit of information concerning the deer in the area. Deer can leap a fence as if it were a lump of dirt on the ground. At least this is true of most fences that we will encounter in either ranching or farming country. However, in spite of this ability, deer do not always fly over a fence. They often go under it or even through it. And when they do, some hair might be caught on the fence, and some telltale tracks left under the fenceline itself. So, this is a little bit of sign that we can look for if we just happen to be coursing along a fence row. Again, I would not go looking for a fence just to see if deer had been climbing through it or going under it.

Reading sign is part of deer hunting, and part of successful deer hunting. I think when we interpret our findings with a lump of salt, then we are OK. I think when we get all swelled up with the idea that we can determine precisely what a deer is doing, has been doing and is going to do in the future by merely observing some sign on the ground, that we are in trouble. The sign is important to us when it suggests that deer are, indeed, in the area, for it fulfills part one of our three-part rule for successful deer hunting: *deer have to be in the area before we can get one.*

The leavings of deer are not difficult to spot, though domestic sheep in some areas can confuse some hunters if they are new-comers to the game. On the far left we see the large pellet of the moose. In the center is the pellet of the elk, and on the far right we have the pellet of the deer.

chapter 6
Deer Hunting Methods

METHODS of deer hunting are the second part in our list of three major means of successfully taking to the field in quest of venison. Breaking down our hunt into three artificial categories may seem unwise; however, we can't talk about all things at once, so we use this means of separating the points to be made. However, I'm pretty sure the hunter knows the final goal is to put all three together; hunting where the deer are; using wise hunting methods; and then being able to master the tools of the chase so there is a hit instead of a miss, and a hit with a proper missile.

If any topic is open to great controversy, that topic is deer hunting. I hesitated sitting down at the typewriter because I could sense the hundreds of letters from shooters who can always tell whitetail tracks from mule deer tracks, doe tracks from buck tracks, and who have used a .25–20 to bag dozens of trophy bucks. Well, areas differ greatly in geography, and deer differ according to their reaction to the habitat. So we have to leave a little room for these variations. With that in mind, let's take a look at some basic hunting tactics.

Still-Hunting

First, there is still-hunting. Still-hunting means just that, being still, or quiet, as one moves through deer country. But it does not mean staying still. That is another method altogether. So, by still-hunting we mean moving through the woods or other deer range. One thing to con-

sider in still-hunting is the fact that the deer are generally still, and the hunter is in motion. It is a matter of hunter psychology, the hunter aware at all times that his quarry is either motionless or making very small movements while he is, in effect, coursing through the trees and thickets or over the open land.

Clothing for Still-Hunting

The first point I'd like to consider is clothing for still-hunting. Wool is quiet. Being from the West, denim type pants constitute much of my hunting wear, but they are not as quiet as wool pants. A season ago, I was hunting in a high country camp in Idaho and two of the camp's members were from the East, the other two from the West. The Easterners were far better equipped than the two fellows from out West, those two being my son and myself. The Easterners had stout wool pants. We on the otherhand, wore the denim type trousers. While the wool remained soft and pliable, our pants became more and more stiff and noisy.

Footgear is also important to the still-hunter. Certainly, the type of footgear depends upon the season of the year and the terrain. But several of the finest still-hunters I know wear sneakers now. They used to wear boots, but they got away from them in favor of a truly soft-soled shoe. Many of us can't get by with low-topped shoes, however, and in my opinion if a fellow wants to use sneakers, he should select the high-tops. Also, for those of us who have broken our bones over the years, and who might have weakened ankles, I recommend wrapping the ankles prior to a hunt. The regular stretch-type support bandage will do just fine for this, and it offers support which has been lost when the high-top leather boot is traded for the softer sneaker.

I use a canvas type shoe called the Maine Hiking model from L.L. Bean for my early season woods hunting. This is a hightop shoe of the sneaker type, but I like it better than regular low-cut "tennis shoes." I only wear them in the woods when the ground is free of snow and hopefully free of mud as well. It is a wonderful shoe in the early season woods because it is quiet.

The soft shoe, soft of sole and soft of top, is murder in the cactus country. I have used these shoes in such terrain and I love them because they are quiet, but once the needles and barbs have found a home in the foot (coming right through the side of the shoe, generally), the hunter is a sorry figure. In cactus country and in terrain loaded with rocks, the leather boot is best.

However, the primary advantage soft shoes have for a hunter, especially good for the still-hunters, is that they make a person walk softly. You don't tend to bang through the woods and bash your ankles up against fallen logs when wearing soft shoes. They also do something else that is excellent—they make you *slow down*.

Still-hunting should be slow hunting. I chastise myself

J. Wayne Fears walks a seldom-used road in Alabama. That is, the road is seldom used by vehicles, but Wayne found enough sign in the area to convince him of deer numbers worth looking into. He still-hunts on the road for a distance and then circles into the growth and back out to the road again, moving slowly. (Photo courtesy J. Wayne Fears)

The L. L. Bean Maine Hiking Shoe is a soft-soled shoe with excellent gripping power for the rocks or any terrain composed of loose materials. It is a quiet shoe for the forest as well. Of course, no one shoe or boot serves all purposes, and the hunter must be aware of trade-offs. While this shoe, a favorite of the author, is quiet in the rocks, the hunter must be cautious in his movements so that his feet do not receive rock bruises.

regularly for getting too curious about what is deeper in the woods and hurrying too much. If a hunter has chosen decent deer country, he need not try to set a record in getting through it. I should make this clear: I don't believe in pussyfooting all day long. There are some areas which dictate that a hunter put on some speed and get the heck through it and on to better things. I once watched a man crossing an open meadow. He was maintaining the same pace he had used while in the woods. It looked downright funny. While the slow-stepping was perfect for the dense cover, it was truly pointless out in the wide open. There was scarcely a twig in the meadow for a deer to hide behind. The man would have been better advised to pour on the speed and get across the meadow and then continue his slow motion methods when he was once again in the thick of it all.

Moccasins are also wonderful for stalking, but I want a bit more sole between my feet and the good earth. Some moccasins, however, have just enough sole to offer protection, while at the same time forcing that hunter to virtually feel the ground with his feet as if he were running his hand along the back of a catfish to avoid the spines. I suppose if we were shod in moccasins from childhood the soles of our feet would be tough, and we could enjoy stomping over broken twigs and rocks. Maybe that's why we have been called tenderfeet by the true and tough frontiersmen of old.

I won't go further into the clothing necessary for still-hunting. I'm sure we all get the picture. The soft flannel shirt, the soft-soled boot or shoe, the quieter materials for our pants, that's what we need, I think.

How and Where To Still-Hunt

As said before, in still-hunting the hunter moves slowly and quietly through the forest in an attempt to find deer within range. But just how quiet can we be in the woods? Well, it certainly depends upon the hunter. Some hunters are naturally more quiet, more coordinated afoot than other hunters. I know I am more noisy than some, so I do one thing, aside from softer clothing, to cut down on the noise I make. And it, again, is slowing down. If I walk very slowly, I can cut out some of that blasted noise that I tend to make as I go through the woods.

Moving quietly while still-hunting or stalking is extremely important because of the hearing ability of deer. Deer can hear so well that no man alive can depend upon always being quiet in terms of sneaking right up on deer all the time. But with the wind just right and the ground soft, it is amazing how close a hunter can get to a deer. My closest stalk to a buck was 5 yards with my son Bill looking on. I got 5 yards from the buck. It jumped from its bed, for I had spotted it bedded with my binoculars from a distance, and I put a round ball from my muzzleloader through the buck at 10 yards. But the ground was soft. That was the secret.

Over some terrain I defy any man to walk quietly. I have seen days in the northwoods in which the ground was covered with thousands of dry leaves. Again, all we can do in such cases is slow down and try to stay, perhaps, in shady spots which may hold a bit of moisture, thus deadening the sound.

I love still-hunting. It is much more interesting to me than sitting, though at times the latter method is great. I try to still-hunt in country where the deer are going to be "catchable." I am especially fond of hunting in "transitional cover." Some hunters call it "edge." It is, in some cases, the division of actual life zones, but more often simply the meeting of two different vegetation types. Much of the edge is found where a forested area meets a brushy area. It is this edge terrain then that often contains low browse or brush that is deer food. I like to still-hunt so that I can see some of this edge and yet be within sight of good deer cover too.

The still-hunter needs to know the edge country, the likely deer spots. He needs to go and search out that blowdown of timber instead of just walking past it because it is more convenient to walk past it. He studies the old burns and will not pass up a place ravaged by a fire a few seasons ago or longer because he knows that the sunlight can now strike the ground in these areas and new life in the form of deer browse is likely to spring up. He uses his horizons. There is nothing wrong with showing yourself at a meadow's edge. You may have to. But you do not burst into view. The still-hunter will also not

This is good "edge" country. At the edge of the timber, a new and different type of vegetation thrives, and this vegetation is very often deer food. The small plants have been given a lot of sunlight, and yet the protective forest is nearby, a good place to look for deer sign.

appear at the edge of a meadow until he has looked into the meadow and along its edges with great care, preferably with optics. He will not show his head over a rise all at once. He will step forward a bit at a time, looking at the new land in front of him bit by bit before he allows his full body to come into view. He tries to move without too much movement. A man can swing and sway his way through the woods or he can keep the upper half of his body less animated. The latter is better for the still-hunter.

In snow, the still-hunter uses tracking in his favor. We have talked about reading sign, and in snow the hunter can say things he could not say without the white carpet underfoot. He can see a track and call it fresh. If it has recently snowed, the age of the track becomes somewhat pinpointed. An older track in snow has a tendency to lose its sharp edge, so a hunter can usually tell a fairly fresh track from an older one just by the clean sharp cut of the newer track *vs.* the dull, less sharply outlined older track. He may spot a bit of yellow stain in the snow as if sprinkled there, and he can then call this sign that of a buck, even though he has not seen the animal. In deeper snow, he may locate a place where the genitals of the deer made a mark, saying "buck" again.

All geographic areas are not necessarily excellent for still-hunting, but still-hunting can be used almost anywhere if the hunter so desires. However, trying to still-hunt an area which is so dense that the hunter can't see 20 yards in front of him may call for other measures, such as a drive or even a stand. But I have still-hunted in brush so thick that I had to force my way through some of it, and I have gotten shots in that type of terrain, but it is hardly an ideal situation. Still-hunting is also not recommended for areas with a large number of other hunters.

The skills of a good still-hunter are several. But those skills are often less important than attitude. The still-hunter needs stamina. In other words, he ought to be in good physical condition, and as for those skills just mentioned, eyesight is certainly a plus factor. So are the skills of fast gun-handling and straight shooting should a buck jump cover. But more important than these is the attitude a still-hunter assumes—that of believing in what he is doing. The still-hunter must have confidence. It is easy to become lulled into a terrible lack of attention, so that when the golden second arrives and that deer is either in sight on the move, or standing still, the hunter can act with calm decision.

I will say this again, no doubt, but most of us who still-hunt a lot have one big failing. We walk too fast. There is a lot of interest in still-hunting, interest created by, "I wonder what is over that next hill?" As a result, the hunter tends to force ahead. When the hunter moves too quickly, many bad things happen. First, he is generally noisier. I do not believe that there was ever a man who could *always* walk quietly in any type of terrain, especially the fall countryside where crisp leaves litter the ground. But a hunter who moves slowly has a better chance of keeping the noise level down. A hunter who moves slowly is more thorough in his search, too. Instead of walking past an area, he may take the time to really look for that deer. While we are not talking about a skill here, we are again talking about an attitude, and the hunter simply must adopt the attitude that during much of his still-hunting, slow is better than fast. To be sure, there are specific areas which are not highly productive for deer, and a hunter may then wish to speed up and get past that terrain and into more productive country.

How much ground is covered? The slow-moving still-hunter may spend a whole day looking over a deer area no more than ½-mile wide and ½-mile long. Or he may know special little places in the country, which means he might hunt a ridge during the morning, then hotfoot it over to another area during late morning, take a little time out at noon, move into different territory for early afternoon and then head for a special spot for a late afternoon prowl. The latter is very often my method of hunt-

(Above) In open terrain the still-hunter has to be very aware of "topping out" carefully, that is, appearing on the horizon slowly while looking ahead for deer. He must also make certain that his path takes him into likely deer "hangouts," and that his field position is such that he can get a shot if he jumps a deer. The still-hunter has to be ready to fire quickly, but with accuracy and safety always in mind.

(Left) Another example of still-hunting along "edge" is demonstrated here as a successful black powder hunter tugs his trophy back to camp.

ing an area I know well. I like to cover the ground in between places I really want to see, and I mean cover it at a reasonably fast pace, slowing down when I reach that special "pocket," that particular ridge where I saw deer food, the area where beds seem evident, and so forth. No particular range estimation can be made for a still-hunter. I have walked 6 miles in whitetail country, and then at other times I have barely covered ½-mile straight away from my campsite. It all depends upon the lay of the land and the sign that goes with it, and prior knowledge gained of the area and its deer.

We tend to talk about whitetail hunting *vs*. mule deer hunting, and it is certainly true that our whitetail is generally a creature of denser cover and a creature of more delicate ways. Certainly, we must hunt differently depending upon the terrain. But of the basic methods of hunting described here, it is sometimes startling to see how well each particular method works on *either* type of deer. Many fine whitetail deer were taken by still-hunters, and many big mule deer bucks are taken on drives, even though many hunters of the West don't recognize that the deer which they harvested was driven.

The still-hunter gains special increases in possible success when he knows the terrain well. This is why I uphold the pre-scouting of an area as a major tactic in annual success. Earlier, I said that I might slow-hunt an area and then hotfoot it over to another area. Without prior knowledge of the country, such actions are pointless.

What if a deer is jumped and a shot is impossible? Should a hunter abandon the chase on that animal? A still-hunter will, without a doubt, experience several such cases. He will certainly jump bucks which give him the slip. Should he follow up? It all depends, of course. Given fresh snow and a deer which is not really spooked, but seems to more or less leave the country with little panic, I would follow up for a while. What can it hurt? Even if that deer is not sighted again, it may be heading for darn good country where other deer are hanging around. On the other hand, I have seen deer, both whitetails and mulies, simply clear out. The idea of these deer running in a wonderfully perfect circle and ending up right back to where they started from is sometimes sound, but a hunter who counts on cutting the buck off "at the pass" is usually going to be disappointed when that buck is making tracks because it has been spooked. I have seen deer in more open country which were still running ½-mile away. If they were making a circle, it sure was a funny circle. It seemed to me the deer was trying to prove that the shortest distance between two points is a straight line, and the straight line it was making was as far away as possible from me.

But I have jumped a buck and then gone back to the same area and found that buck again, and this has happened to me all of about three times in 30 years of deer hunting. Once in Mexico I saw a whitetail buck across a canyon. It was rather thick terrain, too, but from one knob a person could see to another knob. I missed

Deer abound in this area. The hunter knows it. He uses the road as a guide post, hunting back into the bush slowly and then back out to the road again. (Photo courtesy J. Wayne Fears)

the shot, but I had a good chance to see the buck before I fired and its antlers were extremely light in color. They looked white. They were heavy. They were, in short, easily identifiable. I hunted a series of small pockets, depressions filled with brush, in truth, all around the area where that deer jumped. And remember, I had fired and missed besides allowing the buck to see me. I hunted all day, poking around those pockets. Finally that buck came out and I managed to collect him. It was the same buck. I'd bet my deer rifle on it, for the buck had that same white rack, the same thickness of beam, the same number of points. He had not gone far after being spooked by me.

Staying Still

Still-hunting is interesting and can be productive. It is one good way to find a buck. But it is hardly the only way and not always the best way, either. Sometimes a hunter's best bet is to stay still instead of still-hunting. After all, still-hunting is a mathematical condition, is it not? There is only so much terrain out there, albeit often miles of the stuff, and there are only so many deer in that cover. We hope that there is a buck deer in that area and that our still-hunting will bring us to that buck. We use up the terrain bit by bit, covering it with reasonable quietness, as thoroughly as possible, hopefully at slow throttle and with our eyes doing much of the walking for us. We reduce the odds the more we still-hunt, the more ground we cover. That is fine, but not for all the time, and certainly not for everywhere. The key to successful stand-hunting or drives is having a hunter in that opportune spot, a place where a deer is likely to cross. We have already mentioned some of these locations, such as edge terrain, old burns, meadowlands and such places. First, let's speak in general terms and then we will get more specific. How about trails for stand-hunting? Wouldn't it be great to sit on a trail and wait for a deer to come by? I suppose there are times and places where this works out. I have hunted various terrains, and I simply cannot report that deer use trails during shooting hours the way we sometimes tend to think they do. All in all, it is up to the individual hunter in his particular locale. While I personally have not had much luck on trails, others no doubt have had luck where they hunt.

By far, I prefer a crossing. I trust a crossing for deer more than I trust a trail in terms of seeing game. I consider a trail a single-file type path cut into the landscape. A crossing is more a natural area which, because of the lay of the land, if you will, is an easement for game. When

(Above) Being on stand means different things to different hunters. Essentially, the hunter on stand is staying still; he is not in a situation where he is going to indulge in much motion. Preferably, he will have a background which helps his form blend into the surroundings, and he will have sufficient cover all around to prevent a deer from seeing him. Yet, he can see the area in front and around him very well. Here, the hunter is crouched (seated on a rock) into a small cleft in the side of a canyon.

(Left) Here is a natural crossing. The tracks do help here in indicating how much activity there is on the abandoned logging road. Also, the little road, mostly grown in with vegetation now, leads into a meadow. We have what is known as "edge" where vegetation types of a varying kind come together.

By remaining still, a hunter may find that a deer will come quite close to him, even when he does not have camouflage clothing on. However, when a hunter makes a move, he can fairly well count on being seen. These deer are very close to the hunter, but he has not yet moved.

I was a beginning whitetail hunter, my brother and I got a lesson in crossings from a seasoned hunter.

The country we were hunting was choked with plant life. A man could hardly move through the thickets. In fact, we saw a good number of deer, if you count tails disappearing in the brush and a flash here and a flash there. But we got no shots. Back in the small town, we consulted a friend of ours, an older person, concerning our problem. He hunted the same choked area.

The next morning he told us to sit in a spot which was actually a converging point for several hills. It is hard to explain it exactly, but the hills were tall and steep, except for this pancake flat spot that seemed to join the hills together. There was no distinct trail through that pass, but it was a pass. I wondered why there was no cattle path at least and then realized that the waterhole was below and that the few livestock in that area did not need to climb up to where I was for feed or water. So, we sat in the pass. Nobody was driving. But deer came by. We had gotten on the stand before light by using our flashlights to guide the way. The first hour of light we saw several bucks. Our aim was big heads at the time, but we did not see a big animal. A fellow seeking venison, however, would have had his in a few moments following first light.

Perhaps it is too bad that every area is so different, and to add to that, the movement of deer in various places differs, too. Nobody can give a blanket statement for North American deer hunting. What we can do, those of us who have devoted thousands of hours to deer hunting, is speak of our findings and hope they apply to the reader's situation. I say this because a friend of mine uses a field as his deer stand and has managed to put a buck down every year for the past 15 seasons—good-sized animals at that. There is no one trail to this field. But there are about four trails that I could find which did show sign after I had swept them clean. The deer did use those four pathways to the field. They also used no trails at all in many cases, merely heading for the field in as straight a line as they could manage. While this situation

existed in that one field, there was a different situation in another field I hunted.

The second field is rather small and surrounded by natural hills fairly loaded with deer. In fact, the deer put one man out of business, or at least this is what he said before he sold out. He told me in plain language that he could no longer put up with the ravages of the deer in his field. One could argue that taking a stand on a trail by this field would have worked because deer did appear like clockwork in the later afternoon, almost toward dusk, and they did come in on trails, mostly. But the trails were actually situated between hills and were more in the category of natural passes, I think. At any rate, we filled our second deer tags in and around this field, and we are still doing so to this day by simply taking a stand and waiting.

Let's suppose that we elect to take a stand. What makes stand-hunting, staying still, effective and what causes failure? My first thought along these lines is my own lack of patience. I am not at my best sitting my hindmost parts on a stump and waiting. I have cost myself deer because of my lack of patience. On a hunt in South Dakota I took what I thought was a good stand in a "natural pass," and the pass consisted of a draw which connected two big sections of woods. Deer moving from one wooded area to another, I felt, would use this brushy draw rather than walking out of it in the open. I was right. But I did not wait around long enough. The hunter who did wait long enough bagged a whitetail right where I had been sitting. Meanwhile, I was still-hunting in the thick of it and not seeing anything for it.

So, the hunter should control himself. Being cold is one sure way to get a person moving. So, the hunter might want to look at his outfit very closely if he intends to take a stand. A neighbor of mine uses electric socks when he is on stand and he says they have made the difference for him.

A stand can be a stump that has some cover around it, or it can be a more elaborate setup. The biggest problem with a stand is having a good clear view of the

(Left) Here is an Amacker blind called the "Brella Blind" Model B 1000. The hunter can see out but he cannot be seen while in the blind. It prevents rain, sun and insects from coming through and as can be seen, it is camouflaged in nature. The total weight is 5 pounds, folding into a 7-inch by 34-inch package.

(Right) The hunter who wants to be above it all might look into a tree stand as one means of staying still. Still-hunting is not the only way to bag a deer by any means and this hunter has a good chance of seeing venison before the day ends. (Photo courtesy J. Wayne Fears)

Taking a stand may be as simple as sitting in a strategic spot. This small opening was loaded with deer tracks and the hunter decided to rest here a while and watch the location.

area while at the same time insuring that the deer do not have a good clear view of you. Motion is the killer. I have had deer walk up to within spear-chucking distance of me even when I was not totally concealed. But one move of the pinky finger, and they bolt. Movement is a sure way of alerting incoming game. Therefore, the hunter may wish to build a blind. The idea of a blind is to have good cover which conceals the hunter while the hunter can see out. But more than this, the hunter's motions are blocked from view by the blind. If he wants to sip a cup of coffee, he can do so without his movement spooking deer that might be coming toward him.

Where legal, tree stands can offer a few advantages over the blind, though certainly a good blind located in the right spot can be highly effective. In truth, there is but one big reason for tree stand success—it is harder for the deer to see the hunter and easier for the hunter to see the deer when the hunter is up in the air. We can make all sorts of wise statements on this subject, but that is what it all boils down to. The tree stand, being up in the air, allows the hunter to look down into the area. He can see better from up there, and deer, while they do look up depending upon conditions and locales, do not tend to look up with the frequency that they look around themselves. Looking up, in short, is not a major action taken by deer. Therefore, our simple statement, I think,

This is what might be called a "natural blind." It is a small open spot near a deer trail. The hunter, when he ducks his head a little, is quite hidden, and yet he can see out very well, making the cover serve as a blind. Even without any form of camouflage clothing, the hunter will not be easily sighted, yet he has command in front of him of an open area and a deer trail. Getting a shot off will be no problem.

makes sense. The tree stand is useful because the hunter can see better and the deer do not tend to look upward very much.

Some hunters feel that full camouflage is called for on stand. However, we must look at the law. It may not be legal to hunt without the orange or brightly colored clothing called for by the law. Where legal, the hunter who believes in camo may as well go all the way, to include face and hands, for these are quite easily visible. Up in the air in a tree stand, or concealed by a blind, I do not feel that camouflage is necessarily going to do a lot of good, but others would disagree. Movement is the big problem. That a deer will see. This is why the tree stand hunter or blind hunter makes certain that he can quickly put his hunting tools into play and with as little evidence of his movement as possible.

A tree stand in some areas is dynamite. A friend in Texas has taken photos of deer from a tree stand, and he had to leave his 400mm lens for his 35mm camera at home in favor of a 200mm lens because the deer were simply too close, and he could not get the whole deer in the picture with the 400mm lens. Occasionally, a natural blind will present itself to the hunter. In Idaho, I found a blind which had a screen of small brush in front of it and a perfect view of a pass. It was natural. In Wyoming, I located a place on a bluff which was a perfect stand for wild turkeys, but I also saw deer from it. It was natural, too, simply a high spot above a meadow.

The location of a tree stand or a blind is going to vary with each bit of variation in the lay of the land. It is impossible to give a summary statement concerning the placement of a blind, therefore. The hunter is going to have to select that site based upon the specific factors at hand. There is no guarantee that a deer will come in from left or right, back or front, and this statement applies to trails and openings as well as any other parcel of land. The main thrust of stand/blind placement is that of deer sign. I have seen blinds placed at the edges of cultivated fields which show signs of deer feeding. They may be placed near small openings in the brushland. Common sense and specific conditions must dictate where a blind is located, and the same goes for the tree stand.

So, the hunter can place himself on a stump, find a natural blind which is more concealing, set up a man-made blind or use a tree stand. I suppose it almost goes without saying that when on stand we shut up and look a lot and listen. If a sound is heard, cup the hands about the ears as previously mentioned and use the direction of the hands like "radar" to pick out the direction of the sound. It works.

Wayne Fears can elect to bag this small buck or wait for a bigger one to come along. He has a bead on the buck from the advantage of his tree stand (see in background). He can have a muzzleloader harvest if he wants it. (Photo courtesy J. Wayne Fears)

Although this hunter has the advantage of being in a tree stand, he is also wearing camouflage, including a face mask. Camouflage is one more trick used by bowhunters to secret themselves from their quarry. Some hunters feel that the reflection from a lighter-skinned hunter's face may be a warning sign to deer. (Photo courtesy J. Wayne Fears)

maybe as many as four, and alternating driving and sitting jobs. The wind direction is very important in a drive. A young friend of mine bagged a whitetail buck because he was placed at the head of a little draw, and his dad and I simply meandered along the lower areas letting our scent work up the draws. A whitetail buck sneaked right into the boy, and the young man won first place in a state contest with that buck.

Using the natural pass in combination with a drive is good, and the hunter who is walking, I think, should still-hunt. While it may be useful to carry tin cans, horns and bongo drums while trying to scare a tiger out of the jungle, I think that the unavoidable noise and human scent are enough to make a whitetail or mule deer move *when it wants to sneak away* from the walking hunter. Watch the wind. The hunter on stand should have the wind in his face, in his favor in other words, while the still-hunter, in this case, has the wind at his back. Naturally, this is not the way to still-hunt when we have no one on stand. The very last mule deer buck that I got, as I write this, was in a thickly forested area of Idaho. The 4-pointer (10-point eastern count) was "driven" to me by my hunting partner, Dean Zollinger, the gunmaker.

Dean simply still-hunted a huge ridge, walking back and forth in the timber, not trying to make noise and at the same time using the wind in my favor instead of his. The buck moved out of the thick cover, had to cross the area in which I was on stand, and I got him. My only

Here is the Hide 'um Hunter portable blind, which can be set up for deer hunting. One hunter can easily set the blind up, and its camouflage is very effective.

If the rut is on, and in some areas it will be, then the scrapes which are, in my opinion not very effective out of the rut, might be productive. I have deer hunting associates who tell me that they can take a stand near scrapes, preferably in an area which contains several scrapes close to each other, and do very well. I have other friends who claim that they have watched scrapes even in the rut and have nothing to show for it. Take your choice.

In the rut the bucks are on the move whereas before the rut they were much more sedentary. In one locale, the bucks, mule deer by the way, are so sedentary that if a hunter is not very good with binoculars or a very persistent still-hunter, his chances of getting a deer are small. But when the rut arrives, these deer are on the move. Unfortunately for the hunter, the rut begins after deer season in this area, and the only reason I know of the deer's activity there is the fact that I hunt wild turkeys in the area during the deer rut.

Drives are, in effect, a mixture of still-hunting and sitting still. I like mini-drives, just a couple of hunters,

This specific locale marked a well-used pass. The pass is directly in front of the person who is pointing (left), and consists merely of a passageway from the high country to the lowlands. This particular slope was heavily tracked, and in the evening, deer were often seen moving down from the higher areas into the lower areas, out of the trees to feed.

observances on that stand were to remain quiet, concealed and motionless as possible. The buck never saw me.

Sometimes the wind plays less of a role. Depending upon the terrain, a hunter can go on stand on a higher point and his companion or companions can simply circle around him. I don't care for this as much as I do waiting in a natural pass, but I have seen it work. They say that the big bucks cut back on themselves and sometimes work in circles. I do not know this to be a fact, but I have seen a hunter walk right next to a buck. The buck allowed that sportsman to go by and then got up and simply walked back in the same direction from which the hunter had come. That I have seen more than once.

So we have these very basic methods of deer hunting to start us off. The master deer hunter has more tricks up his sleeve than still-hunting and staying still, but even the old venison-taker of the hills finds himself using these two ways as long as he's a hunter. One point we have not elaborated on is field position, however, and I think it deserves a few lines of special attention here.

Field position goes with both still-hunting and staying still, but more with the first. It is the hunter's awareness of the land, and this awareness is vital to bagging a buck much of the time. I have seen hunters who seem to pay no attention to field position. They are rarely in a position to shoot if a deer should present itself. I like to play a little scenario in my mind as I still-hunt. I like to imagine what I would do at any given moment if a buck should emerge in front of me.

In this way, I know when I have lost field position. It is a seemingly simple point to make, I know, but let us use an example to show how important field position is. Let us say that a hunter is approaching a small rise

in the ground. All around this rise there is downed timber, deadfall if you will. What does he do? Well, he can skirt the rise or mound and work around the edge of the deadfalls, but what happens when he does this?

First, he has cut off his view from all of the cover on the other side of that mound. Second, he is on ground level with the deer. If he gets a shot, there's bound to be some form of twig or branch between him and the deer. On the other hand, if the hunter exerts himself only slightly, he can climb the mound and then he has increased the area that he can view, plus he has given himself a much better chance for a shot. To be sure, he must not rush up the hill and show himself all at once on top, but he should move up on that mound slowly and look around. He might also stay up there for several moments, too, because a buck might just be hiding below him and that buck could easily sit still and let the hunter pass, but by staying a while the buck might get nervous and show itself.

Field position is also hunting on the backbone of a ridge so that there is a view off of both sides of that ridge. It is using promontories for field glass work. It is hunting above the deer when possible instead of below them. Field position is all of these and more, and the hunter should be able to tell immediately when he has gained field position and when he has lost it. Stop. Look around. Can you get a shot if a buck jumps? Can you see those likely spots which might secret a buck, or are you in fact out of field position?

Driving Deer

Driving deer is a highly successful and worthwhile means of taking home some venison to eat. A deer drive can be elaborate or small, "maxi" or "mini." Furthermore, deer drives work just about anywhere, not only in the terrain generally thought of as whitetail habitat. Drives are seldom used on western mule deer, but I have taken some good bucks with mini-drives, often only two hunters strong. Driving is not still-hunting, and it is not stand-hunting; yet it is both at the same time. Most importantly, the hunter should recognize that driving deer, where legal, is not a "sissy" way of getting one. The lack of harvest is, to my way of thinking, much less sporting than pushing a deer out of its lair and toward a hunter.

Driving takes teamwork, and teams seldom function very well without a leader and a plan. I would not be a part of a drive which did not have both. Each participating hunter must settle his mind upon two things: First, he must make up his mind that the leader *is* the leader. If the individual hunter is to be a driver instead of a person on stand, so be it. If the hunter is instructed to remain on his stand until 12:30 PM, then he should follow those instructions.

Second, the plan is of utmost importance in a drive. We may have from two to perhaps 40 hunters involved in a drive and each must follow the plan. As a hunter friend of mine from the whitetail country of the South says, "I have never known of a hunter being injured by another hunter on my farm, but we always insist that each hunter be able to recite the plan of the day exactly before we begin a drive." We said this was a team effort, and it is. The effort begins by knowing the terrain and hopefully something about the deer in that area.

A plan is devised where so many hunters sit on stand, and so many walk. The hunters on stand generally have the better chance of seeing a deer, and this is why it is only fair to first "draw straws" as to which hunters drive and which sit, and then alternate positions when possible. Those who bag a buck, by the way, should consider themselves a continued part of the hunt. I am not impressed with hunters who drop out the minute they "get theirs." The plan is no good without the leader, for he has to have knowledge of two things, where the stands are and what path the drivers should take toward those stands. I cannot relate the thousand and one possible drive/stand relationships which can exist. But I can say this: The location of stands and the paths taken by drivers must coincide with the lay of the land more than any other factor. The hunter on stand must be located so he can swing into action swiftly, and yet he must be at least placed so that he's not spotted instantly by a deer. We should remember that background makes good camouflage, and this means a hunter backing up to a brushy area. Safety is the most important aspect of all, of course, and the hunter must be unobtrusive and yet visible as a hunter.

This is not so hard to realize. The hunter dressed in proper color will be seen by his drivers. Though scientists have changed their minds about deer seeing in color, suggesting now that deer do indeed see color, the fact is,

motion will alert these deer far more than a blaze orange cap. The drive which works is organized. The organizer has to know what he's doing. In a tree farm one time I was shown the pattern used for a deer drive. There was no season, but it was clear that the leader of that drive knew what he was doing. The stands were set up where deer would have to burst into the open in front of a hunter, and the paths were actually the deer trails which led from heavy brush into cultivated fields.

The driver can consider himself one of two things: He can react simply as a device to push deer or he can act as a still-hunter. In my opinion, the single factor which governs this is safety, again. Given a couple hunters or a half dozen hunters, it's usual that the drivers still-hunt, trying in fact to get a shot themselves as they penetrate the country. This is usual. The situation is usually one of hunters moving toward other hunters, knowing where each man is located, and the man on stand knowing where the drivers are coming from. When the driver acts as a still-hunter, he need not be quite as stealthy as he would be if he were truly still-hunting, for pushing deer is still the major object here or it would not be a drive. But any hunter can be certain of one thing—his normal movements will be heard by deer. The only big problem is that a deer may "hunker down" as the hunter approaches and then we no longer have a drive.

This is why some drives are built around hunters on stand, and these indeed are the only hunters. The rest of the party, the drivers, are simply instructed to stay on certain paths or on certain prescribed courses and make all the noise and commotion they want to make, and the more the better. The idea, of course, is to get the deer moving and if the leader knows the "traffic patterns" taken by the deer, then a hunter on stand is going to get a shot.

A big factor in a successful drive is having the drivers get into position intelligently. Obviously, if the drivers push the deer away from the hunters on stand before the drive even begins, nothing is accomplished. So the drivers skirt the area. They flank it. They make a big circle and then converge into their patterns. Timing is vital. If the drivers in the center move too fast, the deer may move out to the sides and move far enough to be out of the path of the other drivers. In fact, it is often better to have the drivers on the ends move a bit ahead. All of the deer in the area cannot be expected to rush straight toward the waiting hunters. But with intelligent positioning, the drivers should be able to push something toward the hunters on stand.

What about the wind? We must remember that our deer use the sense of smell as a main method of detecting the presence of hunters. Therefore, a drive can change its pattern based upon the currents of air moving about. In fact, when a drive is only workable from one direction, the wind can just about scuttle the best laid plans of mice and men. If the wind is all wrong, should a drive be attempted? I think so. Of course, if the drive can be reversed, so that the drivers have the wind to their backs while the hunters on stand have the wind into their faces, all the better. But if the drivers are arranged in a U-shape pattern, even the scent of the hunters on stand coming toward the deer may not dissuade them from going forward and away from the very obvious noise-makers which are moving upon them. So the drive may still produce a harvest.

Of course, a deer drive is a natural when the brush is thick and a still-hunt a poor method of getting a deer. Therefore, the geography of the locale may dictate a drive. But I think the western hunter often misses a good opportunity when he fails to try a drive, ever, and many western hunters never use the drive method at all. Let us suppose that a party of four hunters is out in the high country of the Rocky Mountains. Let us also suppose that they work the land still-hunting, but within sight of each other.

Now they get together. Up ahead is an aspen grove. Is there a big mule deer buck bedded down in the aspen grove? Why not? There could be. So two or three of the hunters flank the grove, move into it, preferably still-hunting, wind at their backs, while the other hunter or hunters take position on the off-side, the wind in his face. A deer may well move out ahead of the drivers in this case, giving the hunter or hunters on stand a good chance at a shot.

We have used this method in the high desert, too, where long ravines may secret bucks. A hunter takes a stand at a place along the ravine, wind in his favor, as another hunter or hunters move into the ravine, wind at the rear. A buck may leave its bed and sneak right into the waiting hunter. It happens. In fact, we used this method on the lowland deserts around Yuma, Arizona. With a topo map, it was easy to see that the drainages, long sandy dry washes, lead down from the regions of slightly higher elevations to the lower elevations. A hunter would position himself at a little bend in the wash, as his friends worked down the wash, sometimes a driver in the bottom and one on each side. While this particular method is not certain to produce results, it is one more trick to try.

Finally, there is what I call a "natural drive." A hunter was seated on a very brushy knoll one season as I walked by, and since it was noonday and there wasn't much going on, he beckoned me over and I went. In the course of conversation he told me that he had taken a deer on or near that point almost every season for a dozen years in a row, failing only twice. His method was simple. He knew that hunters often parked at a small lake down below. From that lake, they moved up into the country. They simply had to walk right into the spot occupied by the sedentary, but well-located hunter on stand. It was a case of the deer moving naturally in a certain pattern and that pattern put them within range of the waiting hunter. I promised not to use the man's special knoll and proceeded to camp.

This hunter is on a drive, his assignment being to "flank" the woods on his right. Hunting whitetail deer in South Dakota, this particular drive was designed to push a buck down a narrow strip of timberland. Open ground on both sides of the timber allowed hunters to keep the bucks headed forward instead of slipping out of the timber. With the wind behind him, the hunter slowly moves ahead. Any buck coming to the edge of the timber will, at least in theory, move back into the timber and continue moving ahead of the drivers in the woods. If the plan goes well, finally, the deer will emerge in a clearing where hunters have been posted.

Dogs and Deer

The idea of chasing a deer with a dog or dogs often repels hunters. It is also quite illegal in many areas. For most of us, it takes an open mind, where logic overcomes sentiment, in order to understand the motives of such hunters and the actual reason for dogs being used to push deer toward hunters. Is it sporting? I think I have to respond by saying that it is more sporting than a low harvest and an inevitable die-off. Of course, the big problem is control over the dogs. Dogs running loose wreak havoc upon deer. In fact, one of the big factors in deer kill can be dogs in some areas, and I mean house pets, not wild animals. Therefore, to have dogs on hand which are actually encouraged to chase deer means that these dogs must be kept under control not only during the deer season, but out of season as well.

Hunting deer with dogs is, on the other hand, quite different from the imaginings which some of us might hold. The dogs are not even close to what I thought they would be, in fact. Since I had not hunted deer with dogs, I called upon a friend from the South who hunted with dogs when he was a youth. He was almost reluctant to talk about it, now living in Colorado and fearing that a western deer hunter would not understand. But I had been to the part of the South he mentioned, and knew the man was correct about that terrain.

I would dare a hunter to still-hunt that and truly harvest deer in a good biologically sound manner. A human drive would be just about as useless. Some of that terrain is thicker than a bramble bush. The dogs and deer are lucky to penetrate it, let alone a human being. So the need for a harvest having been established, dogs were the only near-at-hand answer. And we don't mean a bunch of greyhounds or black and tans.

The dogs in question are, if their owners will excuse the expression, mutts. I suppose "mixed breeds" is more kind. These dogs do not have the skill or fleetness of foot to catch a deer. Nor will they catch a healthy deer. They chase, all right, and the idea is to push deer into hunters, but no deer is going to be dragged down unless that deer is less than whole in health. The dogs may be used in the event of a wounded deer, of course, and then they could actually come upon a deer, face to face, so to speak.

Generally speaking, we are talking about group hunting again, and we are talking about organized hunting. The dog hunt without a plan would produce but little. Again, we have hunters on stand and then we have the dogs attempting, by reason of the control of the master, to push deer to these hunters. The country must be known well by the leader who controls the dogs, and all of the hunters on stand must obey the rules agreed upon.

Since the range is close in this tight country, the shotgun is at home here, and buckshot can be excellent. This is true of other drives as well, not only dog drives. There are certain arguments concerning the truly effective, humane range for the use of buckshot. I recently read a statement which suggested that 75 yards was an effective distance. I fully disagree and will stand upon that. My own observations on shotgun range using buckshot for missiles is established further in this book.

Where to Hit 'em

Now that we've discussed hunting methods, let's look at where to aim and hit your deer for a clean and humane harvest. Without a doubt the chest shot is the preferred aiming point for the deer hunter who has a shot at this area. The reasons are several and somewhat easily supported. In the first place, the chest is a large area on the deer. Being large, it makes for a good target. But that is just the beginning of the strong points in favor of the chest shot. Not only is the chest area a large one, but it also contains so many vital organs, such as the heart (very low in the chest) and the lungs, which provide a rather large target. We have to note one more thing about the chest strike; normally there is very little edible meat here. I qualify the statement with the fact that in some cultures the lungs are cooked and eaten. In our own culture, whether the lungs are struck or not, they are seldom consumed as food.

So we have a large area and a vital one, and it is an area containing little to no valuable meat. I contend that this is the proper place to put a harvesting bullet. I have, in the past 30 deer seasons, dropped a rather large number of deer with the chest shot. In such cases, the deer generally and almost always fell instantly and was almost immediately defunct. Remember that the nervous system is not totally lacking in the chest area. It is not a matter of vascular collapse alone which makes the chest shot valuable. Because of the high liquid content of the chest cavity, "hydrostatic shock" is also very much at work with a chest hit. I'm the first to concede that the term is somewhat lacking in a few scientific details, but at the same time, anyone doubting the effect of a high-speed bullet striking a liquid area should repair to the gun range with two large tin cans in hand. Fill one with sand; the other with water.

Preferably, both cans should be mostly covered. That is, each can should have very small holes into which the sand and the water is loaded. In other words, the lids are mostly intact. To be sure, a high speed bullet through the tin can holding the sand will be devastating to the can. But the can filled with water will, on most occasions, literally blow up. The shock wave pushing liquid in front of it makes for a powerful force. Remember, we are talking about deer only. The chest shot is not always recommended for other game. We are speaking strictly of deer and not of animals larger or tougher.

Often, we will find an exit hole larger than a clenched fist when we make a strike in the chest cavity. Quite obviously, this was not directly caused by the bullet, but rather by the force in front of the bullet. It only makes sense. For example, let's take a .270 Winchester round using a 130-grain bullet. No .277-inch bullet will expand as flat as a clenched fist, and yet every season hunters will find huge exit holes made with the .270 and the chest shot. Fairly obviously, the bullet itself, directly, did not create this over-sized hole.

Enough on this subject, then, as far as the chest shot goes. If the hunter were to use a non-expanding bullet, in other words a soft-nose too hard to expand on deer, and perhaps meant for game much tougher than deer, the chest shot might be less desirable than we have made it out to be. But today, hopefully, one will seldom encounter such a hard bullet in the deer field, and there need be no concern about a chest shot as long as the bullet does expand as it is supposed to expand on thin-skinned game.

The Shoulder Shot

Since the shoulder is generally going to offer itself no more often than the chest shot, I will go on record as being against the shoulder as a proper aiming point for the deer hunter who is using the proper expanding bullet. Sure, if the bullet is harder than two bricks glued together, then the shoulder may be a more appropriate target. But I am against picking bone out of the meat supply and a bullet into the shoulder means splintering bone fragments. I am not against the shoulder shot. On larger game, the shoulder is often an appropriate area to aim for. But on deer, using proper deer rifles of the day with correctly structured bullets, the shoulder is definitely not as preferable a striking point as the chest cavity.

High Shoulder

A hit through the shoulder blades, high up, more or less close to the spine, can be absolutely dynamite in dropping a deer. In fact, I have seen bull elk drop instantly (and bull elk are terribly hard to bring down instantly) with the high shoulder hit. Then isn't this a better area to go for than the chest? No, it isn't, not if we are talking about deer, and definitely not if we are talking about deer cartridges and correct bullets. Yes, this vital nerve center and locomotive area is a very good target, but the chest shot is going to do just fine, destroying tissue vital to continuance, but not tissue which is normally consumed as food. Again, we are talking about hard bullets, in which case the high shoulder area would be preferred over the chest cavity.

The Neck Shot

On a caribou hunt a number of years ago, a companion of mine filled his three caribou tags with three shots from his .30–06. The bulls went down instantly and cleanly and very little meat was wasted. This was the neck shot, and my friend was an expert in its use. The neck is a totally excellent target in terms of dropping a deer instantly, all right, and if the hunter wishes to perfect his skill in the neck shot, that's fine. I, personally, am not a good enough game shot to use the neck as my main target in deer harvesting. When the neck is struck and the deer falls instantly expired, we can count on one thing being true—the vertebrae were broken. In other words, when we say the neck was broken, we don't really mean the neck, we mean that extension of the spinal cord which constitutes the neck bones.

When a hunter can be sure of hitting this column of bones with its vital spinal cord in the center, all is well. All is well also if the jugular vein is struck by a bullet. The neck, then, is certainly not a bad target, but I do not think it should be considered the best target for taking a deer. Once again, if the neck and chest are both visible, I prefer the chest shot.

Facing Shot

Once in a while, a hunter may have a chance to shoot a deer which is staring directly at him. I have seen this shot made only a few times in a number of years. My brother did harvest a big buck with a head-on shot, and he did it with a bow. The bow, specially constructed for him, pulled at 100 pounds, and Nick was using a Razorbak-5 broadhead. The arrow penetrated the length of the buck.

If a buck is facing head-on, and I use the term buck

because of ingrained habit, we have several choices. The final choice is up to the individual hunter. First, we can try the head shot. Remember that this may destroy the antlers for a Boone & Crockett measurement if the hunter has such interest and if the buck is that large. If the skull is split, the inside spread is all but impossible to determine "legally." However, if the antlers are of no concern, a head shot will certainly suffice to bring the buck down. In fact, I have used the head shot where the range was close and I felt certain of a good solid hit. Normally, however, the head is rather small when compared with the bulk of the body. If the rest of the body is showing, the head may not be the best choice for a deer facing front-on.

The neck is often an appropriate target on a front-facing deer. Sometimes, only head and neck will be showing in the first place and a shooter can line up on the neck and make a very clean harvest. If there is no other target, then the choice may be limited, and if limited to head or neck, it could be best to take the neck shot when the head is going to be mounted or the antlers hold specific value for the hunter.

Where neck joins body, the hunter has a pretty good aiming point and since we are talking about deer and not elephants, rhinos or water buffalo, this shot is a good one for a head-on target. The bullet may break the neck if it strikes higher than the intended point, and if the point of aim is hit squarely, then the bullet will range into the chest cavity anyway. It is a good shot. Meanwhile, the shoulders should be left off limits. A shot in the shoulder on a deer facing the hunter can mean a broken shoulder and not much more, the bullet not necessarily taking the vitals in on its tour.

The Raking Shot

The south end of a deer which is headed north is sometimes all a hunter has to shoot at. Of course we can certainly suggest that the deer be allowed to run off in such a case, but let's be practical here. A fanny shot on a big buck can drop that buck in its tracks and most hunters know it. I am not in favor of this shot and in fact will personally try to put a bullet at the juncture of the neck and body instead of the hind end. But with a deer caliber and a good bullet, especially the larger rounds, and here we refer to the .270, .280, 7mm Mag, .30–06 and so forth, the bullet is quite likely to drive forward into the chest area. I do not wish to be indelicate, but in truth, the raking shot can be a mess, meaning a gut-shot animal. Or the hip can be broken, very costly in meat and also a mess. I may miss my target, but the deer headed straight away from me is going to be aimed at where neck and body join. In fact, I'd rather try a neck shot, not my all-time favorite aiming point, rather than putting a bullet into the tail end of a deer which will result in lost meat.

The Quartering Shot

Seldom do we have a perfect side shot in terms of a

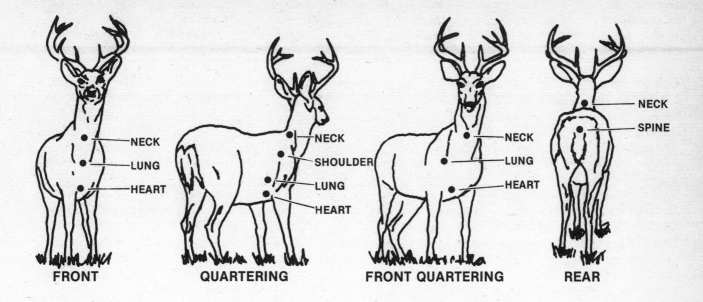

FRONT   QUARTERING   FRONT QUARTERING   REAR

moving deer. Yes, it happens and happens often, but just as often there will be some quartering angle to consider. The key to this shot is in the word "angle." All the deer hunter need do on the quartering shot is try for the chest, not the front part of the chest so much as the rear portion of the chest. In this way, the bullet will angle forward, generally taking a shoulder on the way out. If the deer is standing and feeding, I always wait for a side shot, and I avoid the quartering shot. But when a deer is on the run, a quartering shot may be the only one available.

Sometimes a deer will be quartering toward the hunter rather than away from the hunter. In such a case, the same shot called for above in the head-on stance is recommended. It is not the best of all possible angles, the head-on quartering shot, but the strike into the frontal chest area is not without effect.

Arrow Placement

The aforementioned chest shot is again preferred for the archer. The arrow will not encounter overly large bones in the chest area, only ribs, and good penetration is the result. Also, since an arrow harvests game by the bleeding process and "medical shock," loss of blood, then this area of many capillaries and veins, and some arteries, is a good one. Of course, there are some huge vessels in other parts of the body; however, we are once again speaking of the best place to shoot, taking all things into consideration. The hepatic vessel, for example, may cause very quick dropping of the deer if struck by the sharp broadhead, but one cannot risk a shot into the paunch of a deer in hopes that this vessel will be struck. The chest area, then, is much better as a target for the arrow.

Shot Placement with the Black Powder Projectile

Because tissue destruction is a bit less with the slower-moving black powder projectile, slower than the modern bullet, that is, then the hunter can use the following rule of thumb—if the chest area is visible and the shot is within 100 yards or so, put the ball or conical into the chest cavity. Over the past decade I have harvested more deer with a smokepole than with a modern rifle and all have dropped quickly to the chest shot. If the deer, however, is over 100 yards away, the electrifying blow associated with the high shoulder hit can be more sure. At 100 yards or more, the slow-moving ball or conical will not destroy as much edible meat as its fast-moving counterpart, the modern jacketed bullet.

These are offered the reader following experiences from the field and not from the text book. There will be individual hunters who have perfected their own shots and who should stay with what works for them. But for most of us, the safest strike on a deer, and a very humane one, remains the chest cavity.

We have considered still-hunting, staying still and driving deer as the major hunting methods. But we will move forward now in our walk along the deer hunting trail and our topics will be many. Deer hunting is a diverse, sweeping topic, an involved activity, especially when hunters wish to reduce the luck factor and upgrade the annual success rate for their own personal deer hunting. In this quest for success, we deer hunters will sometimes still-hunt and we will sometimes stay still, or we will drive deer depending upon the conditions confronting us. Knowing when to do which is a part of hunting maturity and a matter of experience.

chapter 7
The Eye of the Hunter

IN MY 30 years of seriously chasing the deer of the plains, woods and mountains, I have come to rely upon one tool almost as much as my rifle. That tool is the binocular, with the spotting scope ranked in there somewhere as well. I have honestly found more good bucks, big bucks, both rack and meat, with the glass than with any other instrument or means at my disposal. And yet, some hunters tend to use binoculars as if they were at the opera or football game, looking at something they have already found with the naked eye, rather than employing the glass as a tool for *finding* game.

If I had to choose between a cheap glass and an expensive rifle, or a top quality binocular and a cheap rifle, I'd go the latter way. The glass I will use hundreds of hours in a season, the rifle for a few shots. As long as that rifle is well equipped with sights, reliable in function and is accurate, I will get by. A good surplus military rifle with a carefully mounted scope sight will put so much venison in the bag that it's remarkable. But I won't stand for a binocular that lacks definition and rugged as well as accurate construction.

But you have to find that deer first, and the binocular can be a tremendous boon in this task of locating a buck. That is why I call it "the *eye* of the hunter." My binoculars are my eyes. They are better than that. They are extensions of my eyes. I have found deer feeding, deer bedded tight, deer just resting in the sun, deer in canyons, deer in the brush and deer in the open with the glass.

The binocular is not for all the time, of course, but neither is still-hunting for all the time, nor is staying still for all the time. The binocular is a tool, however, a tool which is as much a part of my hunting kit as my boots. I hope for one thing—let the reader disagree with my still-hunting methods, and let him disagree with my thoughts on trails and scrapes and reading sign. But please let him try the glass, not as an appendage stuck in front of his face, but as a tool which requires special use, special practice and special talent, a talent that *can be learned*.

I want to point out that even though I do 90 percent of my deer hunting today with black powder muzzle-loading rifles, I still use the glass, and not only for finding game, but also for the safety factor inherent in the process. The binocular, in short, can help us be more safe in the field.

I'm not talking about jumping a buck at 30 yards and sticking a glass up to the hunter's face before shooting, of course. But I am talking about those many occasions when a deer is really seen as only a part of a deer. Then the hunter has time to look with the aid of the binocular. Is that really a buck in the brush? Or is it a doe? And more than that, is it a deer at all? I don't care if a hunter has been at it for a half century, at times it is not possible to tell at a glance just how big that buck is, or whether the shot will be blocked by a hunk of limb. The glass will tell us.

But won't the scope on a rifle do the same thing? Well,

Although the hasty glance is not advised as a *finding* method for deer hunters, we do not wish to leave the idea that a simple quick glance through binoculars is worth nothing at all. This is not the case. John Fadala takes a fast look at something in the distance, following the spotting of a movement in the brush. The movement turned out to be a doe mule deer with fawns.

I like the binocs better because I do not care to aim my rifle at something unless I am certain that I want to fire. I'd rather look with the binocular first. Also, the three dimensional view of the binocular helps perspective, visually speaking. The 3-D view means gaining a sense of proportion out there, and I have made out an avenue for my bullet or round ball only after looking with the glass first. Again, I realize that many bucks are jumped right under our noses. And I am not talking about the binocs under those conditions, but I am speaking of the many other times that glassware can help us be safer hunters.

The thrust of this chapter, however, is using the "eye of the hunter" as a finding tool. There is more to it than simply sticking the glasses up to the face and peering through them. I am aware that there are as many opinions on deer hunting as there are expert deer hunters, and I bow to the knowledge of others who chase venison religiously. However, I have little use for the intrepid outdoorsman "glassing for deer" with the binoculars pinched twixt thumb and forefinger as if he were at the opera watching *Madama Butterfly*.

Which Glass to Buy?

First of all, we have to select a hunting glass, and this means a precision instrument with built-in quality. The problem is that all glassware looks great in the store, and if a hunter steps out on the street and takes a look at the

bright neon sign down the block the view is going to be just beautiful. So, on this basis, we can walk out of the store with our new purchase thinking we really have something. Well, maybe we do. Probably we don't. Bargain priced glasses are seldom a bargain for deer hunters, though they are usually great for football games.

Why does the hunter need a better glass? The first and most obvious reason is the difference between sitting in the stands watching a football game and actually making our way through wood or mountain. A glass which is fragile in any respect has no business as a mainline deer hunting tool in the outdoors. But there is something even more important—the inside construction of that glass.

A binocular is much more than optics. It is a precision mating of two different barrels that must remain perfectly aligned or the hunter is headed for a headache, literally. Even though we cannot see the misalignment of the barrels in some cases, that is we do not see it consciously, when it is there, we pay for it later on with eye fatigue. So good glasses are not purchased for the optics alone, but also for the internal construction. Fortunately, we have a good means of locating well constructed glasses. In this case, brand names really mean something. I am not going to list a series of brand names here, because I will surely miss a good one, leaving it out unintentionally. However, the names are well known to most of us.

The better glass will usually cost more money. With modern technology, some perfectly adequate modestly priced deer hunting binoculars are available today, however, and I don't want to give the impression that a

These small binoculars are very popular with today's hunters, for the optics are good, yet the size is small. These are 8x21mm, armored and camouflagged from Apollo.

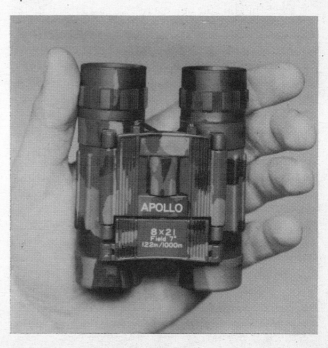

man has to spend his monthly paycheck in order to buy a quality set of binocs. That isn't true. However, the specs on special for a few bucks are probably not the ones to select for lifetime hunting companions.

So, we should look for a good brand name and a glass that is above the bottom of the line in price range. We want rugged construction so that the barrels will remain aligned and so the internal optical elements will also remain lined up. But there is another feature of the glass which is vital to the hunter, and that is definition. I was going to include all sorts of charts and explanations, to suggest what optical definition is, lines per millimeter read and so forth. Actually, the deer hunter can do better by making simple tests with different binoculars in order to determine for himself which glass possesses better definition qualities.

What is definition? In hunting talk and for our purposes, I want to give an example I have used before. I had a pretty fair set of binoculars and I thought a lot of them. But my friend John Doyle felt otherwise. He did not believe that my glasses had sufficient definition as compared with better binoculars. He, in fact, loaned me his glasses to take out and compare with my own.

Both glasses looked good to me for a long time that day. I could see well through both. But in the afternoon, I had a startling thing happen to me. I was glassing in the distance, and I had an oak tree in sight. My own binoculars, of the same exact magnification power as John's, showed me clearly the distinct leaves on that oak tree. I was more than satisfied. But then I looked through my friend's binoculars, and I could actually distinguish the edges of those leaves, the pattern that they made. That is definition. The definition of the better glass, for our hunting purposes, came out clearly to me in that little demonstration. But why worry about definition? I want to give you one more example of how important definition is.

We were hunting the mountains that season, and it was a good year for us. We had seen some good bucks and were still looking for old mossback. I caught sight, in my binoculars, of a rock that disturbed me. I did not know why, but the rock seemed out of place somehow if a rock can indeed be out of place. Finally, I realized that the texture of that rock was wrong. The rock was a deer. I was sure of it. The fine optics of that glass had not only found a buck for me at a distance far greater than most readers would care to believe, but it did so on the basis of actual texture of that deer as compared in contrast with a boulder.

I moved a couple hundred yards closer and looked again. I could be wrong, I knew, for I had not seen my rock move. And as I watched the rock it almost magically turned into a deer as a paint-with-water picture materializes on the page.

Recently, I was hunting out West with my friend Val Forgett of Navy Arms Company. We were walking a ridge in the high country and I was glassing often as we went. I saw a deer. The deer was brushed up, but I found a single eye showing in the brush. There was a log right in front of the deer. The buck was going to stay put, I figured, because it was looking right at us, but within that tight cover it'd probably just remain still. We walked right toward the deer until we were only 75 yards away and then the deer and the log both got up and began a slow walk up the side of the mountain. My superb binoculars could have distinguished the log as a deer, too, but I was concentrating on the deer in the brush more than the obvious "log" out in front of the brush. All the same, the good optics of my glass certainly were at work in finding the eye of a deer in a screen of brush. That is definition, by our hunting standard, at work.

Considerations Before Buying

Exit Pupil

The hunter seeking a pair of binoculars will need to know several terms in order to understand how glasses are rated. One of these terms, exit pupil, is quite simple to derive. Exit pupil is obtained by dividing the diameter of the objective lens (lens farthest from the eye) by the magnification of the binocular. For example, the exit pupil on a 7x35 glass (7 power with an objective lens diameter of 35mm) is five (5). An 8x30 binocular will have an exit pupil of 3.75, 30 divided by 8, in other words. In order to actually visualize the exit pupil, the glass is held out at arm's length pointing toward a source of light, such as the sky. The little bright circle which appears on the eyepiece is the exit pupil. The diameter of the exit pupil determines the amount of light transmitted to your eyes. The important point for the hunter to keep in mind is the fact that his binoculars must be efficient in light transmission as well as ruggedly constructed. Using the exit pupil as only one of the items of selection, however, we only get a raw figure, a useful number, but this number does not say "excellence" or lack thereof. It is simply a useful number to keep in mind. The higher the number, the larger the lens diameter and the more light the lens will let in. An exit pupil of only 3 will serve the eye in good light. An exit pupil of 5 is satisfactory for most dimmer atmospheres, such as twilight. And an exit pupil of 7 is about all the eye can actually use. Also note, however, that small exit pupils cause a bit of "blackout" if the glass is moved much. An example would be in bright light when the exit pupil of the human eye is about 2mm wide. If the exit pupil of the glass is 5, then we have a leeway of 1.5mm. Extra light gathering power is nice to have on a hunting glass, but remember this—in order to obtain this good factor, the objective lens has to increase in size. As it does, the binocular gets bulkier and heavier. Those extra ounces around your neck throughout the hunting day can certainly get mighty heavy and mighty annoying.

Relative Brightness

Another useful factor in determining which glass to buy for hunting purposes is *relative brightness*, or the light

Here is the Steiner 7x50 Commander binocular, a high quality glass for the dedicated hunter. It has a built-in bearing compass, a distance scale and electric illumination.

The Bausch & Lomb Compact Waterproof glass is a favorite of hunters who are weight-conscious. The author uses this type of glass quite often when weight is a factor, alternating these with his B&L 9x35 glasses.

Good hunting binoculars exhibit a high degree of optical clarity and definition. These qualities are especially useful in early morning light and later afternoon light. The Leupold Company is now offering both 7x30 and 9x35 Hunting Binoculars with these features.

gathering capabilities of your binoculars. In this case, the diameter of the exit pupil is squared and that is all there is to the formula. Above, we learned that the exit pupil for a 7x35mm binocular is 5. Therefore, the relative brightness of a 7x35mm glass is 25, or 5^2. Our exit pupil for the 8x30mm glass is 3.75. We have a relative brightness factor of 14 here. Although the relative brightness factor has some value, it is not a complete story, because magnification is not included in the formula. Yes, the binocular with the larger objective lens did win in relative brightness above. However, higher magnification aids our eye in determining detail in low light situations, and that is why the *twilight factor* formula has been developed.

Twilight Factor

Here, we multiply the diameter of the objective lens by the magnification of the binocular, and then we find the square root of the product. A 7x35mm binocular will now have a twilight factor, sometimes called "twilight performance" rating of 15.6. Now let us see how an 8x30 compares. We multiply 8 times 30 and we arrive at 240. Now we must find the square root of 240. It turns out to be 15.5. If we multiply 15.5 times 15.5 we end up with 240.25. So, the twilight factor for the 8x30mm glass is 15.5. In short, the 7x35mm glass and the 8x30mm glass

end up with about *the same* twilight factor, which is correct and which can be seen in the field, all other things being equal.

A 10x40mm glass would then end up with a twilight factor or twilight performance of 20. The higher the number, the better. We can "see more" then with the 10x40mm in low light than with the 7x35mm in low light. We would be able to detect a buck in the lower light of afternoon better with the 10x40 glass. While this is a fact, the hunter must weigh other things as well as twilight factor, including the size and weight of the binocular and the fact that using higher magnification takes a steady hand. The magnified shake of the body (hands) is more evident, of course, with the stronger glass.

Magnification

Just as higher ratings in exit pupil cannot always be used by the eye, since the eye can only open up to an exit pupil of about 7mm anyway, it is also true that a point is reached where higher magnification is more trouble than good. Unfortunately, it is impossible to give a standard rating for all human beings. We differ in the amount of body movement we must live with. We do have "steadier" people and "shakier" people. The latter type is in a real fix when he sticks a pair of 10x binoculars

(Left) Hunter picks a high spot to do some glasswork. Sometimes it is amazing how far deer can be located in open terrain. And perhaps more amazing is the location of a bedded or feeding buck in a forested area.

(Right) One of these bucks was located with the binocular and the other one was spotted without the aid of a glass. The use of optics is very important to the deer hunter, and it is one major part of his entire bag of tricks, not his only one, but an important one.

to his eyes. Furthermore, we have to consider how willing the hunter is to get steady. I am very willing to do this. I carry a Moses Stick, and I use it faithfully. When I glass from the sitting position, I get steady before I attempt to look. If I have been walking, I let my body calm down before attempting to glass for deer.

In open country, I like a 9x to 10x glass, and feel I can use this much "power" with total effectiveness. But in brushy terrain, I carry a pair of 7x binoculars and feel that 6x would also be good. Twilight factor is very important to deer hunters who want to have an advantage in spotting game in the later afternoon hours, but legal shooting light makes the finding of game at dusk somewhat academic. Therefore, in a trade-off, I have 9x35mm glasses and 10x40mm glasses which I find good for my uses. I also have a small 7x24 glass which serves me well when I want a small unit.

Field of View

Field of view is taken at 1000 yards from the binocular. It is a linear measurement in feet of the diameter of the view seen through the binocular. As an example only, we have 6x30 binoculars with a field of view of 450 feet. We have 7x35mm glasses with a field of view of 380 feet at 1000 yards. There may be a 7x50mm glass also with 380-foot width of view at 1000 yards, and we may have an 8x30 with a 330-foot field of view. Taking the latter into consideration, for comparison purposes only, we may also have an 8x30mm glass with a field of 390 feet. So the hunter can study the factor of field as an *individual*

quality for each specific binocular.

There are wide angle glasses and extra wide angle glasses, too. Generally, the edges of the "picture" in the wide and extra wide style is not as sharp as the edges are in a standard glass, but many hunters get a lot out of the wide angle feature, for it seems easier to use, bites off a big hunk of terrain and encourages the user to hold steady and allow his eyes to scrutinize the field rather than moving the glasses a lot in order to scan the area. As for me, I am not in favor of the extra wide angle glass as I see no real useful value in that much field. The wide angle glass is fine, and so is the standard. I find sufficient field of view in the latter and that is what I own.

Other Factors

We can go on for a great length of time discussing all of the possible features to be found in a given binocular. This would soon lead us pretty far afield and away from our topic, deer hunting and glasses for deer hunting. We want a glass which has magnification commensurate with our needs, a good twilight factor trade-off (in other words good light gathering ability in a glass we enjoy carrying), a reasonable field of view, high image quality and sharpness, lack of distortion, good "edge" quality in the picture, rather than fuzzy perimeters, as often found with cheap glasses, lack of color fringing, in other words no halos of light dancing in the view of the glass, only a clear "white" picture, and of course, top grade construction which will keep those barrels in alignment. We also need a fairly weatherproof glass. If it rains, my binocs get tucked under my clothing, to be sure, but I do not want a fogged glass just because the atmospheric conditions changed. Good glasses will not fog easily. They have air-tight construction.

The old standby in the world of binoculars has been the 7x35mm, a size I can't argue with, provided the quality is there in the glass, with coated lenses, top grade lenses, and so forth. As a hunter grows more proficient with his binoculars, and if he needs the range (open terrain) he may wish to look into the 9x35s and 10x40s and similar glasses. One thing a hunter must not do: He must not peer through those cheap glasses and declare them bright and wonderful just because some neon sign down the road shows up brightly in the view of that glass. The hunting binocular is used a lot, and it can last for generations. It's worth buying good glasses to begin with.

Being Steady

The next important thing to consider, after obtaining a good pair of glasses, is learning how to find game with them. Getting steady is a primary rule. The hasty shaky picture in a glass will not show a hunter all he needs to see. I want to point out that a shaky glass can only be looked into for so long before a headache sets in. Even a good quality binocular will tire a hunter if the picture is not steady. So, the first thing we must do is get steady. If a hunter wants to, he can sit, preferably with something at his back, such as a boulder or a tree, and he can use his knees to steady his elbows, holding the glass with two hands.

I do a lot of glasswork from the standing position, but I use my Moses Stick for that work. What in the world is a Moses Stick? Well, that is a story unto itself, but suffice to say that a Moses Stick is a walking staff with a padded top. On this padded top I rest my binoculars. It is very steady and the resulting picture is very clear.

What Else Does a Glass Do?

Aside from the obvious advantages of magnification, hopefully with a clear picture of high definition, the glass isolates areas for scrutiny. The glass bites a hunk out of the terrain and calls the hunter's attention to that bit of real estate. That isolation means concentration, and concentration can produce game.

The glass is useful in open country and even in the mountains for keeping track of fellow hunters, too. Often, I have spotted a partner of mine or he has spotted me from a great distance through the use of the optical aid. I have studied landmarks with binoculars, and I have located distant roads to which I have packed my game because the glass told me whether a scar in the distance was a natural element in the land or a man-made road.

How to Use the Glass

For heavens sake don't look for a whole deer. You stand to be disappointed in your glasswork if you do. Deer don't stand out like a pimple on a pretty lady's face.

The use of the Moses Stick, a walking-shooting staff, is shown here. The binoculars are rested firmly atop the stick so that the hunter, Dean Zollinger, the Idaho gunmaker shown here, gets a good steady picture. Note that Dean cups his hands around the binocular for extra-steady viewing.

87

During the later part of the day, this buck was feeding when spotted and then stalked for a close-range shot. Nancy Fadala harvested the deer with her 6mm/222 rifle, one shot, 87-grain Hornady bullet. She found the buck for herself with her 8x36mm binoculars.

Binoculars are useful even in this very thick cover. Note, for example, the little open spot in the lower left of the picture. A deer could easily feed out into this type of opening, and deer have also been known to bed down at the edge of such openings in the forest. While it is more difficult to see, there is another such opening almost in the center of the picture (slightly left of center) and a hunter with binoculars could glass this opening from a slight rise in the ground.

They blend in. Chances are a part of a deer will be found before a whole deer is picked out of the terrain. Of course, there are many exceptions. I have seen deer feeding on open grass meadows and even right out on the plains, and then a view of a whole deer was the rule. But more often, the hunter is going to have to train himself to that glitter of an eye in the brush. That bony projection which is antler and not tree limb. That horizontal line that somehow simply does not fit into the pattern made by all those vertical trees, that soft ear in the brush whose texture belies it as a leaf. All of these and more will the patient glass user find.

But you have to study the scene. It takes concentration and dedication. The man who truly wants to find game with his binocular looks "behind the rocks and through the trees." He scrutinizes the area. He does not merely gloss over it. He never looks for the obvious. He always looks for that little piece of a deer that gives it away. I have seen the throat patch of a whitetail buck that was bedded in brush. And I have seen the creamy rump patch of a feeding mule deer on the next mountain.

I am not suggesting that everyone will be good with the glass. But I do think everyone will be helped in some

way by truly using binoculars as hunting tools. Some have more skill than others, more patience, a better "knack" for finding game with a glass. My wife is much better at this than I am because her patience level is much higher. She sees more deer than I see. Also, I find myself getting lazy when I am with her because I know she is good with the glass, and I expect her to locate game before I do. That is a sorry condition, for the hunter should maintain his steady search rather than waiting for the other guy to find something first.

The "eye of the hunter" is a first line tool with me. I hope the hunter will truly give the glass a try. No *one* method and no *one* tool will do it all for the deer hunter all the time, and the binocular is certainly not the end-all of deer hunting. It is a solid addition, however, to our other tools and no matter if the hunter is in the thick of the woods or the thin mountain air, he can find use for a good, high quality glass.

Today, the small specs which I used to dislike are now very worthwhile, too, so there is no excuse for leaving the binocular home to save the bulk. The littler glass of high optical quality can aid in the finding of game. For the big hunt and for the open country, the larger glass

The Bushnell Rubber Armored spotting scope is available with an eyepiece which adjusts from 16x to 36x in "zoom" format. Such an instrument is highly useful to hunters of mountain areas. Even when the terrain is thickly vegetated, a hunter can often find game "on the other side" of the canyon with a spotting scope.

John Fadala learns to use the spotting scope on a pre-hunt trial run for small game and varmints. The spotting scope is a fine addition to the deer hunter's list of gear, especially for open country areas. Here we have the Bushnell Trophy model. made for outdoor use.

Optical companies note the need of good glassware for hunters. Redfield's 30X spotting scope is only 7.5 inches long with a weight of 11.5 ounces. The open country deer hunter can easily pack along such a scope in his daypack.

is still king, but I have both and very often will carry my smaller binocular with me, especially on black powder hunts or when I may be in close cover. The binocular does not seem to interfere with my sense of primitiveness when I am shooting black powder. After all, optics were here long before the Hawken rifle. Jim Bridger, by the way, carried a telescope.

Jim, according to the fine document by Osborne Russell, *Journal of a Trapper (1834-1843)*, page 52 of the Aubrey Haines edition, was always with his telescope. To quote from the book: "Feby. 22d Mr. Bridger according to his usual custom took his telescope & mounted a high bluff near the encampment to look out for 'squalls' as he termed it..." The old mountain men knew that optics could increase the odds for finding things important to them, from food in the form of game to hostiles in the form of Indians. Today, the serious deer hunter should know that optics can also help him find game.

The spotting scope has not been mentioned because it has a more limited application than the binocular. But there are three spotting scopes among my family of five hunters. Sometimes, in the big mountain country, we will pack along a spotting scope, tucked into the daypack riding on the packframe, or salted away not too far out of reach in one of the compartments of the bigger pack-sack. I also have a tiny tripod I take along, and I have more than once examined the far country through the powerful optics of the spotting scope. While the spotting scope loses the important aspect of three dimensional viewing, it is still a terrific tool for locating game at great distances, and I find myself using it more and more where it can be applied.

So much for optics. For those who feel they have no use for glassware, let them try the smaller specs of little weight and size and see if their minds are not changed. For those who want to employ the glass to its utmost potential, the full-sized binocular could be the best bet. I intend to continue with both types for the remainder of my hunting days, with a spotting scope tossed in for good measure.

chapter 8
The Deer Rifle

THE AMERICAN INDIANS had a saying for it. "Any gun good that shoot good." I doubt that any Indian ever said any such thing, but the statement bears truth all the same. In other words, no matter the shape of the stock, the condition of the finish, the style of the action, or length of the barrel, if a rifleman hits the mark with a specific firearm, then it's a good gun. With this philosophy in mind, we can work toward a body of suggestions concerning the deer rifle. I believe that there are many important criteria to consider. In spite of the fact that a good deer hunter can probably get by with what amounts to the wrong rifle for the circumstances, it is advisable for the shooter to select his deer harvesting rifle with great care and thought. Nothing said here is intended to throw any disgrace upon anyone's favorite deer rifle, of course. If a rifle feels right, handles well, points with ease, has decent sights and trigger, and if the individual shooter hits the mark regularly with that rifle, then it's a good model if the caliber is legal and prudent.

Deer Rifle Criteria

There are a great many criteria to look at when buying a deer rifle. As with the purchase of a car, no one factor should sway the buyer. For example, a car may look pretty fine, but if it only gets 10 miles to the gallon and if the buyer is on a budget, then looks will simply have to take the back seat, so to speak, to mileage factors. The same holds true of picking a deer rifle. The hunter must look

at a range of criteria and then make his selection based upon a balance of those criteria. The big problem in choosing a deer rifle today is the fact that the gunmakers have truly gone all out. There is a wonderful selection of firearms with numerous good features, a plethora of excellent deer calibers, a wide price range, and perhaps most important of all, a high degree of reliability built into all of the deer rifles we tested. American shooters have long forgotten the fact that firearms once had to be chosen on the basis of function and safety. Today's over-the-counter deer rifle functions superbly and is safe. In my tests I have not found one modern deer rifle which did not feed rounds neatly and extract empty cases smartly, nor was there one model which was built of incorrect steel.

1. Caliber

Later, we will discuss this very important point at greater length. However, caliber is a strong criterion for selecting any deer rifle. Basically, we are interested in ballistics which will "get the job done" at the range we intend to shoot. Fortunately, there are absolutely dozens of such rounds available to the American shooter. But a shooter may also have special reasons for choosing a caliber. He may wish to use his deer rifle for other activities, for example.

Supposing a shooter wants to hunt deer once a year, but intends to shoot varmints at long range. Can he have

The Model 70 Winchester Featherweight is a very popular bolt-action rifle available in numerous deer calibers. Here we have the smooth lines of the Featherweight without sights. The stock is classic in style, a flowing design of good taste and function both.

The Smith & Wesson bolt-action Model 1700LS Classic Hunter. There are two action lengths. The standard handles the .270 and .30–06, both fine rounds for deer, and goes just under 7 pounds. The short action is chambered for the .243 Win., and overall weight is again just under 7 pounds. This is a six-shot rifle.

The Weatherby Vanguard rifle is equipped here with the Weatherby Imperial scope sight in 3x–9x variable format. The scope is mounted on Buehler mounts.

a varmint caliber and deer caliber all wrapped up into one firearm? He can. In fact, the very existence of the .243 class of cartridge, being the .243 Winchester, 6mm Remington, .240 Weatherby and similar, is for varmint/ deer flexibility. I would carry a 6mm caliber arm loaded with a strongly-constructed 85- to 87-grain bullet at 3200–3300 fps with total confidence for deer hunting, using that same ballistic arrangement for varmints, though a thinner-jacketed bullet would be used in place of the deer bullet.

Another type of flexibility is seen when the western hunter chooses a caliber which will work for both deer and elk. There are several rounds in this department, ranging all the way from the .270 to big .30 Magnums and even larger calibers. In the ballistically powerful rounds, such as the .30 Magnum class, the deer hunter can use a strongly constructed bullet for both elk and deer: for elk because of penetration qualities and in order to keep the bullet intact instead of fragmenting and for deer because the harder bullet will tend to disrupt less edible meat.

2. The Action

The deer hunter does have to face a choice when it comes to the type of action his rifle will possess. The gun/ hunting writer of the past had it made when it came to this problem. There was nothing to it. He simply told his readers to pick the caliber and then let the action go along with the selection. That is impossible today. A good long while ago, though not that long when one considers the entire span of time, if a shooter wanted a semi-automatic deer rifle, he had to stick with calibers on the order of the .401 Winchester, the .25, .30, .32 and .35 Remington calibers and so forth. There was or is nothing wrong with these calibers then or now. However, even though the .257 Roberts was around, for example, and the .25-06 was a wildcat back in the 1930s, one did not chamber the autos for these rounds. The Krieghoff semi-auto was available in a sporting rifle chambered for the .30-06, but this was a somewhat esoteric firearm and hardly found at the crossroads sporting goods shop.

The same facts surrounded the slide-action deer rifle. Very fine calibers were offered, but the longer-range, more powerful rounds were not chambered in the pump gun. The lever-action was much in the same boat. True, the excellent Savage Model 99 was around early and chambered in the fine .250 round and .300 round, but even these were not the .30-06 ballistically. Taking a look at the same Savage Model 99 today, we find several powerhouse calibers, as well as the fine .250 and .300 offerings. Therefore, when the gunwriter of a few decades ago spoke of actions, he talked about calibers in the same breath. Not us. We can't do that. Want a lever-action with enough "stomp" to put down a moose? Well you don't have to go to the big bores of yesteryear to get it if you don't want to, though the superb .45-70 is still

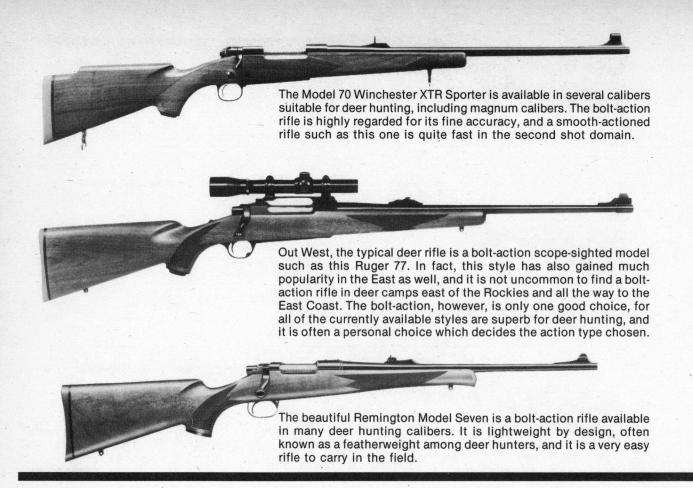

The Model 70 Winchester XTR Sporter is available in several calibers suitable for deer hunting, including magnum calibers. The bolt-action rifle is highly regarded for its fine accuracy, and a smooth-actioned rifle such as this one is quite fast in the second shot domain.

Out West, the typical deer rifle is a bolt-action scope-sighted model such as this Ruger 77. In fact, this style has also gained much popularity in the East as well, and it is not uncommon to find a bolt-action rifle in deer camps east of the Rockies and all the way to the East Coast. The bolt-action, however, is only one good choice, for all of the currently available styles are superb for deer hunting, and it is often a personal choice which decides the action type chosen.

The beautiful Remington Model Seven is a bolt-action rifle available in many deer hunting calibers. It is lightweight by design, often known as a featherweight among deer hunters, and it is a very easy rifle to carry in the field.

chambered in the Marlin 1895 rifle. However, Marlin's lever-action is also available in .356 Winchester caliber now. Here is plenty of punch in a medium caliber which can "shoot flat" out to 200 yards or more, plus the rifle wears a scope sight wonderfully, and it's a lever-action. How about the Browning lever-action? Same story.

The semi-auto fan can find a rifle in modern long-range calibers, not only .30-06, which is certainly a good one, but also the .280 7mm Express Remington, 6mm Remington, and even the .338 Winchester round. The single shot is available not only in the big calibers of old, such as the .45-120 (from C. Sharps), but in all the modern numbers as well, such as the 6mm Remington, the .270 Winchester, 7mm Remington Magnum and even the .338 Winchester. My point is simply this: the deer hunter no longer selects his rifle based upon the action style combined with the caliber. He bases his choice on the action style for reasons other than caliber, and then he simply chooses the type of caliber he wants.

Deer hunters must pick actions today on the criteria of handling, and many other reasons, but certainly not caliber. In order to say anything intelligent about deer hunting rifle actions today, we need to leave caliber out of the picture and cling to specific virtues of each style. After the hunter decides upon the action style he likes for his own personal reasons, then he can talk caliber. In any of the action styles, from bolt to single shot, he will find a caliber which will take care of any game in North America, not only deer but moose, elk, bears and so forth.

The Bolt-Action: In the hands of a practiced hunter, the bolt-action can fire rapidly enough for most deer hunting situations. Although there are single-shot bolt-action rifles, by far the bolt is a repeater with a magazine capable of holding several rounds. The capacity varies, of course. My Model 70 Winchester custom 7mm Magnum magazine holds three rounds. The magazine on my wife's 6mm/222 Sako custom will hold six rounds. Shooters like the bolt-action because it is thought of as an accurate lock-up system and a very safe one. Because the action is rigid, reloaders find that cartridge case stretch is minimal and cases last well and can be reloaded several times each. When returning a case to full-length resize, if the case was used in a bolt-action rifle, there is little problem, even for full throttle loads.

The bolt-action is reliable, and we have admitted that it can be fired rapidly, though not in the same speed class as some of the other action types. Another factor which put the bolt-action on the map, so to speak, is action strength. With all of the bolt-action systems used today in new firearms, the locking lugs are designed to hold far more pounds per square inch pressure than found in factory-loaded ammo. In other words, the margin of safety is a high one. The bolt-action is very strong.

As far as overall rifle balance and handling, a bolt-

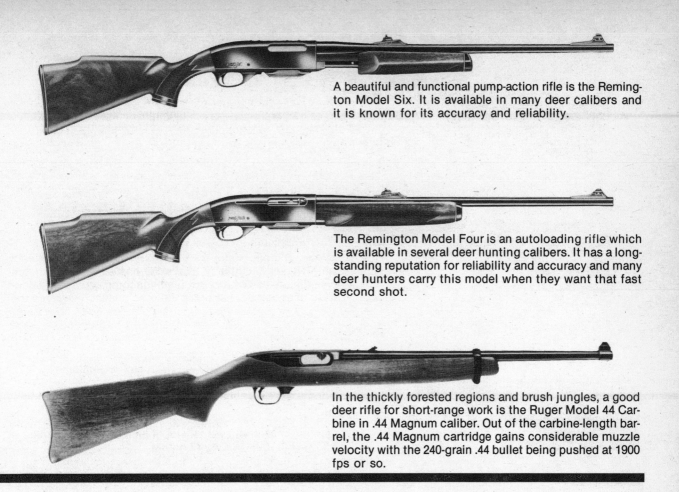

A beautiful and functional pump-action rifle is the Remington Model Six. It is available in many deer calibers and it is known for its accuracy and reliability.

The Remington Model Four is an autoloading rifle which is available in several deer hunting calibers. It has a long-standing reputation for reliability and accuracy and many deer hunters carry this model when they want that fast second shot.

In the thickly forested regions and brush jungles, a good deer rifle for short-range work is the Ruger Model 44 Carbine in .44 Magnum caliber. Out of the carbine-length barrel, the .44 Magnum cartridge gains considerable muzzle velocity with the 240-grain .44 bullet being pushed at 1900 fps or so.

action is all right. I feel that the bolt generally makes up into a rifle which is very steady in the hand, very solid in feel. I do not take the bolt-action rifle from my shoulder in order to work the action; therefore, I find that in my own bolt rifles, speed of second shot is certainly rapid enough. All in all, the bolt is a fine choice for the deer hunter, especially the deer hunter of the West, but with the featherweight, short-barreled bolt-action rifles now becoming so popular (again), there is no way I could in good faith tell a deer hunter to stay away from the bolt because he hunts in the East. Probably, other action styles are more appropriate for the deep woods, but certainly the bolt-action rifle is suitable for taking deer anywhere a rifle is legal and prudent for deer hunting.

The Pump Action: Slide-action is probably the more sophisticated term for this type of repeater; however, the pump has also been affectionately called a trombone action as well as slide. Once again, magazine capacity is more than sufficient and always has been in the pump gun. The speed of operation is right on the heels of the semi-automatic. In fact, when I was shooting a pump style .22 rifle one day, a fellow with a semi-auto challenged me. We both loaded 10 rounds, my friend using a Winchester Model 69, while I was using a Model 61 Winchester pump. I fired 10 rounds before my friend got his seventh off. The pump is fast.

It is natural for most shooters to work the actions of the pump, lever or semi-auto with the rifle shouldered. The slide-action is very easy to operate, and it is soon a natural function to aim, fire, pump and then do it all over again as the rifle stays pretty much on target. The new slide-actions are rigid enough to offer good reloading characteristics for expended brass cases. I have used full-length resized rounds fired in a modern pump and they gave no trouble. I think the bolt-action is still king in the department of case stretch, or rather lack of it, but cases last well enough in the pumpgun, too. If the cases are brought to full-length resize religiously, they will function as new rounds very smoothly in the slide-action. Now, in the reliability department we have to give the bolt a 10 out of 10 score. If the pump uses new or newly dimensioned cases, I think the same score applies. If cases are expanded and not back to original dimensions or close to it, then the pump is not going to be as reliable as the bolt. In terms of "camming power," there is nothing which will beat the bolt-action. But we are talking about deer rifles and deer hunting. There is no reason that a hunter can't use new or once-fired cases in his slide-action rifle. He can save the older cases for the range, where total smoothness of function is not crucial.

The strength/safety factors of the slide-action rifle are well established. The bolt is stronger, but there is no slide-action rifle manufactured today which will not handle its rounds with total safety when those rounds are factory spec or reloaded to approximate factory pressures. While

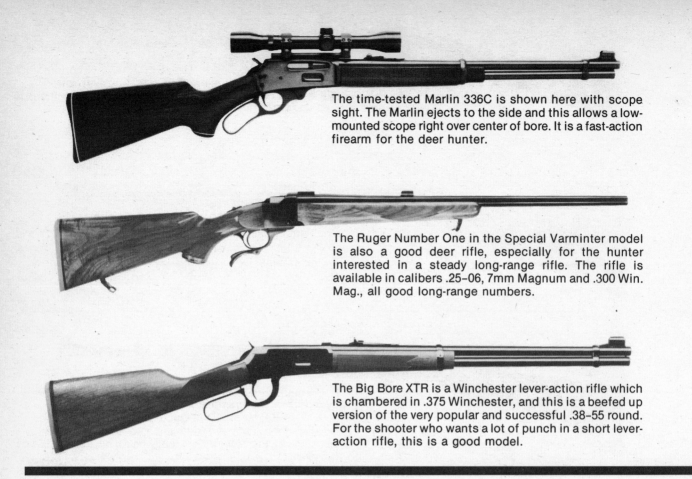

The time-tested Marlin 336C is shown here with scope sight. The Marlin ejects to the side and this allows a low-mounted scope right over center of bore. It is a fast-action firearm for the deer hunter.

The Ruger Number One in the Special Varminter model is also a good deer rifle, especially for the hunter interested in a steady long-range rifle. The rifle is available in calibers .25-06, 7mm Magnum and .300 Win. Mag., all good long-range numbers.

The Big Bore XTR is a Winchester lever-action rifle which is chambered in .375 Winchester, and this is a beefed up version of the very popular and successful .38-55 round. For the shooter who wants a lot of punch in a short lever-action rifle, this is a good model.

we include the feature of action safety here, we do so simply to take notice of this criterion, but not because a deer hunter has to concern himself about the safety of any of the action types using ammo for which the action was intended. Overall, the pump rifle is fast in the handling department, and shooters who love their pump shotguns find the slide-action deer rifle a particular joy to own, carry and shoot in the field.

The Semi-Automatic: In terms of speed, the semi-auto ranks number one among deer rifles, in spite of the fact that the slide-action fan can often, but not always, train himself to match or come close to the rapidity of fire found in the semi-auto. Many shooters like the idea of simply pulling the trigger, with nothing else to concern them. For these shooters, the semi-auto is the deer rifle of the day. Obviously, we have a repeater again, as with the slide-action and bolt, and magazine capacity is far more than adequate in all of the semi-auto types of both today and yesterday. As for reloading, there is more case stretch in the semi-auto than in the bolt-action, but all that we said concerning the pump and reloading can be applied to this action style, too. Full-length sized cases which are carefully returned to original tolerances can be fired with confidence in the semi-auto. Older cases, stretched cases, dirty rounds and any ammo which is not purely up to snuff should be left out of the semi-auto for field work. But can't we truly say the same about all

of the other action styles? I think so.

The semi-auto rifle is a deer hunter's choice where a fast second shot is desired. Some hunters feel that a semi-auto encourages rapid fire just for the sake of rapid fire. I do not think this has to be the case. I have hunted with outdoorsmen who used semi-auto deer rifles, and I found no trigger-happy, fill-the-air-with-lead attitude present at all. I have never personally felt a need for a semi-automatic deer rifle, but countless others have and I do not thwart their choice one bit.

The Lever-Action: Here is the old American favorite. Again, we have a fast action, certainly faster than the bolt-action for the average shooter, and if two seasoned hunters put on a contest, one using the bolt, the other the lever-action, I will wager that the one shooting the lever will get off more rounds faster than the bolt-user every time. Once again, the rifle need not be lowered from the shoulder. I have seen excellent shots who do not, however, take this course. They always lower the lever-action rifle, lever in a new round and then re-mount the rifle, feeling that this total sequence gives them a much better *flow* of smoothness in the operation. I can't argue with this. A sequence of operation can be important. In shooting the longbow, for example, the great Howard Hill said that a certain speed should be maintained for each shot. If Hill drew an arrow rapidly from his backquiver, he also strung it on the bow quickly, drew quickly, took fast

The Browning Lever Action big game rifle is a modern version of the ever-famous repeaters in the lever-action mode. In fine deer calibers, and with a clip feed, this is a fine model for the modern deer hunter.

The Model 94 Standard is an ever popular model among deer hunting. In caliber .30–30, this particular lever-action rifle style has taken a great many deer over the many years of its production, and it will harvest a great many more.

The Thompson/Center Single Shot Rifle is available in several deer calibers, including the .30–06, 7mm Magnum, .243 Winchester. This made-in-America rifle offers accessory barrels; therefore, a hunter can own a few different calibers by purchasing various barrels.

aim and loosed the shaft within a short time span. If he drew the arrow slowly from the quiver, then he nocked it with less speed, took longer to aim and loosed the arrow with less quickness or lapse of total time.

For reloading, the lever falls into the same category as the pump and auto. New styled levers have locking type lugs in some cases, rather than a more conventional lockup system, and cases stretch less than the older models allowed. But I have reloaded for the older lever-action arms and have been able to use a case several times with no hangup whatsoever. So I do not consider reloading factors to be detrimental in this action type, though the bolt still remains the least offender in case stretch. Reliability? I have never in my life had a round hang up in a Marlin lever-action rifle, a Winchester lever-action, or any other I have used.

The lever-action rifle is plenty strong, of course, for the rounds that it chambers. All things considered, it is no wonder that the lever remains highly popular to this day. Generally, the lever-action deer rifle has fine balance and handling is quick. In short, if the deer hunter wants to pick a lever-action rifle, he should do so with no reservations. As we have noted, caliber selection today is wide in the lever-actions with ballistics suited for any American hunting, not just deer but all big game.

The Single-Shot: One may think that we have to discount speed of action here altogether. After all, what could be slower than a one-shot rifle? Nothing, I suppose. But I want to point out two facts: First, I have touched off second shots at deer out West in the open places, and I think any practiced shooter can do the same with a single-shot. If a second round is handy, there is no excuse for a lack of a second shot when a buck is working up a hillside and the hunter has the "drop" on him. Second, at least in theory, the single-shot encourages marksmanship. The deer hunter who knows that he has but one round to fire in a woods situation may take that one shot quite carefully, picking a little opening to shoot through and making that one round count. Even in the West, the hunter who *can* get off a second shot with his single-shot rifle is also encouraged to make the first one count. So, speed of action is certainly not in favor of the single-shot, but a lot of us feel that it is of little practical consequence. Given a situation where I need a fast second shot, I'll take a repeater. But let's not condemn the single-shot for lack of firepower.

As for reloading, I note that most single-shots do better with full-length resized cases. In my opinion, I put the single-shot with the actions above, suggesting full-length resizing when reloading deer hunting rounds, and this goes for all actions except the bolt, and even then the shooter should full-length resize for the hunting field in spite of the bolt's camming power. Reliable? Of course the single-shot is reliable. It is a simple action, on the face of it at least, and one can call the single-shot more

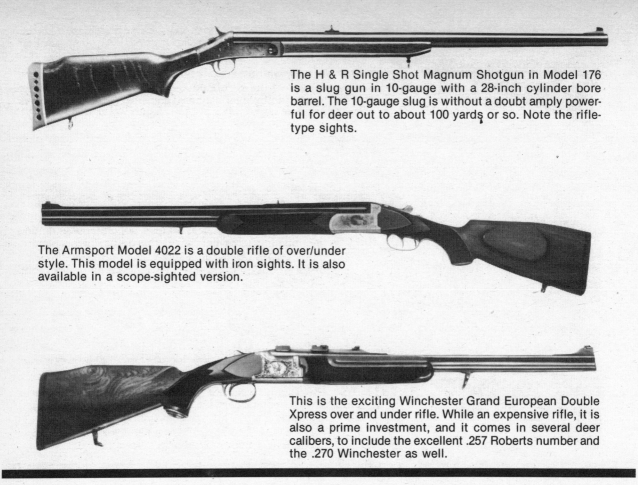

The H & R Single Shot Magnum Shotgun in Model 176 is a slug gun in 10-gauge with a 28-inch cylinder bore barrel. The 10-gauge slug is without a doubt amply powerful for deer out to about 100 yards or so. Note the rifle-type sights.

The Armsport Model 4022 is a double rifle of over/under style. This model is equipped with iron sights. It is also available in a scope-sighted version.

This is the exciting Winchester Grand European Double Xpress over and under rifle. While an expensive rifle, it is also a prime investment, and it comes in several deer calibers, to include the excellent .257 Roberts number and the .270 Winchester as well.

than reliable. It is highly strong, too, being able to handle the hot rounds of the day. As for overall balance and "feel," a number of shooters like the single-shot in this respect. The single-shot action allows for longer barrels without getting into long overall lengths. More on this in a moment.

The Drillings: This is a rather expensive action style and one which will not be normally encountered in the fields of American deer hunting. However, we should point out that drillings have a place in the scheme of things and are available to shooters who wish to buy them. A drilling is a combination firearm. It is usually, but not always, a side-by-side shotgun with another attached and regulated barrel, that barrel being for a cartridge. There are several combinations available, far too many to include here, and on special order, just about any conceivable blend can be included in a drilling. As an example, let's think of a side-by-side 12-gauge shotgun with a .30-06 barrel. That is a drilling. The attributes of the action correspond with the single-shot, with the exception being, of course, multiple firing ability. The drilling would be useful for those deer hunters who also hunt upland birds at the same time. Even in the West, I have been quail hunting only to jump a whitetail buck, in season, deer tag in pocket. Instead of watching the buck make tracks, the hunter with a drilling could have a chance for harvested venison in this situation.

The Double Rifles: The double rifle often associated with African and Asian hunting is available to American deer hunters, too, in suitable calibers of course. Again, the caliber possibilities are too many to include. One can have .30-06, 7mm Mauser, .243, .308 Winchester, .375 Winchester and so forth, not to mention a host of good European calibers. Everything we said above about the single-shot applies here. Of course, the double has two shots instead of one. It may be a side-by-side or an over-and-under model. With two fast shots, a well-constructed double can be a good choice for a deer hunter. Scopes can be mounted and the better doubles are regulated so that the barrels shoot to the same point of impact at a given range.

3. Overall Dimensions

Another criterion for selecting the deer rifle is overall length and the total weight of the firearm in question. Some of this ties in with action, of course. The configuration of the action dictates the overall dimension of the finished product. However, in most cases, a light rifle can be built on *any* action type, and there are bolt-action rifles which are very light in weight. As for length, short barrels, while noisier than longer barrels (depending, too, on the powder capacity of the cartridge case), are feasible. For example, in one test we took a .270 Winchester with a 24-inch barrel and chronographed it. With a 130-grain bullet the velocity was 3,144 fps at the muzzle. We took that very same barrel and cut it down to only 20 inches. With the exact same handload, the 130-grain bullet gained a muzzle velocity of 3,024 fps. Individual firearms will vary here. But short barrels are possible with any of the action styles.

The single-shot, as well as drillings and doubles, of course, allow for modest overall length with longer barrels since the action is much shorter on these types. There is some advantage here. A friend of mine chronographed his .270 Ruger Number One and obtained 3300 fps with the 130-grain bullet in the 26-inch barrel.

As for weight, I think Jack O'Connor said it all when he suggested that a deer rifle should weigh as much as your wristwatch when you carry it, but when it's time to shoot, the rifle should suddenly weigh over 10 pounds. A heavy rifle is steady and recoil is reduced, of course, as rifle mass is added. But we do seek a lighter rifle for ease of carrying. Since I generally carry a deer rifle on a sling, the sling looped on a special strut of my packframe, I don't mind a deer rifle that weighs a little over 9 pounds total when I am in open country. In the brush, where it is often wiser to keep the rifle at the ready, lighter weight is appreciated.

I have handled a bolt-action .270 with a special fiberglass stock that only weighed 7 pounds, scope and all. So it is not possible to say that bolt-actions are heavy rifles. I have a single shot that weighs about 10 pounds because of a heavy barrel. Lightness of rifle depends upon the design, all right, but any action style can be used to obtain a lightweight deer rifle. If the hunter wants light weight, he should turn to the pages of a big gun book, such as *Gun Digest*, and peruse the dimensions of the arms given therein. If he wants ultra-light weight, he can turn to the featherweight styles or he can have the rifle customized by a professional who can trim off a lot of weight through metalwork and stockwork changes.

4. Balance

Each shooter handles a rifle a bit differently. A rifle has good balance, then, commensurate with how it is handled. I do not mind having a center of gravity which rests out toward the end of the fore-end. I have long arms. Other shooters would find a rifle so balanced unwieldy for them. However, the deer hunter should consider balance as one of the criteria used in the selection of his personal deer rifle. While many specific firearm attributes cannot be tested in the gun store, balance can be. A hunter who picks up a rifle and finds that "it fits him" just right is experiencing in part the balance of that firearm in his hands. The balance of a firearm will affect the handling features of that firearm. But handling is more than balance. Balance is simply how that rifle settles in the hand, either just right (on the level), butt-heavy or barrel-heavy.

5. Handling

Handling means how the firearm functions in the hand.

Individual build will play an important role here. Being long-armed, I have an awful time with rifles that have very short lengths of pull, the measurement from the trigger to the buttplate. My face lands too far forward on the stock with these rifles. In fact, shorter-stocked rifles "kick" me, to use the vernacular. So handling means stock fit. It also means action. I do not find any of the action types clumsy to operate, but other hunters do. This used to be more true when the left-handed shooter was forced to operate a rifle, especially the bolt type, right-handed. Today, there are left-handed actions available. But there are shooters who prefer a lever over a bolt, for example, finding a bolt clumsy to work smoothly. Handling, then, is a sum total of how that rifle feels in the hands of the individual, right down to how the firearm loads and ejects its ammo.

6. Accuracy

Of course it makes sense to pick a deer rifle based upon the accuracy of the rifle. But this is not a cut and dried proposition. What is hunting accuracy? Is it a minute of angle? I doubt it. I doubt that we can put a figure on this topic which will please everyone, so I am going to state what I feel personally on the issue. For the open spaces of the West where I might get a shot at 250 yards or better, I like minute-of-angle accuracy, approximately.

A minute-of-angle means that I can get a three-shot group of an inch at 100 yards, 2 inches at 200 hundred yards, 3 inches at 300 and so forth. It's nice to have minute-of-angle accuracy when a buck is across a canyon. But in fact, a rifle of two-minute accuracy would suffice, in my opinion. For closer range shooting, where 100 yards is a long shot, and there are places where this is a fact, a rifle capable of putting three bullets into a group size of 3 or even 4 inches at 100 yards is going to put a lot of venison in the freezer.

I have not put accuracy way up front on the list of criteria because *every* deer rifle that we tested to date has been capable of putting three shots into 4 inches at 100 yards and most rifles, no matter what style the action, managed 3-inch or smaller groups at 100 yards. I know of no currently available deer rifle which will not manage a 4-inch group at 100 yards. But aren't bolt-action rifles always more accurate than the other styles? Not always. All in all, the bolt is a very secure lockup system and the producer of fine accuracy, but I have tuned rifles of other style actions which produced one to two minute groups.

In short, the available deer rifles are all accurate enough for deer hunting. If a shooter wants special deluxe accuracy, then he will have to tune the rifle or have a professional do so. However, I am not worried about accuracy potential among modern deer rifles.

7. Recoil Factors

Recoil is a function of Newton's Third Law, with every action having an opposite and equal reaction. Therefore, the mass weight of the firearm and the "power" of the

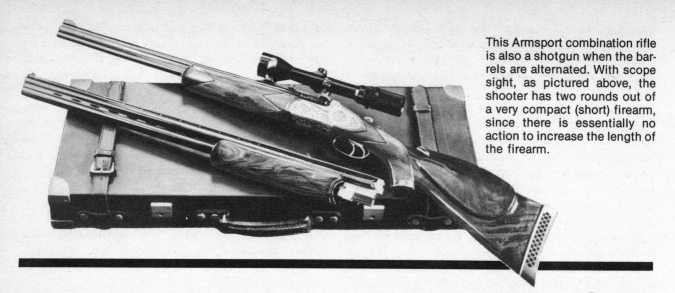

This Armsport combination rifle is also a shotgun when the barrels are alternated. With scope sight, as pictured above, the shooter has two rounds out of a very compact (short) firearm, since there is essentially no action to increase the length of the firearm.

round add up to actual or real recoil. The force presented by a fired round acts equally in two directions. The expanding gas is pushing the bullet out of the bore, but this same force is pushing back on the rifle, hence we have recoil. We can compute free recoil energy. We end up with a foot-pounds rating. A .30-06 in a 9-pound rifle kicks more than a .243, and this is all we need know as deer hunters. It is also nice to know that "visible recoil," how much the rifle seems to "buck back," has no effect on accuracy. The bullet is gone from the muzzle before critical damage is done to aim. Photos taken at a millionth of one second show the bullet to be on the way before there is muzzle rise.

So, the deer hunter can look at recoil as bothersome, but not as a hindrance to his hitting the target. The above expression of recoil is actual. There is also "felt recoil." This is not totally scientific in nature, but it is very real and very important to the shooter. The felt recoil is the thrust of the actual recoil as it affects the individual shooter. Let us use an example. We have two rifles. Both are chambered for the .30-06, and both are using identical loads. Both weigh precisely 9 pounds. Therefore, both recoil exactly the same. However, one rifle is designed with a rather straight stock, a slightly sloping cheekpiece, correct length of pull for the shooter, a wide buttplate, a good fore-end allowing a little bit of felt recoil to be taken up by the left hand (but don't squeeze down on the fore-end while shooting) and so forth. The other rifle has a narrow buttplate and a stock which does not fit the shooter well. Obviously, though both rifles have the same recoil energy, recoil the same, the design of the first mentioned will give less felt recoil to the shooter. There are many other factors, such as buttpads and location of fore-end sling swivels and features of stock drop and wrist size to consider. But the real consideration is in the shooting. This is individual in accord with the build of the shooter and his shooting style, plus his sensitivity to recoil.

Recoil is an important factor in selecting a deer rifle. In the field, the recoil of modern deer calibers means little, for none kick hard enough to hurt a shooter or cause him to miss a deer. In fact, in the excitement of shooting, I doubt that a shooter recognizes that he has been "kicked" unless he has been shooting a very large caliber or a medium caliber in a very light rifle. Mainly, recoil trouble happens at the bench, at the target range and during informal practice. Here, the hard-kicking firearm teaches the hunter to flinch, and he may carry that habit into the field. Therefore, though that one round fired at a deer hardly hurts the shooter, he may have flinched due to previously learned patterns and missed the target.

A cure? For the recoil sensitive, I like to consider a good rubber buttpad and a rifle designed to deliver the recoil straight back instead of up into the cheekbone. Also, there is no reason to shoot long strings of high power ammo in practice sessions. My wife has a custom .284 Ruger and it is super light in weight. Dean Zollinger, the Idaho gunmaker, put it together with weight factors in mind. But the stock is straight and the buttpad is of high quality rubber. She shoots modest target loads in practice, turning to full power loads for field use only. My Frank Wells 7mm Magnum, on the other hand, wears a steel buttplate, but Frank designed the cheekpiece so that the stock actually recoils away from my face. I have never been bothered by that rifle, not even with strong handloads of 160-grain bullets at 3100 fps.

8. Cost Factors

Cost is a consideration, and the deer hunter should look at his selection with cost in mind. If a rifle doubles for a varmint piece as well as a deer-harvester, then a few more bucks might be invested with extra use serving to justify extra cost. At any rate, the shooter can buy a used firearm in excellent condition with many models to choose from at modest cost. I consider cost to be of small consequence because a good accurate rifle can be purchased cheaply, and it will last more than a lifetime. Used firearms can be a bargain, too. Often, a rifle will have been fired only a comparative few times, but the owner may have decided to move into another caliber or style for his own reasons. My son recently purchased a used .30-06 for $150 in like-new condition. It had a cheap but workable scope on it besides. A good deer rifle does not have to cost a lot, though the hunter may consider every dime he spends on such a rifle an investment in a very long-lasting tool.

9. Looks

Perhaps this factor should have no bearing on the purchase of a deer rifle, but I think we'd be off base not to suggest that it does. Deer hunters often select a rifle based in part on appearance. There is nothing wrong with this. Tools have always been embellished as works of art. I would not select a deer rifle based on looks alone, but if a hunter likes Rifle A better than Rifle B strictly on appearances, and if both function well, he should purchase the rifle he likes best in overall terms, and the "looks" of the rifle will play a big role in many cases.

Geography and the Deer Rifle

We cannot really speak of the East and West in terms of deer hunting geography if we are always going to think of the East as close-range shooting and the West as long-range shooting. On the average, it's probably true that the cover is more dense in the East and the shots closer, so this is a fair appraisal. It follows, then, that we look at western deer hunting as more open with longer shots available. With this in mind, let's transcend actual geography and talk about environmental conditions instead.

If I were in a thick area, I'd like to have a somewhat shorter deer rifle, a rifle which would mount quickly and point well. I'd like the latter to be true in spite of the fact that my close-range rifle would probably wear a 2.5x scope sight. While I'd not concern myself with the action type to any great extent, I'd prefer a lever-action, pump or auto for this type of deer hunting for reasons of a fast second shot if needed and if available. The caliber would be somewhat less important to me than the actual handling qualities of the rifle. Instead of attempting to shoot through brush, I'd prefer to put a bullet between the openings. But there can be a slight benefit in larger calibers for the brush and with that in mind, I'd be more inclined toward the .35 Remington, .358 Winchester, .356 Winchester, .44 Magnum, and similar rounds than to the faster numbers.

My brush rifle would have a barrel of short length so that the rifle could be handled well in the brush. A barrel of 18 to 20 inches would be good, I feel. Many modern rifles fit the patterns we are establishing here, and the hunter would have no problem finding a host of different firearms to suit his close-range deer hunting needs. In fact, I fear the real problem will be in deciding which one to pick. Just to offer a checklist, let's list a few attributes of our close-range deer rifle:

1. The caliber is .30 or better, with calibers such as the

.375 Winchester and .356 Winchester, .35 Remington and the like, considered ideal.

2. The rifle is not overly heavy in weight. With scope sight, the total weight falls in the 8-pound category, roughly.

3. The barrel is short. There is no need for a long barrel here. We can gain all the ballistics necessary from a barrel length of only 18 to 20 inches.

4. The rifle can handle a scope sight, though it is up to the preference of the hunter as to which sight is placed on the rifle.

5. The action is auto-loader, pump or lever-action repeater for fast second shots.

6. The handling and balance of the rifle make it easy to mount quickly and get off a fast, well-placed shot.

As for that long-range rifle, other qualities would be useful to the deer hunter. Listing those might satisfy the criteria very well, so let's try to do that here.

1. The caliber of our long-range deer rifle would be such that a flat trajectory would be possible. If the hunter wanted the rifle as a varminter as well as deer-taker, something on the order of the .243 or 6mm would be just right. If the hunter wanted a deer rifle only, a .25-06 or .257 Weatherby would serve, with larger calibers working for deer and elk, beginning with the .270 and going up.

2. Weight of rifle can be quite important in open terrain, and in some cases more critical than brush country hunting, though this is a forced point to be sure. However, in some of the mountainous areas the heavy rifle becomes a millstone about the hunter's neck, so to speak. Out West, the featherweight deer hunting rifle is highly admired. On the other hand, the rifle of modest weight does offer the "ballast" necessary for a steady hold. It's a hunter's choice. But accuracy is certainly available in the lightweight rifle today, and I think most hunters would be happier leaving some of the bulk out of the deer hunting scene by using a featherweight firearm.

3. The barrel of our long-range rifle would probably be from 22 to 26 inches in length, allowing for a modest but sometimes helpful increase in muzzle velocity over a shorter barrel, hence a little flatter trajectory. We are dealing in small figures here, mere inches of drop, but in open country the longer barrel is no problem to carry so we might as well strain a little more muzzle velocity out of our deer rifle.

4. This is a moot point; however, we will follow the numbers here and suggest that the long-range deer rifle be suited to a telescopic sight. I can't think of one which isn't so suited, however.

5. Since long-range calibers come in all of the action types today, it would hardly matter which action is selected. However, the most popular action for western deer hunting is the bolt. I think a single-shot is extremely good for open country hunting, too. A second shot is possible if necessary, and the rifle can have a longer barrel while

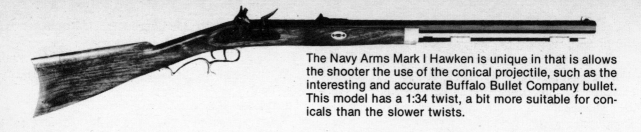

The Navy Arms Mark I Hawken is unique in that is allows the shooter the use of the conical projectile, such as the interesting and accurate Buffalo Bullet Company bullet. This model has a 1:34 twist, a bit more suitable for conicals than the slower twists.

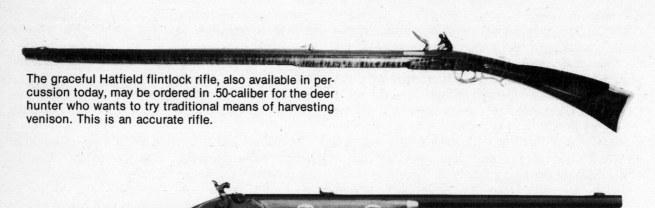

The graceful Hatfield flintlock rifle, also available in percussion today, may be ordered in .50-caliber for the deer hunter who wants to try traditional means of harvesting venison. This is an accurate rifle.

The strongly constructed Browning Mountain Rifle is available in deer calibers and is built for good black powder loads. (See *Gun Digest Black Powder Loading Manual* for loads and ballistics.) With the many special black powder hunts available to the deer hunter, such rifles have gained much popularity.

not growing in overall length. We are a bit less concerned with overall length in an open country deer rifle. Even Western mule deer terrain which is not forested can have a few tight spots to walk through and overall length of deer rifle is still a consideration. Not only that, but a rifle has to be packed for transport, too, and again the shorter models are easier to work with from home to camp and back again.

6. While it is nice to have fast handling action in any rifle, the open terrain deer rifle may serve better to offer good steady holding qualities, with rapid handling qualities taking a back seat if necessary. For example, I have a bolt-action deer rifle which is built so that it "hangs" very well. It rests nicely in the hand for a sitting shot, and it steadies on a padded boulder or similar object in the field very nicely. It does not snap to the shoulder as quickly as some other rifles I know of, but its steadiness makes up for that fact.

So much for our close-range and long-range considerations. These must be blended with all of the other features we have discussed concerning the choice of a deer rifle. As we have admitted, the selection is complicated by the fact that there are so many good choices. I suppose, however, it is better to have too many than too few.

Trends

I think the deer rifle of the future is rather self-evident today. In the bolt-action category, we are coming up with more and more featherweight rifles. Although it is quite true that heavier rifles are easier to hold steady when it comes time to shoot, hunters reason that they have to carry a rifle for hours and even days, but they shoot it darn little. Of course, if a shot were missed because of a lightweight rifle, then all of the easy packing in the world would not make up for it. However, this is not going to be the case. Light rifles can be quite accurate and they can be managed well in the field.

The pump is still alive and well and apt to stay that way for a very long time to come. The newest slide-action which I personally saw, the Remington Model Six, is a finely balanced rifle with a 22-inch barrel. The bolt is shrouded in style. Fast-handling is the big feature in this firearm. Calibers are several, including a 6mm or .243 for those who wish these for deer, and they are good choices, along with a .270 for some heavy-duty long-range work, a .280 Remington for the same, the venerable all-around .30-06 and the .308 Winchester, a fine deer number. The pump has maintained its tradition, then, of fast-handling, rapidly delivered second and third shots, and yet the modern slide-action is easily scope-sighted and it comes in many up-to-date calibers.

The semi-automatic rifle is trending toward a fast-handling mode, with positive lockup features and many excellent calibers. The Ruger .44 is ever popular as a close-range fast-handling semi-auto, and then we have the Remington in its new Model Four with about the same

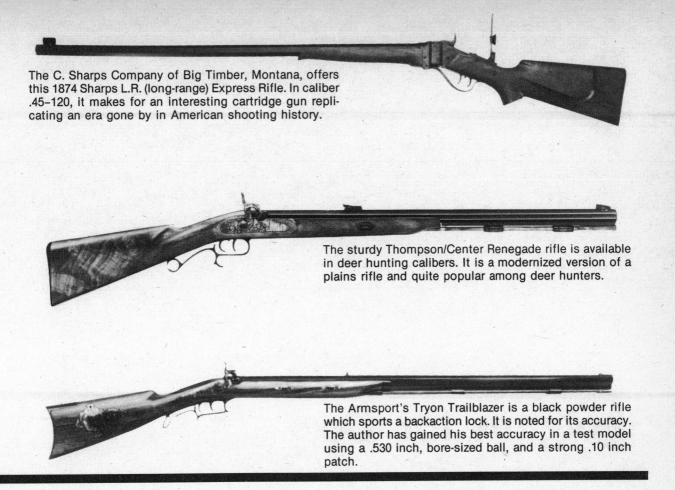

The C. Sharps Company of Big Timber, Montana, offers this 1874 Sharps L.R. (long-range) Express Rifle. In caliber .45–120, it makes for an interesting cartridge gun replicating an era gone by in American shooting history.

The sturdy Thompson/Center Renegade rifle is available in deer hunting calibers. It is a modernized version of a plains rifle and quite popular among deer hunters.

The Armsport's Tryon Trailblazer is a black powder rifle which sports a backaction lock. It is noted for its accuracy. The author has gained his best accuracy in a test model using a .530 inch, bore-sized ball, and a strong .10 inch patch.

features as enumerated for the pump Model Six and the same calibers. I firmly believe the trend will continue here, with light, handy semi-autos available in modern calibers.

The lever-actions have made some changes recently, the main changes being in caliber offerings. Lever-actions in powerful calibers are the trend today. As an example, we have the .375 Winchester round, the .356 Winchester and the .307. The .356 is quite close to the powerful ballistics of the .358 Winchester, and the .307 is not far from the .308 Winchester in performance. Winchester has also updated the famous Model 94 with the Side-Eject model for better scope mounting. This is the trend, then, with the lever-actions, high power, such as found in the Browning and Marlin and Winchester, and all with good scope-mounting characteristics.

The single-shots are strongly represented today, especially in the fact that good accuracy is obtained in a rifle of modest weight and length. Calibers are too numerous to mention; the deer hunter has his pick from the .243 up to the magnums. Drillings and doubles are not going to be overly popular in the deer hunting field, mainly due to high cost factors, but they remain in the running and are available for those who want them.

This just about wraps up our discussion of deer rifles for the modern hunter. However, there is one more rifle style which deserves mention. Coming out of the past to be represented in the future by modern deer hunters is the muzzle-loading rifle. There are special black powder only deer hunts in many parts of the country, and where these hunts are lacking, the muzzleloader may still be used during the regular seasons in all of the areas I checked into recently. Over the past decade, I have been using the muzzleloader more than other rifles for my own deer hunting, though I have never abandoned the modern deer rifle and have no intention of doing so.

chapter 9
Shotguns for Deer

WHILE IT MAY BE a fact that America is a land of riflemen, the facts also prove two other things: First, America is also loaded, if you will excuse a pun, with shotguns; and second, shotguns are the only legal firearms for deer-taking in a number of areas. You see, the deer have indeed staged a comeback. While, at the turn of the century many locales were devoid of deer, several factors have turned this around. So we now have deer which have to be managed—harvested in other words—and these deer dwell in such close proximity to people population that the only two answers are archery hunts and shotgun hunts, with a possible third choice of round ball black powder arms in some areas.

We are, very obviously, looking for an effective tool for deer harvesting, but we do not want that tool to possess a great range potential. The shotgun is ideal in this department. With buckshot and even with a single slug the projectile range is not nearly as great as that of a modern high-power rifle. I certainly do not mean that the range is so limited that a hunter need not be extremely careful. The range of a single slug from a 12-gauge shotgun is several hundred yards. Buckshot will get out there, too.

First, let's take a look at buckshot as a deer harvesting medicine. Perhaps some shooters, especially those who live in areas where buckshot is a traditional deer-taking missile, will disagree totally with me, however I do not find it possible to rank buckshot with a single slug when it comes to harvesting "power."

Let me point out that if a hunter suggested using a round ball from a black powder muzzleloader in a rather small caliber just about everyone would cry out against this procedure and some buckshot lovers would rent the sky with their protests. Yet, the buckshot load is, for all intent and purpose, no more than a handful of small round projectiles very much like those used in our squirrel rifles for those of us who shoot muzzleloaders.

Ah, but the difference, you say, is in the fact that we have multiple projectiles here, and right you are. But we still must look at each individual pellet as one round ball, that and nothing more than that. Bear with me. I am not condemning buckshot. I just want to gain an accurate perspective on exactly what we are dealing with when we use buckshot on deer.

So that we will be more than fair about it, we will look at a double-ought (00) pellet. The 00 pellet goes .33-caliber, or .33-inch. I want to point out that most of my round ball hunting for rabbits up to wild turkeys takes place with a .36-caliber black powder squirrel rifle using a .350-inch ball, slightly larger than a single 00 pellet, in other words.

Using the formula to decipher the theoretically perfect weight of a pure ball of lead ($D^3 \times .5236 \times 2,873.5$), we find that the .33-caliber pill goes 54 grains. My .350 ball weighs 65 grains. However, we can look at this another way. A modern 12-gauge hull may be loaded with

Today's modern buckshot loads are better than ever, though still best held to modest range. The Federal buckshot load is shown here in component form. Note the filler (far right) which buffers the buckshot and aids in retaining the shape of the shot.

No doubt the most powerful missile fired from a shotgun is the slug, or "rifled" slug. These are the excellent Federal brand slugs, showing here the 12-gauge, left, with a big 10-gauge slug, right.

a dozen of these .33-inch balls, so we have a total projectile mass weight of 648 grains. That is a substantial missile! Let's compute what we would have for a muzzle energy if those dozen 00 pellets were stuck together like cold meatballs and all of them hit the target *en mass*. We would have a muzzle energy rating of 2,432 foot-pounds if the charge of pellets left the muzzle at 1300 fps, as they do in the handload I use.

So, out of this 12-gauge shotgun firing a dozen 00 pellets, we have a muzzle energy rating of 2,432 foot-pounds. A .30-30 with a 170-grain bullet at 2200 fps is rated at 1,828 foot-pounds, so we are certainly dealing with a deer-taking force here. But will each and every pellet strike the target? From a few yards out, they will. In fact, when I was trying to concoct a powerful buckshot load for my double barrel Armsport hammer gun, cylinder and cylinder bores, I was surprised at the tightness of the pattern at 10 yards. But much beyond that, the pattern began to open up. At deer ranges, say 30 yards for the woods, I do not think that there is much chance of every pellet hitting the deer.

So we are forced to study the energy of each individual pellet by itself. Now, at a starting velocity of 1300 fps, we have only 203 foot-pounds energy rating. So, each 00 pellet is going to have 203 foot-pounds of energy at the muzzle. But, as with all round ball projectiles, the ability for the sphere of lead to retain this energy is limited. Just as a ball park figure, let's suggest that the .33-caliber 00

buckshot is still doing about 1000 fps at 50 yards. If so, then we would have a striking energy at 50 yards rated at 126 foot-pounds. What if only a couple of these hit the deer at 50 yards? Well, as I said earlier, I am not out to make light of the buckshot load. In fact, history has shown buckshot loads to be very effective. All I wanted to point out was the fact that the buckshot load is meant for close-range shooting where multiple strikes are the rule rather than the exception.

Looking at a standard 12-gauge slug we find a missile of about an ounce weight. There are 437.5 grains in an ounce; therefore, our rifled slug in 12-gauge will go 437.5 grains weight. In my handloads, 1500 fps for this slug is not a hard velocity to achieve. Now we have a single projectile which is certainly going to have to strike either as a unit or not at all and at a muzzle energy of 2,186 foot-pounds. I also want to point out that the Lyman 12-gauge cast slug goes 443 grains and it, too, can be driven at about 1500 fps from the muzzle. In fact, one Lyman load, page 156 of the first edition *Lyman Shotshell Handbook* shows a 443-grain slug leaving the muzzle at 1575 fps which will have a muzzle energy rating of 2,441 foot-pounds.

Before going further, I would like to point out that a deer hunter with a double-barreled shotgun can use an old-time load which has been called "buck 'n ball." The buck 'n ball loads have been prepared in two ways over the years. One I will not vouch for because I do not con-

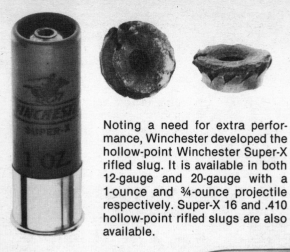

Noting a need for extra performance, Winchester developed the hollow-point Winchester Super-X rifled slug. It is available in both 12-gauge and 20-gauge with a 1-ounce and ¾-ounce projectile respectively. Super-X 16 and .410 hollow-point rifled slugs are also available.

one gun with which to "make his living," I think that one gun might well be a shotgun. I will stick my neck out and suggest that it ought to be a double-barrel model. Further, that it should be as simple as possible, the side-by-side model, in fact. With this one firearm, I think a dedicated and resourceful person could bag enough edibles to make a go of it. Of course, terrain varies and a shooter might find himself where even a slug would not be ideal as far as range is concerned, but I think a hungry hunter could find a way of getting within 50 to 100 yards of a big game animal under almost any circumstances.

While this little scene is just for fun and has, in fact,

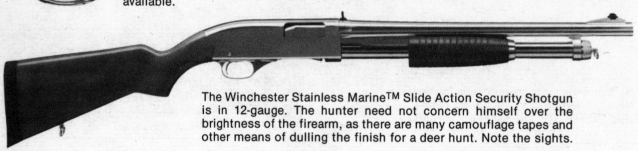

The Winchester Stainless Marine™ Slide Action Security Shotgun is in 12-gauge. The hunter need not concern himself over the brightness of the firearm, as there are many camouflage tapes and other means of dulling the finish for a deer hunt. Note the sights.

sider it correct, but I mention it because it is historically recorded. This is a load which has a round ball in the breech topped with some shot. I am against this practice and will not recommend it. I do not like the idea of adding to the mass weight of a "projectile" in this manner, for surely a person may try to add the shot on top of a ball which is already loaded with a correct but optimum charge of powder. However, the other type of buck 'n ball load, I am in favor of. But you have to have a double barrel for it to work out.

This load simply calls for a single projectile to be loaded in one barrel while the other barrel contains a charge of buckshot. Now the hunter is ready for a very close and fast shot at a deer in the thick, where he will touch off a load of buckshot for a sure hit. But he is also prepared for a little longer shot where he will send out the single missile instead of the buckshot charge.

Also, while I do not like to consider anything but an instant kill as proper, it could be that a deer taken at very close range with a buckshot load could be instantly approached and before it had a chance to regain its feet, a hunter could fire up close with the slug from the other barrel, keeping the deer down.

I have tested the buck 'n ball theory, and it is sound. In my own black powder shotguns, I have a buck 'n ball load which is certainly adequate for deer hunting, and I want to explain that load soon. For now, let's continue with a few more general points about using the shotgun on deer. The first consideration in favor of the shotgun, I think, is it versatility. The second is its general fast-handling characteristics.

If a person had to set out into the wilderness with but

no bearing on reality, I use it to suggest that the shotgun is in fact a very versatile tool. As for its fast-handling nature, a shotgun is a pointing instrument as much as an aiming instrument. Given that a target is very close and moving, I'd just as soon have a shotgun as any tool. Given that a big game animal offers a standing shot at up to 100 yards, I think the same shooter with the same shotgun can manage a solid hit.

My friend Dean Zollinger, Idaho gunmaker, is quite good with a shotgun firing slugs. I have witnessed him hit a 6-inch bull at 50 yards with almost every shot using a side-by-side double gun and slugs. Therefore, though a double gun such as my friend's may not wear sights, it is possible to make a hit using only a bead to line up the target. On the other hand, we have shotguns made for deer hunting. Now this is another matter. These are shotguns which have rifle-like sights, and they work.

A current example of such a shotgun is the Remington 870 Deer Gun. It is a 12-gauge pump shotgun with a 20-inch barrel, and it wears a set of rifle sights. The rear sight is on a ramp and is adjustable. The front sight is on a ramp, and it is mated with the rear sight for a standard sight picture we expect from a rifle. The Ithaca Model 37 LAPD is another shotgun which will serve the deer hunter wishing to fire slugs where it is legal to use slugs, but not legal to use a high-power rifle. The shotgun is also 12-gauge. It wears a sling, has a 5-shot magazine, and it comes equipped with rifle sights. The Winchester 1200 Police is the Defender model except that a set of sights are available. These are short-barreled handy guns, and the rifle-like sights make them ideal as slug-shooters for deer hunting.

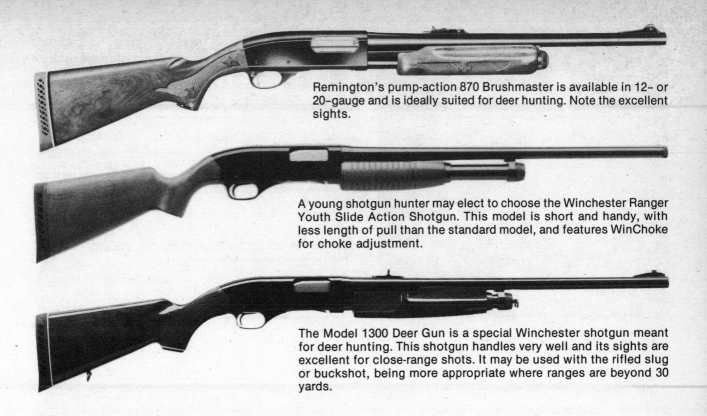

Remington's pump-action 870 Brushmaster is available in 12- or 20-gauge and is ideally suited for deer hunting. Note the excellent sights.

A young shotgun hunter may elect to choose the Winchester Ranger Youth Slide Action Shotgun. This model is short and handy, with less length of pull than the standard model, and features WinChoke for choke adjustment.

The Model 1300 Deer Gun is a special Winchester shotgun meant for deer hunting. This shotgun handles very well and its sights are excellent for close-range shots. It may be used with the rifled slug or buckshot, being more appropriate where ranges are beyond 30 yards.

For slug shooting, a scope sight may be mounted on a shotgun, and there are now a number of scopes which would serve well as shotgun aiming devices. We can look at the Burris 1.75-5x which gives a field of view around 70 feet at 100 yards, and this scope can be cranked up to 5x (actually over 6x) for longer shots. Weaver still offers its popular 1.5x scope, too. Swift has a 1.5-4.5x. Bushnell's Scope Chief VI may be purchased in a 1.5-4.5x model which gives a field of view at 100 yards rated at 73.7 feet on its lowest setting. The idea of rifling on a slug is to make it rotate. In other words, since the smooth bore of the shotgun has no rifling, then putting "fins" of some sort on the projectile itself will give the projectile rotation. The idea is rather interesting; that it works quite that way is rather doubtful. Evidence has it that a rifled slug does not rotate on its axis like a bullet, but rather it flies point forward because of distribution of weight.

We have to remember that as a projectile grows in mass, it requires somewhat less rps (revolutions per second) to stabilize it in flight around an axis. Therefore, we do not need a great degree of "spin" to stabilize a big rifled slug. I can also vouch for the fact that a rifled slug is sufficiently accurate from a standard shotgun to offer a good chance of hitting a deer-sized target at close range. At 50 yards from a bench rest, I have produced a 5-shot group of only 2.5 inches with an Ithaca Deerslayer. This would translate to a 5-inch group at 100 yards though slug-shooting with the shotgun is a close-range deer hunting proposition. No one can put a strict limitation upon the effective range of the slug, because the slug certainly has ample remaining energy at 100 yards to drop a deer; however, surefire projectile placement might be thought of as no more than 100 yards, with 75 yards being a more conservative limit. The slug flies "point on" due to the aerodynamic attitude of the lead projectile itself. We also know that as the mass increases in a projectile, stability and inertia change in a positive direction.

If I lived in an area where I intended to hunt deer with shotgun slugs on a regular basis, I would do the following: First, I would prefer a 12-gauge to anything smaller. Second, I would purchase a slug-shooter type shotgun, the ones we mentioned above and several others of a similar nature being examples. In other words, I'd select a shotgun with a short barrel. While I'd probably be content with the good sights available on this type of gun, I just might be happier yet with a scope. With something of the 1.5x range, preferably a variable, I would sight in to strike the bull's-eye at 50 yards, and if I saw a deer feeding or bedded or "frozen" at 100 yards, I would have no compunction against taking it with a carefully sighted slug-shooting shotgun.

The very first thing I would do with my own deer-taking shotgun is sight it in, of course, but I would also make certain of shooting at various ranges from 25 to 100 yards. I also suggest that a shooter take his shotgun with slugs to the range and try it at 200 yards. I have. I was convinced that at least in my hands I could not shoot accurately enough for this distance. We still have a short-range tool when we use slugs in a shotgun.

If a hunter will sight in with the slug and treat the slug-shooting shotgun as a rifle, taking advantage of its sights or adding a scope sight, I think this tool becomes a very

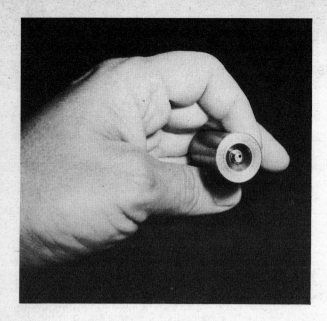

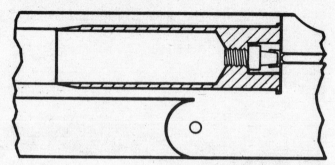

(Left and below) The Instant Muzzle Loader converts your shotgun to a muzzleloader. Uses percussion caps and black powder. No permanent modification of the shotgun. Inserted or removed in seconds. One can see the nipple, as it were, in the base of the shell. On this projection, the percussion cap, No. 11, is fitted.

viable deer-taker. As we have been careful to point out, the range is still going to be limited. However, deer hunting in the woods is *generally* short-range work, though long shots are sometimes a possibility across meadows and from one ridge to another.

The shotgun hunter must address himself to the fact that his methods have to coincide with his firearm. Field position, as already mentioned, has a very strong bearing on shotgunning for deer success. When a stand is taken, that stand has to be chosen on the basis of shotgun range, not rifle range. The still-hunter needs to stay on his toes in the woods because things happen so fast. If his field position has him so situated that a shot is nearly impossible, what good will it do if the hunter does jump some bucks? So, moving in near slow-motion speed, our still-hunter with shotgun in hand is ready for fast action. He is prepared to shoot at a quick target. He plays a little game in his mind when he goes. The game is one of fantasy, perhaps, but as he peers over downed timber, he imagines what he would have to do in order to bag a buck that might break from that tight cover. When he nears a meadow, he considers how he would approach in order to get a shot if a deer were bedded at that meadow's edge. If he climbs a small incline in the forest, he readies himself for an encounter with a buck that could be bedded on the other side. Most of the time, his fantasy will go unrewarded. But somewhere down the pike, he may indeed fulfill an imagined harvest. That harvest that he previously worked out in his mind as a "trial" or "dry run," may come true.

Well, there is always argument in all hunting. The argument ranges from which firearm is best to which method is best and then how in the heck to cook what was harvested. This little tale has its built-in controversy, too. I have leaned toward the slug and the 12-gauge, and

I might as well toss in the fact that a friend of mine who owns a 20-gauge double gun has been so successful that I know he's going to call me down if I do not mention the fact that he has bagged several deer with one 20-gauge slug each. All right, Norm. There it is. But in general, I still think I'm going to recommend the 12-gauge for all-purpose deer hunting conditions.

The deer hunter who uses a shotgun as his tool of harvest may wonder if he has to buy a special shotgun for the task. The answer is no. A shotgun which is suitable for hunting ducks or upland birds will handle factory shotgun slug ammo, too, and usually with sufficient accuracy for the short-range deer hunting available in shotgun-only terrain. There have been arguments as to the accuracy of a slug from a choked bore; however, in my own testing I have not found any problem with shooting a slug from any degree of choke from Improved Cylinder to Full. However, the special deer hunting shotguns which are equipped with rifle-type sights are the best choice when slugs are to be the most used projectile in that shotgun. Special deer hunting shotguns are now offered by several arms companies because they make sense, not only from the standpoint of better sights for where aiming instead of pointing the gun is necessary, but also from the standpoint of overall dimensions. The slug-shooting shotgun made for the job generally has a more appropriate barrel length (shorter) for this work.

Now what about black powder? The first point I wish to make is that a shooter can try black powder without having to run out and buy a black powder shotgun. There is a device which bears mention. This is the Instant Muzzle Loader unit from Sport Specialties. The Instant Muzzle Loader is in effect an all-steel shotgun hull or case. It is offered in 12-gauge, and it employs a standard No. 11 percussion cap on a sort of "nipple" situated at the base of the shell. Obviously, the spark from the percussion cap flies through a flash hole and into the main charge, which is located, naturally, at the "bottom" of this case per normal.

To load an Instant Muzzle Loader case, one simply pours in the powder charge, the proper wads, the shot, buckshot or single round ball, which I also tried, and he then inserts an over-shot wad to hold it all in place. The unit may then be fired in a modern shotgun. I much prefer using a double-barrel shotgun as it is easier to clean up. Remember, with black powder, we must clean up after use. Black powder is corrosive. It is not so terribly

New all-brass battery cup shotgun shells are available in a *very* wide variety of gauges and can be used in any shotgun to shoot black powder or smokeless powder. The 4-ga. 4-inch model is a monster!

Here is a short and handy shotgun, Model 1212, from Armsport. It is a 3-inch magnum shotgun and with such speed of handling would make a dandy close-range deer hunting tool.

corrosive that it eats metal like high school kids down hamburgers, but it certainly does no particular good to the bore left uncleaned. There is something worse—black powder is hygroscopic. That means it has a love affair with moisture. Fired black powder residue will attract moisture and hold it. This means rust.

A single-shot or double allows for easy access and easy cleaning. Of course, I have used my Model 870 shotgun with black powder loads, and I simply pull the barrel and clean it up, and I also clean the mechanism. An auto is more trouble. A person wishing to shoot the black powder unit mentioned above should probably avoid the autoloader unless he is willing to do a complete clean-up on the mechanism.

Let me give one example of a load which I would not mind using for deer at close range if I were to employ the Instant Muzzle Loader on a deer. In my fast-pointing Armsport Model 1212 hammer gun, 12-gauge, with its 20-inch barrels, I'd load a single Denver Bullet Company round ball. This ball weighs a full 494 grains, by the way, and depending upon how large the ball actually "mikes out," it can weigh more. In my actual test, the ball miked out at .695-inch and the weight was 502 grains.

Using 110 grains of GOEX brand FFg black powder, followed by the ball patched with a .015-inch Ox-Yoke Precision patch, and a CCI No. 11 percussion cap to kick it off, the velocity at the muzzle was 1115 fps. Muzzle energy with this load is 1386 foot-pounds. At 100 yards, this ball is down to 881 fps with an energy of 865 foot-pounds. However, a ball of almost .70-caliber is a bit more authoritative than the raw figures show, and I have no doubt of its effectiveness after tests.

Now how about a load in a regular black powder muzzle-loading shotgun? Looking at the Navy Arms Classic side-by-side double, we can drive a load of nine

00 buckshot with 80 grains of Fg, or we can turn to a single round ball in one barrel and the buckshot load in the other barrel. This is our buck 'n ball load, of course. That ball, by the way, weighing from 494 to over 500 grains, depending upon the precise size of the ball itself, can be driven at about 1000 fps from the muzzle with an 80 Fg load. That is GOEX black powder, 1F (Fg) and a single patched ball.

Another good shotgun for deer in black powder hunting is the single, and we can load up the Magnum Cape Gun, offered by Euroarms of America, with the same 80 Fg load and the round ball mentioned above for about the same ballistics. In these round ball shotgun loads, the firearm can be treated as a musket and loaded with powder, an over-powder wad such as the cardboard type to protect the felt wad, then a felt wad soaked first in liquid lard or Crisco. The ball will sink into the felt wad and this works well. I caution that an over-ball wad should be used in any instance where there is the slightest chance of the ball rolling down the bore prior to firing. A spaced load is very dangerous, risking probable blow-up of the firearm and possible personal injury.

The shotgun as a tool for deer hunting is indeed a viable firearm for the job, and all that must be remembered is to hunt in accord with the range factors presented by the shotgun. However, I think we should consider buckshot less lethal at ranges over 30 yards than is sometimes presented to the public.

In my own tests, I have collected buckshot pellets fired into sawdust (damp) at 100 yards. The idea is to shoot several times at a large box filled with damp sawdust and then examine the pellets found in the medium. It is my firm belief that we can count on barrel deformation of the pellets. In short, before the pellet is out of the barrel, it is deformed to some degree. The shooter is invited to

This Leather Shotgun Sling from Michaels of Oregon is just right for deer hunters who want to pack their shotguns during the season. Note the padded shoulder section.

Euroarms of America offers their "Magnum Cape Gun," a special black powder shotgun in 12-gauge. It has a strong receiver, and it is excellent for round ball shooting. With 80Fg GOEX, that is 80 grains of Fg (one F) powder, it will propel a 494-grain round ball at over 1000 fps at the muzzle.

This is the Navy Arms Classic, available in 10-ga. or 12-ga., and with a buck 'n ball load, it can be very effective at close range.

test this and the effective pellet range for himself. All he need do is set up a 12-inch black circle and shoot at that circle from 40 yards and then tell me what he found out. He will find out that fewer pellets struck that circle than he'd hoped for. In my own meager tests, I got best results with a modified choke using buckshot, not a full or an improved cylinder. However, beyond 30 yards I would not feel confident that a buck would be mine every time even if I centered that deer in my shotgun pattern.

For pellet size, we have already alluded to how truly small buckshot is. Even the 00 pellet is only .33-caliber and more important, weighs but 54 grains. The 000 pellet is .36-caliber and it only weighs about 70 grains. Each must be considered a unit, and if only one or two strike a deer, even in the chest area, a certain instant kill cannot be guaranteed. Multiple hits are necessary when using buckshot on deer.

So take your favorite tube out and enjoy its potential, but if you do hunt with buckshot, make it where the shots are going to be terribly close, and I mean 20 or 30 yards. Then pick the larger buckshot. If you have a 3-inch Magnum, use it. If you can, buy its best load of 000 buckshot. If you get close and hit a deer, do not be shy about shooting the deer again before it regains its feet.

The shotgun is a useful deer-taker, but if I move to

where I must use one almost exclusively, I am going to buy one of the special deer hunter models. I am probably going to put a scope on it. I am going to sight the thing in as if it were a rifle. I am going to use a single slug when and if allowed. If I use buckshot, I am going to pick 00 or 000 and am going to use the load which provides the greatest number of pellets for my shotgun. I am also going to pledge to hold my shooting down to maybe 30 yards and hopefully less when I am using buckshot on deer.

If I hunt with a side-by-side black powder shotgun, I am going to use the buck 'n ball load. One barrel will carry the most number of pellets which I can use according to the sanctions of the gunmaker. I will not overload. But I will use as much shot and powder as the manufacturer recommends as totally safe in that black powder shotgun. The other barrel is going to carry one patched round ball. In a good shotgun, the load is going to be 80 Fg. I have tried more powder than this with a single .690-.695-inch round ball, but velocity did not seem to increase enough in my test guns to warrant much over 80 Fg in the GOEX black powder brand.

Given short-range deer hunting conditions and either of the above, the modern load or the old-fashioned black powder load, I will enter the fields with confidence.

chapter 10

Handguns for Deer

DEER HUNTING with handguns is common practice these days, and there have been sidearms capable of deer-harvesting power for a very long time. In the 1800s, for example, there were the big bore horse pistols, firing large projectiles at modest velocity, often with energy ratings which surpass some of the handgun calibers listed today as legal for deer hunting. Replicas of these, such as the Navy Arms 1858 Harper's Ferry and the Lyman .54 pistol, offer plenty of deer hunting power today. However, there are several considerations for the would-be handgun hunter, and in this chapter we will touch upon them. The most important of these considerations, I feel, rests with the hunter himself. He must be committed to the extra challenge inherent in handgun hunting, that added dimension of difficulty and the consequent chance that he may go home with no venison *because of* his firearm's lack of long-range potential.

In short, if a deer is standing broadside at 200 yards feeding on a bush and the handgun hunter can't get much closer than 200 yards for reasons of terrain or other conditions, then the hunter is going to have to settle for a look at a legal deer, but not a shot at the deer. Obviously, there are a few handgunners who are so proficient at their sport that they would argue with the above. However, in general, we must concede that handgun hunting for deer is a specialized activity, and the hunter has to put in some extra effort if he wants to take his venison regularly and cleanly with a sidearm. He has to stalk to reduce the range. He must be able to put his firearm into play accurately and quickly at close range. Increased challenge is the rule in handgun hunting for deer. The hunter willing to accept the challenge can, however, bag his deer cleanly and regularly with a sidearm.

Calibers and Power Legalities

Calibers are considered in another part of this book; therefore, we will not go into a discussion of the individual rounds which could be employed as deer-taking numbers. Legality, however, is the prime consideration for the would-be handgun hunter. It is, of course, the total responsibility of the hunter to locate and digest the laws governing any deer hunt. Game departments will include in the laws those calibers deemed legal for deer hunting with the handgun. As an example, the laws of my home state say:

The Wyoming Game and Fish Commission has approved the following cartridges for the taking of all BIG or TROPHY game animals; .41 Remington Magnum, .44 Remington Magnum, .44 Auto Magnum, .45 Winchester Magnum, and .454 Casull. Any firearm meeting the above qualifications is allowed.

Laws governing calibers are not always easy to interpret or to enforce, of course. However, the hunter who reads the above knows he can use the specific calibers listed plus those calibers which equal the "power" of the listed rounds. As an example to work with, let's see what happens when we take the .41 Remington Magnum, one of the legal rounds listed for the state of Wyoming, and compare it with another cartridge. Using the 210-grain Hornady hollow point, the .41 Remington Magnum develops a muzzle velocity of 1450 fps (*Hornady Handbook,* Third Edition, p. 349). The muzzle energy rating would be 981 foot-pounds. The .30 Herrett can use a 130-grain bullet at a muzzle velocity of 2200 fps (p. 371 of aforementioned manual). This is a muzzle energy of 1,397 foot-pounds. It must follow, then, that the .30 Herrett is legal in the above-cited situation for Wyoming deer hunting.

We will not belabor the issue of handgun cartridge legality here. However, it is important to restate the fact that the hunter must first determine which rounds are legal for handgun hunting and which are not legal in the deer field. There is one other consideration—ethics. Even if a handgun caliber is legal, it is up to the hunter to

The tremendously powerful .45 Casull is more than ample for deer hunting. Casull ballistics call for a 225-grain bullet at a muzzle velocity of 2000 fps for a muzzle energy of 1999 foot-pounds. This is more than a .30-30 has at the muzzle with a 170-grain bullet at 2200 fps out of a 20-inch barrel.

Wayne Fears enjoys taking deer with many methods and tools, including archery hunting, black powder and the handgun. He poses with a nice buck he harvested with a handgun. (Photo courtesy J. Wayne Fears)

determine for himself whether that round should truly be used for deer harvesting. A perfect example of this arose when I studied the game laws of one state which actually allowed almost any handgun caliber for deer. Just because the law has not prescribed a minimum caliber in this case does not excuse the hunter. He still has to choose a suitable deer round for his handgun all the same.

The hunter may also be faced with a remaining energy law. As an example, the deer round may have to have a remaining energy at 100 yards of 500 foot-pounds. Cartridge companies, as well as bullet-making companies, offer ballistic information which will show the hunter what is legal in the way of remaining energy and what is not legal. The Winchester ballistic sheet, which I am using here for a reference, gives a 100-yard retained energy figure in foot-pounds for all of the centerfire handgun rounds the company manufactures, from the little .25 ACP all the way to the big .45 Winchester Magnum. The .25 Auto shows a retained energy of a mere 42 foot-pounds at 100 yards. The .45 Winchester Magnum has a retained energy of 636 foot-pounds at 100 yards. The Hornady loading manual has a complete ballistics table included in the book.

Trajectory Pattern

If cartridge legality and power constitute the first criterion for the selection of a handgun round, trajectory may well be thought of as the second criterion. While we are not concerned with long-range shooting here, having already admitted that the handgun hunter is generally going to have to consider his deer-taking tool as having less range potential than a rifle, there is still a consideration to be made in terms of trajectory for the sidearm deer hunting round. Therefore, we are not out to condemn any given round on the basis of looping trajectory. We

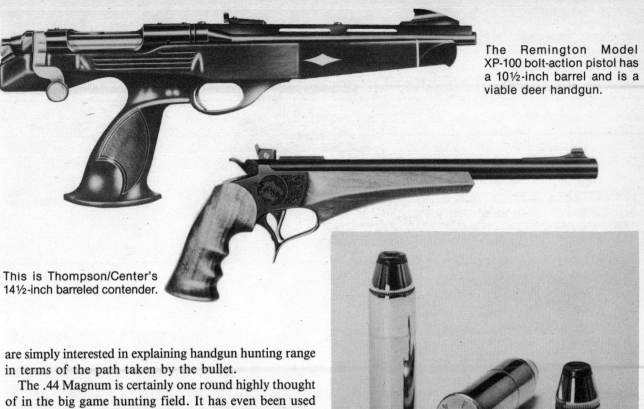

The Remington Model XP-100 bolt-action pistol has a 10½-inch barrel and is a viable deer handgun.

This is Thompson/Center's 14½-inch barreled contender.

are simply interested in explaining handgun hunting range in terms of the path taken by the bullet.

The .44 Magnum is certainly one round highly thought of in the big game hunting field. It has even been used in Africa on elephants with some degree of success, though I do not think of the .44 or any handgun as an elephant stopper. Given a 240-grain bullet at 1400 fps, a possibility in the standard handgun with a 6- or 7-inch barrel, with the handgun sighted in for 50 yards, the bullet would drop about ½-foot at 100 yards. However, we could sight in 3 inches high at 50 yards and be on at 100 yards. This would put the bullet about a foot low at 150 yards. Handgunners have taken deer at over 200 yards with a .44 Magnum; however, in terms of remaining energy and trajectory, it seems wise from the information that we have to confine our deer hunting to 100 yards or so.

All of the larger bore handgun rounds offer a trajectory pattern not too far from that described above. In other words, sighted for 3 inches high at 50 yards, the bullet will again cross the line of sight at *about* 100 yards. If the hunter prefers, he can sight about 2 inches high at 50 yards with the .44 Magnum class hunting load, which will put the bullet on again between 75 and 85 yards and just a couple inches low at 100 yards. These figures are close, but of course not to be considered totally transferable to any .44 Magnum. The .44 240-grain bullet at about 1400 fps, however, will describe an arc of trajectory pretty much as we have outlined it above.

The other trajectory pattern to consider is that of the modern pistol of the Thompson/Center Contender type. The added barrel length can mean an impressive increase in velocity for standard rounds. For example, while a 7- to 7½-inch barrel developed about 1400 fps in our .44 Magnum tests with the 240-grain bullet, a muzzle velocity of 1750 fps was earned by a T/C Contender with a 14-

Here is Federal's new high-performance .44 Remington Magnum cartridge with 240-grain jacketed hollow point bullet.

Choosing the correct ammo and/or bullet is of utmost importance in handgun deer hunting. The .44 Magnum is shown here with a 240-grain bullet (left), and a 265-grain bullet (right). The 240 will expand much more on a deer than will the 265. One must consider expansion *vs* penetration in this case and make his choice. Probably, the 240 will be the best choice for deer.

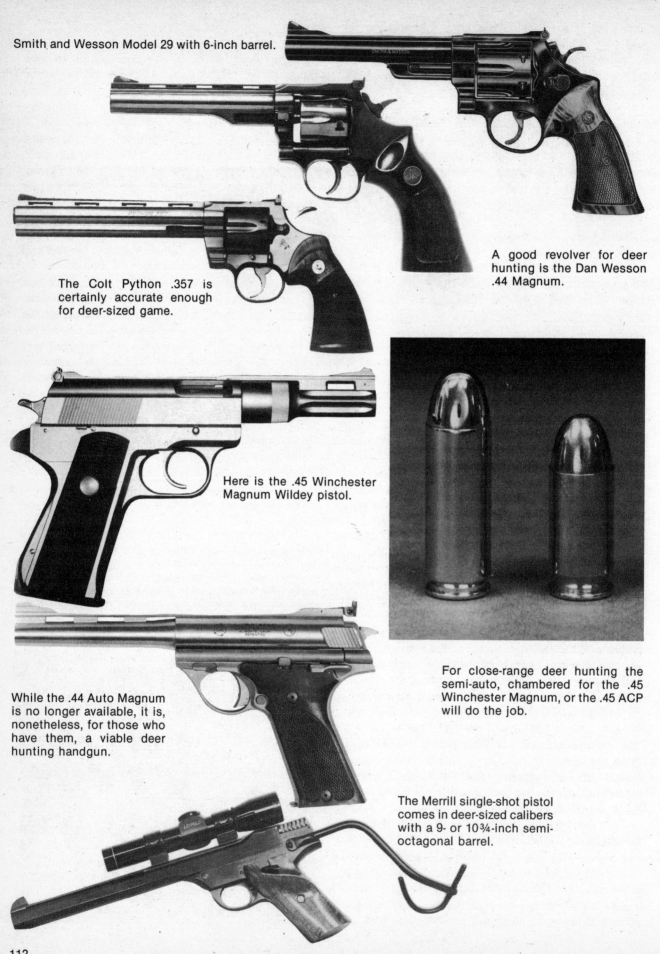

Smith and Wesson Model 29 with 6-inch barrel.

A good revolver for deer hunting is the Dan Wesson .44 Magnum.

The Colt Python .357 is certainly accurate enough for deer-sized game.

Here is the .45 Winchester Magnum Wildey pistol.

For close-range deer hunting the semi-auto, chambered for the .45 Winchester Magnum, or the .45 ACP will do the job.

While the .44 Auto Magnum is no longer available, it is, nonetheless, for those who have them, a viable deer hunting handgun.

The Merrill single-shot pistol comes in deer-sized calibers with a 9- or 10¾-inch semi-octagonal barrel.

inch barrel. If we were to sight in with this load, we could print about 2 inches high at 50 yards and the bullet would cross the line of sight again at 100 yards and at a full 150 yards, the 240-grain bullet would only be about ½-foot low.

Obviously, the range has increased here due to flatness of trajectory, but it has also increased in "striking power." At a beginning velocity of 1400 fps, the 240-grain bullet reaches 150 yards with a remaining velocity of about 1000 fps and an energy of 533 foot-pounds. When the very same bullet begins at a muzzle velocity of 1750 fps, it will reach 150 yards doing about 1130 fps for an energy of 681 foot-pounds. While the latter is not an amazing increase, it does amount to slightly more than 25 percent more "punch."

However, if we were to pick up a Remington XP-100, just as an example, custom barreled for the 7x45mm Ingram caliber (7x233 Improved), we would have a 139-grain bullet moving out at a muzzle velocity of 2250 fps. We could sight in for a strike only 2 inches high at 50 yards and this would put the bullet back on aim at a full 150 yards from the muzzle, and less than 3 inches low at 200 yards. At 200 yards, the bullet would still be doing about 1900 fps for an energy rating of 1114 foot-pounds.

Choosing the Deer Hunting Handgun

The above discussion has already taken us a long distance down the road toward choosing a big game handgun for deer hunting. When we are picking our sidearm for deer, we certainly must observe caliber choice in light of legalities and in terms of our own limits of "power" which we feel to be correct for the type of hunting we do—mainly the range at which we can normally expect to get a shot at a deer. We may also wish to consider trajectory in our selection. If we are hunting in the West, or anywhere where longer shots are common, then we may elect for a longer-barreled firearm, one capable of picking up some extra muzzle velocity and a couple inches of trajectory. Or for that matter, we may put the long barrel and a modern pistol caliber together for the longer range shooting.

Personal ability with the handgun must enter here. For me, I believe I could use my Smith & Wesson Model 29 with its original iron sights for deer hunting up to 100 yards. After that, I would look for a little flatter trajectory coupled with a scope sight. I have friends who can, however, hit a mark at 200 yards with the same handgun. They do not hunt deer with 200-yard shots in mind when using a standard iron-sighted sidearm in a handgun caliber. If they were pressed to hit a deer-sized target at 200 yards, they could do it. I believe that the hunter should look at trajectory and remaining energy factors, coupled with his own ability to use a handgun, and then decide upon the handgun of his choice using all three pieces of information—power, trajectory and personal marksmanship.

Revolver or Pistol?

Both are capable of good hunting accuracy. In fact, the handguns which are suitable for deer hunting, in either revolver or pistol style, are all adequate for the job at hand, especially if a hunter will stalk so that the range is not too great. In my own tests, I managed groups of an inch at 25 yards with revolvers, such as the S&W M29 in .44 Remington Magnum caliber with hunting loads. From a rest, I kept 5 shots in a 6-inch bull at 100 yards with the same firearm. I like to think of a 4-inch group as good hunting accuracy, generally, and I believe that from a bench with the right sights, especially glass sights, the hunting handguns can produce smaller than 4-inch groups, center to center, with regularity. Therefore, I feel we can toss out the accuracy question. Both revolver and pistol are accurate enough for deer hunting.

As for "firepower," the number of shots which can be gotten off in a short space of time, there is no contest. The revolver will obviously offer faster shooting than the single-shot pistol. The auto pistol, such as chambered for the .44 Auto Mag or .45 Winchester Magnum, will beat either in getting away a number of shots in rapid succession. In closer range shooting, I lean to the revolver or the semi-auto pistol. I have hunted a limited number of big game animals with both the single-action and double-action revolver and have enjoyed the fact that a follow-up shot was available. Let the hunter choose the style he prefers and can shoot best, of course, but I'd suggest the revolver or semi-auto for close-range hunting, with the single-shot

Certainly, the handgun hunter must consider accuracy potential as one of the major criteria for his selection of a deer-taking sidearm. Here, the Navy Arms Company Grand Prix Silhouette Pistol in .44 Remington Magnum was fired at 50 yards from a benchrest. The group size and pattern indicate that this pistol will perform to satisfactory deer hunting accuracy levels. This group is a bit under an inch center to center, and several 1.5 inch groups were easily managed from the bench at 50 yards using the target sights of the pistol.

Although this Navy Arms Company Silhouette Pistol is intended for competitive shooting, its caliber, .44 Magnum, and its good handling qualities also render it a deer hunting handgun.

The Sterling X-caliber single-shot is offered in .357 Magnum or .44 Magnum, both adequate for deer.

pistol being used for longer range hunting.

The single-shot pistol is hardly new. Stevens, for example, offered single-shot pistols in the early 1900s. They were generally called target pistols, and the ones I have seen were only in .22 rimfire caliber, though Stevens did have a single-shot in .410 gauge, too. Stoeger offered a variety of single-shot pistols. These old-time firearms, about a half century back in time, were also in .22 rimfire caliber. But they were break-open designs and very much like the fine Thompson/Center Contender in appearance. With 10-inch barrels, sight radius was good. Scopes were not generally mounted on handguns at the time of the Stoeger pistols.

Today, the break-open design is featured in the single-shot of the T/C type, and a bolt-action is available in the Remington XP-100 model. The big features of the T/C Contender are its automatic safety and its interchangeable barrels. One Contender pistol is many Contender pistols. Many fine calibers are offered, not only for deer hunting, but for small game hunting as well. The owner of a T/C Contender, then, can choose a deer hunting caliber and a small game or varmint caliber as well.

The barrel of the Contender is normally 10 inches long; however, a 14-inch barrel is also available in some calibers. As an example of the flexibility offered by the multiple barrels of the Contender, a shooter could select a .22 Hornet barrel (very accurate) for small game and varmints, loading down for small game and using harder projectiles. He could also have a barrel for the .30 Herrett, in which case a 150-grain bullet could be driven at 2000 fps muzzle velocity.

The octagon tapered Contender barrel is a bull barrel in configuration, and it wears a ventilated rib. With the 10-inch barrel, the overall length of the handgun is 13¼

inches and the weight is about 43 ounces. While this firearm is fitted with good iron sights, it is also drilled and tapped for scope mounts. The gun is very comfortable to shoot, accurate and highly effective. With a scope, such as the Bushnell Phantom, a deer hunter is all set.

The good features of the single-shot pistol are many. It is nice to handle; comes in many excellent deer hunting calibers of good power and range; allows for easy scope mounting; has good trigger pull qualities; accurate; and is well constructed for strength and reliability. All of the features one could ask for in a deer hunting tool can be found in such a handgun, and our comments apply to the Remington XP-100 single shot as well as the Contender model.

The revolver has all of the above features, too, with one trade-off. The revolver allows for fast follow-up shots, whereas the firepower of the single-shot is more limited and tied to the ability of the individual shooter. On the other hand, the revolver does not have the wide range of strong deer calibers offered in the pistol. However, the new Remington .357 Maximum is offered in the Ruger revolver, and this cartridge is suitable for deer hunting. But if a shooter wants to use a 7mm BR Remington caliber, he will have to turn to the single-shot pistol, and the same goes for rounds such as the .30-30, .35 Remington and .357 Herrett, at least as this is being written.

Single- or double-action? While there is no use whatsoever that I can see for double-action capability in the revolver, there is also no harm done in having it. The famous S&W M29 in .44 Remington Magnum is certainly not harmed by the fact that it is double-action. Nor is the Ruger Redhawk in the same caliber. But the single-action, such as the Ruger Blackhawk model, is equally well suited to deer hunting. As for fast repeat shots, the single-action can be fired with more than ample speed.

Auto pistols are somewhat limited in terms of deer hunting. There is the Auto Mag, which dates back to 1971, of course. Handling the big .44 Auto Mag round, this is a very powerful pistol capable of taking deer. A .44-caliber bullet is certainly pushed at magnum velocities out of this pistol, a 200-grain Hornady at a maximum of 1600 fps, for example, with the 240-grain bullet leaving the muzzle at 1450 fps and the 265-grain flat point going out at 1300 fps.

Another auto pistol which is not seen often in the deer field, but which would make the grade in terms of power, is the Wildey Auto Pistol. I have never handled one; however, the data shows this pistol chambered for the powerful .45 Winchester Magnum round.

Black Powder Sidearms

My friend and mentor, Professor Charles Keim, well-known Alaskan Master Guide, had told me about the handgun exploits of famous handgun expert, the late Al Georg, before I was involved in black powder shooting. What interested me so much at the time, aside from the fact that Mr. Georg was so proficient with the handgun as a hunting tool, was the fact that this dedicated hand-gunner had taken big game with a black powder revolver. In fact, now that I have tested black powder revolvers and pistols, I am aware of just how good Mr. Georg must have been. While he was able to harvest big game cleanly with the black powder revolver, I think this is a case of

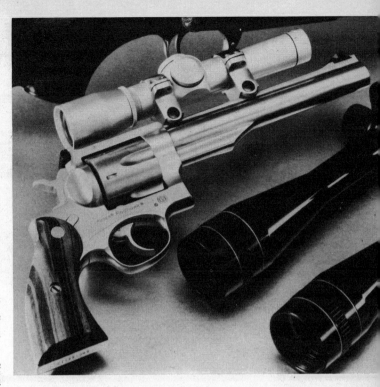

The Leupold 2x Handgun Scope called the "2x Silver" is shown mounted on a Ruger Redhawk revolver. The eye relief on such a handgun scope is extended so that the shooter can hold the sidearm at the proper, normal distance and still enjoy a full field of view in the scope. Furthermore, the eye relief is not rigid in this scope, being from 12 to 24 inches.

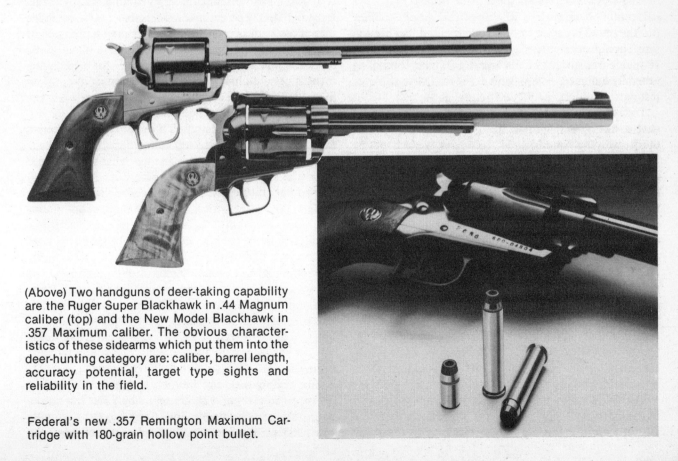

(Above) Two handguns of deer-taking capability are the Ruger Super Blackhawk in .44 Magnum caliber (top) and the New Model Blackhawk in .357 Maximum caliber. The obvious characteristics of these sidearms which put them into the deer-hunting category are: caliber, barrel length, accuracy potential, target type sights and reliability in the field.

Federal's new .357 Remington Maximum Cartridge with 180-grain hollow point bullet.

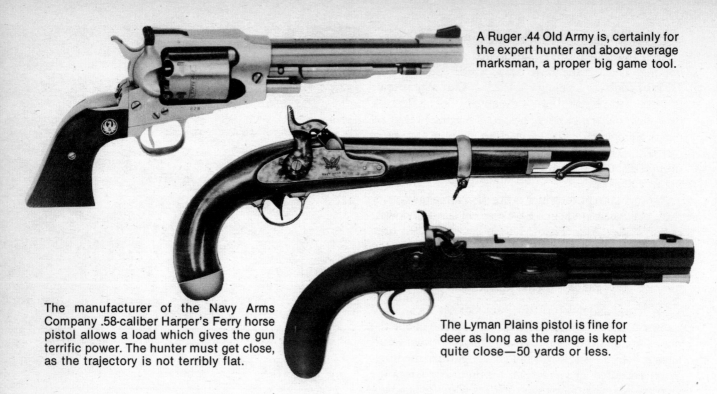

A Ruger .44 Old Army is, certainly for the expert hunter and above average marksman, a proper big game tool.

The manufacturer of the Navy Arms Company .58-caliber Harper's Ferry horse pistol allows a load which gives the gun terrific power. The hunter must get close, as the trajectory is not terribly flat.

The Lyman Plains pistol is fine for deer as long as the range is kept quite close—50 yards or less.

what can be done by a true expert. I feel that the black powder revolver, while perfectly adequate in the hands of a true expert hunter and shooter, is not powerful enough to be considered a proper big game tool in the hands of the average marksman-hunter. Remember, we are talking about black powder revolvers now. We will discuss the black powder pistol in a moment.

Let us first examine a Ruger .44 Old Army, a black powder revolver capable of heavy loads, and then we will look at a Richland Arms 3rd Hartford Dragoon 1851 revolver. Are these two revolvers adequate for taking deer? The highest energy which I recorded in my own testing of the Ruger Old Army runs as follows.

The 40-grain charge of Pyrodex^R P (pistol powder) gave a starting velocity 1047 fps from the muzzle. Muzzle energy with this round was 348 foot-pounds. At 50 yards, the .457-caliber round ball of 143 grains weight was down to 859 fps and energy was rated at 234 foot-pounds. Because of obvious chamber restrictions as to how much powder can be seated along with the space taken up by the projectile, the use of a bullet in the black powder revolver did not appreciably raise these energy levels, though some hunters may argue in favor of the bullet anyway in terms of retained energy and penetration. Black powder handgunners of wide experience do not report marked increase in actual field effectiveness with the bullet in the black powder handgun, however.

There you have it. Compared with a .357 Magnum, which I certainly consider minimal in terms of deer-taking force, the superb Ruger Old Army .44 does not match up in sheer ballistic force. On the other hand, shooters who know what they are about as deer hunters bag wild boars with black powder revolvers like the Ruger Old Army. I do not go on black powder hunts without my

own black powder revolver along, but I do suggest that if a shooter is going to use a black powder revolver, he get close and take only good shots. The Richland 3rd Hartford Dragoon 1851 .44 revolver tested out at only slightly more forceful than the Ruger Old Army. I concede that the black powder revolver in the hands of a good shot and careful hunter has bagged all kinds of game, including deer; however, all I ask is that the shooter take into account the power level he is dealing with when he employs the black powder revolver. These guns can be scoped, by the way, and everyone knows that bullet placement is certainly still the number one point to consider in lethality. I only suggest care and caution with any hunting tool that does not deliver a heap of punch.

The black powder pistol is a horse of a rather different hue in a few cases. I am only going to discuss two black powder pistols here, but they do show what can be gained when the limiting factor of a chamber is eliminated. Remember, in the pistol we are loading essentially the same as we would with a black powder muzzle-loading rifle. This does not mean we can overload a pistol. Not at all. The pistol must be kept within the limits imposed by the manufacturer.

Looking at the Lyman Plains Pistol in .54-caliber, we see what can be done with black powder power in a sidearm. For example, the 40 GOEX FFFg charge developed 952 fps with 224-grain round ball. Now, you say, the muzzle energy is only 451 foot-pounds, so what makes this suitable for deer? Well, if range is kept quite close, I think 50 yards or less, we have to consider the fact that we are dealing with a projectile which is over ½-inch in diameter and about 224 grains in heft. In test media consisting of clay blocks, the .54-caliber ball from 40 yards and a .357-caliber load created wound channels not

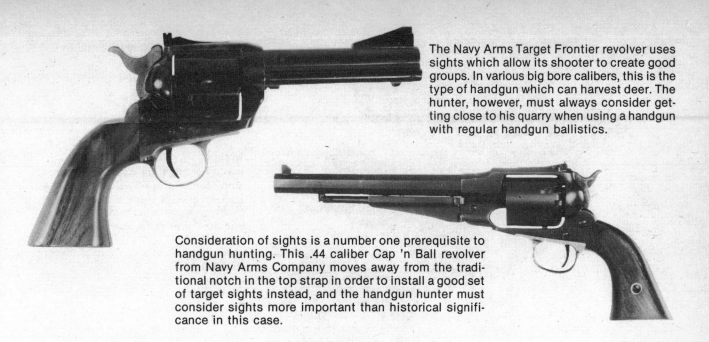

The Navy Arms Target Frontier revolver uses sights which allow its shooter to create good groups. In various big bore calibers, this is the type of handgun which can harvest deer. The hunter, however, must always consider getting close to his quarry when using a handgun with regular handgun ballistics.

Consideration of sights is a number one prerequisite to handgun hunting. This .44 caliber Cap 'n Ball revolver from Navy Arms Company moves away from the traditional notch in the top strap in order to install a good set of target sights instead, and the handgun hunter must consider sights more important than historical significance in this case.

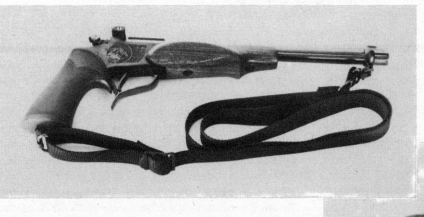

(Left and below) Uncle Mike's swivel and sling for the Contender Super 14S is just right for the hunter. Pachmayr grips are used.

so different from each other. I would call the .54 Lyman Plains Pistol adequate for close-range deer hunting. Though we stayed with 40 FFFg in our tests, the data allows as much as 50 FFFg. Now we would have a starting velocity over 1000 fps.

Another black powder pistol I would call a deer-taking tool is the big Navy Arms Company Harper's Ferry 1858 model. This is a .58-caliber pistol built with a bolster and a heavy lock. A Lyman-moulded No. 575213 Minie ball left the muzzle at 802 fps pushed with 60 FFg GOEX to gain this muzzle velocity. Recoil halted further loads, we felt, and we did not want to add more fuel. However, though the muzzle energy is only 750 foot-pounds, we have to consider the effect of a bullet of .575-caliber and a weight of 500 grains as a sufficient force.

Now let us look at a round ball from the big .58-caliber pistol. A charge of 60 FFg GOEX earned a muzzle velocity of 975 fps and an energy rating of 587 foot-pounds. At 50 yards, the velocity has dropped to 839 fps and energy has fallen to 435 foot-pounds, but still enough to do some work. The bigger 525-grain Lyman Minie at a starting velocity of 802 fps clocked at 766 fps at 50 yards for a

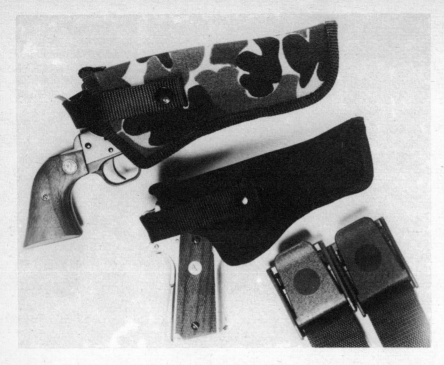

Holsters are very important to all handgunners, but especially to those who take to the fields after deer. A holster should protect the firearm, but even more important than that, it should maintain the sidearm in a safe posture at all times. These Uncle Mike's holsters do the job at a very modest cost.

retained energy of 684 foot-pounds. So, at 50 yards, the .58 "Horse Pistol" has more retained energy than a .357 Magnum has at the muzzle, looking at the max load on page 346 of the 3rd Edition *Hornady Handbook* (593 foot-pounds, 158-gr. bullet @ 1300 fps).

Suppose that we have the Navy Arms .58 caliber 1858 loaded to full potential, and we have scoped the pistol to boot. Would we have a deer-taker for close-range hunting? I think so. If we use the minimum cartridge ratings for deer established by some game departments, the answer has to be yes.

Why Handguns for Deer?

Having looked at the handgun as a deer hunting tool, and having shown, I feel, that the handgun has the power and the accuracy for deer hunting, along with excellent sidearms of high quality and good sights, the last question we ask may well have been asked earlier—why handguns for deer? Some handgunners would probably use the old mountain climber's reason for scaling cliffs, "just because they are there." I believe that two big reasons stand out, however. First, I feel that the extra challenge is a calling card to deer hunters who use the sidearm. There is a special reward here not only in the taking of a deer with the handgun, but also in the actual hunting of deer with the handgun, having to generally get a little closer, even with the scope-sighted models and high-power calibers.

After all, even some of the fine rounds, such as the 7mm handgun calibers, don't match up against the flat-shooting trajectory and high remaining energy of the longarms in the same caliber. A 139-grain bullet at 2200 fps in the 7mm BR Remington round is fine for deer, but the exact same bullet at 3350 fps in the 7mm Remington Magnum is quite another story. Plus, a handgun is still a handgun not only in range and power, but also in necessary skill for well-placed shots. In short, I think the average hunter shoots a rifle a lot better than he shoots a handgun. It takes more skill for a hunter to bag deer regularly and cleanly with a handgun, I think. The challenge *is* greater.

Second, I believe that hunters enjoy the lack of size and weight which is inherent in the deer hunting handgun. Even the longer-barreled models with 10- to 14-inch barrels are much smaller and lighter than rifles. And the revolvers and pistols of ordinary length are more convenient yet. The use of both hands while climbing and the fact that the deer harvesting tool is tucked into a holster instead of slung or in hand, is a plus for convenience. The longer pistols can also be carried with slings. Again, they are lighter and less cumbersome than the rifle.

So much for hunting handguns. They are not for every deer hunter, but they are for the outdoorsman who is interested in the sidearm and who is willing to practice and learn his shooting craft. The modern handgun can be a perfectly legitimate deer-taking tool. The hunter interested in this form of putting venison in the freezer should make his way carefully, looking into the calibers offered, selecting the round which best suits his needs, and then purchasing the handgun which offers the chambering of that round. Fitted with proper sights, such a sidearm will prove itself worthy in the field.

chapter 11

Calibers for Deer

IF THE HEART of this book is methods for deer hunting, then the pulse is this look at viable deer rounds. Again, we have based our entire project on the three main factors inherent in any successful deer chase. The game has to be in sufficient abundance to offer a mathematical opportunity for the hunter that is reasonable. The hunter has to have some mode of operation going for him, a plan; and then when that opportunity does present itself, the hunter has to capitalize with a harvest instead of a sad story. He has to hit instead of miss, and he has to hit with a cartridge worthy of the game.

There is no way on earth that a chapter of this sort can be other than a combination of three things. First, there is personal experience. No one hunter has taken deer with all of the calibers that are going to be listed here. So we have to rely on transfer of knowledge. In short, if we have cleanly taken deer with a certain round and there is another round which is a ballistic twin, then it is safe to say we are on the right track picking that similar cartridge. Fortunately, I was able to get in on some of the more open deer hunting in the U.S. and also in Mexico. I also consider it good luck that I am able to harvest a couple deer in my home state now and a couple out of state annually, because I have made it a point over the years to try several cartridges rather than sticking with one, even though I ran across many rounds that served me well. My love for firearms almost forced me to use different calibers just to "see what they'd do."

I have not used all of the following, but I have used or I have seen used many of them. I have also called upon the reportings of many deer hunting friends in order to help compile the data below, if indeed we can call a few brief comments truly data rather than opinion. My overall feeling at this stage of the game is that we have badly over-done our qualifying of rounds as great, good, not so good and lousy for deer hunting. I know this does not sound very exciting, but in fact the very great majority of rounds in the "high-power" class are just plain fine for deer and often of much more punch than is necessary.

If a hunter hunts, stalks, gets close enough for good placement of his projectile, he's going to bag a deer so swiftly and so cleanly that he can take great pride in the fact that he puts meat in the freezer rather than buying it pre-butchered. A man with any of the reasonably powerful rounds chambered in a rifle he can shoot, or a handgun for that matter, is going to "make meat" and no doubt about it. Accuracy, coupled with a good bullet, coupled with a hit in the vitals, combined with the distance from which the bullet was fired all add up to a "clean kill."

Rifle Calibers

6mm/222

I am including this wildcat round as the smallest I would allow any of my family to hunt deer with. But I am also including it at the bottom of the cartridge listing for deer because we have had a solid 10 years of experience with this round on deer and antelope. Furthermore, I can say with witnesses to vouch for my story that our own little 6mm/222 has put more game into our freezer and the freezer of others than any other round in any other rifle that we have used or I have used in the 30 years I have hunted deer.

On the face of it, the 6mm/222 is just barely in the ball park when we consider raw energy. We use two bullets, in the main, and we very carefully considered how we would load our own 6mm/222 before the rifle was made. These two bullets and their ballistics I'll lay out shortly. However, more about the rifle first because this background is very important to understanding the round and its amazing record. Each year my wife, for it is her rifle, and my daughter, for she always uses the 6mm/222, carry this rifle. But it is also loaned out to many visitors, and it is not impossible to find the husband of the owner using it on occasion.

Frank Wells made the rifle. We decided upon a Sako L461 action. We wanted a round which could be counted on to take deer and antelope, mainly whitetails, I might add, at very reasonable ranges, about 100 yards with 200 yards being as far as we would allow ourselves to shoot. My own experience with the .250-3000 Savage came to mind. Friends and I used the 250 Savage with the original 87-grain bullet at about 3000 fps, and we never lost a deer and only had to shoot a couple more than once. I made up my mind that my wife Nancy could get by with the power of a .250-3000. But I wanted her to have a small handy rifle with a short-throw action. Frank Wells and I sat at the planning board for a very long time before the rifle was born. We ran many ideas over the scratch pad.

Finally, we agreed that if we had a very strong-actioned 6mm/222, we could make our minimum-power rating. In short, we could, with Ball-C-2 (BL-C-2) powder from Hodgdon's, gain sufficient ballistics for a whitetail/antelope rifle. The strong 6mm/222 case could withstand a reasonable charge of BL-C-2 and we could drive an 80-grain bullet at 2900 fps from the muzzle or an 87-grain bullet at 2875 fps from the muzzle. The rifle was constructed, and I took 20 cases and loaded them and fired them with top loads 10 times each. The cases still showed no signs of excessive head expansion.

Now, 10 years later, we can report the taking of many deer and antelope from very close range to a maximum of 200 yards, nothing lost, nothing wounded. Why this record? I suspect that people can shoot this little rifle so well that our "average" hit on a deer is in the neck or at least in the chest cavity.

Not to dwell too long on the 6mm/222, which is of course the .222 Remington necked up to hold 6mm (.243) bullets, but I felt it important to admit to an absolute minimum in a rifle, and we think this is our minimum. With the 87-grain bullet, we have a muzzle energy of 1597 foot-pounds. At a full 200 yards, the velocity of this load is down to *about* 2350 fps and the energy has fallen off

to 1067 foot-pounds. But, as I like to point out, if you believe in energy ratings, then you have to like even this little 6mm/222 at 200 yards, for it has more energy at 200 yards than a .44 Magnum handgun round has right *at the muzzle* if you consider a 240-grain bullet at 1400 fps (a muzzle energy of 1045 foot-pounds). And it falls behind the original .250 Savage load by only a few foot-pounds at 200 yards.

.243 Win./6mm Rem.

Might as well lump these two together. They are alike as two new pennies. In the new *Lyman Reloading Handbook,* 46th edition, we find the .243 driving a 100-grain bullet at around 3000 fps and the 6mm pushing the same bullet at about 3100 fps. I have taken deer with these ballistics, and I have seen deer taken with them. A friend of mine says that he has used a 6mm Remington for a long while now, and he can tell no difference whatsoever, between his 6mm and his .270 or .30-06 on a chest-hit deer at 200 yards. Well, I think I have seen some differences in the actual wound channel here, but I know what my buddy means. After all, defunct is defunct. A chest hit on a deer at 200 yards with a 6mm 100-grain bullet that began its journey at over 3000 fps means a deer in the pot, provided a good bullet has been used—more on bullets at the close of this chapter.

.240 Weatherby

Here we have a 6mm round which fires that 100-grain bullet at about 3200 fps from the muzzle. Obviously, what we have said above applies again here. I might add that we have not included anything under the 6mm class because I do not consider the .22 Hotshots right for deer. Heaven is going to toss lightning bolts at me for saying so, I know, and I have a hunting companion who is allowed the use of the .22-250 for deer in his home state, and he gets 'em with one shot darn near every time. I admit to knowing that the Swift and other hotrock .22s can do it, and I used to hunt deer with a .22 varmint load myself. But I found some strange effects of little bitty pills pushing out at super speeds and for every day, day in day out, the "average" gunner for deer ought to get a 6mm or larger and leave the varmint rifles for varmints. Many game departments feel the same way.

.25-20

I do not consider the .25-20 an adequate deer rifle round, though I saw a whitetail dumped with same and though I have an acquaintance in central Wyoming who used the .25-20 until the game laws of the state made it illegal to do so. Although the 86-grain bullet at 1750 fps gains about 585 foot-pounds of muzzle energy, we have no big bullet to make up for lack of energy, and this fine round should be used on game smaller than deer. I might add I will get into grave trouble later on when I consider other lower powered rounds in terms of raw foot-pounds ratings. I'll try to worm my way out when I get there.

The .257 Roberts has always been a fine deer caliber, and though it was put in the back seat for a long time, its worth as a deer round has always proved itself. Here we have the Winchester loading of the .257 Roberts, its 100-grain Silvertip bullet shown in upset form.

The .257 Roberts in the Winchester loading is also available with a 117-grain Power Point bullet, shown here in the upset form. This ammo is known as the ".257 Roberts + P" ammunition and it provides higher velocity than the former factory loads.

.256 Winchester Magnum

Consider a "hotter" .25-20 and you have the .256. It is not truly a deer round. With its 86-grain bullet at about 2200 fps, the muzzle energy is 924 foot-pounds.

.250 Savage

The .250 Savage in the hands of a cool shot is just as good as the .243/6mm class of cartridge. It will drive a 100-grain bullet at about 3100 fps and the ballistic coefficient of a .25 caliber 100-grain bullet is sufficient for good "carry-up" at a couple hundred yards and even a bit more. The original 87-grain 3000 fps load has, obviously, been surpassed by the new powders, and yet the original 87-grain bullet at 3000 fps worked fine for many a deer hunter, to include my departed friend Clifford Black and Mr. Black's brother, who did good work with the little .250-3000 in Alaska when I was just a boy.

.257 Roberts

For all practical purposes, the .257 Roberts is in the same circle with the .250 Savage. It's a good one.

.25-06 Remington

I have seen a couple dozen deer taken with the .25-06, and I have taken two with this round myself, both mule deer bucks, and both harvested to the turf with one shot so quickly that I could not see where they had fallen at first. The same 100-grain .25-caliber bullet found in the .250 Savage and .257 Roberts is now driven at about 3300 fps from the muzzle. Recoil is very manageable. The .25-06 is a long-range number.

.257 Weatherby Magnum

As I write this, there is a .257 Weatherby standing in the corner waiting further testing. Thus far, it has proved capable of starting the 100-grain .25-caliber bullet at a muzzle velocity of over 3500 fps. At such speed, the energy rating is 2721 foot-pounds. At 500 yards, not that I am suggesting anyone shoot that far, but for the sake of conversation let me go on—at 500 yards, this bullet which started at about 3500 fps is still doing about 2100 fps with an energy of about 980 foot-pounds.

6.5x55m Swedish Mauser

A friend in Alaska who is also a guide uses the 6.5 on moose to gather up his winter meat. He seldom has to shoot more than once. I have included the 6.5 as an example. It can drive a 100-grain bullet at about 3050 fps, a 120-grain bullet at about 2900 fps and a 140-grain bullet at about 2600 fps. The long 160-grain bullet, which is used by my Alaska friend on moose, is pushed out at about 2400 fps. Yes, this round is strong enough for deer.

6.5 Remington Magnum

Super popularity does not belong to this 6.5 number, but it most obviously is good deer medicine with a 100-grain bullet at about 3000 fps and a 120-grain bullet at over 2800 fps. I might add that I know of long-throated 6.5 Rem. Mags. to chronograph at about 3200 fps with that 100-grain bullet and 3000 fps with a 140-grain bullet. Of course it is enough for deer.

.264 Winchester Magnum

At this juncture, we have to start considering whether we are going overboard in our ballistics for deer. When we have admitted that a .243 is a good deer round, does it seem reckless to include the big .264 as a deer round, too? After all, we have a long 140-grain bullet skipping out at 3200 fps in some rifles and surely 3000 fps with milder loads. Well, I think for everyday deer hunting the .264 is larger than needed. But out West where a shot may be taken at a few hundred yards across a canyon, this round can reach its destination with much authority remaining. In fact, if we start at 3100 fps with the 140

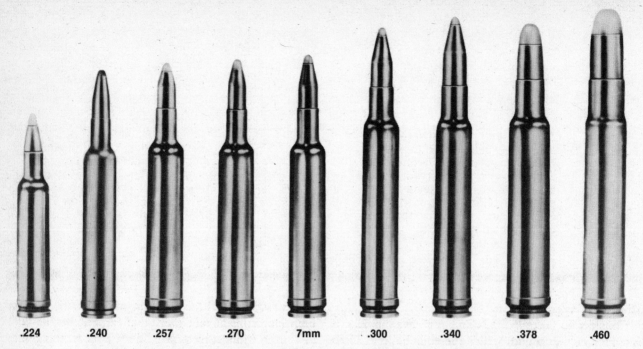

The famous line of Weatherby cartridges contains some very fine deer numbers. The .240 Weatherby Magnum fires 6mm bullets at high velocity. The .257 is another long-range powerhouse for deer, as is the .270 WM, 7mm WM and .300 WM. The .224 is mainly a varmint round, and the .340, .378 and .460 are for game larger than deer.

| .224 | .240 | .257 | .270 | 7mm | .300 | .340 | .378 | .460 |

pill, we will arrive at 300 yards still doing roughly 2450 fps and that is worth 1866 foot-pounds, more than some deer rifles gain at the muzzle.

.270 Winchester

Prejudice is going to show here, and I know it. The famous Jack O'Connor wrote so well on this round that a great many of his fans, including this one, went out and bought a .270 and were never ever sorry for it. Certainly, the 130-grain bullet can be pushed along at 3100 fps from the muzzle and a fellow shooter here in Wyoming, Richard Reitz, gains considerably more than this from his 26-inch barreled single-shot rifle. He also shoots a 150-grain bullet at over 3000 fps in the same rifle. I have taken record class heads with the wonderful .270 and up to caribou with the same round. It gets the job done. What more can I say? At 300 yards, the 130-grain bullet that started off at 3100 fps is still churning along at about 2350 fps with an energy rating of 1595 foot-pounds.

In the 1950s I used to use a 140-grain bullet in the .270 Winchester. My memory tells me it was a 2D bullet by MGS. The 2D meant two diameters, the shank being about .277, but the ogive about .270 inches. My handloads at that time gained over 3000 fps with this bullet, which is no longer offered. But Hornady has now come out with a 140-grain bullet, and the data I have chronographed shows the bullet making about 3025 fps in our

rifles. At 300 yards, this one will be doing about 100 fps faster than its 130-grain cousin which began at 3100 fps. The standard .270 is a great one for western deer.

.270 Weatherby Magnum

Here we have regular .277 bullets, as used in the standard .270 Winchester, perking along at about 3300 fps for the 130-grain number. With that bullet, the .270 Weatherby is a shade hotter than the .270 Winchester and can be used for the same purposes.

7mm-08 Remington

This round represents what I call commonsense ballistics for deer hunting. Essentially, we have a .308 Winchester case necked down to shoot 7mm (.284-inch) bullets. Even with the short 18½-inch test barrel used by Hornady, the 139-grain bullet started off at 2600 fps. For most deer hunting, where a shot at 100 yards is far more likely than a shot at 200 yards, and a shot at 200 yards about as common as finding a $20 bill stuck in your hamburger at lunch, the 7mm-08 is going to do just fine for deer.

Because of the short case, this round will allow for some modest-length actions to be used, and I foresee featherweight rifles chambered for the 7mm-08. While happy with the ballistics of this caliber, I would suggest that the western deer hunter who wants the extra punch at longer ranges take a look at the .270 or similar. However, for so very much of the deer hunting actually going on today in America, this round will do the job. Remember that the same 139-grain bullet shown at a starting velocity of 2600 fps here can be made to do 2800 fps in a bit longer barrel. This cartridge was developed, in part at least, for the serious silhouette shooter who wanted a light-recoiling rifle using a 7mm (.284-inch) bullet from a case of modest capacity. As it turns out, the round is a very fine one for the modern deer hunter. A 150-grain bullet can be driven at over 2850 fps from the muzzle. Anything which we can say for the 7mm Mauser or .284 can be said for the 7mm/08, which offers good power from a small case. I predict the cartridge will be popular.

7x57 Mauser

I owned a single-shot original Remington Rolling Block in this caliber and never found it lacking in strength for deer hunting. My friend Dean Zollinger of Idaho has built a custom 7x57 for his wife, and she has done well with it, as had Dean himself when he wanted to pack a handy rifle and begged to borrow his wife's 7x57. The 7x57 is a light-kicking number, and it has plenty of power for deer.

From what I have seen, if the hunter sticks to a modest range, certainly not over 200 yards, the 7x57 has sufficient force to put larger-than-deer game down with one shot when the chest cavity is penetrated.

The 140-grain bullet can be pushed out at about 2900 fps in the 7x57 and a 150-grain bullet can make 2850 fps and more. I count the 7x57, ancient that it is, a fine cartridge for modern deer hunting, with its mild recoil and good ballistics.

.284 Winchester

I remember growing excited over the announcement of the then new Model 88 Winchester as well as the Model 100. Both were sleek, modern-looking rifles and a fellow could get ".270 ballistics in a lever-action" with the Model 88, or at least we were told we could. In fact, we could. But the M88 faded out, and so did the Model 100 and the .284 simply did not set the world on fire. I liked it, though, and thought of the round as a short .270. In fact, my wife ended up with a .284 Ruger totally customized by Dean Zollinger.

This rifle was not meant to take the place of her little 6mm/222 custom deer rifle, but it would serve on an occasional elk hunt and certainly put a black bear away, and on the rare occasions when we hunted big canyon country where she might want to fire across a canyon at a heavy buck, we might have the .284 along.

The .284 is indeed in the same league with the 7x57 Mauser, or 7x57 mentioned above. It gains, roughly speaking, about 100 fps in velocity over the 7x57 and of course it makes a good deer cartridge.

7mm Express Remington

A rose may smell just as sweet by any other name, but the blasted things might not sell as well. That is certainly the case with the 7mm Express Remington. Here we have the very good .280 Remington with a new catchy name. Singers, actors and others have long known that a name can make a difference, and I am very happy that Remington decided on a name change here. Interestingly, I knew of fellow "gun writers" who lauded the wildcat 7mm-06, which was surely no more and even a hair less than a .280 Remington, but when the latter came out, I did not see too many hats tossed in the air with glee.

Now that we have the fine 7mm Express Remington with us, this may change. Actually, ballistics match up with the aforementioned .284 Winchester, and we need not repeat them here. The .280 Remington—pardon me—the 7mm Express fires the 140 class bullet in the 3000 fps domain. It is plenty for deer. We have, essentially, a .30-06 case necked to 7mm caliber, but the Express is a bit longer. The standard '06 is 2.494 inches long and the Express case is 2.540 inches long. (Author's Note:Remington has reversed its decision on the title of this cartridge. It is once again called the .280 Remington.)

7mm Remington Magnum

I surprised myself when I finally agreed to yank the action from my pre-'64 Model 70 Winchester in .270-caliber and have Frank Wells build a new rifle around that action, but in 7mm Mag. instead of .270 Winchester. It almost took courage to make the decision. Surely, the 7mm Mag. is more than powerful enough for deer. At a full 300 yards from the muzzle a 160-grain 7mm bullet taking off at 3100 fps, chronographed not only on my machines but on the test range of Jensen Custom Ammo shop in Tucson, Arizona, is still doing close to 2500 fps. The energy rating at 300 yards with this load would be over 2200 foot-pounds. That is more than the .30-30 at the muzzle with a 170-grain bullet.

In the years that I have owned and fired the 7mm Magnum, I always felt it was more than I needed for deer. In fact, I feel that every deer I ever bagged with the 7mm I could have taken cleanly with the .25-06 or less. There is only one exception to this viewpoint, and that exception happens to be a particular series of canyons where I have seen some very large bucks and a fellow may have to shoot across the canyon, for it is difficult to see deer on "your side" of the hill, which is steep, brushy and rocky. Then, I like the 7mm Magnum, but all in all, it's a bit much for deer.

My own 139-grain bullet load drives off at about 3300 fps and with this load the 7mm Mag. shoots about as flat as some of the hotrock items touted for their stretched-string trajectory. With a 175-grain bullet at 3000 fps or a 160-grain bullet at 3100 fps, the 7mm Mag. can take elk or other larger-than-deer game. It's a very good round. It might be more than the average deer hunter needs unless that deer hunter is also an elk hunter.

7mm Weatherby Magnum

Ditto. This one is much in the same arena with the 7mm Remington Magnum, as is the 7x61 Sharp & Hart.

.30 M1 Carbine

This cartridge is illegal for deer where I live. I agree. It is OK for smaller-than-deer game, and of course it can kill a deer. So can a ball peen hammer. The 100-grain short-jacket can be driven at about 2100 fps for a muzzle energy of 980 foot-pounds, which is more than a .357 Magnum gains at the muzzle. However, as long as we are going to use a rifle, then we might as well have it chambered up with more authority.

.30-30 Winchester

Most of the deer hunters at one time considered the .30-30 and the short rifle that went with it as a standard for venison-taking. Today, the .30-30 is no longer considered No. 1 in the deer fields from the sources of information I have on hand. But this round was always ample for deer at close range; it always will be. A friend, Glen Carlton of Tucson, Arizona, used the long-barreled M94 Winchester in .30-30, and we learned from his

The Marlin 1895S lever-action rifle has been popular with sportsmen for many decades. It is chambered for the .45-70 round, a very strong caliber for deer hunting at modest range.

harvests that the soft-nosed bullets were best. Therefore, I think something on the order of a 170-grain soft-nose, with ample lead exposed at the tip, is certain deer medicine for the woods.

The rifles chambered for the .30-30 were always popular. I can shoot the old-timers very well, with the 26-inch barrels or similar length. Levi Packard, the well-known Arizona game warden, used a .30-30 with great effect. One season I asked Levi what firearm he was going to fill his antelope tag with, and he said his old .30-30. For him, the challenge was enjoyed. The .30-30 is no long-range round, but with a 170-grain bullet at up to 2200 fps, and a muzzle energy of about 1828 foot-pounds, this number will do the job.

.300 Savage

When I was a kid, the ads for the .300 Savage burned in my subconscious. There was a picture of a fellow packing a .300 in the Model 99 Savage, and he was in the process of taking a moose with this rifle. Obviously, the .300 Savage is fine for deer. It can drive its 150-grain bullet at up to 2800 fps, after all. I have seen deer taken with 180-grain handloads, too, and the job was sure and clean.

I don't feel sorry for anyone who owns a .300 Savage for deer hunting.

.308 Winchester

For all intent and purpose, the .308 Winchester is the same as the .300 Savage if we want to talk deer hunting. While it can propel some bullets at higher velocity than is normally possible in the .300 Savage, this is neither here nor there for deer, as the .308 with a 150-grain bullet at 2900 fps is all one needs for deer with the rare exception of shooting across some western canyons for those big mule deer, a situation I have seen so seldom as to make it hardly worth the mention. Then, I might elect for a big 7mm Magnum. Most of the time, the .308 and its ilk will do just fine.

.30-40 Krag

Still with us is the .30-40 Krag. I once used a .30-40 on a deer hunt, and it seemed to me that this round will do whatever a .300 Savage will do, speaking in general terms. Up in the northland, in the Yukon and parts of Alaska, I spoke with hunters who had bagged moose and bear with their .30-40s and they were satisfied with them. Give me something larger for grizzly, but we are talking deer right now, and the .30-40 is certainly an adequate deer-taker. It is not a long-range high velocity round, however.

.30-06

Everyone knows that the .30-06 is versatile and that countless game has been taken with this caliber. Anything I would add would be something like putting a quart of water into a pint jar. My son Bill has taken a large number of deer, antelope and some elk with the .30-06, and using a 165-grain bullet for all his hunting has had good luck all the time. The new 165-grain Hornady boat-tail can be pushed at over 2900 fps from the standard .30-06 case and even up to 3000 fps with some powders. I think this speaks for itself.

.300 Winchester Magnum

This round represents what can be done with a bit more case capacity in .30-caliber. I will include in my comments that whatever we feel about the .300 Winchester Magnum, we can fairly well apply to the .300 H&H, the .308 Norma and that whole class of wildcats based upon the magnum case in 30-caliber. The 150-grain bullet can be propelled at about 3400 fps maximum from my data, and the 180-grain bullet will reach about 3100 fps. Son Bill has taken to the .300 Winchester for one very unique deer area we hunt out West, where the canyons are huge and seeing game on your own side is often difficult.

The 150-grain bullet at 3400 shoots flatter than some of our so-called varmint rounds. The 180-grain at 3100 is certainly adequate medicine for larger-than-deer class game. If a person feels a need for this much power, the .300 Winchester should certainly answer his wishes. Naturally, such power is not needed for general deer hunting and for deer at woods ranges using a .300 Winchester is like swatting a fly with a two-by-four plank.

.300 Weatherby Magnum

Many of the world class hunters I know use this round and speak highly of it, men such as Victor Ruiz of Sonora, Mexico, and Spike Jorgensen of Tok, Alaska. We have a 150-grain bullet at 3500 fps and a 165-grain bullet at 3300 fps, with a 180-grain bullet at 3200 fps. The 165 pill will still be churning along at about 2270 fps at a full 500 yards, with an energy rating of 1888 foot-pounds.

With this load, the 150 Hornady boat-tail, at a starting velocity of 3300 fps, we can sight in for a full 300 yards by initially printing 3 inches high at 100 yards, and at 400 yards the bullet will have dropped less than 9 inches with such a sight-in trajectory. Using tougher bullets of the "big game" type, a hunter with any of these big .30-caliber magnums would have a long-range deer rifle. For normal deer hunting circumstances and deer in the woods, these are much more than is necessary.

.32 Winchester Special

This round is nothing more or less, in modern day terms, than the .30-30. A 170-grain flat-point at 2200 fps is possible with today's loads. It is a perfectly adequate deer number, especially for woods hunting. It is not a long-range cartridge, of course.

.307 Winchester

The .307 Winchester is a new round as this is written. Ballistically, the cartridge comes close to duplicating the .308 Winchester. Why, then, offer this new number? The round functions in the Model 94 Winchester rifle, and will also be offered by Marlin 336ER (Extra Range) rifle. Therefore, we have these time-honored lever-action styles matched up with cartridges of longer range ability. The .307 is listed with a 150-grain bullet at a muzzle velocity of 2760 fps and a 180-grain bullet with a muzzle velocity of 2510 fps.

8mm Mauser

There are a comparative few 8mm Mausers in the deer field these days, but let it suffice to say that for those who own rifles in this caliber, it is plenty for deer or even larger game. It will push a 150-grain bullet at 2900 fps. My only personal contact with 8mm was in the 8mm/06, the '06 case necked up to accept the 8mm bullet, and the loading data I had, which I feel now was too hot, gave that round a mighty punch. More than is necessary for woods hunting, the standard 8mm Mauser is a good medium-range number.

8mm Remington Magnum

Here is an elk round which some will use for long-range deer hunting out West, and before I get into a pickle, I'd best qualify this by saying I have seen some long-range possibilities in the eastern half of our country, too. Anyway, with a 150-grain bullet at 3400 fps and a 220-grain bullet at 2900 fps, this is a round more in the elk class than deer class. Of course it will take deer at long range, too.

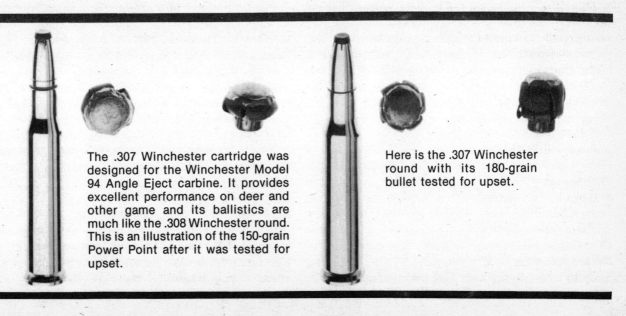

The .307 Winchester cartridge was designed for the Winchester Model 94 Angle Eject carbine. It provides excellent performance on deer and other game and its ballistics are much like the .308 Winchester round. This is an illustration of the 150-grain Power Point after it was tested for upset.

Here is the .307 Winchester round with its 180-grain bullet tested for upset.

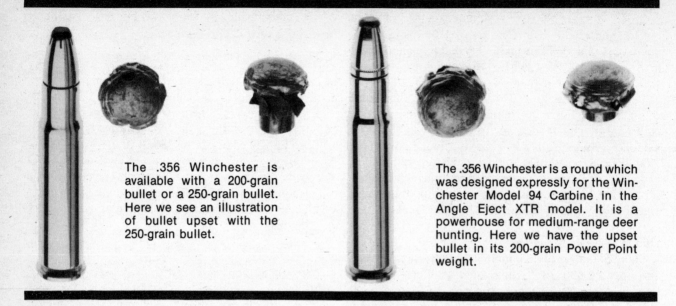

The .356 Winchester is available with a 200-grain bullet or a 250-grain bullet. Here we see an illustration of bullet upset with the 250-grain bullet.

The .356 Winchester is a round which was designed expressly for the Winchester Model 94 Carbine in the Angle Eject XTR model. It is a powerhouse for medium-range deer hunting. Here we have the upset bullet in its 200-grain Power Point weight.

.338 Winchester Magnum

Here is another elk caliber, if you will. My friends Harold Schetzle and Charles Keim swear by their .338s for Alaska hunting where both are guides. With a 200-grain bullet at 3000 fps, the .338 is more than is necessary for deer. And the 225-grain bullet at 2900 is more powerful yet, I suppose. If a hunter already owns a .338 and wants to use it on deer, he should employ the "big game" bullet which will not tend to strip the jacket.

.340 Weatherby Magnum

All that we said of the .338 applies here, only more so. We have a 200-grain bullet at 3200 fps and a 225-grain bullet at 2900.

.348 Winchester

For woods hunting, the .348 is still a good one for deer and game larger than deer. It will shoot 200-grain bullets at about 2500 fps. Since the only rifle for the .348 is the fine M71 Winchester, which has not been made since 1958 following the advent of the M88, we won't dwell on this round. I once sought a .33 Winchester, cousin to the .348, because Ben Lilly, the famous old hunter used one. But dreams are usually replaced with reality and I can say that no one needs a .348 or a .33 Winchester for deer.

.357 Magnum

This excellent handgun caliber is now offered in several rifles. When we push the standard 158-grain bullet at 1700 fps, we have a marked improvement over the handgun at 1300 fps, but this round is still in the short-range class for deer, I think. With its 1700 fps rating, the muzzle energy is 1014 foot-pounds.

.35 Remington

Thanks to companion Max Wilson of Tucson, Arizona, I had a chance to use a Remington pumpgun

in .35-caliber. One could push the 200-grain bullet at about 2000 fps for a muzzle energy of 1777 foot-pounds. This round was always a good one for deer in the woods, and it always will be. It is still offered to this day, which attributes to its usefulness for deer. The round put venison in the pot for years.

.356 Winchester

The .356 Winchester, a new round as this is written, was developed for rifles of the familiar lever-action mode, such as the Model 94 Winchester and the 336 Marlin. The cartridge, in its present factory loadings, is credited with a muzzle velocity of 2460 fps for a 200-grain bullet and a muzzle velocity of 2160 fps for a 250-grain bullet. The round closely approximates the fine .358 Winchester in power.

.358 Winchester

Being a little eccentric, I suppose, it bothers me when a round I consider excellent does not take the fancy of the shooting public. I understand that the good Savage 99 will continue in .358-caliber for a while. I might say that where I could bag deer and black bear and maybe close-range elk all in the same locale, and where my shots were not going to be across canyons, I would feel well gunned with a .358 Winchester. Its 200-grain bullet can be driven at 2500 fps to almost 2600 fps and a 250-grain bullet will leave the muzzle at about 2300 fps. For shorter range work, its a dandy.

.350 Remington Magnum

The .350 Remington Magnum is the .358 Winchester with a bit more punch. It will drive a 200-grain bullet at about 2700 fps and a 250-grain bullet at 2400 fps, and it will perform these ballistics from a short barrel, only 18½ inches in length. Of course it is OK for deer, and it is also more powerful than necessary for forest hunting.

.44 Remington Magnum

We have skipped all of the .35-caliber big-cased magnums, because, as with the .338 and 8mm Remington Magnum, these rounds are truly more powerful than is ever necessary for deer hunting. If long-range power is badly needed, the 7mm Magnum and its kind have more than enough punch. But the .44, while in this case a handgun caliber, turns up respectable ballistics out of an 18-inch barrel. The 240-grain bullet will do about 1900 fps and the 265-grain bullet will make 1700 fps with top loads. For short-range work, the .44 Magnum in a rifle is worthy for deer.

.444 Marlin

This one is more than necessary for deer. But if a shooter wishes to use it in the Marlin lever-action rifle, he should do so with confidence. The 265-grain bullet out of the .444 will gain as much as 2200 fps. The energy here is going to be 2849 foot-pounds, whereas the energy out of the .44 Magnum case at 1700 fps is around 1701 foot-pounds. In the woods, the .444 would work out well, especially for the hunter who might also want to tackle larger game.

as this is being written, one may wish to purchase a box of Remington .45-70 loaded ammo, carefully "pull" the bullets and then reload the cases for the Ruger No. 1 rifle.

There are many old-time rifles in obsolete calibers or calibers which were termed obsolete, but somehow never died. We want to mention the .38-55 immediately because this one always was a good deer round. Today, we have the .375 Winchester round which is essentially an improved .38-55, capable of driving a 220-grain Hornady "compromise" bullet at 2200 fps. The .375 Winchester is amply powerful for deer, of course, and so is the .38-55 with a 265-grain bullet at about 1750 fps from the muzzle.

The .38-40 and .44-40, squat little numbers that they are, do churn up enough punch for close-range deer, too. I'd prefer larger potential in most cases, but the .38-40 will drive a bullet of 180 grains at about 1850 fps, while the .44-40 will toss its 200-grain bullet at about 2100 fps. Up close, both will take deer. They are old rounds, but ammo is still sold in both calibers and the handloader who owns a safe rifle in either caliber can use such a rifle for deer hunting under woods conditions.

There are simply too many of these old rifle rounds to mention each one. The individual shooter knows his own limits with these rounds, or should, and by being

The well-designed Marlin Model 1894 rifle is available in .44 Magnum caliber. It is suitable for deer hunting and many shooters like this short-throw lever-action rifle for woods work.

.45-70 Government

This old round will never say die. Today, it is still found in the field. For deer hunting, even the Springfield 1873 model can be a good deer rifle in the woods with this round, for with under 25,000 CUP at work, a velocity of 1900 fps is possible with the 300-grain hollow point Hornady bullet. Out of the much stronger Ruger No. 1 rifle, I have chronographed the .45-70 at 2150 fps for a muzzle energy of 4158 foot-pounds with the Remington 405-grain bullet. If that is not enough for a deer, I'd hate to have to face such deer in combat. I have also managed to gain 1800 fps with the Hornady 500-grain bullet from the .45-70 in the Ruger No. 1 rifle.

The only caution is to use harder bullets, such as the 500-grain Hornady if the hunter intends to load up his No. 1 for deer with the .45-70. If the 405-grain bullet is selected, the shooter should take care not to strike the shoulder or hip area. In fact, this took place on one hunt and the lost meat was a shame. The Remington bullet in 405-grain size held together a little better than the Winchester 405-grain bullet, but the latter opened up a shade better at lower velocities in our tests. Since Remington no longer offers bullets for sale to handloaders, at least not

careful, can produce a good record of harvests. Recently, a reader asked about using the .32-40, for example, as a deer caliber, and he was surprised to learn that this round developed about 1950 fps with a 165-grain bullet, not too far behind the .30-30 in power. But watch out for the real little guys. While the .32-20 was once sold as a deer caliber, it really is not. Some of the factory-loaded ammo in the oldies is also under par, necessarily so considering the fact that these rounds could find their way into old and unsound guns.

A Few Handgun Calibers

Just to touch on the subject in this chapter, let us look at a few handgun calibers of the day. I think it surprising to some of us rifle-lovers that the one-hand arms have come so far in terms of sheer power. But they have. Some of these rounds gain considerable punch from a small case.

7x45mm Ingram

The 7x45mm Ingram Improved is based upon a necked up .223 case, blown out. The 139-grain bullet can achieve a muzzle velocity of 2250 fps according to my Hornady manual, and this would give us a muzzle energy of 1563 foot-pounds. In this round, I would suggest using the standard bullet in the 130-to 140-grain range for deer rather than any bullet which might be too hard. After all, these bullets were made to handle much higher velocities and might not open up much at lower velocities. Also, while the ballistics here are impressive considering a Remington XP-100 pistol with a 14½-inch barrel, we are still talking close-range work with such a round.

7mm BR Remington

Another round suited for the Remington XP-100 pistol is the 7mm BR. In this, as well as the previously mentioned 7x45mm, deer hunting power can be achieved. The 7mm BR can attain 2200 fps with a 139-grain bullet and 2100 fps with the 154-grain bullet, or only 50 fps less than the 7x45mm with the latter load. If we admit that a 150-grain bullet from a rifle delivering velocity in the 2000-2400 fps domain is OK for deer, then the somewhat ballistically superior 150- to 154-grain 7mm bullet at 2100 fps is going to also get the nod.

.357 Magnum

I include the .357 Magnum round because some of the game departments I checked allow its use on big game. In my own opinion, the .357 is somewhat limited in power for deer, but I have a report of an Arizona hunter who has bagged a few elk with his .357 Magnum, which shows what can be done, of course, when a top hunter and good shot puts his mind to it. The 125-grain hollow point can be fired at about 1550 fps from the 8⅜-inch barrel of the S&W Model 27 revolver. The 158-grain hollow point gains about 1300 fps from the same revolver, the latter developing about 593 foot-pounds of muzzle energy. A .22 Hornet with a 45-grain bullet at 2900 fps is worth 841 foot-pounds.

.357 Remington Maximum

New as this is being written, the .357 Remington Maximum round is an elongated .357 Magnum, for all practical purposes, almost ⅓-inch longer than the .357 Magnum case. As loaded by the factory, the round is given a fairly "hot" pressure allowance, and the case is thicker than .357 Magnum brass. The 158-grain .357-inch bullet chronographed at about 1600 fps in a 7½-inch barrel with experimental ammunition. Whether or not this will be the over-the-counter ballistics is yet to be seen. However, with a case of about ⅓-inch extra length than the standard .357 Magnum, there should certainly be added punch as a result. This is not an elongated .357 Magnum case, remember, but a newly designed case. In the hands of the good shot, it will be used for deer with some success. That it is to become a deer hunting round will remain to be seen.

.41 Magnum

Having owned a couple .41 Mags., I can attest to the fact that they have sufficient power for modest-sized game at close range, but can speak no further on the subject with personal experience at work for me. The 210-grain hollow point will leave the muzzle at up to 1450 fps according to my figures, and this means a muzzle energy of 981 foot-pounds. At close range, and in the hands of a good shot, the .41 will take deer.

.44 Special

Supposing that one has a firearm which could handle more than low pressures, the .44 Special could be a deer cartridge in the same way other handgun rounds are deer cartridges. The old *Lyman Reloader's Handbook* No. 42 shows loads for the .44 Special which would qualify for deer, such as the 180-grain lead bullet No. 429348 at 1400 fps.

.44 Remington Magnum

I cannot argue with the words written on page 352 of the *Hornady Handbook*, 3rd edition, which say, "The 44 Magnum is effective on deer, black bear, elk, and other large species." In fact, at least one hunter has taken elephant with a .44 Magnum handgun. Well, it is always interesting to me that when we are dealing with the largest in any category, such as the strongest commercially available handgun round on large scale availability, we tend to forget how we felt about other rounds, especially those fired in rifles, which we did not think strong enough to get us by in the game fields.

I bring this up because I have been told by .44 Magnum fans that a muzzle-loading rifle was not enough for deer, even a .50- or .54-caliber muzzleloader. So, let's look at the .44 Magnum out of the handgun with nothing but that round in front of us. We have, let us say, a 240-grain bullet at 1400 fps. That earns a muzzle energy of 1045 foot-pounds. Is the .44 Magnum a deer caliber?

You bet it is. But even though expert shots have downed elk and even elephants with the .44 Magnum round in the handgun, I think we should recognize that it is a close-range round in terms of surefire efficiency. I have seen good shots hit a large tomato can at 100 yards with a .44 Magnum, and I consider the round my favorite in my own sidearm and would hunt deer with it. But I don't think I'd want to shoot at very long range without considering exactly what kind of punch is left out there. At 50 yards, we would be down to less than 800 foot-pounds with the above load, which is plenty for deer. At 100 yards, we would be down to about 625 foot-pounds.

The .44 Remington Magnum handgun round is a dandy, as anyone can see, and it is a deer caliber. He who practices with his handgun, even scopes it, is packing a formidible tool. He who stalks for good close shots as well, is even better off.

.44 Auto Mag.

The .44 Auto Mag. is listed as having 1450 fps muzzle velocity with the same 240-grain hollow point bullet discussed above. Comments on the .44 Mag. apply here.

.45 Long Colt

Here is another round allowed by game departments in some locales. With a 250-grain hollow point bullet at 1000 fps, and in the hands of a good shot willing to get close, the .45 Long Colt will take deer.

T/C Contender Loads

.30 Herrett

A Thompson/Center Contender round, the .30 Herrett, out of a 10-inch barrel, will shoot a 150-grain .308-inch bullet at 2000 fps. Obviously, we qualify this one as a deer round.

.30-30 Winchester

Also chambered in the T/C Contender, the .30-30, according to data by Hornady, does not offer quite the accuracy found in the same fine handgun chambered for the .30 Herrett. As for ballistics, however, the .30-30 in the 10-inch barrel arrived at the same 2000 fps earned by the .30 Herrett in the same handgun and would suffice for deer hunting.

.357/.44 Bain & Davis

Hornady shows a muzzle velocity of 2100 fps with the same bullet used in the .357 Magnum at 1300 fps. Very obviously, here is some handgun power. The muzzle energy with this load is 1548 foot-pounds. If game departments allow the .357 Magnum, then this round, which is a .44 Magnum case necked down, has to be included in the list of deer rounds.

.357 Herrett

The .357 Herrett fires the 158-grain hollow point at 2000 fps and is in the same class as the .357/.44 above.

.44 Magnum

In the longer 14-inch barrel of the Contender tested by Hornady, the .44 Mag. earns 1750 fps with the 240-grain bullet. The muzzle velocity with that 240-grain bullet gives a muzzle energy of 1632 foot-pounds. No more need be said here. It is obvious that this round is enough for deer as it surpasses the .44 Magnum in its shorter barrel loads.

.45 Long Colt

The .45 Colt gains 1350 fps with a 250-grain bullet when fired in the T/C Contender with a 10-inch barrel. It will take deer.

.45 Winchester Magnum

A 250-grain hollow point is driven at 1550 fps out of the 14-inch T/C Contender barrel. We have to call it a deer round.

Black Powder Calibers

Black powder firearms do not defy the laws of physics. Contrary to much romantic consideration, the muzzleloader which fires a reasonable projectile in terms of mass at a reasonable velocity will get the job done. Lengthy tests and a long list of field experience has lead us to believe that the black powder firearm is a deer-taker. But the black powder arm is not going to be a high velocity proposition. Therefore, we look to the larger calibers to gain power.

.32-caliber

Not suitable for deer. This is a squirrel number and will bag game up to wild turkeys and maybe *javelina* on

The .44 Magnum gains 1750 fps with the 240-grain bullet in the T/C 14-inch barrel. This cartridge is certainly enough for deer.

Though limited in power, the .357 Magnum can be used successfully on deer if used by a good hunter.

129

Various calibers for muzzleloaders are shown here. In the box, and immediately in front of the box, we have the .310 Hornady swaged round ball for the .32-caliber squirrel rifle. This fine ball is superb in the small game field. The conical shown is called a Maxi ball, and in caliber .50 can weigh over 370 grains. Then we have an array of ball starting with the .310, and .350, the .395, and the .445, the .535 and a .690.

a regular basis. Its 45-grain ball will leave the muzzle at 2000 fps or more.

.36-caliber

Not suitable for deer. With a 65-grain ball, which has gained as much as 2023 fps in our Hatfield Squirrel Rifle, the muzzle energy is 591 foot-pounds, but at 100 yards from the muzzle the little ball is only doing 956 fps for an energy rating of 132 foot-pounds. This is a fine caliber for small game up to wild turkey and *javelina* size. But getting close is still the name of the game even with the higher velocity loadings.

.40-caliber

I have dispatched but one larger game animal with this caliber, an antelope at close range and with a neck shot. The buck went down instantly; however, I consider the .40 an absolute minimum for deer, and then only at very close range in the hands of an experienced rifleman. The .395 ball at 2000 fps will gain a muzzle energy of 826 foot-pounds. At 100 yards, expect this energy to have dropped to about 215 foot-pounds.

.45-caliber

With a 133-grain ball at 2000 fps we get a muzzle energy of 1182 foot-pounds. But this ball will be down to about 325 foot-pounds at 100 yards. The 220-grain Maxi ball, driven at 1748 fps in the T/C Hawken, gives a muzzle energy of 1493 foot-pounds and a retained energy at 100 yards of 584 foot-pounds. This is the bottom line, we feel, for deer when we consider the fact that we do have larger black powder calibers. But the .45 can and does bag deer every season.

.50-caliber

We have put down a rather large number of deer at ranges up to 125 yards with a 177-grain round ball at 2000 fps. However, in our hunting we generally shoot much closer, more like 50 yards, where one will find the .50 ball or conical quite effective on deer. A muzzle energy of 1572 foot-pounds is earned from a .490 177-grain ball at 2000 fps, a velocity obtained in our tests with a Navy Arms New Model Ithaca Hawken rifle. A 358-grain Lee moulded (special) Minie gained 1456 fps from a T/C Hawken in caliber .50 for a muzzle energy of 1686 fps and a 100-yard retained energy of 826 foot-pounds.

.54-caliber

A great favorite of many black powder deer hunters, the .54 in a strongly built rifle can fire a 224- to 230-grain round ball at 1900-2000 fps. My own custom .54 drives a 230-grain lead pill at an average muzzle velocity of 1975 feet per second with a muzzle energy of 1993 foot-pounds. I have had to shoot very few game animals more than one time with muzzleloaders. A bear took two hits from a .50 and due to shooting a bit too far away, I have had to finish an antelope anchored with a 230-grain .535-inch lead ball. But I have yet to need more than one 230-grain ball out of my custom rifle on a deer.

The T/C .54 fired a 400-grain Denver Bullet Company Maxi ball at 1499 fps for a muzzle energy of 1996 foot-pounds and a retained energy of 1149 foot-pounds at 100 yards.

.58-caliber

Firing a 600-grain Minie from a Navy Arms Hawken Hunter rifle, we obtained a muzzle velocity of 1358 fps with an energy of 2458 foot-pounds. The highest velocity reached with a 625-grain Minie was 1500 fps for an energy of 3123 foot-pounds. The .58 is enough for game larger than deer. Certainly, it is sufficient for deer.

There are some black powder firearms which shoot lead balls of .60, .70 and larger calibers at modest velocities. We have stopped at the .58 because it has been proved to us by actual field experience that the .50 and .54, using the round lead ball, will cleanly harvest deer. Getting close is the secret, and of course ball placement is important, too. For steady day in and day out black powder deer hunting, the .50 and .54 are good choices.

Calibers and the Game Laws

It is important to note that over the years, a great many calibers have been outlawed for deer hunting. In some cases, the outlawing has made good sense. In other cases, it has not. A list of outlawed rounds would be difficult to compile, for such a list would have to go back several decades. Furthermore, rounds which have been outlawed at one time or another have been reinstated later on, in the same area. However, there are a number of rounds which are *generally* thought of as sub-par for deer, and which have been outlawed at one time or another. These are the following, and remember, this is only a representative list: .22 rimfire, .25-20, .32-20, .38-40, .44-40, .38-55, .40-82, and so forth.

Let's take just a moment to consider a couple of these rounds. The .22 rimfire, I think we can agree, is no deer caliber. It should be outlawed for deer hunting, in spite of the fact that there is no doubt that many deer have been dropped with the little rimfire round. A person I know in Old Mexico has used the .22 rimfire for deer for many years. He is a rancher in Sonora. He hunts as a stalker and gets close. However, I still find the .22 rimfire too small for deer even in the hands of a great hunter. The .25-20 was never meant as a deer round, and though with a handload it can drop deer pretty well at close range with good hits, I think it best to leave the .25-20 out. The .32-20 was advertised as a deer round to begin with. Yet, even with handloads, it's not much in the high energy bracket.

The other rounds, all black powder numbers to begin with, gave low energy yield with their black powder loadings. When the factories began to load these rounds with smokeless powder, they kept charges very mild just in case a shooter had an old rifle which would not withstand much pressure. This is why they were outlawed for

deer. However, in good rifles of sound condition, these rounds make fine deer calibers. For example, the old .38-55 will drive a 255-grain jacketed bullet at a muzzle velocity of 1805 fps (see p. 342, *Lyman Handbook* 46). This is a muzzle energy of 1845 foot-pounds, much more than a .44 Magnum handgun. The old .44-40 can push a 200-grain jacketed bullet at a muzzle velocity of 2079 (same manual, p. 343). This is a muzzle energy of 1920 foot-pounds. However, these figures are of no consequence. And the law is the law. If a round is outlawed, it is outlawed. And that is that. Furthermore, it is the responsibility of the deer hunter to *find out* what the *current* laws are in his hunting area. It is not the responsibility of any agency to *tell him* what the laws are through any form of contact whatsoever, with the exception that the game department is obliged to have printed laws available for the hunter to seek these and study them.

In addition, game departments have also outlawed rounds on the basis of remaining energy figures. The standard is not a standard, by the way, and one state may call for 1000 foot-pounds of remaining energy at 100 yards from the muzzle, while another state calls for 500 foot-pounds of remaining energy at 100 yards. The concept is a good one. Enforcing the law is somewhat difficult, I would say, for the handloader can often improve upon a round which, for one reason or another, was never loaded to full potential by the factory. Therefore, in order to enforce the law, a game ranger would have to seize a suspect firearm and its ammo, chronograph the load and then determine mathematically (easier than trying to chronograph remaining V at 100 yards) just how much muzzle energy the load does have left at the set distance from the muzzle.

These are some of the calibers used on deer in North America. They are sometimes minimal in ballistic force, but sufficient, and they are in some cases truly more than required to cleanly and quickly drop our venison. The serious deer hunter should study the field, try to gain some experience with various calibers and then decide, mainly, what firearm style and type he likes most and can shoot best, and if any one of the deer calibers is chambered in that rifle he is in business.

The forest hunter has countless rounds to choose from, for the high speed numbers are not useless in the woods. The long-range hunters have to look at the high intensity, high velocity numbers that reach across canyons with great retained energy levels. But one thing is for sure—there is a cartridge and a firearm to hold it which is just right for every deer hunter out there.

chapter 12
Bullets for Deer

MY WIFE spotted the four bucks. They were mule deer, high on a ridge, bedded together in a grassy depression. The only problem was the small fact that Nancy was 8 months pregnant. The climb up the side of the ridge, through grass which hid hundreds of rocks, turned me off on the whole deal. I wanted her to get a buck. After all, she located the foursome. But I did not want her to slip on the rocks. Finally, desire overcame reason, and we began a stalk with the promise that we would "go slowly." We did a good job of stalking and came up on the grassy pocket with the deer no more than 125-150 yards away.

Nancy kneeled for the shot. "For heavens sake," I said. "You always sit for your shots. Get a good sitting position." Nancy listened. She got into the sitting position. However, her large tummy wouldn't allow her to get a good steady shot. By now, the four bucks had figured out that the two creatures which had interrupted their *siesta* were trying to gather some venison steaks, and they scrambled up and began a dignified, but hasty retreat. Simply stated, Nancy did not get a clean shot so she did not fire at all.

For 2 days we hunted. On the morning of the third day, what with Nancy's condition and time running out, Nancy got a nice 3 x 3 mule deer buck, and we got the animal to camp. On the last afternoon of our hunt, we were back in the same general area where Nancy had spotted the foursome of bucks. Just for the heck of it, I glassed up into that grassy pocket, knowing I would see nothing but grass. But there, resting in the shade, were four mule deer bucks, certainly the same group we had previously spotted.

"Better get up there and get one of them," Nancy instructed me. I scrambled up the side of the mountain, but something must have gone haywire for when I reached the top of the rise, there were no bucks in the grass. I looked back down where the trail appeared about as big as a long narrow worm, and Nancy was looking up at me. Through my binoculars I could see what she wanted me to do. She was pointing with her walking stick in a sign that said, "They went thataway."

I quickly paced in the direction she indicated and made my way to a bluff. There was a drop-off of sorts on the other side, but there was also a trail, and at the bottom just coming up the opposite side were the four mule deer bucks. I had a moment to look them over. Two could be eliminated right away, not because they were small, but because the other two were larger. One of the other two had a much better than average rack on a modest body, while the second of the pair had a fine thick body and a fair rack. Without much hesitation, I held about ½-foot or so in front of the nose of the big-bodied buck and put a round ball into the back. The buck was mine and the lost meat on this thick-bodied animal would hardly fill a teacup. I already knew that I was more interested in meat than antlers.

132

I tell all of this for a reason. The hunter may have to make a decision between stopping power and salvaging edible meat. He may, indeed, have to decide between a bullet which is explosive in nature and will always anchor the deer with a chest hit, or a bullet which is strongly constructed and will not always drop a deer instantly with the chest hit, but which may indeed break bones better than the bullet which is more fragile. Hunters of long experience argue vehemently as to which bullet is best for deer, a bullet which indeed comes apart inside the deer, thereby "leaving all its energy there," or the bullet which passes through the deer and smacks into the hill behind the animal with plenty of remaining punch.

Actually, we have to end up with some type of compromise. The Greek Golden Mean comes into play—the middle of the road instead of either extreme. But I think we can reach a point of agreement, roughly speaking, on what a deer projectile should be. I believe that we have three major criteria to consider. First, we have to match the bullet to the cartridge. A bullet which is perfect for deer hunting in the .30-30 is not going to be perfect for deer hunting out of the .300 Weatherby, in general. Next, we must match the bullet to the game. A bullet constructed for use on a rhino would probably be less than perfect on deer, though of course there is room for argument since someone might suggest that a .45-caliber 500-grain bullet of tough construction would be OK for deer, wasting less meat than one might think and still killing well. Third, we have to decide what we truly want.

Do we want the deer to go down in a heap at any cost in meat salvation? Do we really care if the exit hole looks large enough to drive a Mack truck through? Or are we terribly concerned that if we do not put that bullet directly through the lungs and if that bullet does not hang together we will indeed lose precious meat? I guess I am in the latter category and that is why I told of my decision when confronted with a choice between a good rack or a very good body on a deer. By the way, just to keep things honest, had that rack been gargantuan, I would have gone for the rack! I'm talking good rack *vs* good meat. Day in and day out, I am a meat-hunter. But I thrill over the majesty of a big rack, too.

Well, looking to our first criterion, we must match the bullet to the cartridge. Essentially, we are again dealing with "averages." I will explain. On the average, we might take a deer at 150 yards in a given type of terrain. So, if we are going to use a .30-30, then we must consider the fact that at 150 yards the velocity of the bullet has dropped off to about 1600 fps. I am considering the 170-grain bullet here because, though I have seen deer dropped quickly with the 150-grain bullet, all in all, I suppose the .30-30 is best with the 170-grain bullet.

Now, in order to have some expansion, the 170-grain .30-30 bullet must be soft enough in jacket thickness and proper in design, meaning lots of exposed lead at the tip of the bullet, to "open up." We want a bullet to expand because of at least two things: First, the expansion of the bullet changes the form of the shock wave in front of that bullet which, in turn, makes a tremendous difference in the wound channel and exit hole if there is an exit hole. Second, change of shape is in effect a transfer of energy.

(Left) These two projectiles are very different in construction, of course. The bullet on the left is a .44-caliber Hornady in the 265-grain weight. It is intended for use in the .444 Marlin round, and when used at the lower velocity of the .44 Magnum round in the handgun it reacts by opening very little; however, penetration is high. The all-lead projectile also penetrates very well due to the molecular cohesion of lead and the mass of this big Minie.

This 130-grain bullet is mostly jacket with only a trace of lead left. It struck the pad of a prickly pear cactus on the way to the target and hit the game sideways.

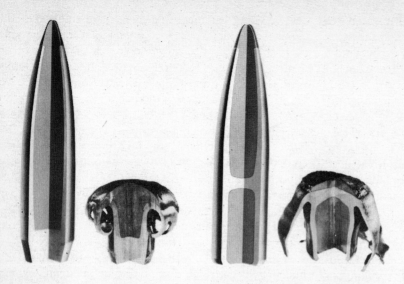

The Nosler solid base bullet, this one in 7mm, 162-grain weight, is another of the innovations from bullet makers of the day who want to offer more than "just a bullet" for hunting purposes.

The Nosler partition bullet (right) insures that the base of the bullet will remain intact, even if a part of the forward core is lost. The solid base bullet from Nosler shows a somewhat different "upset pattern," but both retain a substantial part of their original weight.

But a bullet which will expand at 150 yards with a standard .30-30 starting velocity will be too "soft" for the velocity attained by the .300 Weatherby. Therefore, looking at this quite simply, we have to build a bullet commensurate with the velocity at which we want to shove that bullet. Is there any hope for a compromise? Yes, there is, but we cannot get too carried away with this. We can, of course, have a bullet which "lives two lives." The bullet is both soft and hard. It is soft in the nose area, hard in the shank area. So, the front of the bullet opens up or peels back, but *only so far*. That is the key to what we call a "controlled expansion." Fortunately, the bullet-makers have given us super products in this area, the Nosler partition bullet being a good example. The partition exists for one reason, to give us two bullets in one, as it were. The front part of this bullet is soft enough to expand, even at modest remaining velocities, but the back of the bullet, the shank section, is hard enough and protected in this case by the partition, and it will not come apart.

The shape of a wound channel in terms of the dozens of autopsies I have made varies tremendously with the type of bullet used. The Nosler generally has an ordinary entrance hole, considerable expansion of the wound channel inside of the game and then a modest exit hole. Remember, please, that it is primarily the shape of the shock wave which creates this wound channel and not simply the direct contact of the bullet with the game, at least not in a higher velocity missile. Anyone who doubts this should consider the following.

I have taken deer with calibers such as the 6mm, .270, 7mm Mag. and .30-06 which have had exit holes about the size of a teacup and sometimes much greater. Is it possible for a bullet of only 6mm or up to .30-caliber (less than ⅓-inch across) to punch a hole the size of a teacup? If a .30-caliber bullet were pounded flat with a sledge hammer it would be very difficult to make it spread out to the size of a teacup. This is not a scientific statement, but in everyday terms we can think of it this way: The bullet enters, sends a shock wave of tremendous force out in front of it; the shock wave punches the hole out the other side of the game when there is an exit hole, and the bullet "falls out" of the exit hole. This is not exactly right, but it gives us a better look at the situation than imagining a bullet expanding to the size of a teacup, which it certainly does not.

Our second criterion for selecting a deer bullet is to match it to the game. A deer is not so large, really. Yet it is not so small, depending upon the individual animal, of course. Deer come in a wide range of sizes, something like human beings. A mule deer buck can dress at 125 pounds, to be sure, but he can also dress at well over 200 pounds and more. Naturally, we have extreme records on both ends of the continuum. With that generalization, we look for a bullet which will expand on what we term a "thin-skinned" game animal. Deer bullets cannot be "full patch" in my book. Solids or full metal jacket bullets are illegal where I hunt and should be, not only for reasons of safety in the field, but also for reasons of "opening up" on deer and other game.

So, our deer bullet is not terribly hard, but neither is it overly soft. It has a jacket construction "just right" for deer, in other words. This is so tenuous and general that it is almost impossible to pin down exactly. I think what we need to know is that the work has been done for us anyway. The bullet-makers of America (and other countries, too) have perfected bullets which are indeed just right for "thin-skinned game." We don't need to lose any sleep at night worrying about it.

A shooter will often find a particular brand of bullet which he admires very much for one reason or another. Often, the criteria used to decide upon a specific bullet vary with the desires of the individual. If a deer hunter likes the explosive nature of a bullet and prefers that type of action from the projectile, then he will select a bullet with a more fragile jacket. If he prefers more penetration, then he will go for a bullet with a harder jacket, and with a good relationship between core and jacket in terms of the two remaining together upon impact and creation of the wound channel. Today, however, the "controlled expansion" bullet is king, and it should be. Generally, we have a bullet in this type which offers a fairly fast expansion at the nose, but which does not tend to peel back beyond the ogive and into the shank of the bullet.

This type of bullet performance excludes the question, "What range is the bullet good for?" The bullet is pretty good at all ranges from a few feet in front of the muzzle to a reasonable and prudent distance. Naturally, no type of bullet construction will make up for sheer lack of re-

tained energy at ultra long range. However, the controlled expansion bullet will open up at long range because of the somewhat (comparatively) more fragile nose as compared with the stronger shank. And yet, the construction will not allow for total bullet blow-up at close range. In other words, we have a sensible compromise in the bullet of controlled expansion design.

Naturally, we have to match the construction of the bullet with the probable striking velocity of the round. This is again a compromise, as it must be, but there are very significant differences in bullets created for lower velocity calibers and bullets designed for higher velocity calibers. There are dozens of examples, but just to name one, let us consider the 265-grain Hornady bullet designed for the Marlin .444 round. The bullet is constructed for the velocity of the .444 cartridge, of course. Therefore, when the 265-grain bullet is used in firearms with shorter barrels and less velocity, the tendency is for a lot of penetration, but not much expansion of the bullet. Sometimes this is all right. Sometimes it is even desirable. If a handgun hunter wanted a lot of penetration without

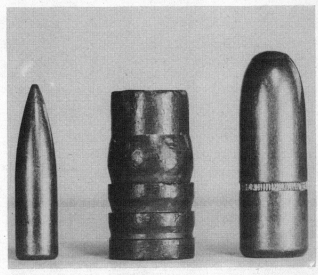

(Right) Bullet construction must vary according to the velocity at which the bullet will most likely strike the game and also according to the intended use of the bullet. On the left is a 140-grain 7mm bullet, capable of withstanding over 3300 fps at the muzzle from a 7mm Magnum round. In the center is a 625-grain Lyman-moulded Minie, generally driven at more like 1000 fps to maybe 1300 fps or so. On the right is a big .458-caliber bullet intended for the .458 Winchester, with a strong jacket for heavy game. Any could be used on deer with varying results, dependent upon striking velocity.

Here is a rather unusual occurrence, a "big game type" bullet which has lost the forward portion of the core. Generally, this situation is not seen. The effect of the bullet was still good, however, and the game was cleanly harvested.

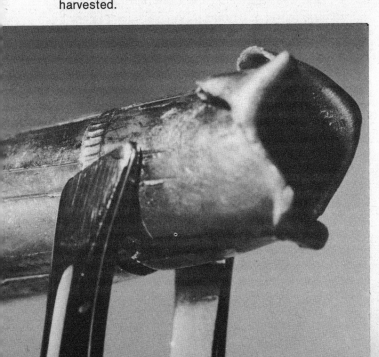

much opening of the bullet, he might use the 265-grain Hornady in his .44 Magnum revolver. For deer, a thin-skinned game animal, this would not be very prudent. On larger game, the bullet might be just right. (One hunter used his .44 handgun in Africa on game larger than plains antelope and found the harder bullet useful there.)

There are many different brand names which tell us of the construction of the bullet. We know that a Silver-tip bullet offers high penetration and does not tend to come apart very readily. The same is true for the Core-Lokt and for many handloader bullets, too. All of the "big game" bullets from Hornady, Speer, Sierra and similar bullet companies offer the controlled expansion feature with the aim being to hold jacket and core together as a unit. The famous Nosler Partition as already mentioned is another example of this feature, and so are

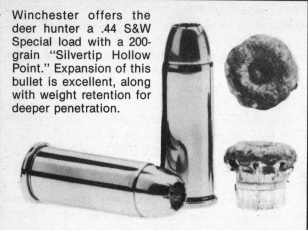

Winchester offers the deer hunter a .44 S&W Special load with a 200-grain "Silvertip Hollow Point." Expansion of this bullet is excellent, along with weight retention for deeper penetration.

virtually taken back by its speed. My deer arms had been the .25-35, .30-30 and sometimes the 7mm Mauser with a 175-grain bullet at nothing like super velocity. The .270 with a 130-grain handload, for I was already a handloader, simply awed us in our youthful enthusiasm.

The first year I owned the rifle I got ahold of some different bullets, trying my handloads to see what I liked best. I quickly found that a controlled expansion 130-

This is a Remington 7mm 175-grain bullet in a "before and after" pose. This is not the Core-Lokt design, and the bullet opens well at the lower velocities found in the 7mm Mauser or other of the non-magnum 7mms. On the other hand, the Core-Lokt design is very welcomed in the higher velocity cartridge cases.

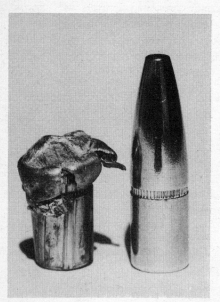

(Left) This is a 165-grain .30-caliber bullet of the "big game" type. The results shown here are equal with 200-yard 7mm Magnum velocity. The core and jacket have held together well, and expansion on game would be quite sufficient.

many other bullet styles, such as the venerable Norma Dual-Core, Barnes, Bitterroot, old RWS Torpedo Ideal, German H-Mantel and others.

But now to our third criteria. What do we, as individual hunters, really want? I had a hunter complain to me that I was way off base in wanting my deer bullets to "hang together." He went on to suggest that he wanted all the energy spent inside of the deer, not on the hill behind the deer. This argument is so good, though I think wrong, that it is difficult to argue it down. On the face of it, you sure would want the energy of a bullet to spend itself inside the game and not on the hill behind the game. In fact, I certainly do want *some* of that energy spent inside the game. But not all of it. I also want part of the bullet's energy spent in making an exit hole, and if there is some steam left and the bullet smacks the hill behind the deer with resounding authority, so be it.

I do not now nor have I ever enjoyed a bullet that blew all to pieces like a hand grenade. I learned the hard way, too. My first "high velocity" rifle was a Model 70 Winchester in .270-caliber and I was, at that distant time,

grain bullet was wonderful. I always got an exit hole, and I never had too much wasted meat. The deer were dropped as if struck by lightning. But I was a sort of experimenter, so I went on to test other bullets. Among these, I ended up with two that were simply too hard for the .270 Winchester. One was a 140-grain 2D bullet, and the other was a 150-grain bullet. For the first time, I found myself shooting deer more than once with chest hits. There was little apparent expansion to create that shock wave and my exit holes looked like entrance holes.

I'd fix that. I then went to a bullet in 130 grains which was known to "blow up." I was hunting with the father of my friend and his brother. We had to fill our second deer tags and I had my .270 along, with its explosive bullets. The old man spotted two deer in a canyon. The deer were not together, in fact, but were about 100 yards apart. He began to take a bead on the closer one, leaning his .30-30 on a fence post. I suggested he try my .270. He dropped the deer with one shot.

Then I grabbed my .270 back and got the other deer, the one farther up the canyon. We were happy. Happy

Here is a 175-grain 7mm bullet which retained sufficient core, but did not exhibit the same qualities found in the "big game" type bullet. A rather large amount of weight was lost here due to part of the lead core departing from the jacket.

An excellent deer caliber, the .257 Roberts cartridge has been updated by Winchester with a special "Cal. .257 Roberts + P" load. Here, a 100-grain Silvertip bullet is shown (right) after recovery in a test medium. Note the expansion of the bullet without breakup. Jacket and core are retained as a unit for better penetration. The round is also loaded with a 117-grain Power Point bullet from Winchester.

This is a .44-40 bullet. At very low velocity, this bullet expanded well due to light jacket. In a higher velocity rifle the thin jacket would not be appropriate.

that is, until we got to the downed deer. The first one had been hit, thankfully, too far back, a paunch shot. I had to admit that the explosive bullet did its work. The deer did drop. But there was a small problem. The exit hole, if you can call that mess a hole, was large enough to ride a camel through, and the meat was badly bloodshot both fore and aft. I will never in my life forget walking up to the other deer. The offside shoulder was off. The front half of that deer in terms of meat was ruined. We soaked the bloodshot meat out, but simply could not save a lot of it no matter what we tried. It looked like a bomb had gone off inside of those deer.

I want a bullet to hang together. I want to drop the deer as cleanly as possible and with utter swiftness. All dedicated hunters want the game to drop this way. But I do not want a bullet to blow up. I do not want the core to go one way and the jacket to go another. I want the core and the jacket to remain wedded together to the very end of the bullet's work. Apparently, I am not the only hunter to feel this way, for we have a whole array of "big game bullets" now available to us, and the very reason

for these bullets' existence is to have a core and jacket remain intact after the bullet has struck home.

My prayers have been answered. With some of the good old designs, such as the Nosler, and with the new bullets now offered by the major companies, we are in business. We have a fine bullet which will open up without blowing up. I think this is just the way things ought to be. Naturally, someone will feel that the bullet which blows the game down by utter shock is the best. But I disagree. I never shoot at a deer without an autopsy just in case *any* style bullet fails to perform as it should. But in the past several years, especially in my son's .30-06, for he has been actually using the "big game" bullet longer than I have, we have no instance of a bullet just passing through the game without telling effect. When it comes to modern jacketed bullets for deer in high velocity arms, make mine the controlled expansion type known as the "big game" bullet. In the old arms of low velocity to medium velocity, the standard bullet with a lot of exposed lead is fine. A .44-40 of my knowledge has taken a number of deer, and due to modest velocity,

The bullet box is a rather simple, yet highly effective device for testing bullets. It is merely a box with partitions. In the first slot goes a balloon filled with water. Then we have clay and large catalogs of the "wish book" type from department stores. The bullet must pass through the water, the clay and is trapped at the back of the box by one of the catalogs. The box has worked very well in showing us which bullets had jackets that would strip and which bullets would hold intact. Also, we have gotten excellent information about the penetration qualities of various bullets at various velocities, for the same bullet is tested at different velocities to correspond with different striking ranges. For modern calibers, we always test a bullet at a remaining velocity for 200 yards. However, we sometimes test for many ranges, to include 50, 100, 200, 300 and so forth. This is easily accomplished by consulting the loading manual for remaining velocities per given cartridge at a specific yardage and handloading the round to that velocity.

One of the extraneous varibles extant in the use of the bullet box is the fact that the media can become wet as tests proceed. Therefore, the test media are not identical shot after shot unless they are totally replaced. However, in most bullet tests, this is not much of a problem, for there will only be a few shots fired into the box for a given bullet and the interior of the bullet box can easily and cheaply be renewed for each shot. Usually, the testing of a new bullet will only require 4 to 6 shots. The results gained so far are of very high positive correlation. In other words, what we got in testing bullets in the bullet box, we got in the field on game. Bullets which shed jackets in the bullet box, for example, shed jackets on game. Bullets which held intact in the box also held intact on game.

even in the handload, bullets are often collected from the game. They have expanded nicely and the jackets have not stripped away from cores. Throw a similar bullet at high velocity and the results are not the same.

Finally, let us expand this third criterion one step further. I think that if game is taken it should be harvested as quickly and as cleanly as possible, but I also feel a strong obligation to save all the meat I can at the same time. Naturally, you cannot harvest game without disrupting some tissue. That would be impossible. But how much tissue is disrupted and to what extent is another story. However, I cannot impose my feelings on everyone, and there will be some hunters who feel that they want the explosiveness of a bullet rather than controlled expansion.

Black Powder Projectiles

All of the above, of course, pertains to the modern jacketed projectile. But we have a rather impressive number of hunters in the field today who are using anything but modern arms shooting modern bullets. Is it possible for these old missiles to perform on deer as we would hope, with quick kills the rule and not the exception?

Yes, the answer is clear. It is possible, but for reasons quite different from those attached to the modern bullet.

But I feel strongly obligated to discuss the potential of black powder in terms of deer harvesting before I go into the prospects of lead missiles on deer. It is of utmost importance that the black powder shooter and hunter understand how to gain power from his firearm, for a world of mythology and magic surrounds this subject. After many black powder harvests and having seen many others put game in the bag with old smoke poles, I think I can speak from the platform of having actually witnessed both success and lack of success in the muzzleloader's potential to drop deer cleanly.

The Missile

I have harvested deer with both conical and round ball. If, and I repeat this to make myself perfectly understood, the hunter is willing to get close, the ball will take a deer as well as the conical. But if the hunter must shoot beyond 100-125 yards, I think he might want to consider the obviously better retained energy levels of the conical.

The reason for round ball and conical wound channel similarity (and I have autopsied a number of deer and

Here we have a plain all-lead bullet with grease grooves as compared with a modern jacketed bullet. When velocities are going to be low, an all-lead or lead alloy bullet is quite useful on deer. For high velocity, of course, the jacketed bullet is the answer.

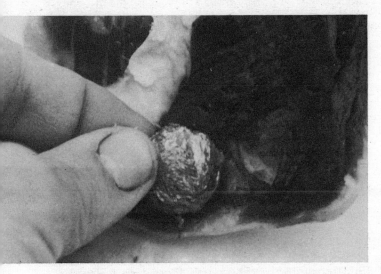

Here is a .535 size round ball extracted from a mule deer buck which was harvested from only 10 yards. The ball traveled underneath the spine of the deer and lodged in the opposite shoulder blade. The ball was pre-weighed before going hunting. It weighed 230.0 grains. The recovered weight is 228.0 grains.

other game taken with both), is the fact that neither can gain high velocity in the ordinary black powder firearm. Therefore, we have a standoff at close range. I repeat again, at close range. I have shot totally through a bull elk and a bull bison with a .530-inch ball of lead, so I know that penetration is there. Up close, at higher velocity, the ball may flatten even more than we want it to and exit holes are not always prominent; however, if one will look carefully at the wound channel created by a round ball at high velocity, he will find that penetration is there. Example—one of my last deer was taken at a mere 10 paces, and the ball was stopped. I had loaded a .535-inch 230-grain round pill to leave at about 1975 fps, so remaining velocity, even for a ball, simply had to be high at only 10 yards. The ball struck beneath the spine and cut across

A family of all-lead projectiles is shown here with one modern bullet for comparison. On the far left is a 625-grain Stake-buster and next to it a 460-grain Minie, then a 625-grain Minie. Our modern bullet is next, a 180-grain .30-caliber, and on the far right is the old-time lead round ball. All serve well on deer under appropriate conditions.

This big .58-caliber Shiloh-moulded Minie is called the Stake-buster design and it weighed an average of 625 grains out of the author's mold. The pure lead of this projectile helps it retain a great deal of its original weight.

to the shoulder blade on the opposite side. The mule deer buck went down instantly.

Trajectory for ball or bullet will be similar out of today's ordinary black powder arms. In fact, we will generally be able to drive a round ball at, perhaps, 1900-2000 fps in a well constructed black powder firearm, such as the Browning or the Ithaca, and we will find the conical doing 1400-1500 fps at the muzzle. Because the conical "carries up" better than the round ball, while the ball starts out faster, we have both ending up at 125 yards with very similar trajectory.

The best advice in black powder shooting is to get close. Get close and shoot one time, with that ball breaking a neck or taking a tour through the chest cavity. Also, it is best to select ball or conical based upon accuracy. Whichever is the more accurate in the given firearm is probably the best bet, provided a reasonable velocity goes with that accuracy! Also, choose the type of conical which works best in your rifle. In fact, there are many fine elongated projectiles for the black powder arm, but they differ and that difference can be seen in accuracy in many cases.

Furthermore, remember that black powder arms do not defy science. Load to a *safe* but optimum level. Low velocity does not suddenly become more potent than higher velocity because the missiles are shot from black powder arms. Physics still rules, and caliber is often the key to black powder "power." Remember that this is true in both conical-shooting and round ball-shooting. With the conical, high velocity is certainly out of the picture, so we go up in projectile mass. In the round ball, yes, 2000 fps is possible and a bit more in some cases, but high velocity in the 3000 fps domain is not with us, so again we go up in caliber to gain "power."

A black powder projectile of pure lead, or as nearly

pure as we can manage, does have a remarkable ability to penetrate when one considers the apparent lack of punch as compared with modern arms. One of the reasons for this fact is what we might elect to call "molecular cohesion" of lead bodies. In fact, in all of the autopsies that I have made where a ball or bullet of pure lead was found, a loss of only a percent of the missile weight was common.

As an example, we took a ball from a bison after it had penetrated the entire breadth of the chest cavity and knocked a hunk of rib *through* the hide on the off-side. Yet the ball only lost .1 (one-tenth) of one grain weight. In another case, a round ball broke the shoulder of a deer and was lodged against the shoulder blade on the off-side and the loss of weight here was 1.0 grain. I weigh each projectile before I put it into my ball bag and carry only 230.0-grain round balls for my .54, only 177.0-grain balls with my .50 and so forth so I can tell for sure what I lost when I recover the ball.

In summary, as far as the black powder missile is concerned, I can only recommend what I have seen work time and again without fail, and this is a good caliber size, a pure lead projectile and as much velocity as can be attained with *safety* and with *accuracy*. No overloads please. I am speaking only of loads guaranteed by the manufacturer. Going ov.. the limit set by the manufacturer is not wise in my estimation. For my own hunting with frontstuffers I choose only those arms which the gunmaker has faith in and shows that faith by allowing me a powder charge which will give good velocity. If he does not trust hunting loads in the arm he imports or creates, then neither do I.

Hunters may wish to start a collection of recovered game bullets. Many of the modern bullets will not be stopped in a deer, but some will. The author keeps some of his collected projectiles in plastic film cases, with information slips inside the cases.

chapter 13

Brush Loads

DEER HUNTERS north, east, south and west may very well encounter a situation where the deer are living in tight cover. Even in open country, such as on the plains of Nebraska in the western part of that state, I have seen deer in brushy conditions. Because of this fact, I have always wanted to know what to load for brush shooting, and more importantly, which calibers were best for this type of hunting. So I set out to learn from some sort of experiment. But first, I should say that taking deer in the brush did not seem to offer much help to me in terms of truly useful experiences.

I had not learned much from actually hunting in the brush. Well, I had learned something. I found out that all of the loads I ever tried were deflected by brush. But I still had no conclusive data as to what made for a "brush load." In fact, looking back at the deer I had taken in the brush, or those harvested by companions, I think we were most successful when we forgot about shooting through brush and concentrated on shooting through openings instead. However, I wanted to study the situation anyway, so for a period of a few years, especially when I acquired a test rifle, I would run out with a few targets, set them up behind brush at about 100 yards distance, then try to put a 5-shot group into the bull's-eye.

As I already suggested, I found out that even a .458 Winchester with a 500-grain bullet at 2100 fps muzzle velocity would, at 100 yards, tour off course when en- countering brush. But we proved nothing. After all, an experiment has to have such validity that the tests can be run over and over again with the same results. Such was not the case with our brush loads. After all, the testing structure offered a heap of "extraneous variables," especially considering the fact that our brush screen was not exactly the same each time we tested each round. Did we end up with anything worth talking about then? I think so.

I think we found out a lot, even though we cannot call our findings proof. The indications were many. As time marches on and more demonstrations, if not scientific tests, are set up, perhaps we will learn more about bullets finding their way through brush. But for now, we can live with what we have compiled. Here are some results of our shooting. Remember, that all we did was set up a target behind a screen of brush. We tried to pick similar conditions and our shooting took place over a period of time marked by several targets and several bushes not just one target behind one bush per each caliber.

The Fast Ones

About the worst brush-busters were the hotrock .22-caliber varmint numbers. I suppose there should be no surprise in this, but I have to say I was surprised later on by some other rounds. The fast .22s were meant for long-range work in open fields and flats where the sighting of a target at a long distance was entirely possible, and

Here is a scene which often meets the eye of the deer hunter, plenty of vegetation to block a bullet. Yet, in this terrain, many hunters annually bag mule deer bucks with great regularity. The key to making a good hit through the brush is in the word "through," in the sense of finding an open spot to shoot through rather than trying to shoot right through the actual brush.

where there would be few to no obstructions between the shooter and that target. Therefore, we are certainly not "badmouthing" the fast .22s because they did not punch through a lot of brush.

The shooting of fast rounds brought us to at least a few special thoughts about brush shooting, however. After we used a .222 Remington up to and including a .220 Swift, we began to wonder what effect there would be in terms of actual bullet energy and brush. Would the .222 fail in brush busting more than the .220? In other words, would the increased foot-pounds of remaining energy in the .220 Swift offer better penetration in brush than the .222 Remington? The answer seemed to be no. Neither did well in finding the bull's-eye through the screen of brush. We did find examples of "exploded"

(Right) The brush screen used for our demonstrations (we cannot call these tests, since the controls are lacking) was fairly light, light enough to allow the target to be seen and an aiming point to be selected. Even this light screen of brush deflected and/or destroyed the bullets used in the demonstrations. It is recommended that a hunter try to shoot at "holes" through the brush if possible, rather than trying to hit a deer behind a heavy brush screen. However, projectiles of higher momentum did do a fairly good job of staying "point on" after going through the brush.

bullets in both calibers.

This term, "exploded bullets" is used for an explanation, but we do not mean actual explosions of course. The bullets, it seemed, broke to pieces, and the target often appeared to be splattered by bits of lead and jacket. As for the bullet actually blowing up on brush, we mean fragmenting. So, this first phase proved nothing we did not already surmise to be the case. High-speed .22-caliber bullets were not the best for breaking through brush.

Since .22 calibers, even the fast ones, are illegal in many deer hunting locales, we tested them only to complete our picture. The next rounds to run the gauntlet were in the .24-caliber range, fired mainly from the .243 Winchester and the 6mm Remington. Actually, I was surprised to find that in some cases these smaller projectiles were not doing so badly, at least not as badly as we suspected they would do. There were, often, neat holes through individual twigs and holes in the black proved to be round, not elongated. But there were some elongated holes in the paper, too. In fact, it seemed that if we could "dead

The .222 Remington was used at 100 yards and of the five shots fired at the target, two printed neat bullet holes in the paper. One may have tilted sideways. The bullet used was a very hard 60-grain projectile with heavy jacket. Note that one bullet was deflected and landed on the 7/8 line. This rifle in caliber .222 can produce near ½-inch groups at 100 yards. The brush disrupted the pattern considerably. Other holes in the paper were caused from exploded bullets and bits of brush penetrating the target.

The entire idea of "brushbusters" has been somewhat overstated in many cases. The individual shooter may in fact try a simple test—behind a screen of brush, set up a target, firing several rounds at the bull's eye. It is not surprising to find bullet holes which indicate that the bullet was keyholing. Here, a big .690 round ball is shown with a 180-grain .308-inch bullet. At 75 yards, neither would rip through a brush screen without going off course, and yet both did strike the bull's-eye with regularity. Again, we suggest picking the hole in the brush instead of trying to cut brush down with bullets. Round balls are very susceptible to brush, incidentally, even in larger calibers, though larger calibers fare better than little ones.

center" a small twig, the bullet would remain on course and hit point forward on the target.

But, all in all, the .24s did not eat up a whole bunch of brush. We had to conclude that if we owned rifles in the .24-caliber range, we would use them on deer in the brush, but the decision was based upon further agreeing that the real advantage would be to look for openings in the brush and trying to hit the deer through these openings, leaving "brush busting" out of the picture.

The Mediums

Getting away from the .222s and .220s and the faster loads in the .24s, we turned to the .30-30 class of cartridge. In one test I used 150-grain bullets and 170-grain bullets and the 170s seemed to win. Now, I was not so sure this would be the case. If we look at sectional density, it would seem that this trait would not be always better in terms of brush penetration. With nothing to guide us besides guessing, the guess was this: A bullet of very good sectional density would be, in the main, long for its caliber. If long for its caliber, such a bullet might tend

Although it is true that there is no such round which can buck brush with perfection, we found a slight edge in the big bore bullet at modest velocity, but not enough of an edge to suggest the use of big bullets with reckless abandon in brush shooting. Here, a 180-grain .308-inch bullet is shown with a Buffalo Bullet Company .54-caliber bullet of 425 grains weight. In our tests, neither bullet provided for a certain bull's-eye on the target at 75 yards when fired through a screen of brush. But both bullets did strike on target well enough to afford a chest hit on a deer at 75 yards, assuming 14-18 inches for a deer's chest.

the .44 Magnum did about as well as either. The .45-70 did all right, but seemed to us no miracle worker in the brush, much to our consternation because this one, prior to testing, was given the nod as *the* medicine for brush in our eyes. Incidentally, once again we had better luck with a harder-jacketed bullet over a thinner jacketed bullet.

What about rate of twist? Here was another good question. At least we thought it was. How would rate of twist affect the ability of a bullet to make its way through brush? At first glance, it seemed that a bullet of high rps (revolutions per second) might in fact be least desirable in terms of penetration. The "centrifugal force" of such a bullet, we surmised, might tend to spin it right off target when the bullet met with a twig. On the other hand, a bullet of rapid rps might in fact remain stabilized even better than a bullet of lower rps. Well, we met once again with inconclusive evidence at best. We even tried some shooting with two calibers in barrels with different rates of twist, that is, the same exact bullet but one fired from a 1:12 twist, the other from a 1:9 twist. No luck. We learned nothing.

Well, we had no good conclusions for retained energy, few good ideas concerning sectional density, other than we did not consider high sectional density a prerequisite for a brush cartridge, and rps seemed to leave us in the cold, too. Pure caliber dimension, however, seemed to offer something. The .35 Remington was pretty good, better than its smaller cousins. Larger than .35-caliber did not seem to help much in our first tests. However, the .45-70 seemed as good, but not truly that much better if any better at all.

Another Look at Velocity

I decided to go back to the .45-70, using a Ruger No. 1 rifle so we could play with a range of loads, with the idea in mind of seeing if increased velocity would play a role in brush busting. As it turned out, I began testing with a 405-grain bullet at about 2000 fps from the Ruger No. 1 and to make this a short story, ended with the same bullet at 1200 fps. Finally, I could suggest something: Do not attempt to lower velocity in hopes that this will increase the effectiveness of a bullet in the brush. At least our .45-70 with less velocity did not improve, and we later tested several other calibers in terms of velocity. About the only improvement we could see, maybe, was lowering the velocity of *some* .22 hotrocks and even then the frangibility of the bullet was such that penetration through brush was poor at best.

Load for full power in the brush. There was no evidence to support a notion to the contrary. As for a .30-30, .35 Remington, .375 Winchester, you name it, the full throttle loads were not behind of or truly ahead of the lower powered loads. Cutting back on the actual velocity, then, did nothing in our little demonstrations, and I think it safe to say that we should enter the brushy areas for deer with loads that are up to snuff, not castrated.

to deflect more than a bullet short for its caliber. Well, in our own .30-30 the 170-grain bullet seemed to reach the bull's-eye a bit more often than the 150, but again, embarrassing that it is to admit, we had no real proof, nothing we could draw upon time and again to show our readers.

Later on, however, it seemed to us that good sectional density was certainly not important in terms of breaking through brush and striking a target. We decided to put the .30-30 up against two other rounds, the .270 Winchester and the .35 Remington. In short, the 200-grain .35 Remington bullet, in spite of less retained energy, got through more brush than did the 130-grain .270 bullet, but the differences were not remarkable. We began, in fact, to suspect that stronger jackets had something to do with brush busting as well as calibers and velocities. This observation came to us as we tested two 130-grain bullets, one of thin jacket and one of thick jacket and the thicker jacketed bullet *seemed* to register more hits on the target. Well, it did register more hits on the target, but I include the "seemed to" because of our test conditions, and I don't want to be too definite here.

The .358 Winchester with a 200-grain bullet kept pace with the .35 Remington in another little shoot-out, and

The Best Cartridge

I do not think we really had a best round, because in fact no round really tore through the bushes in order to punch neat round holes in the target with precise small groups. However, we are back to our old "common-sense" approach when we say that all in all the following did best for us: The caliber was larger rather than smaller. The energy was up to par (underloads did not help the cause). The nose of the bullet was blunt, not sharp. Sharp-pointed bullets seemed to deflect even more than blunt-nosed bullets. Naturally, if we are suggesting larger calibers, then it rather goes without saying that we include heavier bullets as better than light bullets for the brush.

However, when all of the smoke cleared, there was really one glaring conclusion. None of the rounds proved to be at home in the brush. The black powder round balls, even from .58s and up to .62s, did not break through much brush. These, too, deflected on the target with a larger than average dispersal after having gone through some brush. Since we placed our target about 5 yards behind the brush in all cases, we could actually conclude that many of the round balls never even hit the paper, let alone the bull's-eye. On the other hand, the larger round balls at good beginning velocities did the best for us. We might add that in several instances the round ball guns fared no worse than some of the modern arms in terms of putting a mark in the bull's-eye after passing through brush.

One of the rounds which seemed to bore through brush fairly well was the .58-caliber firing big bullets. A flat-pointed 625-grain Shiloh Stakebuster beginning its journey to the target at about 1400 fps did about as well as anything when it came to brush busting.

Even though a 12-gauge slug was also turned aside by brush, the slug-shooter does have a very formidable

The .375 Winchester, left, because of more sheer energy, will probably make it through a little more brush than the .30-30 on the right.

The round ball is very susceptible to being thrown off course by any obstacle. The black powder hunter must be especially aware of this, avoiding brush shots and trying to put the ball through an opening in the brush.

(Left) The big .54-caliber 460-grain bullet from a Dean Zollinger custom black powder rifle printed bullet-hole patterns at 100 yards from the muzzle. The rifle was sighted for preliminary close-range work at the time and was normally hitting low on the target. Therefore, it was fairly much in its normal pattern. All the same, one bullet did strike much lower than usual from this normally very accurate rifle. No rifle we tried, even though a light brush screen was used, put its bullets right on the mark.

missile working for him in the brush, mainly from the standpoint of good energy delivery at close range, with normally ample penetration and a large wound channel, but also for the fact that while a slug will not "bust brush," it does tend to remain on target better than a very light, high-velocity projectile. In part, I think, we have a simple case of inertia, where the slug tends to remain on its path until met by an "outside force," which is the same physics for any bullet, but with the slug we

145

Some experts feel that momentum has much to do with "brush-busting" and therefore a large and heavy missile is better than a smaller and lighter one. Here are some heavy projectiles. These are Federal's Super Slugs, a complete line of hollow-point rifled slugs beginning with the big 10-gauge number, left, found in the 3½ 10-ga. Magnum down to the .410 slug.

have (in 20-gauge and up) more mass to deal with. As we move more and more mass, mass times velocity, our momentum increases. As momentum increases, the path of the projectile is more stable. But a 50-grain bullet does not tend to remain on its original path when it meets with an obstacle, such as a mass of brush.

Suggestions

Our first suggestion for modern arms would be to look for accuracy. Yes, we are supposing a modest caliber with bullets not necessarily pointed, but in fact, in later demonstrations we were to learn the real truth of brush busting. That truth had to do with missing the brush. Here we call upon our firearm to demonstrate at least a bit of accuracy, no, better than that. I think we can make a blanket statement (at last). That blanket statement goes like this: Always choose as much accuracy as possible from the given caliber and rifle of your deer-hunting choice. This means the most accuracy for brush as well as the most accuracy for long-range shooting on the plains.

We can further suggest that a deer hunter learn to shoot through holes in the brush whenever possible. Instead of cutting loose when the deer is in the thickest of its jungle, if the hunter can see that any break in the brush is possible along the path that the deer is taking, he should use that opening to shoot through. I know this sounds like more drugstore cowboy philosophy, but it isn't. In fact, I hunted some plain ordinary jacks and cottontails in the brush a short while ago and I found that I could pick up even on these small targets and follow them with the sights. I could see in the very change of my sighting picture when the brush was less dense. I could also see when I had to fire if I were to get a shot at all.

So, with an accurate rifle, a good full-power load and the thought in mind to follow the game with our sights hoping for an open spot to shoot through, we are now on the road to better brush shooting for deer. Even our 12-gauge slug was turned aside by brush, so this advice seems to hold up. Naturally, range is so very important

to our discussion because we may often find our deer in the brush to be very close and then the accuracy possible from a slug is plenty. In some cases, however, the hunter may have to pick a spot in the brush, perhaps at a distance of more than 100 yards, and for me this means an accurate rifle. With that accuracy working for me, I might just be able to drive that bullet straight to the mark.

What about the scope sight? Is brush a good place for

"Brush buster" is somewhat the wrong name to place upon any standard type projectile fired from any of the arms we would normally use for deer hunting. However, if a rule of thumb were to be constructed, one might suggest that the missiles of higher momentum will penetrate the brush a bit better than those striking with less momentum. The Buffalo Bullet Company .54-caliber bullets shown here (left) with a 180-grain .30-caliber bullet for comparison, was driven from a custom rifle at a muzzle velocity of about 1700 fps and strikes on the target, which was behind a screen of brush, were impressive. The Buffalo Bullet Company projectile shown here weighs 460 grains.

This photo illustrates for the reader just what a shot can be like when a deer is running in thick cover. Note that the buck will soon come into a small clear spot. The smart hunter will pull ahead of the deer at this point, and not fire until the body of the deer is in the little clearing at the right in the photo.

scopes? I think so. I believe that a good telescopic sight is at home in a brushy situation. Since all bullets deflect, then it seems to me we would want to shoot through holes in the brush, and it further seems to me that a good scope sight will enhance the chances of hitting our target. Since scopes of lower power are readily available all over the place, there is no problem in coming up with a model just right for any rifle.

The entire idea of "brushbusters" has been somewhat overstated in many cases. The individual shooter may in fact try a simple test—behind a screen of brush, set up a target, firing several rounds at the bull's eye. It is not surprising to find bullet holes which indicate that the bullet was keyholing. Here, a big .690 round ball is shown with a 180-grain .308-inch bullet. At 75 yards, neither would rip through a brush screen without going off course, and yet both did strike the bull's-eye with regularity. Again, we suggest picking the hole in the brush instead of trying to cut brush down with bullets. Round balls are very susceptible to brush, incidentally, even in larger calibers, though larger calibers fare better than little ones.

I might mount a 2½x scope on a rifle which would see brush country use all the time, but in my own case, I think I would prefer a variable once again as my brush/open country choice. A 2x-7x, for example, would be good. So would a 2.5x-8x scope. Any variable which has a wide field on the lower end of its magnification range would serve us well. Mounted on that "medium" caliber rifle, a hunter would want to load up with a blunt bullet over a sharp bullet, make certain that he is carefully sighted in, and then "have at it" in the brush.

I would not hesitate to hunt a brushy area with a cartridge rifle of the .30-06 type if I could load a blunter bullet and if I had made up my mind to shoot for openings instead of trying to drive bullets through brush. If I lived in the type of terrain where brush hunting happened to be the rule of the day, then I might latch onto a "brush rifle." I suppose I'd go for a .358, .375 Winchester, .35 Remington or one of that clan with bullets in the 200-250 grain class. I further suppose that I'd mount a lower powered scope or a variable which had lower power capability. But after trying to determine just what makes up a brush cartridge, I'd have to conclude that no round truly eats up the brush on the way to the deer.

In fact, my choice of a brush rifle would quite probably rest in the actual handling of that rifle *more* than in its caliber. I would want any rifle to fit me so that when I wanted to quickly bring that rifle to my shoulder I would be greeted by an almost instantly clear sight picture. The rifle would balance well for me, and that criterion may well vary from shooter to shooter. However, one factor would be held in command over all other factors—I would have proved to myself that I could hit a small target through openings in the brush, for this is the true test of the brush hunter, getting that bullet to the target, even when the target may be no more than a few square inches moving through a place that afforded no more than a few small openings.

chapter 14
Sights for Deer Guns

THE FIRST CRITERION for sight selection is to match the sight to the conditions. The second criterion is personal success with a given sight. The first simply suggests that when we choose a sight for a deer gun, be that a rifle, modern or black powder, a handgun or a shotgun, we make the selection based upon the habitat we intend to hunt. The second item asks that a hunter use what he knows how to use. I have heard some very good advice, for example, which speaks boldly against certain types of sights, and yet I have had superior results with these same sights, and I have seen others enjoy the same success. Therefore, even after we have matched our sights to the terrain, from dense brush to wide open flatlands, we still have to look at the personal side of the sight issue—what works best for the individual hunter.

Fixed Iron Sights—The Rifle

If someone had suggested to me about 15 years ago that I would be talking to modern deer hunters about fixed iron sights, I would have laughed. However, with a few million souls carrying muzzleloaders of antique sight style in the deer fields, it is imperative that we talk about these older type sights. Because the fixed iron open sight was no doubt assumed dead as scrap iron, some of us all but forgot how to manage these sights. The fact is, though modern shooters may find it hard to believe, the older sight patterns were quite useful and the consequent sight picture very clear. In fact, a few of the

improvements upon these sights may or may not have offered more for the deer hunter. What we generally have in fixed sights is the following, and remember we are talking about rifles only here.

What we have is, generally, some type of blade front sight. The sight may be "barleycorn" in configuration, or it may have some other shape as viewed from the side, but the important aspect to discuss is the view this sight presents from the cheekpiece of the rifle. This view will be that of a very fine "line." Because of that fineness, we can take a "fine bead" on game. In short, the front sight will not have a true bead at all, but will present a thin aiming point. This front sight is generally mounted on a base, and the base is fitted to the barrel via a dovetail slot. While the sight can be moved from side to side within its dovetail base, we usually consider such adjustment only after we have taken up windage adjustment in the rear sight. Mainly, we want to look at the front sight in the fixed model in terms of elevation. If we want to make the point of aim rise, or to put it another way, if we want the projectile to strike higher, then we take a file to the front sight and trim it down. Be careful when filing down the front sight and go slowly because it is pretty difficult to add metal to the sight if you file it down too far.

We will go into the details of sighting-in the fixed type iron sight in the following chapter; however, all we need to recognize here is that the black powder replica models which bear true resemblance to the originals of days gone

(Right) The fixed rear sight, at a slant here on an Ithaca Hawken .50 rifle, is quite useful and can be sighted in with somewhat surprising results. Some black powder hunters prefer the fixed rear sight for its historical appeal, and also its ruggedness.

In concert with a fixed rear sight, this blade front sight is found on an Ithaca Hawken rifle (now sold by Navy Arms Company). It is mounted low in its dovetail slot. Filing the top of this sight down will raise the point of impact.

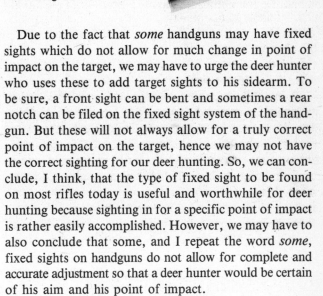

The top of the blade sight has been filed or sanded smooth. This occurred during sighting in; when the rifle was shooting too low, the front sight was filed which made the rifle shoot higher.

by may well have the fixed sight. I want to point out that it is a viable sight. I hope the shooter will give it a chance before turning to some other iron sight just because he may not be familiar with this old-time model. We call these sights "fixed" because they are, in a way, and in another way, they are not. Indeed, they are fixed in place. But they do have the ability to move. As we have pointed out already, the front sight "moves" in that we can shave off a part of it and lower the actual sight in order to raise the point of impact of the projectile. The rear sight moves, too. It moves from left to right in its dovetail slot. Therefore, the front sight generally takes care of elevation corrections while the rear sight handles windage corrections.

The Fixed Handgun Sight

As opposed to the fixed rifle sight, the handgun fixed sights are often very suitable for close-range work, but not totally useful in the deer field. Once again, we may have a blade front sight, and of course it can be cut down in order to raise the point of impact. The rear sight, however, may be a part of the topstrap or even a notch in the hammer nose in the case of some old-time revolvers. Therefore, there will be no possibility of drifting that rear sight in order to achieve a change in the point of impact on the target. We certainly have to concede that we want ultimate control over our point of impact in the hunting handgun.

Due to the fact that *some* handguns may have fixed sights which do not allow for much change in point of impact on the target, we may have to urge the deer hunter who uses these to add target sights to his sidearm. To be sure, a front sight can be bent and sometimes a rear notch can be filed on the fixed sight system of the handgun. But these will not always allow for a truly correct point of impact on the target, hence we may not have the correct sighting for our deer hunting. So, we can conclude, I think, that the type of fixed sight to be found on most rifles today is useful and worthwhile for deer hunting because sighting in for a specific point of impact is rather easily accomplished. However, we may have to also conclude that some, and I repeat the word *some*, fixed sights on handguns do not allow for complete and accurate adjustment so that a deer hunter would be certain of his aim and his point of impact.

The Iron Aperture Sight

Call it a receiver sight or a peep sight if you will, the aperture sight is a rather ingenious device. It is based upon the principle of the eye concentrating upon that point of highest light. In short, the eye will "automatically" look through the very center of a "peep" sight. This is quite a boon. If one will take notice of the fact, he will see that with the open sight the eye must actually focus on three points, the rear sight, the front sight and the target. Young eyes do this well. It is called "visual accommoda-

The aperture or "peep" sight is an excellent device and one can generally do very good shooting with this sight. The idea is to look through the hole without consciously trying to center the front sight in the peep itself. The eye will do that automatically. All one does with a peep sight is find the front sight through the peep. Note elevation and windage adjustments.

tion," the ability of the eye to focus back and forth rapidly on these points.

Given that with open sights when the rear sight is rather far from the eye and there is somewhat great distance between the rear sight and the front sight, even older eyes do fairly well in terms of visual accommodation. However, the old-time rifles of long barrels are, in the main, gone, and we no longer have that long sight radius to depend upon. If one will look at the sights on some (not all) of the old-time longrifles, he will find two things to be true. First, the rear sight is a long distance from the eye. Second, because of the long barrel, we have very long sight radius and even older eyes can accommodate to this fairly well.

But the aperture sight improves greatly upon the situation by removing, as it were, the rear sight. What? But isn't the aperture sight mounted close to the eye? Is it not a "rear sight?" Well, yes, it is. The big difference here is that the eye should not *consciously* concentrate on trying to center within the opening of that aperture sight. In fact, the eye will do this automatically, as it were. Therefore, the deer hunter simply looks *through,* not at, the aperture. He in fact ignores the rear sight as if it were not even there.

In this manner, the eye concentrates on two things only, the front sight and the target. A hunter who wants iron sights for whatever reason and who elects to have a "peep"

sight mounted in his deer rifle must learn to *ignore* that rear sight. He merely looks through it, puts the front sight on the target and squeezes the trigger. He has, for all intent and purpose, eliminated the rear sight. There is nothing new about the aperture sight. Shooters recognized its worth a very long time ago. A glance into, for example, the Ned Roberts book, *The Muzzle-Loading Cap Lock Rifle,* will reveal pictures of several old-time rifles which wore aperture sights. On page 34 of this fine old book, we have two rifles with aperture sights shown, both 19th century models. Mr. Roberts pointed out in his book, on page 35, that aperture sights are very old indeed when he quoted William V. Lowe, who said, " 'I cannot say as to the origin of the aperture sight; I remember that when I was shooting in 1880 or 1883, the aperture sight was spoken of as something new and an improvement on the pin-head, so I think it came into use about that time.' "

Perhaps others can explain why the aperture iron sight did not totally overcome the open sight. I do not have any idea. However, I can certainly guarantee that right to this date the open iron sight will be found on the majority of factory rifles and the aperture sight is more often a matter of addition later on by the shooter, with some exceptions of course. On the black powder models I can understand the adherence to the open sight, especially for reasons of historical correctness and partly for the fact that the long sight radius makes decent shooting quite possible with the open sight. But for modern arms which bear iron sights for whatever reason, the peep is certainly better.

Immediately, someone is going to jump in here and say, "Yes, the aperture sight might be better for shooting at paper, but it is no good when a fast shot must be made." Well, if the aperture sight is saddled with one of those pin-hole inserts, which are intended for target shooting, this is right. But if the hunter will only try, just once, removing that tiny-holed insert, using a much larger insert in its place, he will find that there is no problem at all in getting on target fast, real fast. It is a shame that we have come to believe that we have to use a tiny hole in the aperture in order to gain accuracy. Certainly, for pin-point target accuracy, one wants a small aperture, but the deer hunter owes it to himself, if he has an aperture sight or wants to try one, to shoot with the small-holed disc and the large-holed disc and compare targets. He will find very little difference in terms of hunting accuracy.

Adjustable Iron Sights

We talked about the fixed open iron sight above, and we spoke of the aperture sight. The former is adjustable only in the sense of mechanical manipulation such as filing or moving in a dovetail slot. The latter, the aperture sight, is highly adjustable, sometimes in only ¼-minute increments for a deer hunter to really tune his point of impact. Now we have to make a brief mention of the adjustable sight which is of the open variety. Here, we may have

A leaf sight on an original English 19th century black powder rifle. The dished out section behind the notch is an aid in cutting down on unwanted reflection. The sight has a U-shaped notch.

An adjustable rear sight may be found on a handgun as well as a rifle. This Ruger sight is adjustable for both windage and elevation.

This is a buckhorn rear sight with a very useful notch. The notch appears somewhat large due to the close-up view; however, it is actually quite small and precise. The buckhorns themselves do not in fact add anything to promotion of sighting, but when gotten used to, they can be lived with very well.

several means of changing the point of impact. But in the main, we will perform these adjustments on the rear sight. Generally, the front sight remains in position. We may use a tiny screwdriver to manipulate both windage and elevation on the rear sight, or we may have an elevator bar with steps cut into it, each step either raising or lowering the position of the rear sight. With the latter, we again may have to turn to drifting the rear sight in the dovetail slot in order to affect a change in windage. Suffice it to say that we have duly noted the adjustable iron sight. We will talk more of it in our sighting-in chapter.

Notches

The deer hunter who uses the open rear sight on his rifle is going to have to contend with the conformation of the notch. It is the notch which makes for the name "open sight." This notch can have virtually dozens of shapes, though we usually say that the U-style or V-style constitute major categories. It is rather pointless to go into a long dissertation on which is best. The best is that which performs best for the individual gunner. But there are a few major points to consider. In the main, I'd like to see the deer hunter using an open rear sight which allows for some light to be seen on either side of the front sight as the front sight visually rests within the notch of

that rear sight. In other words, while it may seem very wise to have a front sight virtually fill the notch, be that notch the U-shape or V-shape, this is not truly the case. A shooter needs a point of reference.

The point of reference is taken away when the front sight pattern simply fills, visually, the rear sight pattern. But when a bit of light is visible on either side of the notch, then the hunter has a point of reference. Without this ability to see a relationship between the front and rear sight, we cannot determine if we have things "lined up" or not. We can talk about drawing a "fine bead" or a "coarse bead," but these factors are not nearly as important as being able to determine where, exactly, that front sight visually rests in the notch.

The Buckhorn

Here is a sight which, I do suppose, was offered for reasons long since forgotten. On the face of it, there is nothing wise about bringing "wings" up on both sides of the notch. On the other hand, the fact that part of the target is indeed covered up has had no truly ill effect upon my own shooting. I have a few fine muzzle-loading rifles which have the buckhorn rear sight and while I must admit there is no special value in the buckhorns, the theory that one will not be able to see the target because of these projections is not quite correct. Of course, there

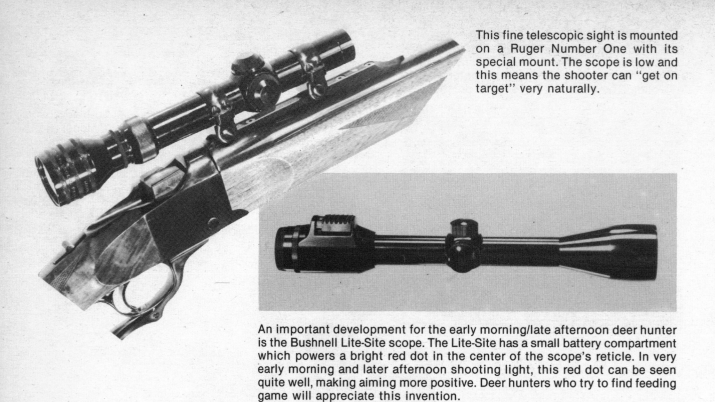

This fine telescopic sight is mounted on a Ruger Number One with its special mount. The scope is low and this means the shooter can "get on target" very naturally.

An important development for the early morning/late afternoon deer hunter is the Bushnell Lite-Site scope. The Lite-Site has a small battery compartment which powers a bright red dot in the center of the scope's reticle. In very early morning and later afternoon shooting light, this red dot can be seen quite well, making aiming more positive. Deer hunters who try to find feeding game will appreciate this invention.

is the matter of distance to the target. As the target is farther away, then of course the "wings" of the buckhorn blot out more of that target. However, with open iron sights we generally are dealing with a short-range hunting tool, and the fact is I have been able to place my shot on deer while using a buckhorn sight. I also have the buckhorn type sight on a few small game rifles and have found no problem placing the shot with these sights. However, just to keep things straight, I will concede that there is no added value that I know of in putting the big "horns" on either side of the notch. It's a romantic style. But it does nothing to improve the sight picture.

The Post

We can get into trouble in our designations here, and I have texts which actually use different nomenclature, but for our purposes the only important point which needs to be made is that we do have a sight picture which is not a blade or even a bead within a V-notch or a U-notch. The sight I mean to discuss has a very *square* notch and the front sight fits into this square notch because it appears flat on top. Therefore, we can very clearly place the top of this flat post within the open square notch so that the top of the post makes a flat line as it meets with the top of the rear sight. Hopefully, there will be a small admission of light on either side of the post as it rests in the notch. Now, the hunter may wish to employ the so-called "6-o'clock hold." Here, we intend for the bullet to actually strike directly on top of the post for the sighted-in distance. In other words, while we may sight in a hunting rifle so that the projectile strikes where we

hold the bead or blade, the square-topped sight picture with the 6 o'clock hold means that the missile strikes just above the actual point above the sight picture. This is a strong and obvious advantage in target shooting. It has but little true application in deer hunting with iron sights where shots will, perforce, be rather close and the target somewhat large and perhaps in motion.

The Telescopic Sight

Without any doubt, the telescopic sight is the very best instrument for precision aiming that we have, be it for target shooting or deer hunting. I am not suggesting that each and every rifle which enters the deer fields must wear a scope sight, but I think there need be no argument that one can place his shots better with the aid of the glass sight. Certainly, this is the case. I don't suppose that we have too many shooters around today who feel that they can produce better groups with iron over telescopic sights; however, this was not always the case.

I personally recall long arguments at the local sport shop where I frequently visited as a youth, and this was in the 1950s. The telescopic sight was strongly entrenched after WWII, in fact, and some may argue that it was already well recognized for its merits long before that. I am speaking now of universal appeal. I am not speaking of the fact that some 19th century fans of the scope sight spoke out strongly in its favor.

However, and I recall this personally, there were still murmurs of doubt surrounding the all around usefulness of a scope sight on a rifle when I was a young man. Naturally, these doubts drifted away soon afterwards and

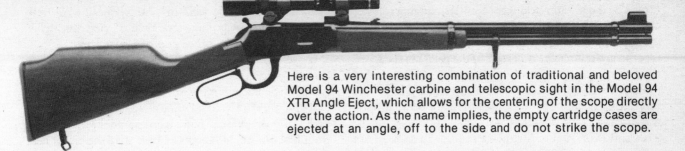

Here is a very interesting combination of traditional and beloved Model 94 Winchester carbine and telescopic sight in the Model 94 XTR Angle Eject, which allows for the centering of the scope directly over the action. As the name implies, the empty cartridge cases are ejected at an angle, off to the side and do not strike the scope.

While the variable scope sight is very highly accepted by today's deer hunters, as shown here by the 3x–9x (top) and 2x–7x (center), there are still many hunters who like a fixed power scope, such as the 4x (bottom). These scopes are offered by the Burris Company.

today the riflemen of the West, almost universally, accept the scope sight as the king of all sight types. The eastern shooters certainly cling to the scope sight as well. Scopes are hardly new. The Civil War saw sniper rifles with telescopic sights mounted on them, and many of the buffalo hunters who cleared the plains of the bison used a high-powered telescopic sight on the rifle.

In light of this, one can see for himself magazine articles dating not that far back in time where the author had to use convincing factors in speaking to his audience, trying to tell that audience that the telescopic sight was for real, strong, reliable and ready for all hunting from brush to mountain. Listen to what a writer had to say about the telescopic sight in 1892. He said: "There is the popular impression that the application of a telescope to a rifle immediately overcomes much of the uncertainty in sighting. This is fallacious; for as you magnify your vision you increase your errors in holding, so much so that few can use the telescope-sighted rifle advantageously in off-hand shooting." (p. 74, *Modern American Rifle,* Gould)

I realize this sounds out of place now, but there was a time, in my time no less, when shooters actually felt that they could not hold a rifle still if it had a scope sight on it. Well, the magnification certainly did show them how much wobble they had in their hold, but, very obviously, the wobble was still there with iron sights, only it was not visually magnified.

So we have a very old idea, really, in the telescopic sight, an idea which has been steadily improved upon until we now have, in my opinion, a telescopic sight which is as reliable as one can ask for. I have carried scope-sighted

arms in the rain. I have used them in rough terrain. I have the utmost faith in the scope. Sure, bang the scope against a rock, and it may be off target. But bang your front (or rear) iron sight on a rock and tell me how sure of your aim you'd be after that. As for "fogging," I admit it used to happen. However, in the past decade or more I have used scopes in all kinds of weather and have never had one fog up on me nor have I seen a fogged scope in camp since the Sunday newspaper cost a dime.

The scope has a flat field. There is no problem with the eye trying to visually accommodate from rear sight to front sight to target or even from front sight to target. There is a flat picture, as it were, and in that two-dimensional image one finds a target and an aiming point. Of course, the viewing of a target, even a magnified target, hardly means that a shooter is going to make his mark. Obviously, all of the other factors of shooting still apply, from breathing to trigger squeeze. Sloppy shooters do not become experts by the mere attachment of a scope sight to their shooting irons.

However, the fact remains that one can see far better with the aid of a telescopic sight than he can without it. The implications here are several, of course. The obvious factor is being able to better place a projectile on target and since we are talking deer hunting then let us say so— the scope-sighted firearm is distinctly the leader in terms of ability to see the target, be it paper or deer, so that a bullet can be exactly placed. Of course, there is another factor which immediately requires mention. A hunter is better able to distinguish his target through the clear magnified image of the telescopic sight, a safety edge.

Field of View

One of the initial reasons for hunters clinging to their old iron sights when good glass sights were available was the apparent limiting factor in the field-of-view. I contend that the notion that we'd never "find a deer" in the scope because of limited overall viewing area was somewhat overdone to begin with. I have a large chart of scopes offered in 1955, and the field-of-view on these models was already in the domain of 40 feet at 100 yards for the 2½x and over 30 feet for the 4x scopes. In short, I see no problem with field-of-view today, and a hunter can sight-in his game, even in the brush, with a low-powered scope sight, and he can do so with amazing facility. I might point out that even those rifles which we normally thought of as "brush guns" are now wearing scope sights. A perfect example is the Winchester M94 "XTR" lever-action which will eject its spent cartridge case at an angle, thereby allowing for the low mounting of a telescopic rifle sight.

Often, we hear that a hunter can't "get on" his deer with a scope sight. When this is true, I suggest that part of the reason is rifle fit. If the fit is all wrong then of course the hunter can't get on his target quickly. If the

with very generous fields-of-view and there are variables which allow for wide field-of-view at the low setting, while of course, swapping some field-of-view for higher magnification on the other end of the setting.

Reticle

The reticle is the aiming device within the view of the telescopic sight. There have been some mighty strange reticles over the years to include just about every configuration that one might imagine. I have tried the picket post in both blunt and sharp forms and I have used dots. I now have a fine scope which has a tapered post and I wish it did not have a tapered post, and of course there is the good old "crosswire."

There are arguments for all of these and more. I would not want to suggest that a person who loves the post or post plus crosswire get rid of it on my account. If it works, use it. I can only speak personally. I like the crosswire, especially the crosswire which is rather heavy until the wires intersect at the aiming point, where they slim down to fine lines. With such a reticle, I can easily pick up a deer moving off at a fast pace, and yet I can get a very fine sight picture at a distant target.

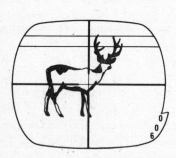
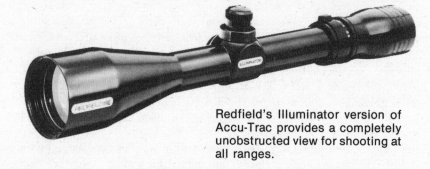

Redfield's Illuminator version of Accu-Trac provides a completely unobstructed view for shooting at all ranges.

scope is not mounted correctly in terms of how the shooter holds his rifle and where he places his cheek on the stock, then of course he cannot get on his game rapidly. If a scope is mounted, then it must be mounted so that the hunter simply mounts the rifle and as he does so, there is no searching around for the sight picture. If the deer hunter cannot see the target in the scope the very second that his deer rifle is mounted, then the rifle and the shooter should both see a gunsmith.

At the gunsmith's shop, the smith, if he knows scopes, scope mounts and stocks, can determine what is wrong and what to do about it. Sometimes this will be a matter of simply adjusting the telescope in its rings, such as moving the scope forward or backward. Sometimes a new ring height will be necessary before the shooter can see correctly through his scope, and in some cases the stock of the firearm will be wrong for the shooter in length-of-pull or drop-of-comb and then the hunter will have to either have some work done to correct these problems or look for a rifle which fits him better. However, suggesting that a shooter can not pick up on game rapidly with a scope is all wrong. There are low power scopes

Relative Brightness

We used to worry much about how bright a scope should be. I think our concern was legitimate. I don't think we have much to worry about today. The scopes I studied before writing this section of the book were all bright, and the optics seemed to be excellent. I grant the reader that in order to truly find differences in optics one must have special equipment and the knowledge to use that equipment, so I am speaking on a "look and see" basis only. Of course there are still differences between various telescopic sights in terms of optics. But all in all, the brightness factor does not concern me personally.

The big argument in brightness centers around which formula a person wants to use. Relative brightness is often thought of as the American way to measure this factor, and it includes exit pupil and the diameter of the objective lens. This is all very well, but there is another way to look at the issue. Twilight factor is often thought of as the German formula and magnification is a consideration. I have no intention of putting myself in the position of having to argue the middle while either side makes a vocal pancake out of me. However, when I want to see a target better in dim light I crank my variable power scope up to more power, not down to less power, so I guess I side with twilight factors over relative brightness factors.

Resolving Power

We might think of this factor as we would consider definition in a binocular. I want to be able to see details in the distance, and better optics afford this luxury. Naturally, magnification is helpful in making out details, but it is not the only factor. Once again, I do not worry about this situation in the modern scope sight because the new scopes, especially well-known brand names, have plenty of resolving power. In fact, I should take this a step further and state that in my tests, which were only cursory at best and did not include sophisticated equipment, I found no scopes with which I could not read a small sign at 200 yards on only 4x.

Eye Relief

This is an important factor and once again I must take my leave of it by stating that I found no scope sights which I could not use because of a lack in eye relief. Eye relief means simply the distance from the eye to the ocular of the scope, and this distance can vary not only from scope to scope but also in the range of eye relief scopes may possess. As an example, the Bushnell Scope Chief VI, 2.5-8x variable shows an eye relief of 3.7 to 3.3 inches. Note that we put the larger number first, meaning that we can "back off" from the ocular 3.7 inches (note this is inches) and still see a full "picture" in the scope. We can put our eye closer to the lens, up to 3.3 inches from it, and again have a full sight picture. So we have a leeway of .4 inches here, or not far off ½-inch to play with. As long as our face hits the stock at a point where the eye is from 3.3 to 3.7 inches from the first lens of the scope, we will have a full picture in the view of the scope.

Looking at the Bushnell Magnum Phantom scope meant for handguns and some other arms, we find a totally different eye relief pattern. Now we have a range from 7 or 8 to 21 inches. We may find some very fine scopes which give a single figure for eye relief, but this is not a problem in any way. Also, I can vouch for the fact that some scopes which have a fixed eye relief are just as quick in the "full picture" department as other scopes which show a range of eye relief. Remember that much is dependent upon the shooter mounting the scope so that it is the right distance from his eye.

One warning—don't shoot a rifle which has the scope mounted in such a manner that the fit of face to stock means the scope's ocular is too close to the eye. I personally wear two scars, small now, from the scope rearing back into my eyebrow area. On one occasion, I was shooting a whitetail buck and in my total concentration paid no attention to the fact that my eye was too close to the scope lens. After my shot, there was an instant flow from a cut that made things very unpleasant for me, but not nearly as unpleasant as the time I did the same thing on the

The mount is almost as important as the scope, for if it does not function properly, the finest scope in the world can fail to hold its zero during a deer hunt.

range, this time shearing a scope off of a .458 Winchester. I still have the rifle and the little broken bits of mounting screws can be seen sheared off in their respective holes. Fortunately, gun writers have extremely thick craniums and this saved me. I was only knocked out for a few moments and was able to butterfly stitch the gap myself.

Therefore, let it serve as a warning—do not shoot a rifle which has the scope's lens mounted too close to the eye. Also, I might add that the shooter should freely and quickly mount the rifle to his shoulder as a friend makes him "freeze" in place the moment the face touches the stock. Now, frozen in place, the distance between the eye and the scope is measured by that friend. The distance should coincide with the eye relief of the scope, yes, but also with safety precautions.

Mounts

We have superior mounts now on the market from many manufacturers. This was not always true. Some of the early mounts were a nightmare, ugly and not that easy to attach to the rifle either. Now we have arms drilled and tapped for our scope mounts, and the shooter can mount his own scope if he is careful about it. Personally, I like a good solid mount which puts the scope low on the rifle. Naturally, the scope must be high enough to allow for the proper function of the firearm, but I'm not much for mounts that are overly high. As for mounts

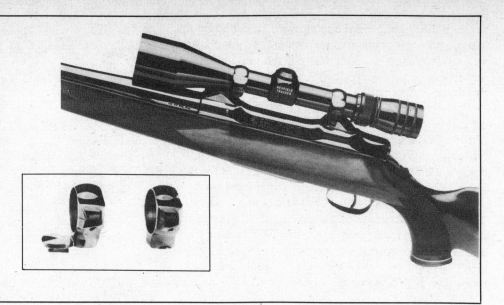

A scope mount must be engineered to fit the individual style of the firearm. This is evident in the Redfield high polish mount with extension rings, specially suited to the Colt Sauer rifle. The standard rear ring offers windage adjustment, while the front extension ring allows for low mounting of the scope.

meant to allow the use of iron sights along with the scope, there are some good ones. I used to have a Pachmayr on a rifle and loved it. The scope was still mounted low, and the mount looked nice. Plus, it did swing out of the way allowing the use of iron sights.

The Variables

My favorite scopes today for deer hunting are the variables. Even for brush hunting, a variable can be handy. Suppose a shooter has a 2x-7x on his rifle? He can hunt with it on 2x in the brush and yet if he sees a deer across a meadow or spots a buck in a distant opening, he can crank the scope power up and enjoy a better image for finer sighting. The real problem with variables is the fact that shooters tend to ignore the feature at times. I have hunted with several outdoorsmen who owned the variable scope and yet they set it at 3x or 4x and left it there. Not me. I have jumped a buck in a canyon and literally switched off of low power to a higher power for a better view of the buck before the animal appeared on the other side of the canyon.

Variables are fine scopes, and they are rugged. My rifles have carried variables for a long time and I have never had a problem with them. The shooter who chooses a variable for deer hunting is a wise fellow. But he's even wiser when he trains himself to take advantage of the variable feature. He is also smart to work the power change back and forth many times when it is new to "break it in." Some (not all) units can be stiff when new, and a hunter may think it impossible to quickly switch power in the field. The hunter should carry the scope on lower power in most deer hunting circumstances, switching to greater magnification when that extra optical power is useful.

When Not to Use a Scope Sight

I suspect that in terribly dense cover, such as I have roamed on the Kenai Peninsula in Alaska, when I lived in Alaska, I would perhaps prefer an iron-sighted rifle for the alders. When a bear print looks large enough to hold a bucket of spring water, then I just may wish to up and point the rifle rather than concern myself with any type of precision sight. Therefore, were I to hunt the little blacktail deer in such a spot, I might elect for a plain open iron sight with a very shallow V-notch. But we are, most surely, talking about a rare circumstance here. Most of the time, make mine a scope sight. Now, the only other instance I can think of where I might leave a scope off, while still enjoying the benefits of other optical aids, is on a muzzleloader of the longrifle class or plains rifle class. Here, we are dealing with a matter of propriety. I do not have a scope on my .54 longrifle, for example, nor my .40 Muskrat nor my .36 Hatfield. But you can bet a buck that I have scopes on my long-range arms and my brush guns of modern style.

Scopes for Handguns and Shotguns

We have not gone along discussing the handgun or the shotgun here in terms of telescopic sights because we can capsulize this right here and now. Both handgun and shotgun deserve scope sights when the target is venison, and there are absolutely superb sights available for both. Should the shooter wish to scope these arms, he may do so. Both the handgun and the shotgun do well with the telescopic sight and as I have said, there is no reason to deny either firearm such a boost in sighting efficiency.

Shotgun Sights

We will not dwell on shotgun sights for the simple reason that if we mount a scope on a shotgun there is no difference in the basic functioning of that scope sight just because we have switched from rifle to shotgun. If we buy a modern "deer shotgun," the sights may be adjustable open type, and again they will not differ from sight configuration and function of the same sight

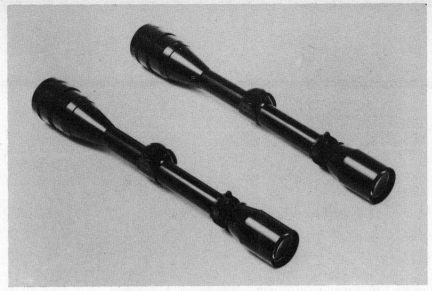

Some hunters, who frequent wide-open terrain, especially in the West, prefer to use a scope capable of high power. This Burris 4x-12x is such a scope (lower) as is the 5x-18x (upper). With the lower settings, a hunter can still pick up a deer in the field of view, while at the higher settings, precision shooting is possible.

The Ruger Redhawk Revolver is another example of a handgun suited for deer hunting. Here, it is shown with the integral scope mount.

The handgun hunter should consider a scope sight for his sidearm. There are excellent mounts and scopes available to him. Here, a Bushnell scope is mounted on a Ruger handgun using a Bushnell mount.

type used on the rifle. As for the common bead, found on the vast majority of shotguns, the bead is a reference point. Beads have been broken off of shotguns and birdshooters have not even known the bead was missing for a month because they were simply pointing the shotgun anyway, not aiming with it. On the other hand, there are shotgunners who do use the bead, even in wingshooting and the bead can be used for shooting the rifled slug. My good friend Dean Zollinger, the Idaho gunmaker, can put several slugs into a half-foot circle at 50 yards with his shotgun using the original bead as an aiming device.

Handgun Sights

Good adjustable sights are a must for a deer-taking handgun. They can be iron sights, all right, but they must offer adjustment for windage and elevation. The target sight style is excellent for deer hunting. One of the best iron sights for handgun hunting can be found on the S&W Model 29. There is a red aiming point embedded in the plane of the front sight on my personal model. And the rear sight is clearly outlined in permanent white. The sight picture is clean and obvious with this arrangement. Any handgun to be used for deer hunting, we can conclude, must have adjustable sights capable of producing an aiming picture of target quality.

Scopes are better yet. And the major handguns of deer hunting quality and caliber are easily fitted with telescopic sights today. There are many excellent mounts and long eye relief scopes on the market. In fact, in my estimation the addition of scope sights to powerful handguns makes the handgun absolutely acceptable for deer hunting. I am sure that many deer have been taken with sidearms which were not fitted with target quality sights and just as convinced that deer have been harvested with calibers which I would not recommend for day in and day out deer hunting. Let's not dwell on the past and let's not use the isolated incident to prove a point. Instead, I think, we should consider the modern handgun for deer hunting with its high-power cartridges and excellent sights.

chapter 15
Practical Sighting-In

THE SUCCESSFUL deer hunter has to have his firearm sighted in on the money if he wants to enjoy the consistency of bagging a buck after he finds that buck. Rifles have never, on the whole, come from the factory totally sighted in. In the past, when the iron sight was truly king, a great many hunters simply went afield with the rifle "out of the box," and they hunted with it that way. I do not think this is true today. I believe that the modern deer hunter is much more sophisticated and recognizes the fact that he surely has to sight his scoped rifle in before he goes afield.

I am saying rifle as a general statement and expedient. I certainly include the handgun in this discussion, and in fact I would not go out in quest of venison with any shotgun unless I had tried the ammo first, on the range, finding out exactly where my average point of impact was, be it with buckshot or a single projectile. However, we have two major things to contend with in sighting our arms properly. First, we darn well have to know how to manipulate the sight changes so that we can move the point of impact. Second, we must know exactly how to sight in a specific firearm in order to gain the most from its potential trajectory pattern.

As for the first, we are going to briefly discuss how to manipulate the sights, how to "move the sights," so to speak, in order to affect a change in the point of impact. As for the second, we will give some, hopefully, useful advice in terms of how to sight a firearm at close range so that it will be on at a longer range, taking advantage of the fact that in the normal parabola, the shape of a trajectory "curve," the projectile will cross the line of sight twice, once closer to the shooter and again farther away from the shooter.

The Fixed Sight

The term "fixed sight" suggests that one cannot move the sights at all. If this were true, the old-time shooter with his muzzleloader would have been in a heap of trouble, and so would his modern counterpart who has taken up the game of downwind shooting in order to get his buck. Of course fixed sights can be moved. We call them fixed because they do not have modern means of adjustment as opposed to adjustable sights. I am going to speak generally here because it would not be possible to anticipate all of the nuances of difference that there may be among various fixed sights. However, we generally move the rear sight within its dovetail slot laterally in order to achieve a change in the windage or "left-right" placement of the projectile on the target. If we want our rifle or pistol to change its point of impact either to the left or to the right, then we move the rear sight (usually) by *drifting* it.

We drift a fixed sight by carefully forcing it to move within its dovetail slot. I use a small piece of wooden dowel and a light hammer to move such sights. The dowel will not mar the metalwork. By placing the dowel up against the base of the sight and tapping lightly against the other end, the sight will generally move. Remember, when moving the rear sight, move that sight *in the direction you want the shot to go*. In other words, if you want the point of impact to change to the left, move the rear sight to the left. If you want the point of impact to change to the right, move the rear sight to the right. Remember, with a fixed sight we are not talking about elevation changes now. Only windage changes are affected by the drifting of the fixed rear sight.

Then how will the fixed sight change point of impact in the "up/down" mode? The front sight does this. All riflemakers should bear in mind that if they present a set of fixed sights to the shooter, they should offer a front sight *higher* than possibly necessary but *never lower* than will be possibly needed. After all, we can file the front sight down. But it is not easy to add metal to the front sight to make it grow taller. We move the front sight in the *opposite direction* from where we want the projectile to strike on the target. In short, if we want the next projectile to strike higher on the target, we trim away some of the front sight, making it shorter and moving it, as it were, downward. If we could raise the front sight, then the next round would hit lower on the target. When a new firearm with a fixed sight system arrives from the factory and the front sight is already too short, then we simply must buy a higher front sight to *replace* it.

The deer hunter must know that when he is dealing with iron sights he has to cut down the height of the front sight in order to achieve a *rise* in the point of impact. In short, lowering the front sight makes the gun shoot higher.

After we have our sights exactly where we want them to stay, then we use a punch and put a dimple or two in the soft metal of the sight base. Remember, the sight base is resting in the dovetail slot. So, by smacking the sight base with the punch, this pushes some of the metal of the base outward to make contact with the sides of the dovetail slot, thereby forcing the base more firmly within the slot and holding the sight in place.

Adjustable Iron Sights

The normal adjustable iron sight generally has all necessary adjustment within the rear sight. There are, of course, a number of ways in which we can affect a change in the rear sight, depending upon the type of adjustment mechanisms. In one popular rear sight, the actual notched blade moves up and down by loosening and then retightening a screw which holds the blade in place. So, we loosen the screw, move the sight either up or down and then we tighten the same screw in order to hold the sight in place after we have made the correct changes. This same sight has a screw which moves the rear sight either to the right or to the left. We do not loosen this screw. We merely turn it according to the directions and leave it alone after it has been moved the proper distance. Period.

Of course there is also the good old elevator bar which rests beneath the rear sight. As we push or pull the elevator bar forward or backward, the sight moves up or down. In some cases, this type of sight must be drifted, just as we previously drifted the fixed rear sight, in order to bring about changes in windage. As we have said, the rear sight is moved in the direction which we want the next hole to appear on the target. Sometimes it is necessary to gain a windage adjustment by moving the front sight in its dovetail slot, in which case we simply drift the front sight. We may have to punch the corners of the dovetail slot downward in order to lock the sight in place after we have moved it in the slot.

The aperture sight may have very fine micrometer adjustments. There is no difference here in terms of affecting a change in point of impact on the target. Read the instructions which come with the sight, and they will relate in which direction to turn the micrometer adjustment in order to have the "peep" move left or right, up or down. An aperture sight is rather easy to sight in. In fact, some have fine adjustments we can measure in ¼-minutes of angle with considerable accuracy.

The Scope Sight

The telescopic sight, be it on rifle, handgun or shotgun, is capable of superb precision when sighting in. About the only thing a shooter has to know is which way to turn the dials and how much movement is inherent in those "clicks" or continuous increments. Armed with these two facts, I think anyone capable of handling a firearm is capable of sighting it in correctly and with rather little trouble. At one point in time it was possible to buy a

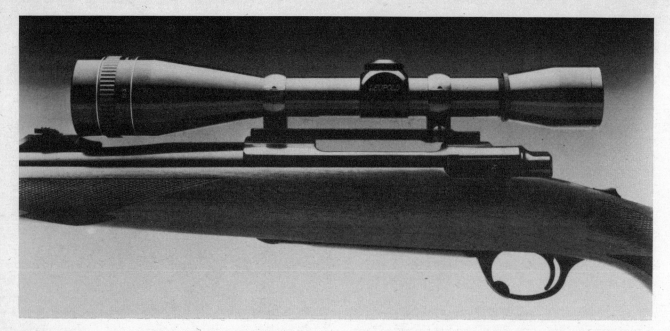

A telescope of this refined nature has superb reticle adjustments. In the early days of scope sights, those sights with the internal adjustments in a turret could not always be counted on for perfection, though they were quite good, really, right from the start. There may have been a little backlash, however, and when an adjustment was made that adjustment did not hold perfectly. Today, this is not the case. This Leupold was tested and the point of impact changed perfectly with the very fine adjustments made.

telescopic sight which had no adjustments in it at all, and I mean for deer rifles. Obviously, we still have a large number of varmint and target scopes today which do not have internal adjustments and which use the mount in order to sight in the firearm.

However, though in the past we felt the deer rifle would benefit greatly by having a scope sight which was free of internal adjustments, we were dead wrong. Today, the bulk of deer rifle telescopes, in fact scopes for handguns and shotguns as well, incorporate the internal adjustment, and they are absolutely reliable in every way. But there is one point which must be made. We must remind ourselves that a great many telescopic *mounts* still have some form of adjustment in them. Therefore, in discussing the sighting in of a deer rifle which bears a scope sight, let's talk mounts first.

The B-Square company offers mounts with both windage and elevation adjustments. Burris has mounts with windage adjustments. Conetrol has mounts with windage adjustments. Redfield has a mount with a windage adjustment. So does Leupold. Let's look at these last two. The shooter who is trying to sight his deer rifle in with a scope sight should be aware that the very *first* adjustment may be in the mount. Looking at a Leupold or Redfield one-piece base we find that we can turn the rear screws by loosening one, tightening the other, which in effect moves the telescopic sight itself to the left or to the right. I always make my initial windage adjustments with such a mount.

The mount adjustments having been made, further groups are fired on the target. Now we turn to the elevation and windage dials situated in the scope turrets. An actual minute-of-angle value may be stated beneath the turret cap. If not, this information will be found in the instruction manual which was provided with the scope. The adjustments are made to correspond with the specific values of adjustment for the particular scope. The movements of correction are then made until the point of impact on the target is centered. Here are some specifics.

First, I insist that one session is definitely not sufficient for sighting in a rifle, be it with scope sight or iron sight. The shooter should first make certain that the rifle's screws and bolts are tight. Of course, there are some bolts which are not to be tightened all the way. Certain fore-end bolts and tang screws are examples. But the bolts which are to be maintained in the fully tightened position must be in that position prior to the first sight-in session. Now, after the first sight-in session, the deer hunter puts his rifle away for a day or two. He then takes it to the range for a second time, first checking for the tightness of the bolts once again, and if a bolt seems to be working free, then Loctite can be placed on the threads of that bolt to help hold it secure.

We also insist upon at least two sight-in sessions because a rifle will often "settle down" after initial shooting. Pressures between wood and metal may optimize, for example. Also, toward the end of the initial sight-in period, the barrel was no doubt quite warm from extended shooting. However, the deer hunter will not be firing a hot barrel, but rather a cold one. Therefore, the first group fired during the second sighting-in session will reveal how the rifle is going to shoot from a cold barrel. In fact, we may suggest that the very first round fired during that second session is one which should be carefully noted,

This Ruger Old Army has been fitted with a telescopic sight, the Bushnell Phantom. It will provide for excellent sighting clarity and accuracy of adjustment. The handgun hunter may wish to check into a scope sight for his sidearm.

The scope sight adjustments are quite simple to make. As can be seen here, an arrow indicates the proper direction to move the dial in order to affect a change on the point of impact at the target. Here, we see the word "up" and the arrow indicating how to move the dial in order to move the point of impact upward.

for it may represent our best information as to where our deer rifle truly shoots with a cold barrel.

The goal for the second benchrest sight-in session is to have the group print precisely where we want it to, 3 inches high at 100 yards, for example, considering a trajectory pattern such as the .270 with a normally loaded 130-grain bullet. In fact, in theory at least, we are even more concerned over where that *first* shot goes on target from the cold barrel. Sometimes, one sight-in session will suffice. Usually, it will not, and the second session is therefore a necessary one. Sometimes there will be dramatic differences in point of impact from the first to the second sighting session. This fact is predicated upon wood/metal agreement in some cases. The barrel and action may in fact "settle" into the inletting of the wood. Of course, loose bolts and screws can also account for variations between first and second sightings. Bolts and screws may vibrate loose during the first benchrest session. Barrel heat, obviously, is a big factor here, too, as suggested above.

During both sessions, the first and the second, we shoot in groups, never one round at a time. Sure, that mythical "one shot group," being the first shot out of a cold barrel is absolutely vital to a deer hunter's peace of mind. He must know how his rifle behaves in terms of that first shot from a cold barrel, but sad to say, no shooter can hold so well that his one and only shot is right where it should be. The reason for a group is to average out error, especially human error. If a shooter fears that by shooting a group he will heat the barrel and "skew" his groups, then he can muster up some patience and wait between shots until the barrel has cooled down. But he must shoot in groups while sighting-in his deer rifle.

While a 5-shot group is good, some call for a larger number of shots with cooling between each shot so that we have a more realistic average to work with. Theoretically, the more "samples" the better the survey of the rifle's point of impact, unless the barrel is allowed to get so hot that succeeding rounds fly out of the actual group. So, our deer hunter may wish to fire 10-shot groups, allowing the barrel to cool off between shots. Doesn't this take time? I should say so. But is it worth it? You bet it is. The deer hunter who buys a good rifle and scope, or a good rifle with workable iron sights, can actually sight in once and then use pre-season trial sightings from then on. We have a few rifles in our possession which were sighted in 10 years ago. We take them out prior to each hunting season to target them, and it is very seldom that changes are necessary in the adjustment of the sights. Not all rifles, of course, are this stable.

Minutes-of-Angle

We hear a lot about minutes-of-angle, and when we know how to work with this term we can use the data provided with precision sights, such as the micrometer aperture sight and the telescopic sight. A minute-of-angle means an inch of value at 100 yards, 2 inches of value at 200 yards, 3 inches of value at 300 yards and so forth.

In order to sight in a deer rifle, be it a muzzleloader as in this case or a modern arm, the shooter must eliminate as many human factors as possible. Even when there is no proper benchrest setup, the shooter can improvise and at least remove some of the human errors inherent in shooting. Here, the author has rigged up a cardboard box with a slit cut in the top of it with tanned leather for padding. This aids in holding the rifle as still as possible for sighting-in purposes.

It can be thought of in terms of a line of departure in that the farther away from the muzzle of the gun the more value the minute-of-angle accrues. A rifle capable of shooting one minute-of-angle would produce an average group per some presubscribed number of rounds of an inch at 100 yards, and therefore 2 inches at 200 yards, 3 inches at 300 yards and so forth. Conversely, this same rifle would produce a ½-inch group at 50 yards and a ¼-inch group at 25 yards.

Of course, we are talking deer hunting and deer rifles now, and not science. The scientist would have a small fit over our playing with minute-of-angle as we have, and he would probably remind us that a minute-of-angle (MOA) is actually the arc that is subtended by that angle of one single minute. Or he might say that it is the arc subtended by 1/60th of one degree, and of course this holds up for any range we wish to talk about. To be more precise, that minute of angle would come to 1.047 inches at 100 yards and not really 1-inch. But we will just call it an inch.

Now let us say that our sight is capable of ¼-minute of angle adjustments. This would be a value of ¼-inch at 100 yards. So, if we turn the adjustment one increment we would change the point of impact ¼ of 1-inch in the direction prescribed by the indicator on the turret or the micrometer adjustment of the aperture sight. Let us look at a minute of angle adjustment on a scope sight, for example. If we see that we want to move the point of impact 3 inches to the left, we move our turret adjustor three increments in the direction (usually an arrow) showing left-hand change. Now, as we come closer to the muzzle, or in other words, as we move closer to the target, these values *increase*. If we want to change the point of

Proper sighting-in requires a good solid benchrest, such as the one shown here. The idea of the bench is to remove as many of the human error factors as possible. The shooter should first be comfortable. The rifle should be rested with forearm, not barrel, over the sandbags. Resting the barrel over the sandbags may change point of impact in some firearms. The right elbow, for a right-handed shooter, should be firmly planted on the bench, preferably with padding underneath the elbow to avoid scraping the elbow on the bench when shooting a powerful rifle which may skid the arm back. Note ear protection for the shooter.

The range which has good solid benches is best for sighting in. Note that these benches are quite solid and well-constructed. Also, the benches are covered so that the elements cannot hinder the shooting. (See the roof sections over each bench area.) The fore-end of the rifle rests on a block of wood which has been covered with carpet, and on top of the block of wood is a bag filled with river sand. Shot bags are used to hold the sand in this case.

impact by only 1-inch at 50 yards, we must move two increments for that minute of angle scope. At 25 yards we have to move it four increments to gain 1-inch of change in point of impact. So, if we start sighting in at 25 yards, which is very intelligent, then for every inch we want to move on the target, with a scope that has minute of angle adjustments, we have to move the scope four increments or "clicks." Now let us say we are 3 inches to the right at 25 yards. With the scope mentioned above, we must move 12 clicks or increments to the left in order to gain a change in point of impact of 3 inches.

Sighting In the Deer Hunting Firearm

In sighting in the deer hunting firearm, start close. Do not back off 100 yards or more and sight in from that point initially. It is a waste of good ammo to take a rifle out of the box, mount a scope, or for that matter shoot with iron sights, and do so from 100 yards or more. For two good reasons, I suggest starting much closer. In the first place, ammo will be saved. In the second place, initial sighting in at close range can produce the perfect parabola curve to gain the most from any given trajectory. As for the first item, it only makes sense—why shoot 10 rounds just to get "on paper?" I have sighted at 25 yards and found my rifle off by several inches even that close. When a rifle is off several inches at 25 yards, the angle of departure makes this a very large figure at 100 yards, sometimes a few feet. I have seen shooters fire a box of ammo before the first round actually printed on paper.

Sight in initially from 25 yards, and if that first shot does not cut paper, then get closer yet, 10 yards if need be. After the firearm is right on at close range, then the shooter can back off to 100 yards and test again. He can

then shoot at 200 yards and even 300 yards depending upon the caliber. Fine sighting in is accomplished at at least 100 yards for a high-power rifle. I move out to at least the 200-yard range for the .270 to .30-06 class and its cousins. When I have access to a bench which is 300 yards from the butts, I prefer to at least try my long-range rifle at that range so that I can see for myself what kind of groups I am capable of printing at that distance from a rest. I might even toss a few from the sitting position as well. Such shooting teaches a hunter a lot.

How to Zero-In

When we talk about zeroing-in, we mean exactly where to sight that firearm in relation to its trajectory. I want us to look at it this way: The sight is above the barrel of the rifle. In fact, the barrel of the rifle, when sighted for deer hunting ranges, is pointing upward somewhat. Our "line of sight" is a perfectly flat line in theory. So we have two lines to deal with. The line prescribed by the bullet we call a path of *trajectory,* and the line prescribed by our vision we call our *line of sight.* The line of sight, in theory, is perfectly flat from zero to the target. Let us take a distance of 200 yards. If we look through our scope sight, our vision is perfectly flat. Our line of sight is direct from our eye right to the center of that bull's-eye.

But the bullet cannot fly along that path! No way. It crosses the line of sight *twice.* It crosses our line of sight on the way up, and it crosses our line of sight on the way down. What goes up must come down, as they say, and the bullet is no exception. We point it up so that it can prescribe an arc from the muzzle to the target. This degree of upward trend is different dependent upon several

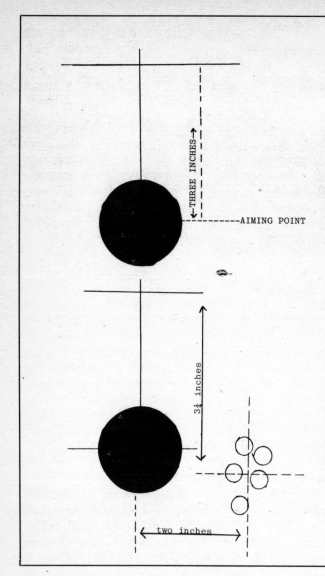

THREE INCHES

AIMING POINT

After careful boresighting or better yet, shooting at very close range, the target is moved out to 100 yards and the big game rifle is fired five times for a good 5-shot group. The shooter must now determine a central mode of the point of impact. This need not be a scientifically correct point, but without it the shooter would not know how much he must adjust his sights in order to achieve the point of impact he eventually wants. In this case, we are trying to sight a .270 Winchester to strike 3 inches above the line of sight at 100 yards. While the black bull's-eye is the aiming point, the cross 3 inches above the aiming point is actually our intended striking point where we want our group to center.

3¼ inches

two inches

This illustration shows the 5-shot group we have made on the target at 100 yards. The central mode of the point of impact has been determined and we now know how much we must move our sights in order to have our next fired group print at the cross above the bull's-eye. Remember, we are not interested in putting our group in the center of the bull's-eye with our .270 Winchester as the example deer rifle. We want to sight in 3 inches high at 100 yards to put our bullet back on at about 275 yards, giving us a very long-range of effectiveness for our trajectory pattern.

factors, including the flatness of trajectory. The distance we can sight-in for varies with the type of cartridge or load we are using.

Let us say we have a .35 Remington in hand, and we want to sight it in for 300 yards. Well, it won't work very well for us. Yes, we can sight a .35 Remington round for 300 yards if we want to, but how high above the line of sight will the bullet have to climb in order to strike dead on at 300 yards? If we use a 200-grain blunt-pointed bullet at 2100 fps, we will have to sight-in 17 inches high at 150 yards in order for the bullet to drop into the bull at 300 yards. Well, a deer's chest might only be 18 inches deep for a big deer at that. With such a huge dispersion away from the line of sight, we'd be in big trouble trying to determine just how far our deer was and exactly how low to hold at about the mid-range location.

Mid-Range Trajectory

We hear a lot about this one. The mid-range trajectory is how high the bullet will have to go above the line of sight in order to strike point of aim. In other words, if

our point of aim for the .35 Remington load above is 300 yards, then the mid-range trajectory is 17 inches at 150 yards. In short, we could sight in 17 inches high at 150 yards, and we would hit on target at 300 yards with the above load. Well, this is not satisfactory. There is too much guesswork involved. Let us try sighting-in for 200 yards with the 200-grain bullet at a muzzle velocity of 2100 fps. Even this is a bit risky. The mid-range trajectory is now 5.5 inches at 100 yards. I would prefer to get that down to about 4 inches. Besides, we picked our .35 Remington round for medium distance and short distance deer hunting. So let us sight-in for it.

Now we try sighting in for 150 yards. This is the ticket. We are only about 2½ inches above the point of aim at 100 yards. We are then on target at 150 yards, of course, since that is our "zero point," and we are only about 6 inches low at 200 yards. So we hold "dead" on a deer from 0 to 200 yards with our .35 Remington and its 200-grain bullet at 2100 fps.

The above has taught us a great deal in fact. We know that we need *not* sight in for 150 yards initially to be on at 150 yards with the above load. We know that we can sight in at 100 yards, but not dead on. No, we need to sight in about 2.5 inches *high* at 100 to be on at 150 yards with this load. This is very valuable information. We can even take it further. Just to get us started off, we can sight about 1½ inches high at 50 yards. So, if I got my hands on a .35 Remington, I would get her on the paper at 25 yards first. Then I would see where she printed at 50 yards, adjusting so that my point of impact was about 1½ inches higher than my point of aim. In short, if I had a scope on the rifle, I'd sight in so that when I held dead center on the bull's-eye, the average striking point for my 5-shot group was about 1½ inches high at 50 yards.

At 100 yards, I would make certain that my average point of impact for the group was about 2.5 inches high. Again, this means when the cross hair of the scope is dead on the bull's-eye, the group actually prints about 2.5 inches high or above that point of aim. Then I might back off to 200 yards just to see how the rifle does at this distance, and to further see that my point of impact is no more than about 6 inches low.

The basics that we have learned here apply to all firearms and certainly we deer hunters can take advantage of it. But, obviously, we can't sight in every firearm to print 2.5 inches high at 100 yards. We must sight in each of the various cartridges according to its own trajectory pattern. The good news is that with most of the high-power rounds from .30-30 on up to .300 magnums we can start at 25 yards and get the arm on the paper and then make our adjustments at 100, 200 or more yards.

The Old-Time Guns

Black Powder Rifles

Looking first at the older arms, since muzzleloaders are once again found in the deer fields, we learn that the ballshooters can gain about 2000 fps at the muzzle in firearms of top notch quality. Well, how do we sight in these old-time deer rifles, for we are talking black powder rifle here? We can start at about 13 yards in all case. Now, the larger projectiles will "carry up" better than the smaller ones. Therefore, we have a little bit of disparagement in the following, but only a little, and we will correct that now. From .45- through .58-caliber with a round ball at about 2000 fps muzzle velocity or conical at 1500 fps:

13 YARDS	50 YARDS	100 YARDS	125 YARDS
0	+1"	−1"	−6"

We can sight dead on at only 13 yards, and this is very handy. With either a round ball at 2000 fps MV or a conical at about 1500 fps MV, we end up with the pattern above, generally speaking. From zero out to 125 yards, the ball or conical will not depart from the line of sight by more than 6 inches, and from zero to 100 yards, the rifle is so close to dead on that we could nip a squirrel in the noggin without any hold-over or hold-under.

We said there would be a bit of disparagement with

a smaller caliber, and since a number of hunters use .40-caliber for deer, we need to look at that one. With a conical at the 1500 fps MV mark, we have the following:

25 YARDS	50 YARDS	75 YARDS
+½"	0" (on)	−2"

So we can sight in about ½-inch high at 25 yards with a conical in this caliber if we had a conical in .40-caliber, and we would be on the money at 50 yards and a couple inches low out to 75 yards. We could hunt deer with our .40 conical out to about 100 yards without undue problem, but after 75 yards such a conical would be starting on a downhill bent. Now, with the .40 ball (.395-inch) at 2000 fps MV, we have the following pattern:

25 YARDS	50 YARDS	75 YARDS
+½"	0"	−1"

Here we have a slightly flatter trajectory, but not for practical purposes. I have not delved into longer ranges with either the .40 conical or the .40 ball because I do not feel either one is real strong deer medicine. Enough said on that topic. The major point to remember for the standard deer calibers in black powder shooting is to begin the sighting-in process at about 13 yards. With the rifle right on at 13 yards, it is going to be very close to on for deer hunting ranges. But be sure to test at longer ranges for "tuning" the rifle to its finest degree.

Black Powder Handguns

Mainly, we should talk pistols here, as the black powder pistol in .54- and .58-caliber is a viable deer-taker. The object is to sight 1-inch high at 25 yards. I fully realize that we have the inherent error of group size when we talk about sighting-in 1-inch high. After all, at 25 yards with a black powder pistol a 1-inch group is about all most of us will manage. But if we shoot enough times, a pattern will show itself, and I think a careful shooter can judge what is 1-inch high at 25 yards by trying to average the center of his group.

Sighted 1-inch high at 25 yards, with the most powerful safe load the pistol can manage, the projectile will strike about on at 50 yards. At 75 yards, the missile will have dropped about 4 inches below the point of aim. So, from zero to 75+ yards, the hunter who has mastered the use of a strong black powder pistol will have the potential working for him to place the ball or conical right in the chest cavity. I think we can agree that the better .54 and .58 loads so sighted do make a deer gun out of the powerful black powder pistol.

Effective Ranges for the Deer Rifle

The .30-30 Class

For the .30-30 and all its brothers in the same clan, such as the .303 Savage, .32 Winchester Special, .30 Remington, and other similar rounds, we can gain sufficient potential range for the majority of deer hunting situations a person will run into, though the western hunter has probably gotten away from the .30-30 class round in the past few decades. Knowing the effective range of a round is very important, of course. As an example, if we keep the above black powder pistol load to within 75 yards or so, I think success will be forthcoming. The .30-30 clan can do some pretty good deer harvesting out to 200 yards of course, and there are some hunters who have gained even more potency from this round.

In talking about how to sight the .30-30, let's concentrate on the 170-grain bullet. We really do not gain all that much in going to the 150-grain bullet in this cartridge. The hottest handload I personally found for the .30-30 produced 2300 fps from a 20-inch barrel. Here is how

we would sight this one in: We would sight in to strike about an inch or so high at 50 yards to begin with. Then we'd move off to the 100-yard range and get the average group to print 2 inches high on the target. This will put us on target at 150 yards and about 5 inches low at 200 yards. We will be about 14 inches low at 250 yards, so I would call the .30-30, so sighted at 150 yards, good to maybe 200 or 225 yards for average conditions.

The .300 Savage Class

We include the .308 Winchester here and the .30-40 Krag, 7.65 Mauser, .303 British and all those rounds which can drive a 150-grain bullet at about 2800 fps. The shooter, after he has his rifle on the paper at 25 yards or less, if necessary, can put his next group about an inch high at 50 yards. Then he should try to group about 2.5 inches high at 100 yards. This will make the rifle maybe an inch high at 200 yards and about 7 inches low at 300 yards.

The .30-06 Class

Now we are getting into the flatter shooters. As anyone knows, if we read the new loading manuals, well-constructed rifles in .30-06 can drive a 150-grain bullet

The target used for sighting-in is very important. A shooter can only group his bullets into a target he can define. This target has been modified for sighting a black powder firearm with iron sights of the open variety. The white center allows for a much clearer aiming point.

(Below) Here is a very graphic illustration of the modified sighting target. At a distance of 75 yards, and with the obvious problems one encounters from taking a photo of this target, the center aiming point is still seen clearly and precisely. Under better conditions, with brighter sun, the bull stands out even more vividly.

in excess of 3000 fps. So we can put the bullet about 1-inch high at 50 yards, then try for 3 inches high at 100 yards. With the 150-grain bullet printing about 3 inches high at 100 yards, it will be between 3 and 4 inches high at 200 yards and on target between 265 and 275 yards, and approximately 3 inches low at 300 yards.

Important—there are a great number of modern rounds which fall into this .30-06 class, some shooting a little bit flatter and others not quite so flat. In fact, the owner of a modern big game rifle, such as the .280 Remington or .270 Winchester can also sight in with the 3-inch high at 100-yard setting. I have tested the 130-grain .270 Winchester load at 3100 fps and found that it will print about 4 inches high at 200, on at 275 and about 3 inches low at 300 yards. The reason for the "about" at 300 yards is the fact that as the group is opening up, it is more difficult to tell just how much of that spread belongs to drop and how much belongs to the actual opening of the group itself.

The .300 Magnums

The holder of the big .300 Magnums will find that the 150-grain bullet will crank out of the muzzle at about 3400 fps. A shooter can sight this hot number in just the way he sights his .270 with the 130-grain bullet or the .30-06 with the 150-grain bullet, the only difference being that when he sights in to strike the bull about 3 inches high at 100 yards, he's going to find that the bullet is less than 4 inches high at 200 yards and will be just about smack on again at 300 yards. In fact, all the way out to 400 yards, these big boys will only be about 9 inches low. We can include in this class all of the magnum .30s and actually the big 7mms as well, for these can drive the 139-140-grain class bullet over 3300 fps in most cases.

The Individual Rifle

All of the above is by way of rules of thumb. After all, I would have no way of knowing the exact muzzle velocity of a shooter's firearm, or the exact shape of the projectile used, or the height of the sights above the center of the bore, or several other factors which relate to sighting-in and trajectory control. But I hope the deer hunter recognizes a fact here, and that fact is that we don't want to castrate even the slower .30-30 rounds by always sighting-in for 100 yards just because there is generally a 100-yard range handy.

I can't relate how many times I have seen shooters at the range, usually a week or less before deer season, sighting in a new rifle or a newly scoped rifle, and trying to print 'em all dead on at 100 yards, even with 7mm Magnums and .270s and big .30-caliber belted cartridges. This is too bad. It is an automatic destruction of the true potential of the round. If a shooter sights his slug-shooting shotgun for about 75 to maybe 100 yards, this is all right, as the potential for more range is not really there. But to have a .280 Remington firing a 125-grain bullet into the center of the bull at 100 yards is to cut off its ability at the starting gate.

Effective Ranges for the Hunting Handgun

All in all, the handgun shooter has much less range potential than the rifle shooter when one considers the big 7mm Magnum and its .300 Magnum brothers, but some of the newer rounds for the strong handguns of the day deserve care in trajectory management. It would be unfair to pass these over entirely, as we have the 12-gauge (and other shotgun slugs) by simply saying "sight-in for 75 to 100 yards." We will briefly look at a few examples:

.30 Herrett

We can sight the .30 Herrett, using the 150-grain pointed bullet at 2000 fps MV, at about 1-inch high at 50 yards, which will put this bullet back on at about 100 yards. Out to 150 yards, the bullet will only drop about 4 inches. The hunter will have to decide for himself how far he wishes to shoot with a handgun based upon his own ability and retained energy at longer ranges, but as far as trajectory goes, the .30 Herrett can be counted on out to 200 yards, where the drop will be around 9 inches.

.357 Herrett

The .357 Herrett can be sighted to strike about 1.5 inches high at 50 yards with the 158-grain bullet at 2000 fps MV. This will put the bullet on at 100 yards, or nearly so, and about 6 inches low at 150 yards.

.44 Magnum

With a 240-grain bullet at about 1750 fps, the .44 Mag can be sighted to strike about 2 inches high at 50 yards and it will cut the bull again at 100 yards, being about 8 inches low at 150 yards.

Shoot Your Own Firearm

There is only one way for the serious deer hunter to really know what is going on with *his* deer rifle, handgun or shotgun and that is for him to take his favorite loads to the range and do his own shooting. Firearms vary. There are many little differences in loads and in bullets. The only way to know for certain what a personal firearm is doing is to go out and shoot it. I think what we have said above is worthwhile because it does give the shooter a strong starting point, a place to begin. He can use this data to good advantage. But the serious hunter is going to fire his own personal shooting iron to determine what it is doing. We only recommend that he begin his shooting at close range and work out to longer ranges, and if there is a 200-yard bench and a 300-yard bench, all the better. Try some loads out there, too, to determine exactly what is going on. There is much to learn in such shooting, and I am afraid that one very worthwhile piece of information might be a warning that some rifles, some handguns too, are not meant for long-range work and the long-range target can show this very vividly.

Bore-Sighting

Before retiring this chapter, I think I had best answer a question which is bound to come up. The question might go like this: "But don't you think that bore-sighting would save a lot of trouble?" I guess I do. But I'm not a great fan of bore-sighting. A couple times in my life I have, indeed, bore-sighted firearms to find that they were right on the money with the first round out of the barrel, but most of the time this will not be true.

Bore-sighting is just that. All bore-sighting accomplishes is one thing—we can rest assured that the barrel is "looking" about in the same direction as the sights. With an optical collimator, if a shooter should have one, there is certainly nothing wrong with bore sighting by inserting the correct spud per caliber and jockeying the scope crosswire or iron sight until both are aligned with each other. In fact, there is nothing wrong with removing the bolt (where possible) and putting the firearm in some holder of sorts and looking through the barrel at the target while manipulating the sights so that the view through the barrel and the aiming point of the sight coincide.

The only thing I don't care for is the fact that some shooters might take this as sighting in, and it is not sighting in. It is simply an act performed to get the first round on the paper, and I have done this countless times by shooting at close range first. If, for some reason, the sights are so far off that 25 yards won't work, then the shooter can move to 10 yards and adjust his sights there just to get the firearm to print somewhere on the paper first and then into the center of the bull or whatever the trajectory pattern calls for. This, I think, is just about as quick and easy as bore sighting.

Two good friends came by recently with a .270 in tow. They had fired the box of 130-grain bullets that they had bought for the new rifle, and they did not have a single hole on the target to show for it. It was a simple matter of the scope being cocked off at an angle because the adjustment in the base had not been looked into. First, we loaded up some .270 rounds with a load they liked. Second, we centered the scope by moving the two adjustment screws on the mount so that they took up about even threads on either side of the scope's rings. Third, we went to the range and fired a group at 25 yards. The rifle was barely on the paper, but it was on the paper with the group far to the left.

We then unscrewed the right-hand bolt on the mount so that the scope would move to the right, for moving the back of the scope has the same effect as moving the rear sight on an iron sighted firearm—the bullet will go in the direction of motion. Then, we adjusted the scope settings, remembering to quadruple the values at only 25 yards.

In 20 rounds we had a pretty good printing of 130 bullets striking about 3 inches high at 100 yards. The shooters returned to the range later and made sure that all bolts and screws were tight and they again printed 3 inches high at 100 yards. They moved to 200 yards and were about 4 inches high and they even tried some 300-yard shooting. They went away with confidence, knowing their rifle was sighted in and knowing where the bullets went at what range.

That is all we are asking for. We simply want to know where the bullets are striking at the various ranges. The firearm is sighted in so that we can hit the mark, of course, but also for reasons of gaining the most from each specific trajectory potential inherent in a round. This does not mean that we are interested in shooting at the longest possible range. A close shot is always better than a long shot. But it does mean that we want to know our firearm and its trajectory, and the only way to gain confidence in any deer hunting tool, even a longbow in a way, is to sight it in.

A Few Tips

The deer hunter should select the day he sights in very carefully. A bright day with clouds is often a good choice for the hunter whose firearm bears iron sight, for direct sunlight on the sights can sometimes cause a degree of sight picture aberration. It is also important to note how the light strikes a target. Even when using a scope sight, the target should be well-lighted when possible. I am aware that one cannot change the direction of the shooting range to correspond with changes in light patterns. However, a shooter can select a time of day when the light is best. On one range nearby I have found that in the morning it is almost impossible to sight a firearm with good results. The range is set up so that the sun strikes the shooter in the face during most of the times of the year when we are normally out sighting in guns. However, later in the day, the sun's position on the target improves considerably.

Obviously, the shooter wants to choose a calm day. Wind wreaks havoc upon the drift of bullets, as every shooter knows.

A benchrest is called for of course. The idea is to eliminate all of the human factors possible, and a solid bench with appropriate firearm management goes a long way in attaining this goal. Under the forearm, and not the barrel, a rest is placed, preferably of the sandbag type, but rolled up blankets will do. The rest is adjusted so that the sights are on the same plane as the target. For a right-handed shooter, a pad should be placed underneath the right elbow. With firearms of even modest recoil, the right elbow can skid over the bench, which is painful. Naturally, a left-handed shooter protects his left elbow. Also, the elbow should be firmly controlled, never held aloft, but always solidly rested. We are, remember, trying to eliminate as many human factors as possible. With the rifle (we are speaking of rifles though the slug shooting shotgun can be treated in the same manner) so rested, the shooter can then concentrate on squeezing the trigger and maintaining the sight picture. Since we have not rested the barrel directly on anything, it is free to "whip" in its normal manner. Had we rested the barrel on a firm object, the gun might shoot away from that object.

With feet planted firmly, both elbows rested, the firearm firmly set up on the bench, the sight picture can be maintained and the trigger squeeze concentrated on. It is wise to use a bull's-eye of appropriate size, too. I like to use the smallest bull which I can clearly define, be the sights glass or iron. If using a variable scope, then I'll sight in on the highest power with a small bull's-eye. With an 8x or 9x scope, the shooter can see a ½-inch dot at 100 yards, for example. However, each shooter can determine for himself what he wishes to use for an aiming point size, and there are a number of sight-in targets available which already have good bull's-eye dimensions.

Of course we sight in with the bullet and load we intend to use for our deer hunting. It would hardly make sense to sight in with a 110-grain bullet handloaded to 3500 fps in our .30-06, later turning to a 150-grain bullet for the actual deer hunt. However, with a flat-shooter such as the .30-06, and the .30-06 is a flat-shooter on the face of it, the variation would not be nearly as great as one might think. If we sighted the .30-06 with the 110-grain pointed bullet at 3500 fps MV to hit dead on at 300 yards, the bullet would rise about 3 inches high at 100 yards and 4 inches high at 200 in order to strike dead on at 300. If we used the 150-grain bullet at 3000 fps MV sighted for 300 yards, that bullet would rise about 4 inches at 100 yards and 5 inches at 200 yards in order to strike dead on at 300.

Cartridges with more rainbow in the trajectory would have somewhat greater variation. However, for modern deer rounds, even those of the .30-30 class, we are only speaking of a few inches variation over normal hunting ranges if we sight in for the lighter bullet and then go a heavier one or *vice versa*. All the same, in the interest of perfection, it is wise to sight in with the bullet and load intended for the deer hunt. Remember, trajectory alone is not the only variation which can occur when loads are switched! And this is the important point here. I have seen rifles which moved a point of impact several inches at 200 yards simply by changing bullet weights. In fact, the exact load with the same bullet weight can change point of impact when a different *style* bullet is used, such as Spitzer to round nose.

If we want to nitpick the issue, we should actually sight in for the elevation at which we are going to hunt. At sea level, the atmospheric pressure will be 750mm of mercury. But I have hunted deer at 8,000 feet above sea level where the atmospheric pressure may have dropped to about 600mm of mercury. Also, we should observe, to a degree, temperature changes along with our altitude factors. However, the differences are not going to be astounding, just barely evident. A 150-grain bullet from an '06 at 3000 fps might shoot, at 8,000 ft., perhaps a third of an inch *higher* at 200 yards than it did at sea level, where it was right on at 200 yards. As for temperature, if we sighted in on a hot summer day, we may find that on a much cooler late winter day our rifle is shooting a bit lower.

The cure? The cure is simple and does not call for drastic measures. When the hunter reaches his destination, if that destination takes him to a much different altitude, he should fire a few rounds from his rifle. Also, it makes sense to insure that the sights were not knocked out of whack on the journey. As for the temperature, a rifle sighted in the heat of summer can be checked again in cooler conditions just to see where point of impact registers. We can get quite carried away with bullet path if we want to. After all, many forces act upon the projectile in flight.

Basically, the important point is to sight in with care. If a handgunner uses the bench along with a rest, such as the Sugar Creek or similar model, with arms planted and as many bodily motions as possible held in check, sighting in usually goes well and pays off with a firearm that is right on the money. If a long trek is in the offing, then a deer hunter may want to check his rifle when he arrives in the general area of the hunt. There is usually some form of range available in almost any hunting area.

We will be better hunters if we sight our firearms with care. After all, we have to hunt where the deer are and we have to find a deer after we get there, but if we can't strike the target after we see it, then the first two conditions do not provide much meat in the larder. The final proof of the pudding is in the shooting, and this is why we have spent a good deal of time on the subject of sighting in.

chapter 16
Triggers for Deer Guns

THE DEER GUN fits the hunter perfectly. He can handle it with speed and polish. Mechanical function is just fine. The sights are excellent and the gun is sighted in just right. Our hunter has it made. Or has he? There is another factor which can throw this rosy picture into the shade. No matter how good the rifle or handgun is, even the shotgun for that matter, if the trigger pull is all wrong, our hunter may be handicapped. I know this is true because I have owned firearms, mainly rifles, a couple handguns, too, which were good in all respects except the trigger pull. In each case the firearm's accuracy potential was unattainable just because of that bad trigger pull.

Even with the sights all lined up, lack of control on that trigger can spell a miss. It is my opinion that every serious deer hunter should know what his firearm's trigger pull is, and he should also know what constitutes a bad pull and a good one. In the main, we think of a "light" pull as just right. This is all right. It's not a false notion. But it is not enough. A trigger pull should be several things, and one of them is modest in the effort it takes to disengage the sear. But lightness of pull is but one of many factors. The deer hunter who wants his game-getting firearm tuned just right must understand that a major criterion in tuning that firearm is that of trigger pull.

Safety

There is no such thing as a good trigger that is unsafe. A good trigger is always a safe trigger. But how can it be that we have a light trigger and a safe trigger pull at the same time? It is not a problem when the initial trigger design is correct. There are several trigger designs which incorporate both desirable criteria, safety and light pull. While it is the obligation of the manufacturer first and the professional gunsmith second to understand trigger design and safety, there is nothing wrong with the deer hunter having an idea on the subject, too. All he needs to know here is that if his rifle is cocked he should be able to take a soft-headed mallet and tap around the trigger housing area *without* the firearm "going off."

The mechanical contact between trigger and sear is not one of precariousness. The idea is not to have the contact so tenuous that a gentle breeze will knock the thing off. Also, and this is very important, a hunter must never consider his firearm trigger safe just because it won't "jar off" when the gun is on safety. The firearm should never "go off" from any amount of contact with the buttplate or side even if the piece is off-safety, though surely we are never going to pack a firearm into the field off-safety. The point is, a safe trigger is one which has a good mechanical design. When the trigger is activated by squeezing, it then releases. But never until it is deliberately pulled.

Pounds Pull

How light should a deer rifle's trigger be? That question is about the same as asking, "What size hat should a deer hunter wear?" Obviously, it all depends. A deer hunter

Triggers can be replaced in many cases. Here is a modern and up-to-date trigger on a Mauser 98 rifle. The original military trigger was discarded and the custom trigger installed by a gunsmith.

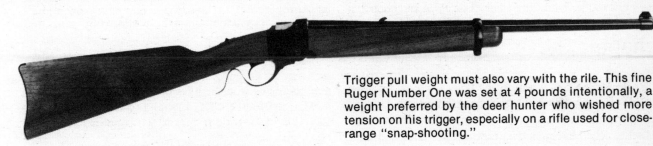

Trigger pull weight must also vary with the rile. This fine Ruger Number One was set at 4 pounds intentionally, a weight preferred by the deer hunter who wished more tension on his trigger, especially on a rifle used for close-range "snap-shooting."

wears the size hat that fits him and his trigger pull weight is gauged to fit the design of the trigger and also, very importantly, the desires of the individual hunter. Some hunters can manage with heavier trigger pulls and some cannot. I cannot. A perfect example of this came to my attention this past deer season. A few days before the hunt a father and son hunting team came by with a new rifle.

They were having trouble sighting the rifle in, mainly because they had started the operation at 100 yards instead of 25 yards or less, but they asked for help. We headed for the range, and I shot the rifle, a good one, at only 25 yards. I thought I was doing a good job of squeezing the trigger and my sight picture looked fine, but the groups, even at 25 yards, were nothing to brag about, not from a modern bolt-action rifle with a variable-powered telescopic sight. Actually, it took me a few moments to figure out what was wrong. But when I did figure it out, I actually managed to control my squeeze even more and the groups tightened up.

For me, the trigger pull on this rifle was an abomination, not from creep or backlash or any other problem real or imagined. It was simply too blasted hard to pull the trigger, and what made it much worse for me is that as a muzzleloader shooter my deer rifles all had multiple lever triggers and my favorite model was set for 7 ounces, that is *ounces,* not pounds. When we got home I pulled out my trigger pull gauge and found that it took 6 pounds

of pull to release that trigger. In fact, on my trigger pull gauge the final figure is 6 pounds, and the rifle did not actually release until the marker on the gauge was *beyond* the 6-pound figure.

I think if I practiced I could learn to manage that trigger pull because there is nothing wrong, inherently, with a 6-pound release. The big problem with that trigger was me. I was spoiled. After shooting multiple lever triggers with 7 or 8 ounces of pull, 6 pounds was just too much to deal with. But I was in for a surprise. After we had that new rifle "on the paper" at 100 yards and sighted so that it was grouping about 3 inches high on the average, we turned it over to its owner, the son of my friend, and he made a fairly decent 5-shot group with it.

In fact, he liked the 6-pound trigger pull. When he tried my bolt-action rifle with a 2-pound pull, he said it made him uncomfortable to have so "little control," as he put it, over the firing of the rifle. I had never thought of a light trigger pull as a lack of control, but I certainly learned something that day. I learned that trigger pull is an individual matter, up to a point. I don't think I will ever be so open-minded that a 10-pound trigger pull will delight me.

At any rate, when I suggested that the young hunter take his rifle to a gunsmith and have the trigger pull relaxed to maybe 4 pounds, he was very unhappy with the suggestion. After a good long hunting season, I had to agree that he was right. The proof of the pudding is still in the shooting, and our hunter did not miss once

A trigger pull gauge will tell the shooter how many pounds pull it takes to make his deer rifle, shotgun or handgun "go off." Hunters do not necessarily want the very lightest possible trigger pull. The pull must be clean and crisp, but most of all manageable by the individual shooter. However, a very heavy trigger pull can do nothing to increase the hunter's chance of placing a shot. If a trigger pull feels very heavy to a shooter, he should have the pull gauged as shown here. If it is heavy, and some have been found to be 9 or 10 pounds, a gunsmith should be consulted.

that year. The first hunt out he bagged a doe antelope on his second antelope tag, and then he dropped a 15-inch antelope buck—two shots, two game animals in the bag. He then filled his buck deer tag with one shot and later his doe deer tag with one shot. To boot, his father borrowed the new rifle and did not miss a shot with it that season.

So much for a bad trigger pull, right? But I still draw a line for myself, and I still have to suggest that a shooter consider trigger pull weight a big factor in tuning his rifle. At the same time, I am forced to agree that trigger pull is a personal matter. A harder pull can be lived with because a shooter can simply teach himself how to control that pull. If I were pinned down to suggest a trigger pull weight for deer rifles, I think I would say whatever pull is totally safe in that rifle, hoping that the pull could be lightened down to between 3 and 4 pounds. As for the handgun, I have had good luck with a trigger pull of 4 pounds. My own custom 7mm Magnum built by Frank Wells on a pre-64 M70 action has a trigger pull of 2 pounds and my .44 S&W M29 has a trigger pull of 3.75 pounds. My custom .54 Dennis Mulford longrifle, with its multiple lever trigger, "lets go" at 7 ounces with the hair trigger set.

These latter figures are not recommendations for anyone else. I point them out because I have trained myself to deal in lighter trigger pulls, but only as long as they are safe triggers. The individual hunter owes it to himself to try various trigger pull weights in order to determine what is comfortable for him. He can even click a few off at the local gunshop if the owner has a safety case he can use to protect the firearm during the "dry fire" period. By trying various trigger pull weights, the hunter may be able to decide what he likes best. The only suggestion I make is to observe safety first and foremost. There is no such thing as a good trigger which is not a safe trigger.

Trigger Pull Gauges

A good trigger pull gauge can be purchased over the counter for a small sum of money. I think it is a good addition to the shooter's gear. Because of my line of work, I own a rather sophisticated trigger pull gauge and a somewhat costly one at that. But I was fairly surprised to learn that the over-the-counter model came up with the same pull figures as my more costly gauge.

The only reason I suggest a gauge for the hunter who wants his rifle tuned-in just so is the fact that it is nice to know what release that firearm has. Though I think of the rifle only when I consider the more delicate trigger pulls, I have absolutely no luck with tough trigger pulls on handguns either. In fact, I tried shooting an older style pistol which had a 12-pound pull, and it was futile for me. At any rate, the deer rifle deserves having a reasonable (always safe) trigger pull, and a trigger pull gauge can show the reader what he is getting in actual terms of pounds release.

Triggers and Trigger Pull Adjustments

Let us say that a hunter has a rifle which has a 7-pound trigger pull. He has tried other rifles with lighter trigger pulls, and he does better with them than he does with his own firearm. What should he do? In my opinion, unless he's trained to work on triggers, he's best off having a professional do the job. There are triggers which have very obvious adjustments and if the instruction manual which came with the firearm allows for it, then

A good modern trigger housing is shown here, this one on a Weatherby Mark V bolt-action rifle. Such a trigger is adjustable in several different modes. However, most trigger adjustments are best left to expert gunsmiths.

the individual shooter can make some form of adjustment in trigger pull himself. My only caution here is to follow the manual and do only what the manual allows. But when it comes to dismantling the firearm and actually taking tools to the trigger system, I think a professional gunsmith is the right man for the job.

Creep

We used to call it "military creep" because the Army rifles we used all had this particular condition. Creep in a trigger is not for me, but some shooters get by with it quite nicely, and as a matter of fact, I have a handgun which has creep in the trigger and I manage to shoot it as well as I shoot my other handguns. I don't want to give the impression that all creep is anathema to shooting and shooters. It isn't. But in general, for a hunting firearm trigger I don't like to have to take up "slack" before the actual squeezing of the trigger begins.

I think this is the best way to think of creep, as slack in the trigger which must be taken up before the actual squeezing of the trigger can begin. I own no deer hunting rifles which have creep in the trigger. My son used to have one. The rifle doesn't have creep now because a gunsmith replaced that military type trigger with a modern sporting single stage trigger.

Trigger Shoes

Should a deer rifle wear a trigger shoe? Again, we are dealing with an individual matter here. I know a number of hunters whose rifles wear a trigger shoe, and they would have it no other way. Again, it is a matter of trying a firearm with a shoe and without one. Then the hunter should choose the style he likes best. The idea of the trigger shoe is to broaden the surface of the trigger itself so that more contact is made by the trigger finger.

Double Triggers

Mainly, the hunter will encounter the double trigger in the fine oldstyle longrifles (and some handguns). However, there are quite a number of double triggers available in modern arms as well. For our purposes only, we are going to discuss the double triggers which are found on the black powder arms, because they are more prominent here. In fact, some of the best selling muzzleloaders of the day have the two-trigger setup. We are further going to deal in a couple terms which are not necessarily out of the old book of shooting. We will use "multiple lever" trigger and "double set" trigger as our two main terms.

The multiple lever trigger suggests that the trigger can be pulled in one of two modes. First, the front trigger can be pulled back and the sear will be released. The gun will fire. Second, the rear trigger can be set, putting into action the mechanical advantage of a multiple lever system, and then the firearm is set off by activating the front trigger once again. Now, why have such a system? Well, the advantage of having the firearm "go off" with the front trigger in the unset mode is simply to allow a fast shot. I have never found it necessary to use this option, but it is there for the shooter who might want to use it. The trigger pull weight will be much higher in the unset position.

The double set (sometimes spelled "sett") trigger will not go off when the front trigger is pulled unless the rear trigger has been activated to set that front trigger. I find no disadvantage in this system, but others might. Have you ever heard of a "hair trigger?" Well, this term is often used to mean any trigger which goes off with very little pressure on it. But I suggest that the old-time double trigger was the real hair trigger, and in fact I have seen nomenclature which termed the rear trigger the set trigger and the front one the *hair* trigger.

At any rate, the whole idea of multiple lever or set triggers is to gain a mechanical advantage which allows for a very light trigger release, while at the same time, and this is important, having a very safe trigger system. I have never been able to cause one of my high-grade multiple lever triggers to go off by pounding the sides of the firearm nor by banging the buttplate on the floor. And we are talking about some triggers which let off in the 6- to 7-*ounce* range. At the same time, I must sound

The set screw should be turned inward a bit to give a nice light release but I always back the screw out a few turns even though I have not reached that point where the release is as light as it can go.

After all, with a good and proper multiple lever design, we can safely reach ½-pound pull on most topnotch systems. Who needs any better? Not me. Or not much better at least. My lightest pull is 6 ounces and 7 ounces is just fine, and 8 ounces is as fine. No sense in abusing a good thing. Use the set screw as a safety factor as well as a controlling factor for trigger pull weight.

Single Set Triggers

The single set trigger is just that—it is only one trigger; however, it can be set. A prime example is the single set trigger on the Browning Mountain Rifle. However, I have seen single set triggers on modern arms as well. The single set trigger has the ability to gain a mechanical advantage and when it is set, it offers a light trigger pull, much like the double trigger arrangements. To set the single set trigger, one merely pushes forward on it. Then the trigger is set and a light pull is achieved. The single set is a nice trigger. I do not find it handier than the double trigger, but that is a personal matter.

The Jonathan Browning Mountain Rifle has a single-set trigger. While it is a set trigger, one can readily see there is only one trigger and not two. The trigger is pushed forward to set it, and in the set position the release is much lighter than in the non-set position.

a warning here—you get used to a truly light trigger pull. You don't simply grab up such a system and have at it.

Whenever I show someone my light pull arms, I always have them dry fire the gun many times before ever trying to shoot it with a charge. I use a nipple protector on the caplocks so that the shooter may fire at will all he wants without having either the cone of the nipple or the hammer nose cup banged up. No hunter should ever use a truly light pull trigger without practice! This is imperative. The hunter must practice with such a trigger if he is to master it. But once he has mastered such a trigger, he has a strong force on his side. Safety is again our main concern.

The Set Screw

On the double trigger system there will usually be a set screw positioned most often between the two triggers right on the plate. This screw increases the mechanical advantage of the system and allows for the "hair trigger" to release at a different amount of pull. As the trigger set screw is turned inward, as it were, clockwise in other words, the pull becomes lighter and lighter. A point can be reached in many triggers where the hair is so light that the trigger will not actually set. Never allow this condition to exist! The multiple lever trigger should not be abused.

Custom Triggers

Most firearms come from the factory with good trigger systems. Sometimes, these triggers can be fine-tuned by an expert. I do not wish to sound like a broken record, but I must once again state that whenever any modifications are made, even as small a modification as tuning the trigger without actual change in any of the parts, safety is the number one criterion to observe. So, it is quite possible in most cases to have a trigger adjusted for a nice letoff. However, there is another option that the serious deer hunter may wish to consider.

He may wish to exchange his standard trigger for a custom trigger. There are several good companies dealing in special triggers, triggers designed to fit most of the rifles encountered today. One such company is Canjar. At last glance, Canjar had at least three choices for the shooter. There was the Improved Trigger, the Set Trigger and the Deluxe. The newcomer may consider the cost of such a trigger on the high side. But they are a one-time purchase and can improve the overall efficiency of a rifle.

Another excellent trigger company is the Timney Manufacturing outfit. They offer some fine triggers as replacement models. They have several different models, such as the Super Lightweight, the Model H for some of the

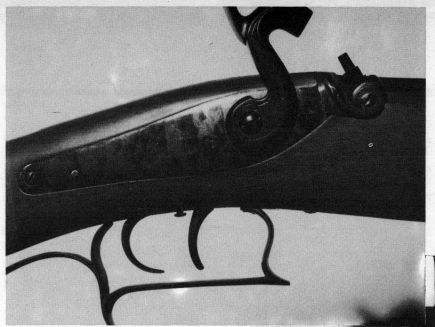

The multiple lever trigger is popular not only on the replicas of the old-style rifles, but certain modern arms also employ this system. Here, shown on an Armsport Tryon Trailblazer rifle, is a multiple lever trigger or "double trigger." The rear trigger is the set; it sets the front or "hair" trigger so that the latter releases with very little effort.

The grooved trigger, as shown here on a Weatherby Mark V rifle, is desired by many hunters. Obviously, the idea of a grooved trigger is non-slippage of the trigger finger.

Mauser type rifles, the Model SP for a large number of rifles, too. And they are modestly priced. The Dayton Traister Company offers custom triggers, at a modest price, and these triggers bear a fine reputation for quality.

There is also a replacement especially for the Mauser rifle. This one comes from the Sherwood Company, and it is priced very reasonably. It converts the Mauser trigger to fully adjustable letoff with a replacement trigger assembly. Therefore, the shooter has a range of selection and he can check with his local gunsmith to determine what might be best for his own specific rifle if he does want to look into a replacement trigger.

So much for deer gun triggers. While it may seem an awfully small point of consideration, any hunter who has a rifle with an unmanageable trigger should simply try a rifle with a truly fine trigger, and he will see what a difference this one consideration can make to straight shooting. The same goes for the handgun fan. While handguns generally have "stiffer" trigger pull weights than do rifles, there is also an important factor here in having the trigger pull a safe, but manageable setting. Even the shotgun should be fitted with good triggers. Most of them are. I can live with a fairly stiff trigger pull on a shotgun, since precision shooting is not generally the goal of the scattergun. But I can't live with creep and a pull so tough that it requires two men and a boy to get the gun to go off. My own pumpgun in 12-gauge has a 5.5-pound trigger pull.

The Goal

I think the goal for a good trigger should be crispness. A crisp trigger has no perceptible creep in it. Some people like to describe a crisp trigger as a small glass rod snapping. The backlash should be minimal, too. In other words, the travel of the trigger, even forward, is limited. The pull is light, but never dangerous. Finally, the trigger pull is right for the shooter and his style of shooting. While I may enjoy and find useful a fairly light pull, other deer hunters may find more confidence in having to pull a bit harder on their triggers. It can be an individual matter. But one thing is sure—no matter if the hunter prefers a light or medium pull, he should be *aware* of his trigger. He should test it by trying other triggers. If he finds that he has a trigger which is not really that satisfactory, he can then seek the advice and aid of a competent professional gunsmith who will either adjust the existing trigger on that deer gun or perhaps exchange that trigger for one which is more refined.

chapter 17
Practice for Deer Hunters

LET'S ASSUME that the deer hunter has the basics down pat. He knows where the deer are, and he knows how to find them. He also has a fine deer gun, be it a handgun, shotgun or the more prominent rifle, and he has his firearm sighted in correctly to gain the most from the cartridge's potential trajectory. There is one thing that this deer hunter can do to improve his already good odds of bringing home the venison. And that is to practice. Mainly, I mean shooting practice, but let's talk about another kind of practice for a moment first.

The other kind of practice is to actually get out into the field on a mock deer hunt. I like to combine this type of practice with my scouting efforts. But it is truly a good and sound method of getting to be a better hunter. Simply, all of the deer hunting tactics are employed with one big exception—no shooting allowed, for we are talking pre-season here. Of course, the hunter can shoot film if he wants to, and he might even find himself with a new hobby if he packs a camera into the deer fields.

The successful deer hunter can often learn a lot about deer habits by studying them during the off-season. Some hunters seem to feel that deer totally change in every respect when the season opens. To be sure, when hunters are in the woods, deer can tend to change some of their habits, but there has to be considerable pressure before they cease "being themselves." Deer, in fact, tend to do the same things during a deer season that they do in the off-season.

Truly, this is deer hunting practice. If I carry a camera, I will try to get close enough to get a photo of a deer, feeling if I can do that, I could have gotten a shot under hunting conditions. But I also like to observe all I can. When good enough to spot a deer before the deer knows I'm around, I will often watch the animal for a good long while. This kind of practice can pay off in big dividends later on. Mostly, I have learned from my mistakes. I have caught myself doing some very foolish things and I tried later, during the actual hunt, not to repeat these foolish things.

Moreover, the pre-season scouting/training run is useful for testing gear. I have learned that a certain pair of boots is not what I hoped for them to be. I have also learned that a particular pair of boots is exactly what I hoped them to be. I have found that my new shirt is just right for moving around in the outback, and I have found that another new shirt is all wrong for moving around in the outback. Plus, there are those many little items that one can try in the pre-season field from calls to lures. Without a doubt, this is the time to practice with those binoculars and get truly sharp in game-finding skills.

So expertise is heightened in the practice run. Tools of the trade are tried. The deer hunter gets into tune. He even gets into shape physically. If he lives simply too far from the deer fields, then our hunter will have a hard time doing his "mock deer harvest," and may have to content himself with getting in shape some other way.

A hunter may elect to harvest varmints or small game using techniques similar to his normal big game tactics. Here, Bill Fadala carries a scope-sighted .22 rifle and he uses binoculars to aid him in locating his quarry.

But he might still be able to get out with binoculars and hike around, and any of this type of experience cannot hurt the cause.

Dry-Firing

Dry-firing is one of the finest ways to learn a "shooting iron" that there is. Mainly, I am speaking of rifle and handgun practice because we are talking more of aiming than pointing, but I suppose a person could gain much good experience by dry-firing a shotgun, too, especially in learning his stance and his swing. Be that as it may, most of my practice in dry-firing has been with the rifle, since that is my mainstay tool.

Dry-firing is a vital practice. It can reveal things a shooter will never find out when he's firing live ammo. For example, when we are shooting a deer rifle, even the milder numbers, we certainly lose sight of exactly where that crosswire was resting or what the iron sight picture looked like at the second of ignition. Oh, to be sure, there is either a hole in the target or there is not a hole in that bull, and that should tell all, but it does not. Yes, if all of your shots are in the X-ring, forget this practice session thing; you don't need it. But could it be that due to a certain habit, maybe a habit of canting the rifle to one side or the other, you missed the bull? Or how about this: Could it be that you actually do snap your eyes shut the split second you think the gun is going off?

Dry-firing will help a shooter determine what he is doing both right and wrong, but most important of all, it will give him a fantastic opportunity to *learn the best possible shooting habits*. I often look out of my backyard window and dry-fire at a rock. Here is what I try to accomplish: I want to get in the habit of "calling my shot," and dry-firing is a great aid on that score. Here is why: In calling a shot, the shooter must know where he was actually aiming when the gun fired. Well, in dry-firing, since there is absolutely no disruption of aim, when the gun goes "click," the shooter can see for himself exactly where his point of aim was. He learns to control the firearm. He learns to master it. He learns how to hold and aim that piece so when it goes "click" the crosswires or sight picture remain centered on target and this is a great boon to later shooting.

Dry-firing also teaches trigger control and stance, and it shows a shooter how to improve on both. My love affair with good triggers for deer rifles came during a dry-fire session a very long time ago. I found that by the time I got the rifle to go "click," my sights were no longer on target. I also learned that while some shooters may be able to hold a dead steady sight picture indefinitely, I cannot. I never have been able to. I never will be able to. But I have taken deer with a passable good record because I have learned to squeeze and control that good trigger and my rifle goes *bang!* when I will it to, not when it wants to. They say that a truly fine squeeze on the rifle will produce a situation where the shooter himself is actually *surprised* when the gun goes off. I believe this to be true, but perhaps overstated.

On the one hand, it is a surprise when the gun goes off if a person is truly squeezing and not yanking or jerking the trigger. But it is, if I may coin a phrase, a "controlled surprise." Yes, we are almost taken by surprise, but at the same time, we have everything under strict control. Our sight picture is steady on the beam. It is always on target. But most of all, and this is the crux of the issue, our gun goes off at the precisely correct split second. If this is important on a standing target, how important is it when the deer is bounding through the wood or for that matter over any terrain? So, yes, there is a sort of surprise element in our shooting piece going off; however I am going to stay with "controlled surprise" instead of simply surprise. The latter suggests that the firearm more or less goes off during the sighting procedure, all right, but not precisely under the control of the shooter.

Dry-firing is simple. All we do is find something which will allow us to shoot the piece without injuring it since there will be no live ammo in the gun during the dry-fire practice. Then we pick a target and we take aim on it.

Naturally, good manners dictate that we choose only safe targets even when we are only practicing with an empty gun. We hold on the target and squeeze off the shot, keeping in mind all of the tenets of good shooting form. And most of all, we look for one thing and one thing only—was that sight picture right on the bull's-eye when the gun clicked?

Practice with the Air Rifle and Air Pistol

Today, powderless ammo is really in force. I must say it has been for a very long time indeed, but for some reason the general body of shooters did not seem to recognize the fact that air power was a vital and real force in modern shooting until more recent times. Air guns have certainly been around long enough. Lewis and Clark, on their 19th century expedition of exploring the Far West carried with them an air gun! In my youth, I of course had the almost mandatory Daisy Red Ryder BB gun, which was presented me by an aunt who "hated guns," to quote her fairly closely, but who thought a "boy growing up in the West ought to be able to shoot a gun in case a rattlesnake attacked him." Anyway, I had my Red Ryder. And when my uncle came home from the war

Crossman's Target Trap allows a shooter to enjoy very important indoor practice through shooting an airgun in a basement or similar setting. It is ricochet proof.

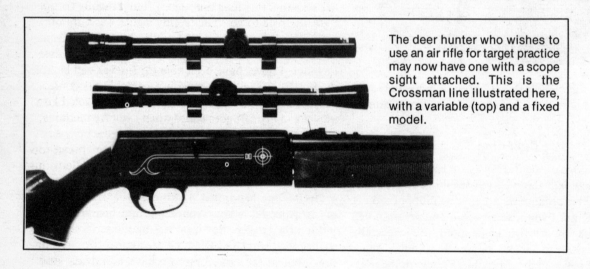

The deer hunter who wishes to use an air rifle for target practice may now have one with a scope sight attached. This is the Crossman line illustrated here, with a variable (top) and a fixed model.

I had something else. It was a fine Diana air rifle, caliber .177. One "break-open" by cranking the barrel downward cocked the gun and it shot with enough force to harvest a few rabbits for me.

Today, rightfully so, the air rifle and air pistol offer some rather obvious advantages for the deer hunter who wants to practice at home. Of course they are very quiet and with the proper backstop in the proper location, such as the basement of the home, they are safe to shoot indoors. About the only thing I would ask of a practicing shooter when using the indoor range is to hold down the participants, and when younger shooters get into the act, I prefer one adult supervisor and one shooter only. For an adult, the idea is to have fun, while adhering to the rules of the shooting game.

While enjoying the delights of the quiet, non-recoiling air gun, the shooter should also consider the enjoyment a serious practice session. He should observe all of the fine points of shooting from stance to trigger squeeze and he should not let himself get sloppy just because it is so much fun to plink away with the air gun. At close range, the air gun is quite accurate, so practice is meaningful.

I think it wise to select air guns which are full size and which have some "game gun" feel to them, be they handguns or rifles. This is certainly no problem today. There are all manner of full-sized air guns on the market. Selection is again a personal matter. All I would ask is that the air gun fit me fairly well. And I think for homerange practice, I might make mine a .177 caliber instead of the .22.

At any rate, the point I want to make is that much good

learning can go on right in the backyard or in the basement of the home with a safely set up pellet gun range and an air gun with accuracy potential. The hunter/shooter can remain in fine tune by practicing with an air gun, and he can have a great deal of fun doing it. The cost of such practice is very low and when one considers a no-noise factor, plus the safety factor, I think air gun practice is a wise move for the shooter and for the deer hunter specifically.

Do I Really Have to Practice?

A very long time ago, my friend John Doyle, the Tucson, Arizona taxidermist, began his business in a small basement shop. The shop, being underground as it were, had a tiny approved range in it. Well, we took advantage of the range and fired at targets several times a week. We felt that we were shooting just for fun because we had both made up our minds that we were "natural good shots." I mean, we had the eyesight and coordination to make our shooting skillful. We were not practicing here in the basement. We were just having fun.

Soon thereafter, John's rather amazing artistic ability came to the fore, and he had to build his own shop in

order to keep up with the demand for his work. Our little underground range was gone. So was our daily or near daily shooting session. There was soon a marked change in our shooting ability. In short, we got lousier and lousier as the days went by. In fact, we missed some game shots which we would have considered none too hard to master. Finally, the truth came clear to John.

One day he said, "Sam, I think I know what's wrong with our shooting." I listened intently. "You know that bit about our being 'natural good shots,' well I think it's all bunk. I think we were good shots because we were practicing our heads off all the time." Well, of course John was right. Oh, there is something to the natural good shot theory, but not much really. It is nice to have decent eyesight and steadiness, but most good shots add another ingredient to that. They practice. They practice a lot. And this is why I consider the practiced shot a better deer hunter, because he is in tune, so to speak, and he will tend to use his practice knowledge in smoothly flowing stance and aim. I think we need to practice our shooting. The above mentioned air rifle and air pistol practice is not a bad way to go.

The Target Range

Briefly, I just want to say that shooters who go out and actually fire their guns are doing the right thing. I do not want to give the impression that dry-firing and air gun practice is the only way to go. Of course actual shooting is irreplaceable in keeping the deer hunter sharp for the coming season. Range shooting teaches control of the firearm, and it gets the shooter "used to" blast and recoil. In combination with other practice methods, range shooting is highly valuable.

The shooter should take his favorite deer rifle out to the range as often as possible and see what he can do with it. The only thing I'd ask for is some "real" practice in the offhand and the sitting positions, even the prone, as well as the standard benchrest shooting which normally goes on at the range. The bench is the place to sight in that firearm. The bench is the place to test for group sizes. The bench is the place to check out new loads. And the bench is certainly good for practice, too. I think a great deal can be learned from bench shooting in terms of trigger control and sight picture. I also know that much can be determined about trajectory patterns and effects of the wind on drift while shooting off the bench. But the shooter should also try some of the more usual stances as well; that is, stances usual to deer hunting. While I have on occasion found rests in the field that were not bad imitations of a solid benchrest, I have yet to find an actual shooting bench set up for me within range of my deer.

Small Game Hunting

Deer hunting practice is certainly carried out in the small game field. If I can lay any claim to being able to take a deer cleanly across the canyon, I owe that ability to the rabbits of my youth. I don't think things have

Silhouette shooting is very lively these days and the Crossman company has devised an airgun silhouette target. These targets are very good for practice sessions and they seem to hold a lot of interest for shooters.

Bagging bunnies in the off-season can sharpen the eye of any hunter. Greg Thompson collects a few cottontails during a winter outing. Using a .22 rifle for these hunts, the practice pays off when Greg picks up his big game rifle in the fall.

changed much on that score. The fellow who can cleanly harvest his rabbits and squirrels for the bag is certainly not hurting himself in terms of later transferring that skill to deer hunting.

I suppose the one major point of consideration here is the fact that we have a moving target in some cases, or a target partially concealed by brush in other cases, a great variation of range if the hunter wants to take advantage of this factor, and in short, quite a number of the attributes one would find in the deer fields. The shooter who can take a small game rifle into the field and do fine work with it is certainly not hurting his chances as a deer shot.

Probably, it is overstepping the facts to consider that a deer hunter choose for his small game firearm the same *type* of firearm he uses for big game hunting. In fact, I think man is more "plastic" than that. I do most of my small game shooting with one of several different firearms. I truly enjoy using a .36 flintlock much of the time. I have a .32 caplock I like very much. I also shoot a .22 pumpgun using .22 Short Hollow Point ammo for cottontails and squirrels. I also have a .22 auto pistol that I enjoy a lot, but am not truly proficient with. Yet, I don't have any trouble in the deer field remembering how to work the bolt on my big game rifle just because I don't happen to use a bolt-action .22 rifle for small game. Nor do I have much problem with my .54 longrifle out deer hunting just because I was so recently taking small game with a .22 pumpgun. Personally, I feel that the small game hunter will gain a lot of skill no matter what style firearm he chooses.

Big Game Guns for Smaller Animals

When my grandfather found out that some good foods could be made from the loins and hind leg parts of younger white-sided rabbits he opened up a whole new world of shooting for me, as well as for my friend Arnold. We knew where the land was overrun with white-sides and the best part, perhaps, was the fact that you almost always had to shoot across wide open canyons to nail them. This meant that we had an excuse to get out and use our big game rifles without having to wait for deer season.

I firmly believe that we learned more about our big game rifles and shooting them in those couple summers than either before or since. A white-side at a few hundred yards, sometimes on the run, presented a very interesting target and we were obliged to make all of our hits "up front," so we'd have the back half to take home to grandpa. We did not know it then, but the fact that that rabbit country happened to have a lot of wind made things even better for us. Arnold had a .270 Gibbs, and I had a .270 Winchester at the time, both fitted with 4x scopes. We learned the meaning of wind drift.

We also found out a thing or two about judging range and holdover, and if you think you were going to get many of these smaller targets at long range by jerking

(Left) It is often wise though not imperative, to select a .22 rifle which is the same action as your big game rifle. Although Nancy Fadala shoots a bolt-action deer rifle, she enjoys her .22 lever-action.

(Below) Using the Moses Stick to support the rifle, this shooter is going to be able to create a good group on the target. What is more, he will be able to asume this position very quickly in open deer country for a good steady shot.

As part of the practice session, varmint hunting teaches several important lessons. First, the eye is trained to locate small animals often at considerable distances. Also, the hunter must learn to control his firearm not only in aim but in trigger let-off, and these are learned as well in the varmint field as on the deer trail. John Fadala poses with two prairie dogs he collected from a village, both taken at about 100 yards with a scope-sighted .22 rimfire rifle. Stalking is another practice often gained in the varmint hunt.

the trigger, you had better think again. So I have had first-hand experience with the use of a "deer rifle" on littler targets, some of them on the move. I can say that it is certainly one way to learn the business of shooting. Naturally, the hunter may have a special varmint rifle for this work, saving his deer rifle's barrel for deer and the like. There is nothing wrong with that. But just now and then it might not be bad to grab up the deer rifle and see how well it works on the smaller critters. Naturally, one must have absolutely safe shooting conditions before he cuts loose with a big game rifle, and certainly a farmer's field is not the best spot to fire a .30-06. But there are very often places where big game guns can be used in safety, and when the possibility arises, it's not a bad idea for the careful shooter to take advantage of the experience.

There are many facets to practice for deer hunters, and the deer hunter with imagination has no doubt a dozen different aspects of practice he could add to our list. The really important point to remember is this: The practiced deer hunter is just like the athlete who stays in training. He knows his equipment and he knows how to use it. And he has one other big plus factor on his side—he has confidence working for him.

chapter 18

Tricks and Tips for the Deer Hunter

THIS CHAPTER is going to deal with some of the tricks and tips a deer hunter may use to bag a deer. At this point in our successful deer hunting adventure, we have delved into the basics of hunting style, and we have talked about hunting firearms. So it is not out of place to say a word or two about some of the less common methods we might try from time to time.

One warning. It is important to know more about our game and we are going to look at the deer for a moment and try to learn more about it. It is nice to know about some of the tricks used over the centuries by successful deer hunters, but I would never want to leave the impression that the tricks are more important than the basics.

The Eyes of the Deer

Deer never look up. Well that's what I have heard. Frankly, I think it is more accurate to say that deer don't look up as much as they look down and on the level. But I have seen deer looking up. I have seen deer, mule deer at that, bedded in deep canyons and looking up at the walls of the canyon often. I have seen them look up on the sides of hills. But as far as looking up into trees for hunters, well, not likely on an everyday basis.

This is why this tip combined with the tree stand then is one good way of bagging a buck when a hunter has picked the right spot to set up his stand. The hunter must not feel that he need not worry about his motions on such a stand, because "deer don't look up." It is good advice to suggest remaining quiet and keeping the movements down when on stand, either resting on a stump or up in a tree stand.

Can deer see color? For years upon years we were told that deer could not see in color. Now the scientific community has reversed on this one and I hear that deer can see color. If they were wrong the first time, I don't think I am ready to put all of my faith in them this time. My best answer is that I have no idea, anymore, whether deer see color or not. The archer, however, is often advised to stick with the camouflage while in the deer field. The gun hunter may have no choice, as he may be obliged by law and safety dictates to wear blaze orange. So I think that where deer eyes are concerned we can so far say this: Sometimes deer do look up but not often, and while deer probably can see color, don't worry about it. Worry about motion much more. Deer see motion way better than they can determine a hunter's coat from a horse blanket.

How well can deer see? Once again, I doubt that there is any sound evidence pointing to exactly how well a deer can or cannot see. I doubt that a deer's first means of detecting a hunter is eyesight. I think that the tremendously long nose has a lot to do with finding out when man is nearby, and I'm convinced that hearing is certainly right in there as either number two on the list if not number one in the detecting realm. But deer can see. They see *motion* beautifully. It depends upon habitat as to how the deer will use its eyes. I am convinced that deer often bed down where they can *see* all around them. They do not always rely on sound and odor to warn them.

Stands and Blinds

The stand can be one of many things. A stump at the edge of a meadow can be a stand. A tree which secrets the hunter can be a stand. A stand can be up in the air, on something as sophisticated as a tower or as light and handy as a commercial tree stand unit. Therefore there are many different types of stands, from a simple stationary spot where the hunter merely remains semi-motionless to a device, permanent or otherwise, which can hold the hunter aloft.

Location

A stand has to be put in the right place for it to offer a chance of working out for the hunter. A good deal of thought must go into stand location, then. The ideal is having a stand located where a deer is quite likely to pass close enough for a clear shot, of course. But arriving at this perfect place is not so simple in some areas. In my mind, the best location for a stand is along any route which leads to special deer food. A hunter acquaintance of mine from Ohio has a stand which has produced a buck for him on a regular basis. It is located near a fence, and if one will observe carefully, he will see that the deer are crossing underneath that fence in reasonable numbers and with some degree of regularity. The ground shows evidence of a deer trail at the fence and the fence is loaded with deer hair. The deer "hole up" in the brush all day and then they move toward the field to feed in the late part of the day.

No one can guarantee that a deer will pass any stand. Deer are creatures of habit, up to a point, but they are also creatures of change. In a couple areas, however, I am totally sure that unless there is a tremendous change in the weather or some other event which completely alters the normal situation, I am going to see a deer and I am going to see that deer coming into a feeding area. My family and I have filled second deer tags (doe only allowed) in such an area, time in and time out.

Having located a place to go on stand, the hunter then decides what kind of stand he wishes to use.

Kinds of Stands

To restate that which we said above, we have the stand where a hunter simply stays put, along a trail, near deer food, at some "edge" country, in a meadow, at a burn, and so forth, using a little natural concealment of course. The commercial stand is mainly the tree type. The first

type of stand needs no special comment, with the exception of the few words offered below on "tips for the hunter on stand." There are some special observations which we will make about behavior on stand, but these observations apply equally to both natural and commercial stands. The tree stand, however, can be viewed with a few major points in mind.

1. The tree stand should be large enough not only to support the hunter in security and safety, but also large enough for the hunter's comfort. I have seen a few tree stands which would soon have me getting to the ground. So the hunter should look at stands which are correctly sized for his own needs and desires.

2. If the hunter must carry his tree stand to a location, setting it up and removing it on a daily basis, he must consider portability. Portability is not only weight, though weight is one factor we need look at. Portability is also design. The hunter will have to look at the tree stand types and decide for himself which design he prefers. Many stands can be carried like a packframe, for example.

3. Setting up is another criterion of the stand. A stand for trees should be designed so that a single hunter can safely carry it up the tree and secure it by himself. There are a variety of stands which offer various means of set-up and security. Which type the hunter picks will have to rest with his own preferences and situation. However,

One of the better "tricks" a deer hunter can use is the tree stand. Here is the Buck-Buster brand with a seat and a platform. It is solidly constructed for safety and stability.

The archer must be able to move sufficiently to operate his bow. Here, the Buck-Buster platform and chair are in use, and note the length of the safety belt so that the hunter can put his archery tackle into effect.

every tree stand should be considered in part on the basis of set-up.

4. The stand must offer support. Obvious as the point may be, there are various types of security offered in different stands and a hunter must consider what he, personally, requires in support.

Tips for Hunters on Stand

Whether simply sitting on a stump, either as a part of a drive or as a waiting measure, the hunter should observe a few points. First, I think, is personal safety and comfort. Only a season ago in Idaho I saw a hunter perched up on a tree stand, and it was evident he was miserable. It was November and cold. He was dressed all right for walking, but not for sitting. A hunter should take the clothing required to keep him warm on stand. When a person gets cold his concentration falls off badly, and whether waiting for a fellow hunter to push a deer to you or just hoping to see a deer walking by a stand, the out-

doorsman should consider taking along the items needed for warmth.

As a part of the comfort idea, there is nothing wrong with having a little food and drink on a stand. A vacuum bottle of hot drink and a couple of sandwiches are not that heavy to carry along, especially in a daypack. Deer hunting can be tough work, but there is nothing wrong with taking some of the hardship out of the experience, and a sip of hot cocoa or coffee and a bite of sandwich can perk a hunter up.

A hunter should make certain what he can do from his stand, what he must be able to do. The archer should be positive that he can loose an arrow in any direction and hit a mark. The gunhunter is in a better position as far as having to maneuver in order to get off a shot, but even the arms user must be in a position to fire without loss of time and with a great degree of accuracy. It is wise for the hunter to "dry practice" from his stand beforehand if possible. This means actual shooting for the archer, but for the gunhunter all that is necessary is to insure that the firearm can be moved into position and aim can be taken.

Don't smoke on stand. Even though we will try to place a stand where the deer is not going to catch wind of us, the truth is simple and clear. The wind changes direction and so do deer. If a drive is in progress, then we have more control over wind direction. But even then, there is no point in smoking on stand. Will the smell of smoke alert a deer that a hunter is nearby? Find me the person who can prove this, and I will ask that person about a whole lot of other aspects of deer behavior! In short, we do not know for certain that every deer in the area will be so sophisticated that it can detect danger from the smell of burning tobacco. But I would have to guess that the scent of burning tobacco would not help the cause of the hunter a bit. I have picked up the smell of cigarette smoke on the air myself, and from quite a distance. However, to be fair about it, I was in Colorado one time and was hunting with a friend of a friend, as it were. The fellow smoked like an old steam locomotive. I did not want to alienate the fellow. I was on his turf and I was his guest. However, I was a little annoyed at the chain-smoking going on.

At the peak of my annoyance, up walked a small mule deer buck, smack into us. The wind had been playing around in circles. I have to believe that the buck could smell the smoke of the cigarette. I did not want to shoot, so I watched instead. The buck got to within about 20-25 yards of us and then caught sight of a movement, I would guess. It turned back to the direction from which it had come and that was that. All the same, and in spite of this and some other examples I have seen of deer paying no attention to the smell of burning tobacco, on stand is probably not the best place to light up.

Movement on stand is unavoidable. But overt movement is not necessary. A hunter can tell himself to keep his motion to a minimum on a stand, especially when simply sitting on the proverbial stump where the deer may have a pretty good view at ground level. Even aloft in the tree stand, unnecessary movement is taboo. No matter what sort of camouflage is used, a deer can spot a hunter if the hunter moves.

What to do on stand is another interesting problem. I have to admit that at times I have moved off stand when hunting by myself with no other hunters to rely on me and no strict plan to follow. Sitting is not always as easy as we might think. Last season, a neighbor of mine told me that he used electric socks on a stand and this made a big difference in helping him sit tight in some semblance of comfort, for it is lack of comfort which often drives a hunter off of his stand. But what to do when on stand is still a problem. Contemplation is my best answer, contemplation without daydreaming. On a quiet stand, a hunter can be alone with his thoughts. It's a good time to think.

Of course we must remain alert when on stand. This means using the ears as well as the eyes. We have spoken often of the hunter's hearing as a part of his "equipment," and I can think of no better time or place to exercise our hearing than on stand. The deer is, indeed, a quiet animal. But it is not a ghost. Twigs are broken when a deer stands on them just as surely as twigs are broken by the boot of the hunter. I have heard deer moving toward me for several moments. How far away these deer were when I first detected them by ear, I have no way of knowing. But I think pretty far.

The Deer's Nose and Scents

Because of that tremendously long snout, the deer is quite a smeller. Anyone who has hunted deer for a long time has seen the nose in action in one way or another. I have watched a deer's head go up with a snap, its nose seeming to test the air, only to have a hunter show up in a brief while. Proving that the nose and not the ears did the first job of detection would be impossible here, but deer certainly can sniff just fine.

So we try to trick them through the nose. This is where the scents come in. Once again, I want to restate the idea that all of the incidental tips and tricks here are in addition to the sound basics of deer hunting. In the first place, there is no doubt that we give off an odor. We are animals, and our sweat glands prove it. I don't know just how far we want to go with this idea, but I certainly know some good deer hunters, smart men, who would not dream of loading down on spicy foods before a deer hunt. These fellows truly believe that digesting onions and garlic and oregano, and other such edibles is a curse to successful deer hunting.

Some of these hunters believe that the Indians ate very mild diets, even avoiding meats, a few days before an important hunt. I don't know about that, but I do know that man has his own odor, and we can mask that odor in several ways. I'm going to name a few here, and the hunter can accept or eschew them. First, we will talk about clothing and how to hide the odors all our clothing holds. A hunter might want to wash his clothing well and then rinse in plain water, no additives whatsoever to be used in that rinse. Then the clean clothes can be placed in double plastic bags and the bags tied shut tightly. The bags are left closed until the morning of the hunt, when the hunter puts the clothing on. In this way, the clothes have not been in contact with gasoline fumes, pet hairs around the house, not to mention the dog rubbing up against his owner—I doubt that dog scent is reassuring to a deer—as well as the thousands of things which can taint clothing with aromas, from cooking to smoking.

While we have mentioned washing our clothing, I

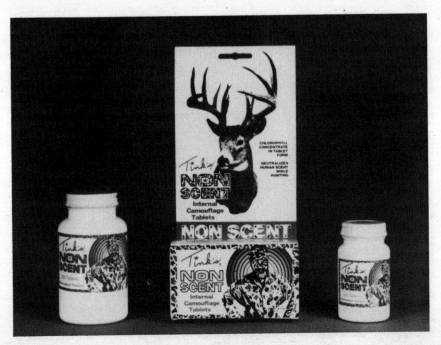

This is another type of cover up device. It is not a scent at all, but a tablet which the hunter is to take according to direction in order to mask his own natural odor.

suppose we could also talk about washing ourselves. It might be well to bathe before the hunt. It's a thought. I suppose the use of scented or perfumed deodorants would be taboo. But maybe the use of natural or neutral deodorants would not be so bad. If I sound tenuous about the whole thing, it's only because I am. I have no real proof of which is best and to give my suggestions here would be to toss guesses into the wind.

We can also try the chlorophyll tablet for reduction of body odor. I am told that we should take the tablet as directed, meaning a few days to a week before the opening of the season. I did this on one deer trek, and the only problem is that I did not have any real evidence to allow me to make a comment on it. I got a buck. But I think I got the buck because of my scouting, hunting the right time of the day in the right place and my glasses which found the animal feeding. On the other hand, who knows? I recall that the winds were sort of fickle that day, almost circling me, and maybe the fact that I was loaded on chlorophyll made a difference.

Masking our odors, then, is a good idea, according to a number of excellent hunters. But we can also use some of the commercial cover-up scents to mask our own scent. I think this is where the apple scents come in, along with similar "perfumes" of the right smell. I really doubt that a deer smells apple scent on the air and then comes charging hell-bent to take a bite out of the hunter, but as a cover-up, surely there is nothing wrong with applying something like apple or similar odor to the clothing.

Now, what about attracting a deer through its nose? Well, it is certainly done all the time in "real life." A deer, especially during the rut, will bury its nose in the ground and follow the object of its affections like a hound dog on a fox trail. Even when the rut is not in full swing, we certainly can believe that messages received by a deer's nose would be interesting to it and it might want to investigate what is making the odor. The attractor odors or scents are generally a bit more sophisticated.

I have hunted with a magnificent elk hunter who also bags a big deer every year. This fellow is one of the most tidy men I know and his home and person are always clean. But not when it comes to elk hunting. When he finds a place where a bull elk has left a scent, this guy will almost roll in it as a trailing hound will sometimes roll in offal. He claims that the odor of elk urine on his person not only masks human scent but also attracts elk which are close enough and curious enough to want to take a look at the intruder. I really don't know if the routine is responsible for the dozens and dozens of elk this man has harvested, but he certainly believes it is.

The scents available today are the "real McCoy," you might say. These attractors are based upon pretty sound principles of deer behavior and knowledge of deer life patterns. Naturally, the hunter who uses skunk musk to mask his own scent is going to do a fairly good job of it, but this is not going to attract a deer. I think that there are times and situations, however, when something like "Tink's Doe-In-Rut Buck Lure" might indeed give an olfactory invitation to a buck that it can't refuse. Certainly, there are a number of documented instances where the hunter believed fully that a deer was coming right toward him due to the attraction of a scent. These scents are what we might call "musks," and they are not artificial apple smells, but rather the heady smells apparently loved by the male of the deer species.

One hunter claims that he has taken several bucks from a stand by using a strong musk as a lure. He saturates a hunk of cotton with the musk, and he then places it where sign has shown recent feeding or other deer activity. This fellow tells of bucks which have raised their heads

Here we have a lure. This is not a cover scent, but rather an attractor. It may be applied to an area with an eye dropper or a dabber.

This is an actual deer lure and not a cover scent.

This is one type of cover scent which can be used to mask the approach of a hunter. It will help to destroy man scent.

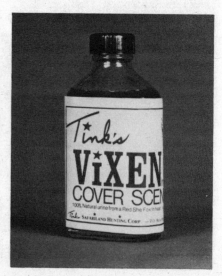

A hunter laces a scrape with scent. If he is in a tree stand above the scrape, this added incentive can be well worth the while. (Photo courtesy of J. Wayne Fears)

Using Its Ears

While the ears of a buck generally tell it what is coming and whether or not to "hunker down" and let that something go by or not, there is another aspect of a deer's hearing powers, and this is for attracting it into the hunter. Of course I am speaking of "rattling up a buck" and "calling a buck." While no deer hunter can possibly have a lot of experience with every kind of deer under every kind of circumstance, we can listen around to others and gain some kind of insight as to how something might work out. Well, I have only had one buck come in to me because I was banging on anything, and it was not a deer season at all. I was simply out fooling around.

Whitetails are supposed to come in better to rattling than do mule deer, but my one and only rattling experience was with a mule deer, and it did indeed come in, apparently looking for some sort of action. The month was November and the rut, in that locale, was in full swing. I had bagged a turkey already and had no intention of turning for home so soon, so I was trying a rattling session, and it worked. I was told later by experienced buck rattlers that I had made some mistakes, but be that as it may, I had a buck come in for a handshake acquaintance.

If I were to seriously try rattling up a buck, I would do the following. I'd select good "live" antlers from a buck I had harvested. I would not use shed antlers. A shed antler, all but the freshest I'd suppose, does not seem to give off that exciting ring that a hard bony fresh antler renders. With a couple fresh antlers in hand, I'd seek a spot where I had reason to believe a few bucks might be within earshot.

I would make certain that I had some cover for myself. If the cover were none too thick, I'd back up into some brush at least. Hiding behind brush can often be less effective in terms of camouflage than backing up into it and having the bulk of the camouflage behind the hunter. I would also use some form of cover up scent, and while I was at it, I would apply a good musk scent to a rag or cotton ball and I would attach that to a bush within bowshot or gunshot distance.

But most of all, if I were to seriously practice rattling up bucks, I think I'd do so only in the rut. I can't imagine a buck getting too excited over a supposed battle for does when the time for battle is not at hand. So, with the rut in full swing, a set of good hard antlers in hand, some sort of camouflage hiding area, plus a bit of scent out there and possibly on me for cover-up, I'd go in for rattling.

Deer calling with an actual calling unit I have done. I have had very mixed results, from exactly no luck at all to the time when my friend Ted Walter and I called up 40 whitetail deer in a single afternoon, and not the same deer over and over again either. Since I lay no claim to knowing how a deer thinks or why it acts as it does in many cases, I cannot offer a theory as to why a buck

100 or more yards from the cotton patch soaked with lure, and then bulled their way right up to the scent itself.

So, a musk lure is an auxiliary, a helper, one of the many methods tucked down into the bag of tricks used by successful deer hunters. I think a lot more personal experimenting is in order before a hunter simply says that lures are not for him. In fact, I know of a long narrow canyon which always holds big bucks, yet these bucks are very hard to approach and I have to pause and wonder if a bit of lure in that canyon would not travel a good distance and perhaps entice a buck to come over and see what the smell is all about.

Certainly, the rut, it seems to me, would be the best time to rely on lures, but, again, there are cases of hunters bagging bucks which they felt were coming in to a lure type musk scent when the rut was still a month away. Once again, I think the lure method should be tried at least once, and I mean tried with good logic, not merely sprinkling it into the air in any old spot, but applying it in a specific location where there is sign of deer activity.

A part of the author's deer hunting gear is a deer call. Although the use of a deer call is not going to guarantee the sighting of a buck, there are specific times and conditions when a call can work very well for a hunter. It is one of the deer hunting tools worth using from time to time.

or doe will rush in to the sound of some squawking on a plastic whistle. Some hunters confidently tell me that the deer is coming in to the aid of a fellow member in distress.

I doubt that anyone can say why, exactly, a deer comes in to a call. I do know that I have had it happen. One year, in September, I was hiking in the Tucson Mountains outside of Tucson, Arizona. This was before everyone had discovered the sun country, and the Tucson Mountains then were composed of rocks and cacti instead of houses. I had a new toy along. The toy was a deer call.

At this time, the little whitetail buck was often seen in the Tucson Mountains. I'm told this is no longer the case. At any rate, I simply crouched in the center of a group of cacti and brush and bleated away on the call. A beautiful whitetail buck came directly toward me within 10 minutes of my blowing. Its head was lowered, but it did not seem beligerant. Trying to assume how it did feel is not possible, but I do know it would not stop coming to the call. I had to have done a lousy job with the call. I had never even blown one until a few days before this encounter. But it came on.

At certainly no more than 5 yards, the buck stopped and its vision seemed to penetrate my "blind" of cacti and brush. At this, it walked around me. Again, it simply had to detect my presence through its nose if not its eyes, but it stuck around. I bleated lowly on the call, and the buck circled a couple of times, and then simply walked

away. It never did run. On many other occasions I have had deer come in to the call. But I must say in all truth that I have never harvested a single deer I have called in. It seems to me that for some reason my success with the call was better either before or after deer season, but I cannot figure what the reason would be.

During the season, I have called in a few smaller bucks I chose not to take, and I have called does in, too. One day my friend Ted Walter and I hid ourselves on a brushy knoll in what seemed to us prime whitetail habitat. I tooted on the deer call and a deer came in and another and then another. I know that there were few to no repeats because we actually stood up from time to time and virtually scared the deer off, and we could also see by size and color that the deer were different. We had about 40 deer come in, to the best of our ability to count, and that is an underestimation not an exaggeration. We enjoyed the calling, but shot no deer.

In light of what I have seen with my own eyes I would have to conclude that deer calling is for real. I consider it another auxiliary method of deer hunting. I think it is a shame we sometimes tend to ignore deer calling because it deserves more trials than it seems to get. In short, after a person has scoured an area, tried to see his quarry, done the basic things to bag a deer, why not give a toot or two on a deer call? Who knows, you may just call in a nice buck.

Now You See Me, Now You Don't

All through this chapter we have emphasized the fact that our little tips and tricks were additions to the main body of sound hunting tactics. Well, here is another such tip. It is not for all of the time, not even for much of the time, but sometimes a hunter may have occasion to try it out.

One October day I was climbing a hill, slowly puffing along, doing a lot of looking as I went, and more or less trying to get over the hill to what I thought would be some good deer habitat on the other side. I approached the crest carefully, so as not to show myself on the horizon all at once and to also give myself a chance to observe the opposite side of the hill a bit at a time. I saw nothing. Finally, I topped the hill and settled down for a few moments, glassing. Still nothing. After a bit of this, I totally changed my plans, decided that I was not that crazy about "the other side of the hill" after all, and I began to retrace my steps because there was an interesting side canyon that needed looking at.

No more than 100 steps back on my original side of the hill I stopped, chastised myself for not following my own plans and sticking with the program, and I once again climbed the hill and was soon standing on the same ground I had recently vacated. Guess what? There was a darn nice buck just walking away from me. It was about 100 yards out, and it had very obviously been bedded within range of my vision the whole time. Because I got that buck, the idea of walking within possible sight of a bedded buck caught my fancy. In other words, you do not burst over the hill, but you take your time, properly, and you sit there and look hard, but if nothing shows up, so to speak, you backtrack over the hill, wait a few moments, and then push your head back over the hill again to see if a buck is, just by chance, leaving the area.

It worked for me a couple more times, though certainly not with any degree of reliability. I only bring it up because it is one more little tip to tuck in the bag of tricks.

The Hearing Aid

I have a friend who is a very fine deer hunter, but he is quite hard of hearing. He uses a hearing aid, and I noticed that he "messes with it" while we are hunting deer. One day, I happened to be looking at him when he was fiddling with the hearing aid and he had me come over and try the instrument for myself. Actually, I felt that it would be very useful for a hunter of normal hearing if he could increase his ability to hear that buck moving through the woods.

Another very useful hint is to use cupped hands to improve hearing. I think the reader will enjoy trying this one and he can do it right now. All one need do is cup the ears deeply into the hands. It works. The cupped hands/outer ear gives much greater surface, as it were, and improves hearing measurably. Recently, I was in a camp and I thought I could hear the wind in the trees below me. I had never camped the spot before, and I did not know the area, nor did my companions. I hooked my ears into my cupped hands and began turning around as if I were a regular sound detector. "That's not the wind, boys. There's a creek down there," I said. Indeed there was a creek in the bottom of the canyon.

The others tried the cupped hands trick, and they were amazed that what was a faint sound a second ago was now quite clearly the sound of running water. I have also cupped my ears into my hands, and picked up the sound of a moving deer. I recently bagged a mule deer buck that was moving in heavy trees across a canyon. I simply could not find it, not even with my glasses, because there was so darn much land over there to survey all at once. Then I cupped my ears into my hands and began pinpointing the sound. After I did pinpoint which part of the hill the deer was on, I found it quickly with my binoculars and put a pretty good mule deer in the freezer.

Shoot, *Look*, Then Leave

While we are talking about deer-taking tricks, it might not be a bad idea to toss in a very important facet of successful deer hunting, and that is to learn to mark the spot in which a deer was standing when you fired at it, and to look, always, before leaving the area. Please take a look. Spend 15 minutes covering the ground carefully, looking for any trace of a hit. I have found a couple of bucks above average in size which were obviously left by mistake. They were both hit right in the chest squarely, and I doubt they walked 20 yards. However, the hunter had not checked out his shot. It is imperative that we always check out our shot, even if we saw dust fly or watched a shower of bark from a tree both of which would seem to indicate a clear miss.

I noticed a tendency in my own young hunters to shoot and then feel that they had missed. In a couple cases, the buck went down so fast that by the time the hunter recovered from recoil, even the mild recoil of a standard deer rifle, the animal was nowhere to be seen. Well, the new hunter, somewhat lacking in confidence, simply thinks he missed. One day this happened to two family members of mine. One of the instances is very memorable because it was my son's first deer.

The buck was nothing that big, but it was a harvestable adult, and I told John to shoot. "Take careful aim," I suggested, "and squeeze that trigger. It's just a target. Think of it as a target, not deer." My boy fired and the buck swept away as if to scorn the boy's shooting. John got up from the sitting position and shook his head. "I missed," he said. Well, I knew better. I was watching the buck in my binoculars as I always try to do when another is shooting, and the animal was struck in the neck. I saw the hair part. The neck bones were intact, but the jugular was hit and the deer was down without so much as a twitch from the 100-grain Nosler Partition bullet from the .25-06. The buck, in fact, had not really run. It had whirled and fallen.

Another time, a buck was dropped so swiftly that we actually could not find it for 20 minutes. It was, of course, only 10 to 20 yards away from a point we had walked by two or three times, but a deer down in the grass is not that easy to see. So I suggest that the shooter always check after he fires. Shoot, but *look* before you leave. It can pay off big. I also think it is a hunter's duty to study the area for cut hairs or traces of blood. Sometimes scrambling tracks can be followed a short distance, and the buck might be down only a few short yards away from where it had been standing or even running. Finally, I also suggest that when possible a hunter take a solid rest. Shooting "off the hind legs like a man" is fine when it is necessary; I think every deer hunter should be able to aim successfully from the standing position. But I like the sitting position when I can get it, and the prone when that is appropriate. From the sitting position, especially with the sling in place, a shooter can produce some rather tight groups that are not necessarily obtained in the standing position.

So much for our tips. Even the old buckskin harvester forgets the raw basics after a while and I always enjoy reading about deer chasing because if I don't learn something new, I at least remember something I used to know but had put in the recesses of my mind.

chapter 19
Black Powder Tactics

SINCE WE are on the topic of tactics, more or less, anyway, I want to tangle with black powder deer hunting for a brief encounter. We do not need a rehash of caliber selections, but a reminder on picking the proper deer gun in muzzleloader form and loading it right are certainly in order, due to the fact that in these times there seem to be more and more hunters annually joining the ranks of frontloader deer harvesting.

There are but two facts I wish to point out in terms of loads for black powder firearms. First, the black powder firearm does not defy the laws of physics and ballistics. Second, each black powder firearm is unique to a degree, and certainly what is a correct load for one firearm may not be correct for another. I'm not trying to be overly blunt about it, but the reader has to remember that over the years some arms have been given us in black powder form which were not always true to correct black powder design or materials.

First, the laws of physics, so to speak. There is no truth whatever in the idea that in black powder the load can be a tiny squib and yet at the same time be devastating on a deer. A target load is a target load. A hunting load is a hunting load. Unfortunately, there seems to be a faction on either side of the broad middle range. On one end we have the "load 'em up" boys and on the other end we have the "pinky load" boys. The first clan seems to believe that you can't hurt a firearm with black powder no matter how you load it. False. You can do damage

with black powder by *abusing* it, and overloads are an abuse. Never, never load more than the manufacturer has recommended, and if the gunmaker has no load limit for his firearm, then as the owner of one of his products, the shooter should insist upon one. If the company who made or imported the firearm has no idea what to shoot in it, certainly no one out there in the field would have the knowledge either.

I had one gunmaker suggest to me that he felt it was up to the shooter to determine what load to use and that there were loading manuals out there. Well, there are, all right, but I think it is nice to know what the manufacturer of the specific firearm had in mind for *that* gun. Not to make too much of this, for most manufacturers are excellent when it comes to giving us margins and parameters for loads. I simply want to point out that these loads are not to be exceeded, mainly because there is no reason to exceed them.

I also point out that what is correct in one firearm as a load may not be correct in another. We are, sort of, back to the max load as allowed by the manufacturer, I suppose, but I have read and heard too often of "blanket" loads. That is, the load is given as "110 grains of FFg in a .50-caliber muzzleloader." What .50-caliber muzzleloader? Any .50-caliber muzzleloader? I think not. We understand perfectly the need for specific loads for specific firearms in smokeless powder shooting. For example, we can look into the *Lyman Reloading Hand-*

book, 46th Edition, and we find loads for the .45-70. On page 348 the .45-70 loads are listed for the 1873 Springfield. But on page 350 there are .45-70 loads for the Marlin 1895 and Winchester Model 1886. Then on page 352 of this same manual we have loads for the .45-70 to be used in the Ruger No. 1 or the Ruger No. 3. Well, it is fairly obvious that Lyman saw a need to give loads for three different categories of firearms based mainly on design and "strength." I hear that we should, in black powder, list only the lowest possible load so no one will get hurt. This effectively ruins the loading potential of all those good rifles and handguns and shotguns out there, does it not? It would be folly to suggest that a Browning .50 be held to a maximum of 60 FFg just because some hard-to-locate Brand-X should be held to 60 FFg in .50-caliber. Enough on this. I only ask that a black powder deer hunter never exceed the maximum load recommended by his gunmaker, and I ask, too, that he load for deer when he is hunting deer and leave the bloopers for the tin cans and paper targets.

Laws of Diminishing Returns

Finally, we must observe the laws of diminishing returns which shows there is not *always* a 1 to 1 correlation between the powder charge and the resulting velocity. The chronograph, a machine so cheap and so handy now that any club can own one, will show us where this cut-off point is. It is very easy to establish the best all around deer load when the shooter has access to a chronograph. Here is what he does: First, we observe the max load. Let's use a real example so we know what we are dealing with. My son shoots an Ithaca .50 for deer. The papers which came with this firearm recommended a maximum load of 110 FFg.

Let us begin with 60 FFg. We get 1493 fps at the muzzle. (See *Gun Digest Black Powder Loading Manual*, DBI Books.) With 70 FFg we get 1505. With 80 FFg we get 1712 fps. With 90 we get 1889. With 100 FFg we get 1912. With 110, our top load, we get a flat 2000 fps at the muzzle. Now let's see. There were increases with all the loads. This is usually true, but we need to see how much increase in velocity we gain for how much powder. Well, in our Ithaca, the increases seem reasonable enough, so we turn to the terrain the rifle will be used in. Frankly, in the forest and at 50 yards, I'd probably call a flat 100 FFg fine, or perhaps the 90 FFg load. Out on the plains, I might look at the 110 with its flat 2000 fps MV as all right.

Now, how about another rifle. I have a .54 which gains 1871 fps with 110 FFg GOEX, 1943 fps with 120 FFg, and 1963 fps with 130 FFg. Well, I think it is plain to see that 120 FFg is my load. I see no reason to add 10 grains of powder for an average increase of only 20 fps.

Wayne Fears takes aim on a whitetail buck using his muzzleloader from a tree stand. (Photo courtesy J. Wayne Fears)

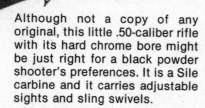

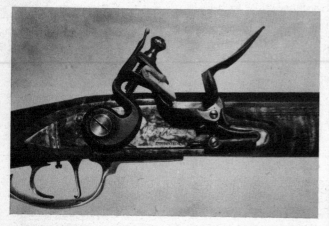

Although not a copy of any original, this little .50-caliber rifle with its hard chrome bore might be just right for a black powder shooter's preferences. It is a Sile carbine and it carries adjustable sights and sling swivels.

The flintlock is not the hit and miss proposition which we so often are told of. If the flintlock system were as unreliable as I have often read, it would be a great wonder that the pioneer managed to "make meat" with it and survive. However, a good flintlock starts with a good lock. This is the lock on the Hatfield rifle and it showers a good spark cluster down into the pan to ignite the pan powder. The cut flint is from the Flintknapper Shop of West Germany.

J. Wayne Fears uses his tree stand as a sometimes part of his black powder hunting style, and he has gained considerable success with this method where he hunts. (Photo courtesy J. Wayne Fears)

That is how I use the law of diminishing returns to determine loads.

The Goal of the Downwind Shooter

The modern muzzleloader deer hunter wants to accept a challenge and then do well in successfully carrying out that challenge. He wants to have a sense of history in his hunting. But more than anything else, he wants to cleanly bag his deer, and there is nothing wrong with that. Here is a short analysis of the black powder hunter's method: He chooses a good muzzleloader. He builds his load for deer in that muzzleloader based on the manufacturer's maximum load and the laws of diminishing returns. He sights in with care. He practices, and then he hunts "heads up" style, alert and watching, but slow on the foot and long on the looking. He uses optics, especially binoculars. He gets close, and he shoots just once. When it goes this way, the muzzleloader deer hunter has a memory as well as a buck to show for his efforts.

The Compromise Black Powder Rifle

Just as I see a muzzleloader as a compromise between bowshooting and modern arms, I see the black powder cartridge rifle as a compromise between the muzzleloader and the modern rifle. We still have a single shot rifle. We still have something old and historical. But the frontloading aspect is gone and those newfangled things called *"cartridges"* can be used. The deer hunter does not have a great array of modern day black powder cartridge rifles to choose from, unless he considers digging up the older lever-action models and including them in the list. Mainly, he's going to run across the Sharps rifle, Remington Rolling Block and the Springfield .45-70 all in newly constructed form. The first he can purchase from C. Sharps Company, POB 885, Big Timber, MT 59011. The second is available through the Navy Arms Company at 689 Bergen Blvd, Ridgefield, NJ 07657, and the latter from Harrington and Richardson.

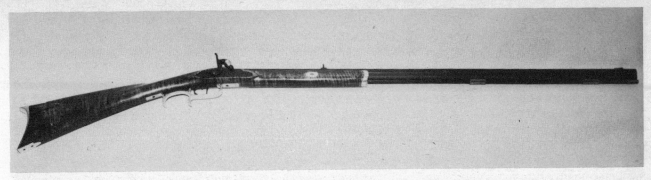

The black powder rifle dictates part of the rule system for hunting with a muzzleloader. This fine Ozark Mountain Arms Muskrat rifle is very accurate; however, it wears iron sights and the hunter must be aware that at dusk, an excellent hunting time, his ability to see the iron sight will be much more limited than his ability to see a deer well through a scope sight. Also obvious is the fact that we have here a single-shot, and a single-shot which cannot be loaded quickly for a second shot. The muzzleloader does dictate much of a black powder hunter's style.

Sometimes it is the little things in a load chain which can cause trouble for the black powder deer hunter. One such little thing is a patch that burns out. When this occurs, a backer patch can be used. Here, the patch on the left is a simple pillow ticking cloth cut smaller than the regular patch on the right, which is a pure Irish linen .013-inch size thickness. The smaller patch simply goes upon the powder charge and the larger is used per normal. If there is any chance of a smoldering patch causing a fire, such as in ultra dry terrain, the shooter may elect to substitute an inert unit downbore on the powder. If so, hornet's nest is ideal.

(Right) Part of black powder hunting success relies upon combining various methods with gear well-known to the shooter. The thrill of bagging a buck with a smokepole is self-evident.

The Readyload

A tip which we can give the black powder deer hunter is to be ready to reload quickly. I am not suggesting that a hunter is going to get a second shot at a fleeting whitetail. But I do believe a basic rule of muzzleloader hunting is to reload the piece immediately after firing. This is so basic that it seems to be overstated, but in the excitement of seeing our buck fall, we may tend to approach with our piece unloaded. It's just good management to do otherwise. I think that with .50 ball-shooter or .300 Magnum, a shooter should be ready to fire again when he approaches downed game. As it is ascertained the game is defunct, the rifle should then be unloaded.

How do you unload a muzzleloader? I suggest that since the hunter is in the field anyway, he aim at a dead stump and shoot the load away. A soft hillside, earth bank or other safe backstop is fine, too, but the idea is to unload the piece. It can be cleaned back in camp later on. The muzzleloader should be cleaned shortly after firing, but it will not hurt the firearm to go the rest of the day without swabbing. If the shooter is worried about his piece eroding in any way, he can swab the bore a few times right there in the field.

But back to that fast second shot—how do you get it? I like the idea of a readyload, a unit that has powder, patch and ball all in one package, so to speak. These are available widely and in various styles. There is the handy unit of plastic and the finely crafted all-metal model. The local black powder shop or gunshop generally carries a supply of these quick-loaders or readyloads. They do work, and they work well.

Loading for Longevity

The black powder deer hunter must also concern himself with a load which will last the day, sometimes 2 or 3 days if need be. This means careful loading. There are some very basic rules to be followed. While we do not wish to go into all of the details of loading here (see Gun Digest Black Powder Loading Manual, DBI Books), we can give a few highlights. First, the deer gun should be clean before it is loaded. It should be free of oil or preserving greases.

When the gun is known to be clean, the charge is dropped. I like to insert a hunk of hornet nest *on top of the powder charge.* This is a very simple matter. The shooter takes a few small layers of hornet nest and folds them over, inserting the nesting material into the muzzle of the bore. Then, with opposite end of ramrod, or with a jag in place, this nesting is thrust to the bottom of the bore to rest on top of the powder down in the breech.

The nesting material will do several things, but mainly it is good for saving the main patch from two devastations. First, it saves the main patch from becoming burned out by the blast of the powder charge. I have located the fired patch with the hornet nest still clinging to the patch. In one case, I used a stout charge of 130 FFg in a custom .54 rifle and recovered the patch with the hornet nest still perfectly intact. It was not even scorched. Naturally, the main patch which had been wrapped around the ball was also perfectly intact. The second thing a bit of hornet nest can do is save the powder charge in the breech from becoming dampened by the lube on the main patch by soaking up any excess lube.

One can also use a double patch. This means a patch down upon the powder charge and then the normal single main patch around the ball. The first patch is run downbore on top of the powder charge just the way we ran the hornet nesting material down. This patch will do the same work as the hornet nest. Some say the hornet nest is better because it will not smolder after shooting, however.

After the patched ball or the conical has been rammed home, the bore should be swiped once or twice with a cleaning patch to dry it. I use a grease substance when I create my black powder hunting loads, such as RIG or

No. 103, and a trace of either will be left in the bore for metal protection even though we run a cleaning patch downbore a swipe or two after loading. However, we do not want a heavy deposit of grease or liquid lube in the bore because this can change the point of impact. I suggest that you sight in with a dry bore and always shoot with a dry bore. By dry, I do not mean squeaky dry, but I refer again to running a cleaning patch downbore after the patched ball or conical has been seated. Of course, we are always speaking of an *uncapped* or *unprimed* firearm. Never, under any circumstances, run anything down the bore of a primed or capped firearm.

Wet Weather

Wet or damp weather does bring about certain problems for muzzleloader fans. But most of these problems can be corrected very nicely. I have hunted in the rain for several days at a time and had the rifle go off perfectly without a hitch. There are a number of rules to follow here. First, I think the hunter should carry his piece upside down in a drizzle or a rain. This means, the ignition system and muzzle will be pointed toward the ground, not toward the heavens.

Second, the flintlock fan can add something like RAINCOAT to his priming powder to protect it from moisture. RAINCOAT is a natural product from Mountain State Muzzleloading Supplies of Williamstown, WV 26187. It is a white powdery substance which is not at all dense and which will do what it is supposed to do when the directions on the container are followed properly.

The shooter can also slip a small balloon over the muzzle. I do not have any data showing any change in breech pressures when a tiny child's balloon is placed over the muzzle of a firearm. If there is any shooter who would prefer to use another method, he may wish to slip a single thickness of plastic sandwich wrap over the muzzle and secure it in place with tape, the tape being wrapped around the barrel, not over the muzzle itself.

An interesting item for the hunter who is going to face the rain during his deer harvest is the Safe-N-Dry Kap Kover from K&M Industries, Inc., Box "E," Elk River, Idaho 83827. The Kap Kover is both for exclusion of rain and for added safety. When in place with the neoprene ring around the nipple (provided), rain would have a hard time invading the powder charge through the nipple.

K&M uses the fine Uncle Mike Hot Shot nipple, modified with a small ring so that the neoprene fitting can be inserted into that ring area around the nipple. Then a metal cover goes over the nipple, making a seal with the neoprene ring. Also, the metal cover makes contact with the nipple seat and thereby will not allow the in-place percussion cap to be detonated by a blow from the nose cup of the hammer. Naturally, instructions which come with the unit must be read and followed exactly or the manufacturer suggests the shooter may not gain full benefit from the product.

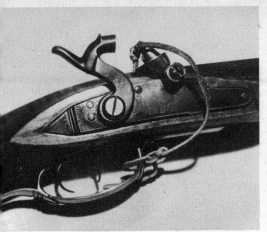

(Left) This is the Kap Kover. It is one of the many useful accoutrements or devices used in black powder hunting. The purpose of the Kap Kover is two-fold. First, it prevents water from entering at the nipple cone. Second, it is a safety device preventing the hammer from falling on a live percussion cap.

(Right) A muzzle may be covered by a balloon to ward off rain. The balloon does not affect the accuracy of the ball, at least not to normally measurable degrees. Naturally, nothing of any substance should be placed across the muzzle, and nothing must plug the muzzle when the rifle is fired.

How Long Can You Leave the Muzzleloader Loaded?

How long can a muzzleloader remain loaded and still be reliable? I suppose no one can put a definite number of hours, or days or weeks on that question. In spite of all of the above rain precautions, I prefer to fire my muzzleloader at the close of each hunting day, cleaning it that evening and reloading it next morning. But in good weather, the hunter may wish to extend the loading time of his firearm as he so chooses. I certainly won't offer any guarantees as to lock time or the possibility of hangfire or misfire, but I can state that I have left my own deer rifle loaded for 72 hours, having loaded it on the afternoon of arriving in deer camp and having taken a buck a few afternoons later. I could detect no loss in lock time and there certainly was no hangfire or misfire.

Cleaning the Black Powder Firearm in Camp

We might want to clean the firearm in camp. The first item needed is a cleaning rod. I use a loading/cleaning rod, such as the N&W unit. Here is a rod which has it all, a muzzle protector, an array of attachments and even a "knocker" to help force free any stuck jag/patch combination. I use it for loading, where I can put about 40 pounds pressure on my seated load, without fear of ramrod breakage, and I use it for cleaning, along with "store-bought" patches, as from Ox-Yoke, or sometimes patches from flannel.

If a shooter wants to flush the bore with hot water or solvent, there are several means. First, there is a unit which is comprised of a threaded base with a neoprene tube emerging from that base. The regular nipple is removed and this unit is inserted in its place. The neoprene tube can be set into the hot water or solvent and a damp patch on a jag run up and down the bore, thereby "sucking" liquid up and down the bore in a flushing manner (by creating a partial vacuum in the bore).

The flintlock shooter can remove his lock and use a device which resembles a C-clamp. There is a watertight fitting which goes up against the touchhole and the same

type of neoprene tube which we just mentioned above acts to bring water into the touchhole and back out the touchhole with the same pumping action we had with our caplock outfit. Simply, the shooter flushes the bore as long as he sees fit to, and on a deer outing he will only have fired maybe once that day, and then he dries the bore with clean patches until the patches remove the fouling therein. After the bore is clean, a patch lightly saturated with some form of oil can be run down a couple times. In the morning, the bore is dried totally with a couple fresh patches before the charge is run home, of course. We don't load a charge into an oily bore. In fact, I also like to detonate a few percussion caps on the nipple of the percussion firearm, pointing the muzzle at a very light object, such as a small leaf or bit of paper. The object should literally blow out of the way indicating a clear channel all the way from the nipple and through the bore.

I like to run a pipe cleaner into the touchhole or the vent on the nipple, too, making certain that all is clear. If a shooter does not want to bother with the hot water flush or the solvent flush, he might simply use a dozen or so cleaning patches soaked at first with solvent and then inserted dry later until the bore is free of fouling. Many black powder shooters prefer this method in camp.

The Shooting Bag

In the field, the successful black powder deer hunter should have with him a number of useful items. Fortunately, these are very small and light for the most part and do not get in the way much. They are generally contained in a shooting bag, such as the fine Uncle Mike all-leather bag. This is a very intelligently designed bag. It is flat and modest in size and it does not hang on the side like a big lady's purse. Called the "Uncle Mike's Full Grain Possibles Bag," it epitomizes what a shooting bag should be for a deer hunter, in this one person's opinion at least.

We can dispense with the terminology quickly by saying that this is really a shooting bag and probably not a possibles bag. I believe, from my study, that a possibles

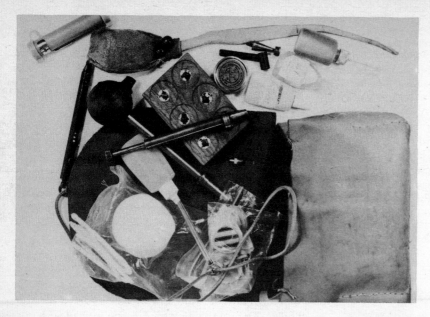

This shooting bag holds a variety of gear essential to the front-loader fan who hunts for deer. Such a kit is necessary to the black powder hunter, especially if he carriess his muzzleloader on a backpack hunt where he cannot return to camp for special items.

bag would have been a larger container holding lots of extras for the mountain man, even to the inclusion of furs and tobacco and gear. Be that as it may, the bag is compartmentalized with a major interior pocket to separate things, and also some loops which can hold an adjustable powder measure and a combination tool and capper.

Looking into my own loading or shooting bag I find the following: First, the loops hold a capper, combo tool and powder measure. Immediately on top is a small pouch of hornet nest material. Then there are my pre-cut patches, and in the same container there are also about a dozen cleaning patches. Then there is a small "bullet bag" to hold round ball. In my bullet or ball bag I have 20 round ball. All are lightly coated with Rig-2 spray. All are pre-weighed to exactly 230.0 grains, so if I should recover any, I can detect how much weight was lost in the game.

I have a small bit of wire, useful for tying the deer tag on the buck, and for other obvious fix-it needs. I have a Forster short-starter with muzzle protector in the bag. There are two Butler Creek readyloads in the bag, but I will put these in a shirt pocket before I take to the field. I have caps contained in a brass box made by Tedd Cash Company. There is an Ozark Mt. Arms nipple wrench and a handful of pipe cleaners. There is a jag and a screw handy, both threaded to fit my ramrod. There is also a worm for pulling a patch.

A small squeeze bottle of "Old Slickum" serves as my lube and my solvent if I should fire, but not use my ready load to recharge my piece. This is from J&A Enterprises and a fine product. I have an extra Hot Shot nipple in the bag, though I can't imagine ever breaking a nipple in the field, and that about does it. I do carry a small powder horn. I have found that the smaller model horn from K-W Company is just right for my needs. It holds plenty of powder but is neat and not bulky.

I think I can get by for several days with only my rifle and that shooting bag with its small and varied contents. The combination tool, from The Hawken Shop, acts as a screwdriver, extra nipple wrench and nipple pick all in one unit. The Hawken Shop capper goes around my neck and holds over 20 percussion caps ready for use. The Uncle Mike's powder measure is adjustable and if I wanted to, I could drop in a light charge and hunt mountain grouse and mountain cottontails where I live. The Old Slickum patch lube and solvent will keep the rifle fit and free of rust in the bore. I also have a sheath attached to the strap of my shooting bag and in that sheath is a smaller knife with a wonderful blade for field dressing a deer. This knife I purchased from Ol' Ephraim Outpost, Rt. 4, Bx 200, Rapid City, SD 57701.

There are numerous "wrinkles" in the muzzle-loading game that we could go into, and of course each shooter is going to finally arrive at the method of hunting which suits him best. We will encounter hunters who carry far less than I do, but I find the shooting bag no problem and I prefer having my gear along with me in the field. Others will load up the rifle, carry a couple readyloads and take off. I often try to remain out a while, and I want to be able to pull a nipple, change a load, insert a fresh load when I want to, and have enough "ammo" along to do some small game shooting if I should so desire.

The black powder hunter, properly equipped, with a carefully loaded firearm, is handicapped as to range and firepower to be sure, but he has more than enough opportunity for success to make up for the handicap. There seems to be more good gear to enhance his lifestyle as time goes by. I recently attained a Hawken Shop sling, for example, which remains rolled up in my pack but can be used to carry the black powder rifle back to camp when the hunter's hands are busy doing other things, such as getting the meat home. By carefully choosing the right tools and using them wisely, the muzzleloader deer hunter has a very good chance of success, both in terms of meat in camp and in terms of pure fulfillment.

chapter 20

The Deer and the Arrow

CERTAINLY archers over the ages have packed meat back to camp, and the modern counterpart of the ancient arrow-flinger has also done a reasonable job in the deer field with his "string-gun." There have certainly been some recent greats in bowhunting, and I'd hate to start naming them for fear of leaving one out. But the good news for archers is the fact that the sport is alive and well, and there is a lot of good information on the subject in magazines and books.

Patience, dedication and supreme interest in the bow can bring a harvested deer. When the hunter has the patience to sit on a well-chosen stump until moss grows to the seat of his pants, or still-hunt so slowly that he's no more than a shadow, the odds for bow-taken venison rise. When the hunter is so dedicated that his bow comes out daily or nearly so, and he is forever getting better through practice on targets, stump-shooting and small game hunting, the odds also increase in his favor. When his interest in the bow is so strong that he reads all of the literature he can get his hands on and then tries the data, keeping what works for him and tossing out or modifying what does not work for him, again the hunter's chances for being successful in the field of archery deer harvesting must at least get a bit better.

The Bow Today

I sincerely doubt that there has been another time in history when the bow was truly more advanced than it is now. I must hasten to point out that I am including the longbow and recurve in that statement, not just the compound bow with its mechanical advantage. All bows are short-range tools when held up in the light of firearms. But it would be folly indeed to suggest that a good archer is helpless beyond 20 or 30 yards. Bows designed to send arrows out over 200 fps are common today, whereas these were considered speedsters only a few short decades ago.

The Longbow

Starting with a very old design, I'd like to mention the longbow. Being historical about this is not my intention. As with all histories, certain primary documentation is sometimes open to interpretation, and a big can of worms opens when one tries to firmly establish the origin of certain tools. But I think we can say that the longbow I am speaking of is primarily the bow of the British. The English longbow was also the style used when archery had its rebirth in this country. The bow was held not only in the hands of the very famous pair, Pope and Young, but also in the hands of Will and Maurice Thompson. The latter wrote some very interesting prose on the bow, including how to make your own archery tackle.

The longbow is with us better than ever. Fortunately, we have some supremely fine bowyers around who can still make a fine longbow, primarily by hand. They make the true longbow. This is a full-length bow, sometimes (seldom) a self-bow, and more often a composite. The

Here is a longbow with a reverse handle. No, the bow is not strung backwards. It is a reverse handle. Howard Hill was known to have more than one of these bows in his shooting career. It is a true longbow and was handcrafted by bowyer John Schulz.

Here are a few memorabilia from the Howard Hill Archery Company. Howard was certainly a great in the entire field of archery, and it is wonderful that we have several interested parties continuing the Hill tradition of longbows and longbow tackle.

The three basic types of hunting bow used in America today are the longbow, compound and recurve. The longbow on the left is a John Schulz creation with reverse handle. In the center is an Arrowstar from Jennings Company and a Hoyt recurve on the right. All are satisfactory for deer hunting, with the compound being the most popular.

true longbow has a very narrow limb and a thick core. The bow nocks are pointed and graceful. The bow is extremely stable. My own longbow was make by John Schulz. It has a reverse handle. That is, the handle points out away from the face of the bow rather than back toward the shooter. This design was not totally uncommon in the past and the wonderful archer, Howard Hill, made mention of, owned and did shoot reverse handle longbows. I mention the reverse handle longbow because it does seem to be a good design for shooting a little bit more in the modern "straight-up" position, though I still cant my longbow considerably, shooting my arrows off the shelf.

The hunting longbow, made by one of the master bowyers, offers more than one might think for the archer. It can be made in darn near any reasonable archery draw weight. Mine is 70 pounds, but 80s and 90s are not uncommon. And it can be fast. I say it can be fast because it depends upon the exact style of the bow, the structure of the limbs and so forth, and it also depends upon what the archer considers fast. My own longbow in 70-pound pull weight has been chronographed at 220 fps with a graphite hunting arrow.

The longbow is light as a wisp of wind. The physical weight of my own model is a bit over 1½ pounds. The longbow is most often shot in the barebow style, instinctively primarily and without sights, though sights can be mounted in some cases. I have often stood in somewhat dumbfounded disbelief as my friends from the longbow camp argued against other types of bows. I have stood in the same unhappy stance when lovers of non-longbow forms condemned the longbows.

I think the longbow is a viable alternative to the compound. It is not better than a compound. Nor is the compound better than the longbow in my opinion, They are just different and what one style can do well, the other may not do so well. There are, however, a few points brought out often which are simply incorrect, and these should be cleared up. Speed without power is one example. I have heard that some bows have speed, but not power. I can only say that an arrow is a missile just like any other type of projectile, and if it goes faster, there is more potential for increased energy. That energy may not be useful energy, but talking about "speed without power" is not a worthwhile subject.

Nor is it correct to speak of a bow with good cast, but its velocity is low. Yes, there can be many factors involved in how an arrow will fly, but when someone speaks of two arrows which are exactly the same, or for that matter, the same arrow being fired from two bows, the faster arrow, all other things being equal, will fly the farther of the two. All in all, arguments in terms of "best bow type" are more or less wasteful.

So, we mention first the longbow because there is a devoted following of this type still strong on our continent and likely to remain so for a very long time to come. Many of these archers follow the traditions given us by the great Howard Hill and certainly no person can impune Mr. Hill's record as an archer. He was simply great. He was both target shooter and bowhunter. His longbows, shooting heavy arrows, dropped all manner of game from cottontails to elephants, and his books can still be located today and will be in reprint form in some number as well.

The Recurve Bow

Some archers call this the Turkish design, with the tips of the limbs bent forward. There are some differences here as opposed to the longbow, but the major characteristics are not totally dissimilar. The tiller is about the same on both styles, and in fact certain aspects of limb length and tiller remain the same on the compounds. The problem with the recurve is that some of the prettiest models were fairly slow-shooters, especially those with huge wide flat limbs and thin cores. But there are now and have been some super fine recurve bows for the archer, and another world famous archer, Fred Bear, did some remarkable work with such a bow.

It seems to me that there should be plenty of room in the world of archery for the various bow styles, but today the recurve bow is not advertised very much at all. It's too bad, because this style of bow is a good one. But archers have more or less split into two camps, the longbow lovers and the compound devotees.

At any rate, there are still some absolutely beautiful recurve bows around, such as the Black Widow, which is still offered by the Black Widow Bow Company, Rt. 2 Box 69, Billings, MO 65610. And there are a number of fine recurve bows which are in the hands of bowhunters. Recurve bows are totally viable deer-takers, and it is the archer behind the bow more than the bow itself which will finally determine success.

The Compound Bow

Certainly, the compound is king today. One may leaf through popular archery publications or visit his local archery shop and he will be confronted on all sides by compounds. The compound bow is indeed a revolutionary tool. On the one hand, it is without question a bow in all aspects of shooting and it is not a "rifle" as some archers seem to think. I was told recently that, "A compound is just a rifle with strings. How can you miss with one?" Well, missing with a compound is accomplished by this shooter without any trouble whatsoever. Hitting the bull's-eye is my problem, and I have found that the compound bow, while it's a marvel and a whiz in many ways, has not made a good shooter out of me. But then, I doubt any bow can do that. I have to do that for myself.

One of the big features of the compound bow is the relaxation factor. In short, as the eccentric cams turn over, we have a condition whereby the archer is now holding less actual "pull weight" at full draw than he was, say, halfway through the draw. This is a good factor, of course. The archer can hold his draw longer. He can draw his bow and wait a moment for that approaching buck. In fact, he may only have to hold about 50 percent of the actual draw weight of the bow. If the hunter happened to be using a 60-pound bow, then he might actually have to hold back on only 30 pounds pull at full relaxation.

There are only two things wrong with super relaxation as far as I can see. First, performance may tend to drop a bit with the bows that have super relaxation qualities. I'm sure some smart engineer will find a way around this,

A compound bow in the 70-pound draw weight shown here is a high performance model from Jennings. The letoff is 25 percent, so we are only holding about 52.5 pounds at full draw.

Here are some bowsights rigged on a compound bow. The topmost beads are for closer range, while the lower sights are for farther ranges. The bar around the sights protects the sight from damage.

but I think the statement holds mostly true at the moment. I have a Jennings high performance compound and the relaxation factor is about 25 percent instead of higher. Second, when the bow relaxes to a great degree, the release, it seems to me, is a bit soft. With the relaxation factor cut back, the string seems to escape the fingers better. But again, the archers who use some form of mechanical release might not have to worry about this factor too much.

The compound bow has a good rating in terms of static hysteresis or efficiency in that the system seems to derive a good ratio between the energy stored in the bow and that amount of energy which finally ends up at the nock of the arrow. This is a very unscientific way of putting it, and as deer hunters all we need to know is that the bow is capable of delivering a high energy rating for the energy that is put into the bow by pulling the string back. Since we are talking as deer hunters and not simply archery enthusiasts about all we have to remember here is that our compound bow is capable of a mechanical advantage that the other bows do not have. Really good archers can enjoy success with all of the bow types.

The Arrow

Whenever we say anything at all these days we open a huge expressway for dissent. But in spite of that fact,

I'd like to suggest that all of the bow styles are perfectly adequate in the hands of a truly good deer hunter, and all will deliver an arrow with sufficient force to shoot entirely through a deer's chest with the arrow whacking into a tree beyond.

I sometimes think the arrow and the broadhead are more open to discussion than is the bow type. There are a few points we'd like to make about the arrow before moving on to the broadhead.

Arrow weight, mass weight that is, has a lot to do with the penetration qualities which will be inherent in the broadhead. But we can't simply say "heavy arrows always penetrate the best." It is not that simple and in fact many engineers who are also archers get very upset when bowhunters simplify penetration down to arrow weight alone, leaving out other factors. In the first place, we have to "spine" an arrow to match the bow. One of the reasons, and please note I said *one* of the reasons, for the faster speed of a compound bow is the fact that the compound is generally capable of shooting lighter arrows (in weight) than can be shot true from noncompound bows of the same draw weight.

If one studies high speed photos of a bow while the arrow is in the process of emerging around the riser, he will see that as the string is released the arrow tends to buckle to a degree and it also tends to "warp" around

Bowhunters have to learn form. Without form, they generally do not excel in the field. Shooting a bow well means doing the same thing each time. In a manner of speaking, the anchor point is like the rear sight on a rifle, and when a shooter takes a different anchor point every time, it is much like moving the rear sight of a rifle at random prior to each shot. Accuracy would be fairly impossible to attain.

the riser of the bow and then straighten itself out. Since, I suppose, the actual initial thrust on a relaxed fully drawn compound bow is not the value of the inevitable full thrust to come, the compound arrow does not need to be quite as stiff as the standard bow's arrow.

We don't want to get spine confused with weight in that it is possible to get heavy spine and lighter weight in some materials. The graphite arrow is a good example of this. The arrow can be quite stiff and yet not terribly heavy. But all in all, we still have to match the arrow to the bow and as we go up in bow pounds pull then we tend to go up in arrow weight. I do not disagree that heavier arrows generally penetrate better than light arrows, but I suppose we should qualify that by saying something about the *energy* of that arrow. We are speaking of the KE (kinetic energy) of the arrow here. So, if we go to a heavy arrow for the weight but cannot drive that arrow at much speed, our would-be penetration values might not be there at all. Fortunately, perhaps, we are generally forced to go higher in bow pull weight when we go up in arrow weight because, in part, of spine factors.

Now, with a graphite arrow this gets cloudy because the stiffness of that arrow allows a rather wide latitude, and one arrow can often be used in several different bows with success in terms of spine. I want to quote some of the work of Harry Mathewson, an engineer with Advanced Composites of Bellevue, Washington. Harry pointed out in *Archery Retailer* a few years ago, the following: "I also would like to make one small comment on arrow penetration. Penetration is a function of kinetic energy (weight of arrow multiplied by the velocity squared divided by two times the acceleration of gravity—32.2 x 2 = 64.4 [64.32 is also accepted]) and not merely weight of the arrow times velocity."

Mr. Mathewson ran, under lab conditions, using a mechanical device to shoot the bow, a series of tests. In short, the theory was fairly well borne out. High energy arrows penetrated more than lower energy arrows. Naturally, lab test medium is never going to match perfectly the hide and bone and muscle of a deer, and we are not trying to complicate matters here. I suppose all we can do is repeat the figures, these being that higher energy arrows penetrate better, and then we can apply the idea to real conditions by looking for that *combination* of arrow weight and speed *out of our bows* which works best. We do this by trying several different arrow sizes and types in order to see which spine and construction flies best from our own individual and personal bows after that bow has been properly tuned. With a compound bow, tuning methods are generally explained in the manual which accompanies the new bow. I also had very good luck using the booklet "Doctor Your Own Compound Bow" by Emery J. Loiselle.

I think the bow test approach itself may be a bit involved for those who want to hunt deer and really do not care about force draw curve, but do care about their

Tink Nathan laced a scrape with his famous lure. Bowhunters generally use a number of methods in order to bag their game. Among the methods we find the use of scents as lures.

(Right) J. Wayne Fears with a whitetail buck he took with the compound bow. The compound bow has become the byword of the American archer but there are still a number of longbow fans around and some recurve shooters. (Photo courtesy of J. Wayne Fears)

personal bows shooting well. However, as a generalized inclusion, we can spend a moment suggesting what a bow test is trying to measure.

1. We need to know how much energy a bow stores when it is drawn.
2. We want to find out how *efficiently* the bow stores the energy.
3. Relation of the energy *stored* to the maximum force which must be put forth to draw the bow is important in rating a bow. The desired condition is an effort/storage ratio that is high in terms of stored energy. How does a tester determine the total energy that is exerted and stored? When the bow is drawn, we measure in 1-inch increments the force necessary to pull the string from brace height to full draw. this information is plotted on a chart and we call it *Force-Draw Curve.*
4. The result here is the potential energy of the bow in foot-pounds. An example would be 51# at 28 inches = 43.23 foot-pounds. Divide 43.23 by the peak weight of the bow, 51, and we have 0.848. So stored energy

divided by peak draw force has given us 0.848 fp/P of draw weight. Therefore, efficiency is the ratio between the actual peak of the bow and stored energy.

Remember static hysteresis. We can look at this as energy *lost* in the system (friction). The system of measuring the actual effectiveness of a given bow goes on into obtaining the kinetic energy of the arrow, and then bow efficiency becomes $\frac{EK}{ES}$ x 100, or kinetic energy of the arrow divided by the stored energy of the bow times 100.

Here is what I really do in order to pick a bow and arrow combination. I have a whole stable of arrows which I use. These vary as to spine and weight, and construction—wood, aluminum and graphite. I select a bow based upon the literature. I then try to mate the bow with the right arrow by first tuning the bow and then trying the various arrows, using the recommended sizes first of course. I don't mean to sound harsh toward intelligent bow testing and I'm not. For example, let's say we have a kinetic energy in the arrow of 32 fp and a stored energy level of 43. We divide, getting .74 or 74 percent. The 74 percent is our efficiency number, and it's great. But I think the bowhunter should study all the materials he can, and then head for the archery shop, picking a bow he may, hopefully, even be able to try out before he plunks his cash down.

In the world of good two-wheel compounds now, he may not even have to tune that bow as he might wish to with a four-wheeler and even this generalization is dangerous. I had a four-wheeler I tuned once and checked over and over again. It did not require further tuning for a year's worth of shooting. Anyway, knowing the bow is in tune, the shooter tries the arrows recommended for the bow, and maybe a few others.

Cedar arrows work well in the compound, by the way, as do the fine and popular aluminum arrows. The latter is the more used today, though I still construct good but very inexpensive cedars for small game and practice, and these work well in the compound by rating the cedar to the peak draw weight of the bow. In short, a 70-pound compound uses a 70-75 spine cedar shaft. Once I find

Criteria for a Good Broadhead

The following are a few ideas concerning the selection of a broadhead to be used for big game hunting. They are only some points which have been gathered over the years and definitely do not constitute the "last word" on the subject. However, some of the points are rather basic, I think, to picking a broadhead which is going to do the job of harvesting with efficiency. First, and I know every archer is aware of the fact, the broadhead must either be sharp when it comes out of the shop or it must have the capability of being made truly sharp. I also know it is a cliche by now, but just to keep the record straight we will once again say that the broadhead kills by causing hemorrhage, rather than relying very much on tissue disruption. In a sense, we can say that the arrow does kill by shock if we use the medical definition of shock which includes the loss of blood in the definition. But we do not mean the so-called "hydrostatic shock" which some people associate with the bullet harvest.

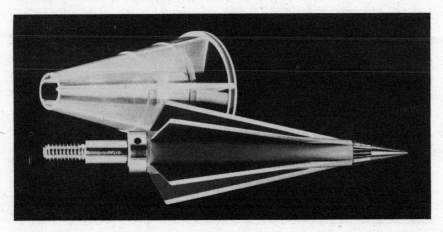

An advanced broadhead design is the Razorbak-5. Today, there are a number of broadheads, such as the Kolpin and others, which are engineered for maximum performance for better results in the field.

the right hunting arrow for the bow, I stick with it and that is that. But I do have more than one arrow type per given compound bow in terms of all-around use. For example, my 70-pound compound uses 70-75 cedars for small game and target work, but I will use graphites and aluminum arrows for serious hunting. In my longbow, I use only cedar shafts at this time, but have had very good luck with both aluminum and graphite arrows in the longbow as well; however, cedar recovers faster than aluminum which means the cedar arrow warps more readily around the riser.

The Broadhead

After a bowhunter has found the bow he likes and he has matched it with the best possible arrow in terms of weight and spine stiffness, he needs to consider a broadhead. The broadhead is to the arrow what the bullet is to the cartridge. No matter the size of the case or the caliber, the bullet has to be right, and no matter the poundage of the bow or the construction of the arrow, the broadhead has to be right.

Second, the sharp head should remain sharp in terms of minor contact with a backquiver, but more importantly it should have the ability to remain sharp as it does its work in the game, rather than dulling or chipping out before sufficient penetration is possible. I also hope that the reader will allow the fact that while our usual concept of shock associated with the firearm is not present in the arrow, there is shock. There is some shock in the layman's definition of the term as the arrow strikes the target, but I think we can stick to the idea that the arrow's broadhead should be sharp and stay sharp in its function so that bleeding can occur.

In a paradoxical way, the more physical shock delivered by the arrow, the better the system is at shutting down bleeding, so we are not interested in delivering a blow to the deer, but only interested in the slicing effect of the broadhead. The flow of blood is curtailed immediately following the striking of a broadhead because the vascular system tries to shut down, and it does so partially, plus coagulation is chemically induced. So the very sharp broadhead, we think, is best because it does not use energy in shape change of the blades, but it uses energy for slicing instead.

Frayed tips of vessels, according to my research, will tend to mend better than cleanly sliced ends of vessels. I suppose we see some of this when we get cut by a new razor blade. I think we are automatically reaching another important point here—the edges of the broadhead should not be so flimsy that they may break or bend excessively. In other words, the edges should remain intact for cutting purposes. Also, the blades of the broadhead should remain in position rather than bending as the theory here is in favor of the blades working together as a single unit for penetration rather than the blades "prying around" and taking different directions, thereby fighting the progress of one another on a multi-bladed broadhead.

Third, there should not be an overly large amount of drag in the broadhead design. Any protrusion which can retard the actual penetration of the broadhead is less than desirable. A broken blade, then, can cause drag and this is not what we want. Also, any protrusions caused by the design of the broadhead will also cause drag. A point

is all a head can do, slice or chop. The problem with chopping is the fact that it requires a lot of energy and that energy could have been better spent in penetration instead. Therefore, we prefer slicing to chopping. Short and wide blades seem to chop. Long and narrow designs seem to slice. An engineer, Andy Simo, suggests that we can draw up a Penetration Ratio which is the ratio of length to width and which results in a raw figure. Mr. Simo has put a bottom line on this figure. He suggests that a broadhead is mostly slicing instead of chopping when the number assigned to the broadhead, via our ratio, is more than two (2). When the number of our ratio is below 2, Mr. Simo suggests that the head is doing more chopping than slicing. As an example, we would have the Howard Hill type broadhead with a PR (penetration ratio) of 2.73. The Razorbak-5 head would go 2.34 and so forth, with some head designs falling to as low as 0.75 in Mr. Simo's tests.

Now, these penetration figures do not include many other important criteria, of course. A flimsy dull head that mushes up on contact with game might have a high

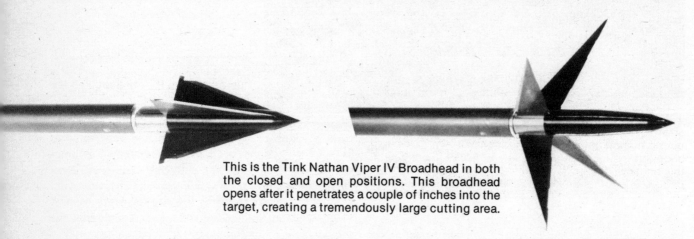

This is the Tink Nathan Viper IV Broadhead in both the closed and open positions. This broadhead opens after it penetrates a couple of inches into the target, creating a tremendously large cutting area.

which bends or even mushrooms a bit can cause drag. Therefore, the better broadhead designs, we think, are those which give a good solid construction, to include a strong cutting edge, and to *exclude* as much as possible any appendage that can grab and hold on, thereby reducing penetration by creating drag.

This will sound silly, I know, but when an associate of mine and I were testing some popular broadheads we used cars at the dump and old bricks as part of our test run. These destruction tests, we felt, were important. We did find some broadheads which snapped and broke and others which did not. More amazingly, the better broadheads of the day withstood a smack into a brick and were not totally ruined for the experience. It may be expensive to run such tests because of the loss of broadheads, but the shooter will find it more expensive to lose game which might have been downed by a better broadhead.

Four, we can consider the mechanics of cutting in two ways, *slicing* and *chopping*. As far as I can fathom, that

PR, but the high PR would not prove of much value in this case. But a strong head with the fewest possible protrusions (which would cause drag) combined with all the criteria mentioned, strength and so forth, *plus* a high PR would be good. We do have to include the force of the arrow in this. A very light bow shooting a very good broadhead could fall behind the effectiveness of a very heavy bow driving an arrow of high kinetic energy, even though the latter is using a chopping type head.

As the reader knows, excellence usually results from a *combination* of good criteria, whether we are judging the penetration qualities of a broadhead or the fine points of a custom rifle. This is why we ask that a broadhead be free of those protrusions which cause surface friction, such as cutouts in the blades, rings, grooves, rivets and so forth.

Five, we have to consider flight characteristics. After all, no matter how high the PR and other factors, if the broadhead does not fly correctly in conjunction with the arrow, then it is of no value to the archer. Of course,

J. Wayne Fears with a whitetail buck taken with bow and arrow. Wayne uses sights on his bow. Sights on a compound make a lot of sense for most shooters, though shooting instinctively is the way to go, generally, with the longbow. (Sights have been mounted on the longbow, of course.) (Photo courtesy J. Wayne Fears)

let's not get carried away. Some fine heads will fail in terms of flight because the arrow is wrong or the bow too light in thrust to give the arrow proper stabilization. We can say that the PR factor does seem to favor good arrow flight because a broadhead with high PR tends to steer less than a broadhead with less of our PR factor going for it.

A high ratio head, in short, has very little tendency to windplane. Aerodynamic steering is mainly a function of blade width and whether or not the blades are in line with the actual plane of the shaft. A wide-bladed broadhead can almost serve as a set of wings, while an offset blade can have a screwing effect in the atmosphere something like the propeller on an airplane. So a broadhead with high PR, narrow bladed, with the blades lined up correctly is less likely to steer an arrow than a broadhead with short flat blades that might also be out of line to boot.

Multiple Bladed Broadheads

How about all those blades? Won't additional blades impede the progress of the arrow? The multiple bladed broadhead is a very good idea in fact, and properly designed will give more than it will take away. The many-bladed head increases the mathematical chance for a blood vessel being struck, and it also increases cutting in the capillary system, which is important because the capillary system is widespread over the surface of an animal.

Broadhead Weight

There can be no rule of thumb as to the weight of a broadhead because the head has to match with the weight of the arrow and thrust of the bow. The arrow must not be dominated by the broadhead. Balance is the key to good flight, of course. We have to include the spine of the arrow as well as the weight of the arrow when we talk balance. I have used a 160-grain broadhead on a very light graphite arrow and the arrow flew well, but the graphite is very stiff in this case. Again, this sounds very costly, but a dedicated archer should take at least one broadhead and actually shoot that head on an arrow, even if the head is dulled on the target. No deer hunter can afford to find out in the field that his broadhead does not match up with his arrow.

Fletching

Today, the plastic vane is used in conjunction with most aluminum arrows. The new and improved vanes are good. Some archers still use feathers, too. The major value in fletching is a drag on the back end of the arrow and the archer must try different fletching styles and materials in order to determine which is best suited to his shooting style and his archery equipment. The longbow, however, must use feathers for fletching. At least, I have not been able to shoot off the shelf with vanes and get by with it. The fletching is quite forgiving when it is feather, and it will collapse on the shelf and allow the arrow to remain on course.

Bowhunting Tactics

The bowhunter is bound by the same tactical maneuvers used by gun hunters. He must first locate a prime area for deer, often determined by preseason scouting, and then he must find a deer and harvest it. The big difference in bowhunting is *range*. If a rifleman finds a deer feeding on a ridge 200 yards away, he has a good chance of taking the animal with one well-placed shot. If the bowhunter sees the same deer, he'd best plan a stalk to within 50 or 60 yards of his quarry. It is somewhat difficult to put an exit limit on bow range for clean deer harvesting. Howard Hill took a bull elk at more than 170 paces with one arrow. However, Hill was not merely an archer by hobby, but an archer by vocation.

I think that 50 yards is about far enough to attempt taking a deer with an arrow *for most of us*. There will be some misjudgement in the actual range of the deer, and I think we can add a plus of 10 yards for that, giving us an extreme practical range of 60 yards. The modern bows can push an arrow fast enough to give it cast sufficient for 60-yard shots. An arrow from a bow of legal hunting weight will, in many cases, totally penetrate a deer's chest cavity at 60 yards. The modern compound bow, such as the popular York model with its Alpha™ Cams and graphite limbs can push heavy hunting arrows at velocities in excess of 240 fps, for example, and in some of our tests with the graphite arrow, velocities of 260 fps and better were reached. Compared with some of the older hunting bows which often achieved something in the 150 fps range, this is quite an improvement. The modern longbow, with composite limbs, has also broken the 200 fps barrier.

Nonetheless, we are still dealing with a short-range tool when we bowhunt. Therefore, our tactics have to match our gear. Getting close is the most important ingredient in a bowhunter's recipe for success.

Clothing

If we are going to stalk for a close shot, then every aspect of our hunting outfit must fit into the realm of quietness. Shoes, for example, should be as soft-soled as practical. Pant legs should not scrape together like cricket's legs in terms of noise, alerting deer to the hunter's position, with the same rules applying to shirts and jackets.

If the hunter is going to carry a pack, then he should

Stalking is a matter of correct wind direction—the air currents coming into the face of the hunter instead of from hunter to game—and it also means quietness and careful use of natural cover. Many longbow hunters, including Howard Hill and, shown here, the nephew of Howard Hill, Jerry Hill, do not prefer camouflage, feeling that motion is the big giveaway and camouflage will not help when hunter motion alerts a deer. Instead of camouflage, these hunters observe wind direction, noise, and the use of cover.

An archer on stand may use the natural surroundings to keep him hidden. However, he must be able to get off a good shot, too. Bill Fadala illustrates a situation in which the archer has to rise "above his blind" in order to get a shot. Since he is standing above a deer trail (his position is very important here), when he does rise to his feet, he will not be seen nearly as well as if he were on ground level with the game.

make certain of the fit, using a pack which will not scrape and rub very much in close-growing vegetation or timber. All of our dress as bowhunters should consist of fabrics which do not "cry out" when we move. Obviously, we must dress for the conditions.

Even the hat makes a difference in bowhunting tactics. The wide-brimmed types can be a big problem. When the archer draws the bow, the string can move into the hat. This can actually cause a problem with clean release of the arrow.

The bowhunter is often allowed to wear camouflaged

clothing instead of safety blaze orange. Of course, this is a matter of local game laws and the hunter is charged with the responsibility of understanding local laws before he sets out in camouflaged clothing. Here, again, we have clothes and tactics blending together. The reason for camouflage is to remain unseen, and the reason to remain unseen is to either get close to a deer (stalking) or let the deer get close to the hunter (on stand). One false move and the deer will spot the hunter, camouflage or not, of course, but camo can aid a hunter in his tactical design for getting closer to his deer.

Stump-shooting is a very important type of practice for the bowhunter. It allows him or her to wander the fields and shoot under a setting very similar to deer hunting. Also, it means some extremely useful range judgement as well. Sometimes such shooting takes the form of "roving," with specific targets and ranges.

(Left) In-the-field practice for the archer is very important. Here, a bowhunter practices on a deer-sized target. He even wears his usual clothing so that the practice is true-to-life.

Tackle

The bowhunter's tackle must suit his methods, and since we are talking about stalking, we mean that a hunter's bow, bowquiver, backquiver, and all his gear be conducive to quietness. First, the bow should fit the situation. Shorter bows are not always better for brush, but if a bow gives about the same performance in either short or long length, the hunter who is out in thick brush may elect for the shorter model. Longbows are so light in the hand and so quiet to maneuver that I do not find them a problem in the brush. The major consideration is for the hunter to pick a bow which he can maneuver quietly, as opposed to a bow which is unwieldy. I had an old compound bow which was built like a couple of planks held together with strings and pulleys, and I was forever banging that thing against something as I tried to carry it in the woods. My current compound bow carries much better.

Bow silencers can make a difference, too. While these devices attached to the string will not quiet the release of the arrow totally, they can help, and if our intent is to stalk and get close to our deer, then we might as well follow up with our plan for quietness with the use of silencers. Why? Because an archer can sometimes get a second shot if his bow has not twanged a message of his location, and more than that, the twang of a bowstring can alert a deer and he can "jump the string." Modern bowhunters do not have as much problem with the latter because today's bows are so much faster than the string-guns of yesteryear. But it can still occur. With the speed of sound being something like 1120 fps, the bowstring's twang will reach the deer before the arrow does, and the animal can actually jump out of the path of the arrow.

All equipment should fit the bow correctly. This goes for bowquivers and sights especially. They should not snag up in the brush. They should be a part of the bow, forming a single unit. All I am saying here is this: The bowhunter should consider sights and quivers which are made for his bow. Other sights and quivers may attach adequately, but do they fit? Or are they protrusions to hang up on the brush? A backquiver should fit, too. Backquivers are excellent. I have used one a great deal. But they should be on the softer side, somewhat pliable, not hard and rigid. The Hill backquiver design is a fine one.

Still-hunting for Archers

I see no great difference between still-hunting for bowhunters or for gun hunters. All hunters have to be somewhat mindful of how they present themselves when they are in motion in deer country. To be sure, no hunter ever born is so quiet that a deer can't hear him move in the woods. But I have stalked deer to within 10 yards by following a few procedures, such as the clothing tips mentioned above. In a nutshell, however, I think the bowhunter should practice one aspect of good still-hunting with great attention— the archer should still-hunt *slowly*, even more slowly than the gun hunter, and the latter should pretend he's a turtle, not a rabbit. On two occasions I have had the chance to watch master bowhunters still-hunt. In both cases, I was pausing in the forest when I saw these two men in action. One was Jim Ploen, a superb archer and hunter. The other was John Kane, who guides and hunts for a living. Both of these men wore clothing which suited their tactics. They had archery tackle which had been tuned to perfection, not only in tillering and those aspects, but also in personal fit. Both men used the ground over which they walked as if they were barefooted and sharpened spikes were protruding up from the earth in all directions. In one case, Ploen was within 20 yards of me before I heard him. Foot placement was part of their quietness, but I think the major contributing factor to their good still-hunting was the slow pace they both maintained.

Standhunting for Archers

Once again, the basics of standhunting, or staying still, pertain to gun hunters and archers alike. An area is chosen not only because it shows sign of game travel, or because it is appropriate for a drive, but also for reasons of tackle handling. If a stand is situated so that the archer has to fully show himself and change his position drastically for a shot, the game will be alerted immediately and chances for a standing shot are going to be small. This is why the tree stand is so often used by the archer. He can get a shot off without changing his position too much and he's above his game so that he can see the area.

One important point, however, needs to be made about a stand for the archer. If a bowhunter is going to use a stand, on the ground or in a tree, or a blind of some sort, he should fire a number of practice shots beforehand. It is more than frustrating to find that the upper limb of the bow hits against a branch when brought into play. If the hunter finds this out before a deer shows up, fine. But if he finds out when the first buck of the day makes his way into the clearing, there can only be a problem for the bowhunter. Also, things look very different from a stand, even a stand on the ground. In other words, we are squatting or sitting. The tree stand is even more strange as far as visual point of view is concerned. I recall firing a group of arrows at a target from a tree stand. My first arrow was a good 2 feet off the mark from only 20 yards away. I adjusted my aim for the angle, and if a deer had later come to that same spot, I would have known how to aim at it. Therefore, I believe that it is an important aspect of hunting tactics for the archer to use some practice shots from his stand prior to any actual shooting at a deer.

The Handling of Tackle

Another aspect of bowhunting is the actual handling of the tackle. It is certainly no good for a deer hunter of any kind to be unable to smoothly handle his tools; however, it is an even larger problem for the archer. I believe that I could fire just about any well-sighted rifle with some degree of accuracy even if I had never before touched the rifle. However, I do not feel the same about a bow. A bow is much more personal to touch. The bowhunter has to personally tune his equipment so that the nocking point on the string is correct for his method of shooting, the arrow rest is proper, the arrows are spined correctly, and so forth.

Every aspect of the bow and its attending accessories should be in tune, so to speak. If a cushion plunger is incorrect, that alone can send an arrow off of the aiming point. The string must be in perfect condition. So must every part of the bow. I once had an arrow rest fall right off the bow just as I released. My son had been working a mini-drive on my behalf and the deer was only 20 paces away when I released. The arrow flew to the earth 10 yards in front of me. The deer did not even run, but instead ambled off into the trees. I think that had I missed for some other reason, I might have gotten a second shot at that deer, for I was fairly well concealed. But my bow was useless until I replaced the arrow rest.

I do not have to tell hunters to take along extra arrow rests and silencers and all other pertinent tackle, so I will not list those items here; however, just as a reminder and nothing else, let's remember that it never hurts to have replacement gear, even an extra bow, back in camp or, for the small items, such as the arrow rest, right along on our person.

Successful deer hunting is a combination of many factors, all working together with a little luck to cement them together. But as archers we can often make a good part of our luck ourselves. We should remember not to create our own bad luck, however, with untuned equipment and lack of practice with our equipment. I was in a gunshop which handles archery tackle when a hunter came in and bought a set of arrows on his way to a deer hunt. The proprietor asked about spine. The hunter was not sure. He had some practice arrows along, but they were cedars and in fact correctly spined for his compound bow. But the hunter had never tried any other arrow. Now he was going into the deer field with an arrow he'd never fired from his particular bow.

He was lucky. The owner of the shop grabbed a few arrows of different spine and the two men headed for the back yard range. When the hunter left the shop, he had an arrow which was right for the bow. But such practice is not in tune with good bowhunting tactics. Bowhunting tactics are much more than field tactics. They are methods which begin long before the season opens.

chapter 21

Getting Your Deer Back to Camp

I SEE NOTHING wrong with driving right up to your downed buck and loading him into a vehicle. By that I mean, I have no "macho" image of hunters being too tough to resort to the iron pony in order to transport the meat back to camp. However, there are some pretty severe problems which restrict retrieving a deer by vehicle. First, and perhaps foremost, is the factor of injuring the land. I know of no rancher or farmer who would appreciate his field being run over by a rig of any sort other than his farm or ranch equipment. By the way, tearing up public land is also to be avoided. Dampness of the earth at times can make even proper dirt backroads off-limits to travel, for the ruts which a vehicle can gouge into the earth may last a very long time indeed. The ruts made by pioneer wagons on the Oregon Trail are still visible on the Wyoming-Idaho border in fact.

However, there are times when a hunter can certainly get close to his downed deer with a vehicle, and I think this method is fine as long as the land is not wrecked in the process of getting the game out. One other thing— no sense in getting hurt when driving up to fallen game either. I am not aware of any actual injuries here, but I am aware of some close calls. I remember a four-wheel-drive vehicle that had slipped off into a wash. The vehicle did not turn over and no one was hurt, but a fender was bent on a rock and it took the party a while to get free of their predicament. They were trying to reach a downed desert mule deer buck.

For the hunter who transports his deer with a motor vehicle large painting tarps are available cheaply at the paint store, so that soiling the interior of a vehicle is prevented. I am 100 percent against mounting a buck on the fender of any vehicle and parading it to camp. If there is any way to avoid toting it on a car fender, I will take that way. Naturally, there may be a time when a hunter has no alternative to this situation, and in that case I would put a tarp down first and fold the edges of the tarp over the deer.

Dragging the Deer

Snow makes dragging quite effective of course, and I have also seen deer dragged over ground as dry as a sand pit. The latter, to my way of thinking, is both hard on the hunter and hard on the deer. It's tough to drag a carcass of "dead weight" over dry ground. Furthermore, rocks and twigs and other obstacles on the way can bruise a deer's edible parts. I don't know that the latter is serious. I simply have had no experience with meat that was bruised in this way, other than to see a deer hanging in camp which, after being skinned, did show bruise marks from dragging. That this ruins the meat, I doubt. That it helps the meat in any way I doubt even more.

When snow is on the ground, however, a hunter can drag a buck over it, and it's better yet when he has help. He may also wish to use the Buckskinner Skinner/Dragger which aids the process. Each hunter in a pair can use the

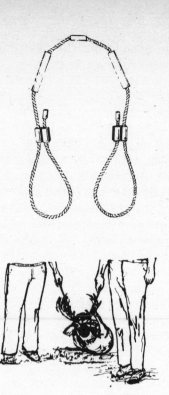

Dean Zollinger, Idaho gunmaker and hunter, uses a Buckskinner Dagger/Skinner (illustrated at right) to help him pull a buck from the woods. The good snow cover protects the carcass from bruising.

handles, one handle on each antler beam. About the only caution I can think of here is to warn the hunter to continue using his bright orange outer garment while dragging. It's the law anyway in most places, but even if it were not, a hunter should be aware that as he stoops and drags his buck his "up and down" profile becomes more elongated and closer to the ground. He should play it safe. If a companion is along, it might not hurt if they talk to each other on the way back to camp so that they can be heard.

The above, of course, is for the good of the hunter. For the good of the deer I suppose we all know that it's best to drag the carcass by the head so the hair on the body will not be pulled out all over the trail. More important than that is the fact that the deer seems to "travel better" over the ground when pulled head first, as the animal is "built that way," more streamlined from head to back feet than the other way around.

Naturally, the deer has been opened up. Hopefully, the hunter used the method of "coring" rather than cutting the cinch bone which will allow the back legs to flop open all the time. With the aitch bone or cinch bone intact, the legs stay together. Also, by not cutting the bone, the hunter has not exposed that good meat in the area of the haunches. The deer will still cool just fine without the cinch bone being cut or split.

Also for protection of the meat and ease of handling, I think that dragging the deer while the carcass is not yet cooled off is best. A cool carcass stiffens up and this means a problem not only with meat bruising, but also with stiff legs hanging up on undergrowth and other objects, some of which may be hidden by the snow.

Pole Carry

I have only tried this one time. Due to lack of skill, probably, it was a miserable effort. I never tried it again. But it looks just great—two hunters with a deer tied to a pole and then one end of the pole over the shoulder of each respective hunter . . . what could be better? As I say, for me it was a bad way to carry a deer out of the forest. We were having a hard time coordinating our efforts, and we almost knocked each other off our feet from time to time, plus the pole dug into the shoulder about like a steel bar. However, there are certainly hunters who do use the method, and it's not for me to dissuade those who find the method useful.

The Shoulder Carry

When I was growing up in southern Arizona, we packed our whitetail deer out over our shoulders. With the ground loaded with rocks and cacti, there might not have been much meat left if we used the drag-out means. I have never known of anyone being accidentally shot while carrying a deer in this manner, but as our human population grows, I think tossing a deer up on our shoulders, while quite romantic and in fact very effective for deer that seldom go over 100 pounds field dressed, is not the way to continue getting our game out.

Even with a big orange rag tied onto the tines of the antlers, I am now going on record as saying I am against toting a buck out of the field via the shoulder-carry method. However, some hunters still do this when they are hunting in an archery only season. I will not condone the shoulder-carry at any time; however, for those who insist upon its use, the only points I can recall needing to mention might be to carry a towel or do as we did, which was to use a T-shirt, and wrap this around the back of the hunter's neck, draping it there without tying it on.

Then the buck is picked up. I used to keep the head on my right side always with one hand grasping the main beam on that side, and of course the hindmost part was trailing over my left shoulder. The opening of the body cavity, theoretically, was to remain closed by the flap of hide on either side of that opening. I have to admit however, that the T-shirt (or towel) about the neck was very nice to have to soak up the liquids. Since our bucks were of the small variety, we let them drain an hour by hanging them in a tree, the country always having a live oak or a mesquite handy. Even then, the shoulder-carry was a pretty tough way of getting a buck out, and yet a way which worked for us then in country where we were pretty much alone.

Given that a bowhunter decides to use the shoulder-carry, I only suggest that he do so with a buck that does not exceed the man's ability. It is hard work. I have a film taken of me on 8mm when I was a young scout, toting what was at the time a record class Coues buck out of the country, and I have watched that film in recent times and laughed at myself. Today, I'm afraid that same buck would have been put upon a pack frame.

The Packsack Method

A deer can be boned in the backcountry and the meat can be placed inside of the packsack which rests upon the packframe. A hunter must be immediately advised

that this method could be illegal where "proof of sex" must remain on the carcass. However, where legal, it is a very workable method. Boning is an art unto itself when we are speaking of boning a carcass out in the field. But it is not terribly difficult to accomplish.

In some instances, when the deer is an elk instead of a regular deer, then the boning process is especially nice. However, we again remind the hunter to consult the law on this matter and to comply with the law before he attempts to bone game in the field. If the law allows, then the hunter can learn to bone game. The first step is to adjust the carcass so that the back is in the upward position and the legs rather underneath the animal. In this manner, it is easy to do step one, which is to slice just beneath the hide all the way from the middle of the head between the antlers right to the base of the tail and even to the tip of the tail.

This important cut is made with a knife that has a sharp point. I use a "full-sized" knife with a blade of about 5 inches or so. My favorite knife is one made for me by Chuck French of De Pere, Wisconsin. If the cape is to be saved for a mount, the cut just mentioned is perfect, for it would be the cut (between the antlers) which would normally be made anyway.

At this point, there are different means of continuing in the removal of the hide. I prefer to make cuts downward behind the shoulder. The hide is continuously cut free in a downward fashion until the *skinned* carcass actually rests upon a "carpet" of its own hide. I was first shown this method of boning by Spike Jorgensen, now of Tok, Alaska, and Spike finished up an antelope in

The pole carry is but one method of getting your deer back to camp.

under 15 minutes. I'm still not that good.

With the carcass bared, so to speak, the first meat to come off can be the shoulder blades. These will actually slice free, and the hunter can remove the shoulders and front legs intact. It is difficult to give a sequence here, because rather than memorizing each step, a hunter more or less *sees* what has to be done as he is working. The shoulders removed, the blade is now used to free the neck meat and the loins by simply slicing along the neck bone and backbone on both sides and carefully cutting out all of the meat. The hide has been worked off of the back legs, and these can be cut out at the hip, giving two large hams, or the meat can be boned away from these hams as the animal lies. Either way, the idea is to get all of the meat free of bones, and then to transport that meat, after it has cooled on the brush or on cloths brought along inside of the pack, into the packsack in which has been placed a large plastic garbage bag.

This method may seem wasteful, but correctly executed as Spike Jorgensen taught me, it is not. The skeleton will be left behind, but the meat will be intact in the packsack. The antlers can be sawed free if this is legal. A belt saw will accomplish this nicely and the object is to cut through the center of the eye's orbit and out the back of the cranium, which will leave the antlers attached to a bony "plate." The hide could be saved, of course.

While this is not as detailed as it would be in a book devoted strictly to game handling, I think the reader has a pretty good start if he has followed along. He will perfect the boning system to suit himself. The boned meat is easily cared for and can be butchered up and packaged with no trouble at all. In fact, with some exceptions, we bone our meat when we reach home, for we do not see much point in storing the bones in the freezer during the year. However, there may be times when some of the bones are appreciated. And if a hunter had to live off of his meat, and if he lacked some of the vitamins and foods needed for a balanced diet, I'd suggest boiling the bones and eating the marrow.

The Packframe

Almost all of my deer are carried out via the packframe these days. It is very easy to cover the deer with orange rags or vests and the modern packframe offers an excellent system of getting a buck out of the hills and back to camp. In the above method of boning we saw the meat deposited in a packsack which was tied to a packframe and carried out on the back also. But this time, we are talking about taking the dressed deer and tying it directly to the packframe. Of course the buck will be dressed in the usual manner, but the hide will be left on to safeguard the meat until the carcass reaches camp.

Two warnings come immediately to mind. We have already told the shooter to tie orange cloth to the deer so that in no way can it be recognized as a deer. But two other points came to mind for safety: First, the hunter should never carry more than he is capable of packing.

Second, the hunter should pick a route back to camp which is a safe one in that he need not ever jump from so much as a small log. Jumping, even from the height of a log, while loaded down with a packframe full of deer can put a mighty cramp in the wrong area.

As for packing too much weight, it is foolish. I frankly do not think there is any problem whatsoever in knowing what is too much. The body will tell you. When the knees and back feel the strain, it is time to forget it. By the way, backpacking meat out is not for everyone. Nor are we trying to talk anyone into doing it. If a hunter is not in shape for it, he'd best find another way, preferably the pack animal approach. I repeat, we are not recommending backpacking a deer except for those hunters who have carried loads in the outdoors.

The man who backpacks as a hobby will often tote 80 plus pounds and keep that much of a load on his back for days and days, so there is nothing outlandish or unusual about backpacking meat or a deer back to camp. Therefore, the byword is for the hunter to use his own good judgement when trying to decide whether to backpack game or use another method in getting the goods back to camp.

One afternoon, I had taken my friend Kenn Oberrecht onto a high country parcel of ground, and he had harvested a pretty nice mule deer buck. We had a little snow on the ground and camp was on a downhill slope, but with all those patches of dry in between the patches of snow, I decided to tie the buck on my packframe and walk off with it. I'm sure I looked mighty sheepish when I tried to get up with the load but my carcass obeyed only the earth's gravity and remained glued to the ground. Finally, I got to my feet and my knees told me to forget it. We had to unlash the burden and forget my backpacking plans on that buck. I had misjudged the weight of the buck which was beyond my limit.

What should a hunter do when he knows the buck is too big for him to backpack out, but he still wants to backpack it? There are two very simple and rather obvious solutions to the problem. First, a buck can be cut in two and shared by a hunting partner who also has a pack. My hunting partner and I always carry our packframes when we hunt together, and we both feel too blasted old and creaky to try toughing out a buck over 150 pounds. My son can manage a buck of over 150 pounds. I never could, not when I was young and most certainly not now.

So, we cut the buck in two. This is very easy. Remember that even a big buck gets whacked down to size when it is cut in two parts. A buck field dressing at an even 200 pounds, which is a pretty darn good buck, turns into roughly 100-pound packages, so to speak, when it is cut in two. All the hunter need do is dress his buck per usual with no differences at all.

Then the buck is cut in two at the end of the loins by severing through the ribs there and of course through the backbone. Please take photos first if you care to have

A good pack frame can be a big a help in getting a buck back to camp. This is the L.L. Bean model with a shelf. The shelf helps to keep the load in place without the load slipping downward. It makes for a very useful packframe when toting out a carcass.

We start out by securing the buck to the pack-frame at the bottom, looping our ¼-inch nylon cord around the animal a few times.

On some frames, such as the flexible Peak 1 model, we can lift the frame up and put a foot under it so that we can slip our cord through the holes in the frame.

(Left) The body of the deer has been securely attached to the frame here, but the head is still loose.

Here is the package ready to be placed on the back of the hunter.

With the hunter sitting down, the loaded pack frame is placed on his shoulders.

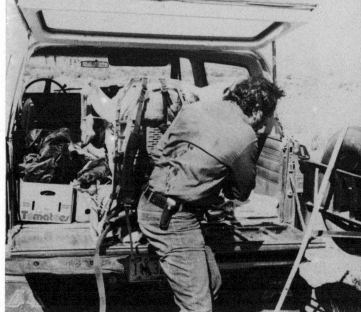

Back at the vehicle, the hunter can use the tailgate to help him slip out of the weight of the packframe load.

(Left) For resting, a hunter can sit on a little ledge and slip out of the packframe by himself. He can then use a stick (in this case our ever-present Moses Stick) to prop up the load.

a photograph of the buck you shoot, because the above operation spoils the appearance of the game. But it also serves to make two packages, both very easy to tie onto the packframe.

The other very obvious approach is to again sever the buck in two halves, but if the hunter is alone he can leave one half at the site of the harvest and go back for it later. Two trips between camp and buck are not going to be bad, and it is far better to make two nice safe trips than to get hurt trying to do it all at once. There is really no more to it than that, and it is my favorite way of getting the buck back to camp.

I prefer using a larger packframe over a smaller one. The hunter can get some very good advice about frames from the local backpack/camping shop, by the way, and he can also find a frame he no doubt likes at such an establishment. I have two frames, one of the rigid type and one of the flexible type and I like them both. The flexible packframe is the large model Peak 1 from Coleman Company. It moves with the body and is constructed of a tough plastic. My other frame is made of tubing, and it has a shelf, which I like because the buck or half buck will not slip off at all due to the shelf on the bottom of the frame. This model is from L.L. Bean Company.

We have recently switched from narrow nylon rope to a thicker nylon rope, the ¼-inch size. The larger rope requires less wraps, and it is much less likely to tangle. It is also much easier to manage, and with packframes that have no shelf, the heavier rope seems to make a better tie-down.

I used to use dead tree limbs to lever my game around if I could not manage to move a buck easily and had no help along. I also used a lever system by tying a long limb to an overhanging tree branch so that about two-thirds of the limb stuck out. By tying the deer with rope to the shorter end, I could lift on the other end and get the buck up off the ground, tying the long end down with rope after the deer was up, not an easy task, but it can be accomplished. I finally went to a hoist. The hoist is a quality item, small and light enough, yet capable of lifting a big load with very little effort on the part of the hunter. This is a nice device when a hunter wants to hang a carcass or part of one, either in the field or back in camp, and it beats the grunt and groan method seven ways from sundown.

Hide On, Hide Off

I like to remove the hide back in camp, but not on the trail. The hide is good natural protection for the meat while the meat is in transit via a packframe or vehicle. Naturally, the boning process in the field removes the hide automatically anyway, but we are talking here of an option. When I have the option, I prefer leaving the hide intact until the carcass reaches camp. Then I much prefer removing the hide, wiping the carcass down with vinegar and water to get off any stray hairs, covering the carcass with a game bag.

The carcass is then safe from flies if the game bag is the proper small mesh, and if it is tied on correctly. We use masking tape around the legs and neck to insure no avenue for flies.

chapter 22
Saving the Meat

SUCCESSFUL DEER HUNTING is more than getting a deer. I believe that a major part of the story lies in salvaging the meat, too, getting the carcass home clean and edible. My family and I have spent a long time trying to develop various means of taking care of the meat from field to freezer so that we would lose none of it. There are several very basic, but important, aspects of meat handling which can insure a good-tasting product, and we will entertain a few of these ideas in this chapter. The deer hunt may only last a day, but the eating of the deer may go on for a few months. Therefore, it is well worth a little extra care and effort expended in saving the deer meat.

In my home state, Wyoming, I see hundreds of deer and other big game animal carcasses being transported from one spot to another, from field to camp and also from camp to the hunter's home, both in and out of state. I'm sure some of this meat reaches home in a tainted state, and I think transportation methods are to blame. Therefore, we will consider transporting the meat as a first step in ending up with something we can not only eat because we feel guilty about wasting, but rather a meat which we want to eat because it is so good.

Transporting the Meat

Mainly, I'd like to speak of getting the meat from the camp to the home. We speak of field to camp transportation elsewhere. In transporting meat from the field to the

home, I think display is the biggest problem. Hunters have a strong urge to display what they got. I can understand the feeling, for it stems from pride in a job well done, not showing off, but honest pride, the same sort of emotion we might feel after winning a football game. Hunting is hard work, and though there is luck involved, just as there is luck involved in winning that football game, there is also skill involved, and a hunter has a natural tendency to exhibit both his hard work and skill as well as his good fortune.

The only problem is that certain types of display can destroy good game meat. We try to get meat cold in order to retard the growth of harmful bacteria. When we cool the meat, but then subject it to heat once more, the bacteria can again grow and the meat can spoil. Carrying a deer on top of a hot roof is inviting the ruination of the meat. To be sure, if a hunter harvests a deer a couple miles from town and simply hauls the carcass home right after the deer has been dropped, there will be little problem. But quite often hunters have a long distance to drive and a deer's meat is going to be ruined by the time the trip is ended.

We often think of deer hunting weather as cold and frigid. In fact, there is a lot of deer hunting weather in all parts of the country which can be anything but cold. I have hunted in the high country of the West Slope in Colorado in October and have seen days which reached 70 degrees Fahrenheit. I have been in Nebraska in the

While these hunters were definitely well-meaning, the fact is, driving back across country with the carcasses exposed to the sun as well as other elements can only mean a problem for the eating quality of the game. In order to save this meat, the carcasses should be skinned, cooled, even butchered and frozen if necessary.

same month and have encountered weather which would spoil meat in no time. Of course, the Southwest and many other geographical locales have warm weather for deer hunting as a rule rather than as an exception. Yet, in all parts of the country where I have hunted, there are deer carcasses, often unskinned at that, perched upon vehicles, the sun beating down on the meat.

I only ask the hunter this simple question—does anyone know of a farmer, rancher or meatcutter-butcher who first puts a cow, pig or sheep carcass on top of a bus or car and drives it around in the sun before processing the meat? What makes hunters think that they can treat meat in this manner and then enjoy it later on?

Therefore, our first point of consideration in getting the meat from the deer camp to home and freezer is keeping the carcass out of the sun. As far as display is concerned, the hunter should bear in mind that few people really care whether or not the hunter "got his." Friends, family and fellow hunters can share in the joys of the harvest, of course, but that is good enough. The game should be skinned in camp. That is my opinion. Studies disagree as to the sweetness of the meat and skinning the carcass—in very cold weather, a hunter may wish to leave the hide intact, and the hide is better on an animal which is being transported from the field to the camp if there is any chance of getting dirt on the meat. I still feel, however, that the hide should be skinned off of the animal back in camp and then the meat protected

with a good game bag. The game bag will keep flies off if the bag has the proper small mesh and if the hunter seals possible entryways around the legs and neck. Then the meat is allowed to cool out totally. When the meat is transported, it can be wrapped in a tarp, game bag still intact on the carcass, *inside* of a vehicle. If there is no room in the vehicle for this, then the gear can be stashed atop the rig and the meat carried inside.

My friend John Doyle came up with the idea of using an old freezer to salvage the meat. He lives in warm country and often takes trips in and out of state during the warmer months of early fall. John found an old freezer small enough to fit into the back of his pickup truck without taking up too much cargo space. The idea is very simple. The carcass is quartered first and cooled out. Then the meat is placed inside of the freezer. The insulating qualities of the freezer will help hold in the coolness, of course, but the idea is to stop at the nearest town and toss in some dry ice. I know that John has transported meat about 400 miles with this method, the meat arriving home cool and in perfect condition. Also, if there is no dry ice available, the meat can be set up on blocks of wood inside of the freezer and regular ice is then used to keep the meat cool. It is best to let the melted ice water drain away by leaving the freezer drain open.

Warning—remember, fellow hunters, it is sometimes illegal to destroy evidence of sex until the animal has been

217

inspected by a game ranger. When this is the case, the hunter must leave evidence of sex in place, but the meat can still be safeguarded with the old freezer method or other methods spoken of in this book. Remember, it is also illegal to waste the meat, so the game department does not frown on ways of keeping the meat edible. Local laws must be adhered to, of course.

Insulation

Even in the fall of the year, when the temperature may rise to a fairly balmy range, the nights will generally cool off nicely. This is an important fact for the hunter because it means that he can cool his meat out by keeping the carcass in the shade, and by allowing the coolness of the night to do its work. I have carried meat home from a deer camp after that meat had been harvested for several days. Insulation saved the meat. Of course the deer is field

bags. The carcasses cooled in the shade that day and all that night. But in the morning we took the carcasses down from the branch which supported them. There was a small woodshed close by, but had there not been, we would have found or made some sort of shelter for the carcasses. The woodshed being there and being abandoned, we used it to house our deer. First, we applied some newspapers to the floor of the shed. Then we put a large tarp down. By driving our vehicle up to the hanging deer, backing right up to them, and then lowering the tailgate so the deer could be let down on the tailgate itself, we were able to make light work of getting the deer carcasses from tree to shed.

In the shed, the carcasses were placed on top of the newspapers and tarp. The tarp was folded over and our sleeping bags were piled on top of the tarp for insulation. The deer carcasses were kept cold for the next few

Skinning the carcasses of the deer, the meat now has a good chance of cooling out and there is no deer hair to contaminate the meat. The carcasses will be wrapped or covered with game bags. Note gambrels in the background, which keep the legs of the game spread for ease of removing the hide.

dressed as usual and then transported to camp. I skin the hide off of the deer in camp next and protect the meat with a good game bag. Then the meat is allowed to cool, not only by using shaded areas for hanging the carcass, but also by allowing the coolness of the night to remove the body heat.

However, after the meat has cooled, it must be kept cool. That is where insulation comes in. This past season, my son John and I both got bucks the first day of the season, but the rest of our party was not due to join us for 2 days. After they joined us, we were in camp for 2 more days while the other two members of our party got their bucks. By the time the hunt had come to a close, our two bucks had been down for a grand total of 5 days, and yet the meat was perfect when we got it home.

After field dressing, the bucks were transported to camp, skinned and the carcasses were covered with game

days by leaving them in the insulation all day long and then rehanging them in the tree by night. Sound like a lot of work? It wasn't that much work, and the meat from two nice bucks made it all worthwhile as we enjoyed good meals for the next several months.

A Cool Spot in the Shade

Sometimes, a handy toolshed is not within reach. But this does not mean that cooling and insulating the meat are out of the question. One time, two of my friends and I were hunting and the three of us found ourselves in very warm country with one buck down and two to go. In this case, we had no place to hang the buck, for it was badlands with few big trees in the area. However, we searched along a dry creek bed until we came to a little green spot and we soon found that the green area was cool and damp. We put the carcass of the buck down into the cool grasses and we chopped tufts of grass with which to cover the carcass. The buck was enveloped in cool grass underneath and on top.

So, without shade we had made some shade. I doubt that this is quite as good as hanging a buck in a cool spot, but in no time at all that carcass was cold to the touch, so it definitely did work out. Certainly, using the cool spot was better than carrying the carcass around with us as we hunted.

Extreme Cold

Another problem is extreme cold. On one hunt, we found ourselves high in the mountains in November. The thermometer pinned to the outside of our wall tent registered 17 degrees below zero at the coldest point in our trip. We had taken game and thought that the extreme cold was good since the carcasses would freeze

skin out after a few days. A fresh carcass is much easier to skin. In the second place, it is difficult to remove spoiled or spoiling meat around wound channels if the hide is left on, for the hunter cannot see where to cut exactly. In the third place, hair from the hide can get on the meat. I prefer skinning the carcass, even in very cold conditions. When the latter conditions do exist, we can protect the meat with a game bag plus a tarp.

Butcher-Package-Freeze and Carry Home

Sometimes, it is very handy to butcher a game animal on an out-of-state or distant hunt, freeze the meat and then carry frozen packaged meat home instead of a fresh carcass home. Remember, of course, to check local game laws. A game animal may have to be checked by local authorities before it can be reduced to packages of frozen meat. On one out-of-state hunt a good 1,000 miles from

This photo sequence shows cooling deer meat by covering it with cut grasses. Since the buck was taken at 10 a.m., and because there was no heavy shade in the area to offer a cool hanging spot, it was necessary to find another means of cooling the meat to prevent spoilage. First, the

buck was totally skinned, since the hide acts so well to insulate and hold in the body heat. Then the skinned buck was placed in a game bag of porous cloth. Still very warm, the buck was then lain in a shallow depression of cool grass which was found by the Platte River.

up nicely. One of the old-timers in camp, however, warned us that if we did not cover our carcasses with a tarp, the meat would be "burned." We took his advice, and the meat did freeze up but was not harmed. However, the hocks which were not covered with the tarp, only with the porous game bag, were dark and crusty and had to be discarded because when the meat thawed out it did not have a good texture. It was damaged. We cooked some of that meat as a stew. Edibleness was a matter of ignoring a rather strong taste.

The hide could be left on to protect the meat under severe cold weather circumstances, but I don't care for this idea. In the first place, the carcass will be hard to

our home, my son Bill and I downed both elk and deer, and it was during a black powder season in the fall of the year with the weather quite warm. Of course, we field dressed our game right away and removed the hides. We washed the meat down with a mixture of vinegar and water, using clean rags, a cup of vinegar (white or any type) to 2 quarts of water.

Then we butchered the meat. The butchered meat was double-wrapped in plastic freezer wrap first and then standard paper. Then the packages of meat were frozen. It so happened that we were able to use the freezer of the friend we were hunting with. However, many towns, even small ones, have lockers which may be rented on

This buck was dragged over snow with the liver tied to a string and coming along behind the buck. If the terrain is not terribly rocky, dragging will certainly not bruise the meat. Snow makes a good surface for deer-dragging.

a short-term basis. Frozen meat can be transported a very long distance by insulating it. Again, sleeping bags, tarps and old newpapers work well as insulation.

Another season we again tried our frozen meat packages, this time hunting out-of-state from my father-in-law's home in Idaho. My father-in-law told us that they used to safeguard meat by freezing it before winter and then laying the frozen packages in sawdust. We put our frozen packages of meat in sawdust in the back of the pickup truck and the packages were rock hard 400 miles later.

When the Meat Gets Home

After the meat has arrived home, the simplest way to continue with its salvation is to hand it over to a professional meatcutting shop. There is certainly nothing wrong with this approach. However, my Old Country grandfather taught us how to butcher our own meat and package it, so we do our own. The first point to consider, however, after the meat has reached home, is the question of aging. Should the meat be butchered right away or left to hang?

Aging

I'm sorry to say that aging has been blown out of all proportion as far as I can tell. In the years prior to my book, *Complete Guide to Game Care and Cookery*, my family and I spent many hours experimenting with wild meats, and we also asked our friends to keep notes for us pertaining to their wild meats. Of course tastes differ, but only one friend out of our association liked meat that was hung "until it's damn near purple," to quote him. This chap also goes for ducks that have been hung up in the shed with a string about the neck and when the body of the duck is "ripe enough," another term of my

buddy's, then it will separate from the neck and it is ready to eat. Taste is personal. I have no right to knock my friend's personal desires in food. But I do think that the average eater would much prefer meat that was far less "aged" than the above. I know we do.

Aging is a process of tenderizing. As far as I can gather, it is, simply put, a process of allowing bacteria to break down the meat. The idea is to impart tenderness, not necessarily a different flavor. I have told the story before of a friend who hung some meat in his garage during a warm spell, saying you had to age meat before you could stand to eat it. All of the carcasses were later sent to the dump.

Aging is best accomplished in a clean area at about 40 degrees Fahrenheit. When a hunter says he is aging meat, but the temperature reads 55 or 60 degrees or more, you can bet he's not aging a carcass. He is rotting it. We have found that if conditions allow, that is, if the temperature is about 40 degrees wherever we are going to age meat, then we might let the carcass hang for 2 days, maybe even 3 or so, and as much as 4, but we have to remember that freezing meat is also a tenderizing process and we have been totally satisfied with taking our venison quite fresh, completely cooled out of course, and simply butchering and freezing it.

Freezing breaks down tissue. There is no doubt about it. I do not believe that we can put an exact figure on this, but I have heard the generalization that freezing meat is like aging it for several days. I doubt that. But I would say that freezing meat most assuredly does tenderize it. Therefore, we have no qualms about taking meat fresh from the field, well-cooled, and cutting it up, packaging it and putting that meat into the freezer. Recently we had guests drop by for a very short stay. They are both totally involved in game meats. I noticed that the package of meat I got out to serve them was venison, and it had not been aged at all. (I can tell the reader exactly what a package contains, who shot the meat, where and how it was handled because we code each and every package that we put away.)

Anyway, the important point here is the fact that this mature mule deer buck was taken during a rather warm spell. The carcass was skinned within a few hours of the harvest, and it was allowed to cool overnight. The next morning, the meat was butchered by us, and packaged by us and then thrust into the freezer. Our guests Bill McRae and his wife Mary were cutting the meat with a fork. This fact is not a surprise. It is the type of venison we have all the time. I have five deer hunters in the family and we bag *at least* two deer each and every year and usually more than that. We have been doing this for several years, so we have had a fairly wide range of our valued deer meat to eat and to remark on. No tough ones yet.

Packaging

Another way to save the meat is to package it well for freezing. The following is only a suggestion. After all, every statement in the book is only a suggestion. The hunter must do what works best for him. But what works best for us in terms of saving the meat in the freezer, and it is delicious a full 12 months later, is double wrapping of each hunk. We first wrap the meat as tightly as possible in a plastic freezer wrap. This is not a household wrap, not a sandwich wrap, but a plastic *freezer* wrap. We find ours at the local Safe-Way Store. Then we wrap again with the standard paper freezer wrap, putting the slick side of the wrap on the inside. We tape with masking tape, mark accordingly and then simply stick the packages in the freezer, trying to spread them out for fast freezing if there is room to do that.

While this is not a very big point, I think double wrapping has helped our meat emerge from the freezer months later in a very good state of eating readiness. It is never "freezer burned" or discolored in any way and it seems to be as good as any other meat we have, fresh or otherwise. So, saving the meat at home, I think, means wrapping correctly. If a person does not want to bother with the double wrap, though certainly venison is well worth the little added expense, I'd suggest that at the very least the paper be ample to truly *wrap* that meat.

Water and Meat

I have been told over the past three decades by many hunters that the biggest disaster to venison is to have water touch it after the meat is exposed by removal of the hide. Well, I believed it at first, but I do not believe a word of it today. Water has never, to my knowledge, harmed a single piece of the venison that we have eaten. Bill Stewart is a teacher who also owns a small ranch. He raises prize-winning sheep and some cattle, and he hunts a lot. Bill, in the past several years, set up a regular semi-professional meat locker on his ranch home. He has all of the processing facilities there at hand. Over the years, whether he has harvested a deer or butchered live-stock, the first thing he does is hang the carcass and wash it totally down with a hose. He has tried other methods and likes this one best and as Bill says, "I think that hair or dirt on the meat is much worse than water."

We actually do some of our meat-washing in the field. When a deer is taken, we hang it by the back legs, head down, and we skin it. With the carcass suspended this way, we now put about a cup of vinegar, white or other, but usually white, in about 2 quarts of water and with a clean wash rag we use the vinegarwater to clean that meat of any hair or blood.

The hunter who has the resource and the time can always take his deer into a meat processing plant in the town nearest his hunt, and there is nothing wrong with this method of saving the meat. In fact, the nation is loaded with fine processing plants and an excellent job can be had at many of them. On the other hand, there is the self-sufficient hunter who might want to do it for himself. Then he must have field know-how to safeguard his valuable venison. At home, he must continue the plan by doing his own butchering/packaging or having a pro do it for him.

chapter 23
Butchering Your Deer

CONVENIENCE dictates that the carcass of your deer be transported to the local meat processing plant. There are many of these plants around the country, and a deer carcass can be butchered quickly and into standard cuts. I'm in favor of the meat processing plant, to be sure, but I think it is also nice for a hunter to know how to butcher his own deer. Successful deer hunting is not merely bagging a buck; it is also field care, and even packaging of the meat. Butchering is just one more piece of know-how for the modern hunter. It is not that difficult to master.

Supposing that the carcass, minus hide, is hanging in the barn, shed or garage right now? What is the first step in butchering? I hang my deer by the rear legs, using perhaps a "gambrel" or rope, forcing the legs apart. First, we remove the game bag. Now we can get to work. Having a few good knives and tools is the best way to go, but I feel I can package an entire deer carcass with a butcher knife, a boning knife and a meat saw. These are all purchased at the local restaurant supply house, and none is expensive. In the field, I have already cut the front legs off at the knee.

Removing the Shoulder Blades

If a hunter/butcher will pull the front leg straight outward and away from the body of the carcass, he will see that it is attached by considerable tissue. So, while pulling on the front leg, the hunter takes his butcher knife and slices *close* to the body of the deer. Slice carefully until the entire shoulder is simply *cut off* of the carcass. In the hand will now be a shoulder blade. Even on a big deer, one man can easily handle a shoulder blade.

The shoulder blade is, in our case at least, transferred into the house as we cut our meat indoors. But the hunter who has working space in his garage may want to set up a butchering table or block. An old school desk top makes a fairly good cutting board, and so does a hunk of formica-type material which can be purchased from the nearest lumber company or home supply house.

I like to cut off both shoulder blades before I start my butchering of the shoulder blades themselves. With both blades resting on the cutting surface, we have two distinct ways to go. First, we can simply call these "blade roasts." If we do so, the blade roast is handled in this manner: We cut off the protruding part of the leg portion right now. This meat will be trimmed off as hock meat for hamburger. If the shoulder blade is from a small deer, it can be cooked intact, one blade to a roasting pot. If the shoulder blade from a small deer is going to go for only a couple or a very small family, it can be cut in two. Naturally, the shoulder blade from a large buck will make up into two blade roasts or even three.

At this point, I make certain that the blades are free of any hair or other unwanted materials and I wrap them, marked accordingly, and drop them into the freezer. If the family is not excited about blade roasts, the meat can be entirely removed from the blade with a boning knife.

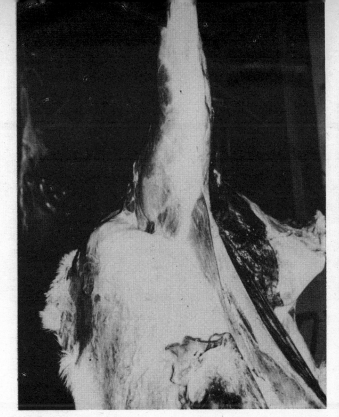

Skinning the carcass is accomplished by carefully tugging at the hide, using the fist to push between hide and meat, and of course by cautiously slicing the hide away with a knife.

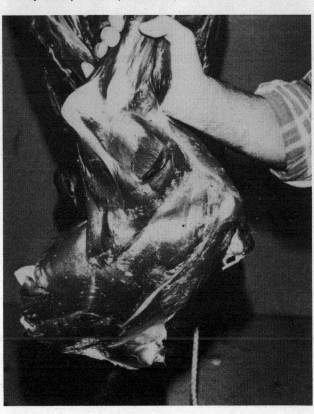

The first step is the removal of the shoulder blade, which is very easily accomplished as described in the text.

A good boning knife should have a flexible blade and should be sharp.

I like to place the blade meat flat on the cutting surface with the outer part facing up, or that portion which was on the outside of the deer. One can see a white ridge clearly, this ridge being separation bone. The tip of the knife cuts along this ridge, and the butcher can see by pulling at the separated meat how and where to continue his slicing until the meat is worked off the bone. There is nothing wrong with having to go back several times on the blade, slicing away right on top of the bone itself until the meat is free of the bone. The meat does not have to be cut into any particular shape at all.

When all of the meat is worked free of the bone and the bone is somewhat "shiny" now, we can discard the actual blade itself, keeping all of the meat that we have cut off in a clean pot, bowl or other container. At this point, we have pure *boneless* meat. The meat can be cubed up and packaged as stew meat, or it can be cut into any irregular shape and ground up into gameburger.

While I saw the hocks off cleanly with my meat saw, others may leave the hocks intact, in which case they are boned out while on the rest of the blade portion. Otherwise, the hocks are now attended to separately, which I much prefer. Given that we have two hocks, or front leg portions, to be more accurate, we simply bone these out. Again, the boning knife is sharp and all it takes is working the meat free of the bone. There is no special talent

The shoulder blade can be cut only once, removing the shank section for burger meat and leaving the major part as a blade roast.

The neck is simply cut off with a good meat saw.

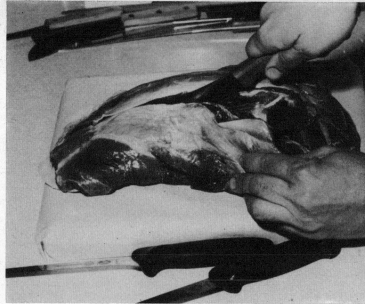

The neck meat is removed by first slicing down the center and then sliding the meat away on both sides of the spine until the spine is clean of meat.

required here, aside from patience and care not to cut oneself in the process. This meat can go in with the burger meat.

The Neck

The carcass hangs now minus the shoulders with the neck protruding very visibly. We simply take the meat saw, and if the saw is properly sharp, a few brisk strokes will leave the neck meat in our hand. Again, some of the bigger bucks may have a neck that is a real handful. In such a case, a hunter/butcher has to be certain that he has a nice clean cloth underneath the neck, or for that matter underneath anytime a piece of meat is being cut off. Then if the neck or any other section falls, due to loss of grip on our part, the meat will remain clean.

Now that we have the neck cut off, what to do with it? I again will break this down into two choices. We can scrub the neck nice and clean and simply package it for freezing. Or if the neck is very large, we can cut it into two halves and freeze these halves individually. Now we have a neck roast to cook (or a couple neck roasts).

Our second choice is to turn the neck into hamburger meat. This is all that need be done: The neck is placed so that the top is facing up. Again, we see a natural line right down the center of the neck. With either the butcher knife or the boning knife, we cut directly down this line right to the neck bones and along the neck bones. Now, with a boning knife, we keep prying the meat away from the neck bones, away and cut, away and slice, away and slice until the meat on the topmost part is totally free from the bone. Underneath, we can again slice up the center or we can start from either side. There is nothing fancy here. Just work the meat away from the bone by slicing

it off a bit at a time. Now we have more meat for gameburger.

I leave it up to the hunter to decide whether or not he should retain neck meat from a deer in rut. I have not had enough rutting deer to present a strong body of knowledge on this matter. We have had a few rutting deer, taken in states other than our own, but in the main, where we hunt, the deer are not yet in the rut. In our modest experience with rutting bucks, the neck meat was less than good.

The Ribs

I was told a very long time ago that the ribs from a very large mule deer buck were as delicious as the ribs from a bighorn sheep. I don't know if I believed the story when I heard it, but I believe it now because I have had ribs from sheep and ribs from deer, and when the deer is truly large, the ribs are simply great. I hastily admit that ribs from spindly smallfry deer are not much, mainly because you need a magnifying glass to find the meat. It's mostly bone.

Supposing, however, that the hunter has a nice mature buck hanging. What about the ribs? We have before us a very clear view of the ribs, and it is simple to remove them from the carcass. I do this totally with a meat saw. The hunter/butcher must take great care to keep his line straight because he's going to be cutting right up against some very delicate and beautiful meat. But using a meat saw is no problem. So let's go at it.

I take my knife and draw a line, as it were, by slicing all the way down the rib cage from top to bottom. Now, in this case, the top is the top as the meat is hanging. So I start my line right up by the end of the rib cage as it

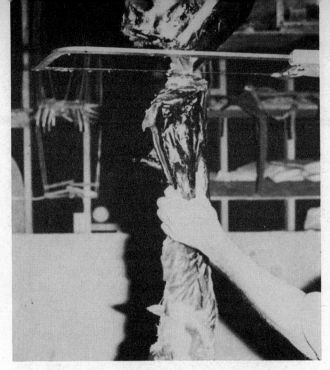

The entire loin section is sawed off just below the rear haunches as the buck hangs head-down.

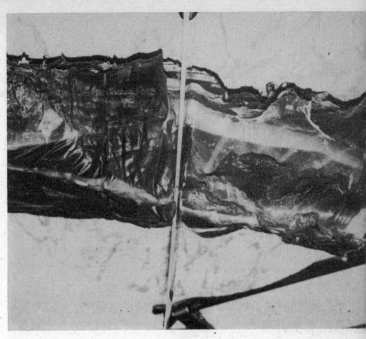

The "upper neck" area is cut away from the true loin section.

would be toward the *back* of the deer. I cut away flank meat. Flank meat is generally very thin on a deer. Others may differ where deer flank is concerned and I only offer this as my opinion. However, Fido gets most of the flank meat. Now, I mean only that meat which is hanging about the area that used to be the paunch, and I do not mean much meat here, just a few scraps.

If the flank meat is removed, whether it is saved or not, one can readily see how to cut the ribs off by staying very close to the backbone and sawing all the way down to where the neck used to be. This will leave the butcher with two halves of deer ribs. Hopefully, the ribs will be meaty. If so, then I like to cut them up and freeze them in packages. I said we could get by with a butcher knife, a boning knife and a meat saw, and we can. The meat saw can be used to cut the ribs up into sections.

With the butcher knife, slice down between the ribs. Then with a cleaver chop through the rib so that it is freed and now separate. This can be done at each rib or several ribs can be left intact for freezing and cooking. I also like to whack the ribs in half with my meat cleaver, thereby shortening them for the package and also making them much handier to eat as well as cook later on.

If the ribs are not very meaty, but not totally bony either, then the hunter may elect to slice the meat off of them and use this meat in his burger.

Loins

A long spinal piece hangs from the two haunches, and this is going to be our fine "filet mignon," or backstrap meats, or loins. I use my meat saw to sever the whole spinal column right where the two haunches meet the spine. This long hunk of spinal area is now brought to

the butcher block or cutting surface. The idea is to bone it. I should point out that some butchers would prefer sawing the spine right down the center and then cutting off hunks of meat into chops. This, I think, is a lot of work to save some bone.

With the boning knife, using the point, a long slit is made right along the ridge of the spine as the piece of meat rests with the back of it upward. In other words, the spinal area is placed on the cutting block upright. I cut down into the spine right along the ridge, dead center as possible, and I continue to cut along this until the flexible blade of the boning knife sort of slips down along one side or the other. Then the idea is to carefully continue slicing longitudinally on the long piece of meat until a very long strip of pure meat is totally removed from the bone.

The best advice is to cut into the bone, not out away from it. What we need is a pure meat removal with bones that are very obviously *clean*. This is the prime part of the carcass. We do not want to leave any of the meat on the bone itself. When both sides of the spine have been cut into and the meat totally removed, the hunter/butcher will find that the portion from up along the neck end of the spine, rather than the haunch end, is not as pure a "filet mignon" as is the meat from farther back. A beginner should cut into this neck end of the loin very carefully, for while it is not truly loin meat as such, it may be hard for a newcomer to butchering to know how much of this to whack off. We do not want to remove the true loin meat yet.

The aim here is to cut back into the long strip of meat a bit at a time in widths of no more than 2 inches for a beginner. This meat is fine for stews and makes top

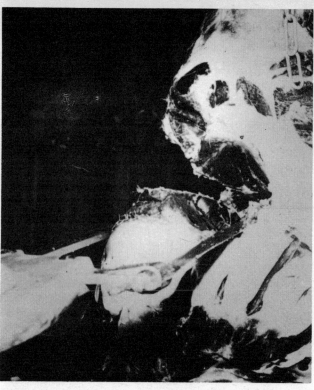

The loin meat is removed from the bone by slicing right down the center of the spine, making sure that the knife cuts toward the bone and not toward the meat.

The haunches are separated into two parts by cutting directly down the center of the spine with the meat saw.

grade hamburger meat but is not true "backstrap." So, how does the butcher know when he gets into the real loin meat? He will know immediately. It is pure filet. It is pure, fine-grain meat and nothing but. The white streaks running in and about the upper end of the cut will no longer appear, just red meat will be left.

So, we end up with a pile of boneless meat from the upper end of the loin cut. This meat can be used in the best of stews and the best of burger meat. We have the two long hunks of boneless pure filet mignon. These long strips should be cut into two halves each. We freeze both halves together because of the size of our family but others may want to freeze a half backstrap per package. These are cooked up much as steak would be cooked, that is venison steak, not beef steak. But I have also broiled the loin sections over coals by basting often with a butter-garlic mixture, heavy on butter, light on crushed garlic, and this will work out. So will larding. But we are getting beyond the scope of this book now and into our *Complete Guide To Game Care and Cookery,* DBI Books.

Underneath the loin area we find the tenderloins. These are terribly tender, in fact, and should be cut away from the bone with the utmost care, soaked out in salt/vinegar water for an hour, dried on paper towels and frozen. They can be butterflied and fast-fried down the road. The tenderloins are immediately recognizable *underneath* the big long bony spinal hunk of meat that we have been working on.

That takes care of the raw basics on the loin cut. We have removed, hopefully, all of the meat and are left with a big long hunk of bone. This bone is highly prized for making soup stock.

The Haunches

Now we have two big hunks of "back legs" still hanging. I swiftly cut these into two separate pieces with the meat saw, aiming dead center through the aitch bone with the blade. There is nothing to it. Inside the house, I like to take a scrub pad such as the "Tuffy Pad," and scrub the inside of the channel which once contained the colon and related viscera. This is accomplished with a clean and soap-free pad, of course, and cold running water. Dried off, the haunch is ready for cutting.

I prefer to cut the haunch into three sections. These are easily defined as the lower part of the leg, which is the hock area and the front part, which is more or less marked off by the end of the canal. We then have what is left over, the large plump middle section. Let us start with that. I like to cut directly into the bone by following the white tissue marks on the meat. In effect, we will end up with some nicely boned hunks of meat which can easily be sliced into steaks, using a long butcher knife later on. The butcher may wish to freeze the hunks of meat he bones from this middle section intact, or he may wish to slice them into steaks and freeze them that way. I go along with the larger hunks. I think they are easier to

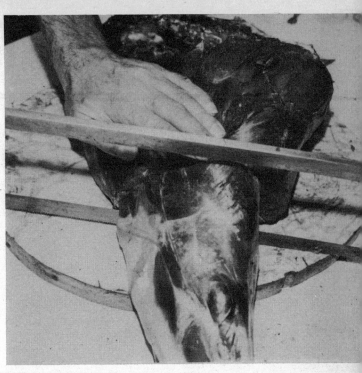

The haunch is divided by first slicing with the knife and then following up with the meat saw. Only two cuts need be made. This first cut removes the hock section. The second cut will divide the meaty parts in two.

Sawing through the hock removes the hock from the meaty portion of the rear ham. The hock is now going to be stripped of meat and that meat will make up into hamburger and/or stew.

wrap and being whole are less likely to be attacked by freezer gases or other problems. After thawing later on, the hunks of boned meat can be sliced nicely into steaks of ½-inch thickness or so.

The meat from the hock end can be made into supreme gameburger or stew. The meat from the end more closely associated with the pelvis can be used for small steaks, especially if the butcher is patient enough to slice the meat out in a boned fashion and then shape with a meat hammer, or this meat also makes fine stew or burger. My wife, being very patient, usually takes over on the haunch area and we end up with more steaks than we'd have if I alone cut the meat up.

In the shed or garage, we now have but one haunch left and of course we follow the same exact process that we used with the first haunch with no exceptions. That is that for the bulk of the deer carcass. It may sound fairly simple. I hope so, because it is fairly simple. I must agree that we do not end up with the more familiar cuts which one gets when the meat is cut on a band saw in a professional way, and anyone who prefers these cuts can learn to make them if he so desires. I suggest looking into books on butchering meat. My plan, as explained here, I suppose comes out of the Old Country tradition. I don't know for certain. I was in Mexico once and I watched an old ranch foreman butcher a deer and his method was almost exactly the same as the method taught me by my grandfather and which I have shared here.

Looking directly into one half of the ham meat we can see that this portion of the deer will turn into steaks. We cut the meat at the natural dividing line which is easily seen here and then slice the meat into our steaks.

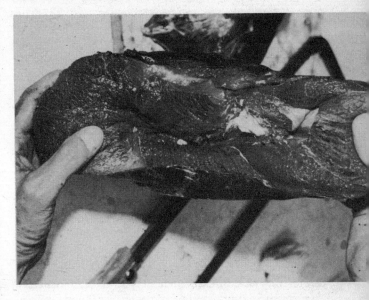

chapter 24
The Deer Hunter's Camp

CAMPING is certainly part of the deer hunter's adventure and a significant portion of his total outdoor memory. Besides, a deer camp is part of a successful hunter's mode of operation. He is, in fact, a better hunter when he incorporates camp knowledge into his deer harvest. I am not saying that a hunter of deer must always camp out, or stay in a lodge, or buy a trailer. Many a great hunt has taken place a short distance from town. Many are the hunters who actually harvest deer on their own land or the land of a friend. But a camp is often part of the deer hunting experience.

The Backpacker-Hunter

Not for all the time, of course, but some of the time a backpack type hunt is a truly enjoyable experience. Furthermore, I want to speak of the backpack as a life-saving instrument and if only this part of the book is listened to, then it shall have been worth the writing and worth the reading, for the backpack can save a life.

Every year, hunters get lost. Every year storms descend upon hunters and trap them in the outback so that they cannot get back to their main camps or their vehicles. Most of these hunters make it somehow. They manage to find their way after all, or they stumble onto a road and meet friendly travelers there. But some hunters do not make it. They get stuck in the outdoors. They become paralyzed by the weather, and they perish. It could happen to me. I realized that a long time ago. You have

heard, no doubt, of the great Ben Lilly, the bear and cougar hunter. It was said he could leave his knife in the swamp one day and go back the next from another entry point, and find that knife.

I'd be lucky to find a big red truck if I left it in an unknown swamp. Because my sense of direction is nothing to crow about, when I hunt country unfamiliar to me, or when I want to venture farther back into the hills at a time of the year when a storm could drop down on me, I have come to use the backpack as a life-saving instrument. Hunters die of the weather. They die from exposure. They don't starve to death, generally. They are not killed by wild beasts, generally.

So it is that I carry a small home on my back. I have with me in my packsack or attached to my packframe, the essentials for life. If I am in country where I can be stormed in for days should I get caught, I have some food in my packsack. This is not the most important thing I carry, however. For attached to the frame I will also have a small sleeping bag, mummy style, compact and light to pack along. If the terrain is really forbidding, I will also have my 5-pound mountain tent along. Should I be caught unawares, I can pitch the tent and I will have shelter from snow, rain and wind.

For hunters who do not wish to carry a 5-pound mountain tent, there is the tarp. A tarp is not a tent by any measure, however, but it is better than nothing. I have seen and used a tarp shelter set up by another hunter and

Here is a full-blown pack and frame outfit from Peak 1.
A hunter can go into the backcountry with this outfit and
stay awhile.

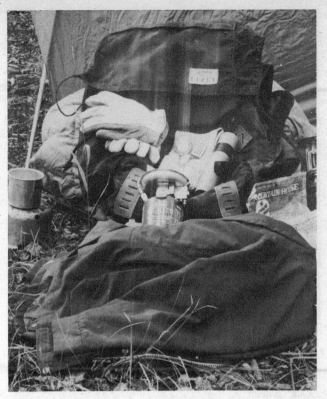

The Peak 1 can carry all the essentials.

in what turned out to be no more than a gentle snowfall;
the tarp was sufficient. On the other hand, I have been
in high country storms which would have made life under
a tarp less inviting than a stay at the best hotel. The tarp
can be used in lean-to fashion with cut and stripped
branches for supports, or rope can be used as a support
to hold the tarp in position.

For me, the packing of a 5-pound tent makes sense
when I am in backcountry I'm not familiar with, or when
I am far enough away from some sort of solid shelter
that I could not very likely make it back to safety if a
sudden storm struck. Since I hunt, generally, with a
packframe on anyway, the addition of 5 pounds does not
bother me. For hunters used to going in the ultra-light
way, the packframe and tent may be a bother at first,
and maybe a bother all the time. I suppose one has to
weigh the trouble of carrying gear against the trouble of
standing up to a storm without the gear.

The particular sleeping bag which I used in conjunction with the small tent is a very light bag. It has a
2-pound fill of down and reduces to a very small size when
compacted inside of a carrying bag. It is not the warmest
bag I have ever used, but it is better than no bag, and
the lightness makes it no burden to carry along while
hunting. Also, the hunter can opt to toss in a light pair
of long underwear to be used as sleeping garments. Of
course, these can come in pretty handy as a dry change
in case the regular long underwear get damp. They are

The backpack hunter can take along a great deal of food
if he will tote the special products which are light and
yet make up into nourishing meals in camp. Here is an
array of such food.

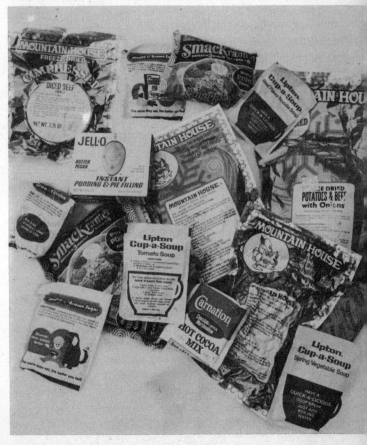

This small tin holds many items which could enhance a hunter's chances for survival in the field. No single unit is enough for a hunter to bank on; however, coupled with other life-saving gear, such as the packframe holding some form of shelter and/or small tent, a little kit like this is a boon. The fire-starter alone could be of great value if a hunter were caught in a storm.

also useful when the weather is pretty good, but not stable. In other words, the hunter starts out on a day which is not that threatening, but several hours later the day has turned into a monster. Now he can stop and put his longjohns on. It might be cool for a moment getting them on, but well worth it.

I have used the packframe for so long now that it is a part of my hunting style. I find that it does not take long to get used to the frame, and therefore I recommend it, especially when the hunter can carry life-saving gear with him, either tied to the frame itself or packed into the packsack. It's nice to have a few other items along in that packframe or packframe/packsack setup. One of these is a safety kit. These can be very compact in size and may contain items more than a little useful to a deer hunter who has to stick it out in the wilds for a little while.

As an example of such a kit, we can look at the Solo Survival Kit, a product which at this time sells for $5.69 postage paid from Marlan Industries, Box 278, Frankfort, Maine 04438. This little kit comes in an aluminum container, and the container looks like a sardine can. It is completely sealed and must be opened by a pull-ring. Of course it is waterproof and will float. The whole can only weighs 3 ounces. It is meant to be retained in the closed and sealed position until an emergency. Here is a complete list of the contents of the Solo Survival Kit:

Band Aids (2)	Compass
Medical Ointment (1)	Sugar Packet (1)
Swab Aid Packet (1)	Bouillon Cubes (2)
Alcohol Prep Packet (1)	Energy Bar (1)
Aspirin Tablets (2)	Tea Bag (1)
Salt Tablets (2)	Chewing Gum (1)
Water Purification	Book of Matches (1)
Tablets (2)	Razor Blade (1)
Safety Pins (2)	Fishline & Hook (12 yards)
Waterproof Ziploc Bag (1)	Firestarter (2)
First Aid Instructions	Wire (2 ft.)
Needle (1)	Duct Tape

In addition to this kit, I like to have items which I can use in a situation which is not an emergency, but which calls for some special aid anyway. I think first of firestarter. At the moment, my daypack is set up with a tube of firestarter in it and I ended up using some of this one time in the past season. There was no big emergency going on, but after being rained on for a half day, I decided to dry out during the noon hour, and it was hard getting a fire going. But the firestarter came through nicely.

It is also good to have a little food along. A man can go a long time without food, but under stressful condi-

This is a well-set-up "mountain rock stove," a camp cooking outfit easy to make and well worth the small effort. The rock by the spatula is for warming foods or keeping foods warm. The rock under the handle of the fry pan is to keep that handle a bit cooler than it would otherwise be. The rock in the fire is used to keep hot things hot. And the rock holding the silverware is useful, too, for holding cooking utensils. Camping is a big part of deer hunting for most of us.

tions, especially bad weather, he's well-advised to keep food in his system. A great variety of edibles can be stored in the daypack, packsack or even in a special bag tied to the frame. There are a number of books on backpacking and these books contain dozens of ideas for the hunter's safety food supply, so we won't go into a long list here; however, it's nice to have along some jerky, maybe some nuts, dried fruit and so forth.

So much for the backpack type of hunter's camp. I have specialized my commentary on the basis of a survival camp for the hunter, but my initial statement concerned backpack hunting, and I'd like to pursue that for just a moment. The backpacker/hunter has a golden opportunity in that he can live in the habitat of the deer on a 24-hour a day basis as long as his food supply holds out and he is comfortable with his hunt.

The backpack hunter can learn his skill in the off-season. Once again, there are dozens of books on backpacking and the would-be backpack hunter need simply get the basics down during the offseason first, hiking into a summer setting, perhaps, and learning to make it with the items he has taken along. My younger son began backpacking by climbing to high country lakes for fishing, this being during the summer months, and with that background he is now capable of backpack hunting if he so chooses.

I suggest a hunter learn his backpacking craft in the off-season. I also think it is wise to read up on the subject first and then take a look at the local backpack shop for all of the latest items there in both gear and food supply. Since my partners and I carry our game out via the packframe, we do not seem to mind hunting with a bit of added weight in the form of edibles, and we have packed in some fairly fancy foods to eat. But the pre-packaged foods are lighter, though not generally as tasty as the fresher fare.

The Tomahawk Shelter

Suppose that the hunter strikes out and gets caught in a storm, but he does not have along the backpack outfit, the small tent and sleeping bag? What then? There are many camps which deer hunters can make out of the environment, so to speak. These camps are very well illustrated in another text, and we will only mention a few of them here. However, one may see several discussed and illustrated in the book *Woodcraft & Camping* by Bernard S. Mason, Dover Publications, NY. I purchased my copy in paperback form from The Sitting Fox Co., 23529 Beverly, St. Clair Shores, Michigan 48082.

Chapter 1 of this book is called "Shelters for the Trail," and this particular chapter is filled with useful information which could save the deer hunter a very bad experience if he gets stuck out "on the trail." As Mr. Mason put it on page 3, "One has no stomach for romance when drenched with rain, nor zest for beauty when shivering with cold!" We might add that one has no zest for deer hunting under those conditions either,

The camp stove of this size makes for easy backpacking and will give the hunter all the heat he needs for camp cooking.

but I am mainly impressed with the emergency aspect of these shelters.

The first emergency shelter in the Mason book is the "Poncho Shelter," and it is essentially our good old tarp used in a lean-to fashion. Mason shows just how to do it with a big log as a part of the unit, with three poles acting as the struts to hold up the poncho or tarp. I think Mr. Mason's idea of a poncho is better than my idea of a light tarp because the poncho does not weigh so much, and it can be worn as well as used for a shelter. I have seen ponchos for sale at backpack shops, incidentally.

The next emergency shelter in the camping book is a brush den. Mason shows two styles of brush dens, one a felled tree, in which case the branches are used for a bit of shelter and the other a cut or dead tree fitted into the notch of a larger tree, the notch made by the branching of the trunk itself. Mason points out that the brush den is a warm weather shelter. Then there is the thatched lean-to, and a quick lean-to of bark. Also shown is an Indian bark kennel. And then Mr. Mason goes into a discussion of "Tents for the Trail."

Mason uses the term "tomahawk shelter" to include permanent structures, and this is right. I also like to think of a tomahawk shelter as any temporary protector from the elements that could be made from a tool as simple as the tomahawk or belt axe. Anyway, the first four chapters of this book are loaded with shelter ideas which could apply to the deer hunter who must take refuge from

Part of any good hunt is a good camp, be it for deer or other game. Sam Fadala, left and brother Nick Fadala enjoy a quiet and peaceful camp-out in a replica sod house, or "soddy," as they are called in Nebraska, where this photo was taken. Note the heavy wood-burning cook stove in the background, used not only for preparing food, but also for warmth.

the elements and that is the important point. There are many other books on the subject, such as *The Art of Survival* by Cord C. Troebst, a Doubleday book.

The Tent Camp

A very common type of deer hunter's camp is the tent. Tents, in my opinion, have come a long way. I don't mean that tents were bad when I was a young man, but they were not, in this one person's opinion, what they are or can be today. There are many different types of tents for camping and all are good. It just depends upon the conditions as to which should be selected. We prefer what we call the "modular" camp tent arrangement.

This means a strong canvas tent as our main tent. This is our family outfit. It is 10 by 12 feet in dimension, has an outside frame, is waterproof and roomy enough for our mealtime and family gathering time. Instead of cluttering this tent with sleeping bags, however, we might set up a couple of smaller tents nearby. These are the sleeping tents. One of the most comfortable nights in the outdoors that a deer hunter can spend is in a sleeping tent if he sets it up correctly.

We use our two 5-pound mountain tents as our sleeping tents. First, it is good for the little tents to be unrolled and set up from time to time anyway, and second, they are roomy enough on the inside to offer plenty of sleeping area. On family deer hunts, the fact is we generally camp in the good deer country and we do so in a nice time of year and we have no need of the mountain tents as emergency measures, so they can be set up and left for the duration of the hunt.

The 5-pound tents we have can be ventilated just right for comfort. What's more, we have purchased some foam pads, a couple inches thick, which fit inside of these tents corner to corner. We first clear the ground of major twigs

and rocks, and then pitch the sleeping tents, filling the tents with a "floor," really a bed, of foam padding. I was hunting with a couple from Idaho and I set up a sleeping tent for them. They both agreed that it was the best sleeping they had enjoyed at any time anywhere.

These days, one can light the main tent with a battery operated unit if he fears using the gasoline lantern. Or he may wish to use a pole upon which he firmly places the gas lantern. By leaving the door wide open on our main tent, which is also our cook tent, we use our Coleman stove for some of our cooking. We also enjoy cooking over coals in camp. If the hunter finds himself in soft wood country, he may even want to carry along a bag of hardwood coals for the broiling of food.

I think the successful deer hunt is a total picture, and a part of that picture is the camping. Tent camps, when executed with pre-thought on the subject and planning, are very good deer hunting shelters. They can be warm, safe and comfortable. Of course, in the later season hunts, one may wish to devise some safe means of heating the main tent. We are speaking of a tent camp for deer hunters in climes which are not dangerously cold.

Cold Weather Tent Camps

Here is another sort of camp altogether. I am not convinced that this type of camp is any more comfortable than the above tent camp, but when one must have a fire contained within the walls of a camp, then the use of the big wall tent, without a floor, is often called for. Such tents are spacious and very well made. They have a reinforced and safeguarded chimney hole in the roof. Again, it is not our aim to discuss this type of tent fully, but here are a few ideas we hope will be worthwhile for the deer hunter who is looking for a big wall tent.

First, I'd suggest a white canvas tent over the olive drab

Even high country late season camps can be comfortable. These two hunters, Tim Kohl on the left and Runo Siren, right, came well dressed for the Idaho tall country and the tent was fitted with a stove.

A cold weather camp need not be a total hardship, even when tent-camping. A good fire with a supply of wood handy is always welcome, and a safe tent heater is enjoyable, too. Also, dressing correctly makes camp life a lot better. Author, left, and his two sons make a cold country camp and enjoy it. Note the tarp covering gear on the ground. This gives more room inside of the tent.

color. This may seem a very small point, but the white tent is much brighter inside and I think more cheerful. The olive drab tent is just that—drab.

Second, floors can be a problem in these tents. I have camped in wall tents which were so soggy that it would have been comfortable only for a frog. Some very knowledgeable campers put straw down for flooring. I suppose this is all right. My only concern would be fire hazard. Of course, he should be exceedingly careful about fire no matter what the floor is made of.

Some hunters use a big rug or series of rugs as flooring in a wall tent. I like the idea of placing some thick throw rugs at the entryway and having hunters wipe off on these before entering the main part of the wall tent. The type of rug which I have seen used effectively is the very porous kind which will help as a scraper for the boot bottom and will also hold quite a bit of moisture.

Heating the wall tent is generally accomplished with a stove of the sheepherder variety. The most elaborate setup for heating that I have seen is that used by a friend in Montana, who has taken regular airtight stoves and designed them to break down so he can pack them in on a horse. They are very heavy, but they will warm a wall tent in the worst weather.

The Lodge

First-class accommodations are generally enjoyed by deer hunters who head for a hunting lodge. Some hunters call this type of deer hunt too easy; others call it luxurious fun. I have only gone on a couple of these deer hunting lodge outings, and I think they can be a lot of fun. I would not want to turn solely to the lodge hunt, but there are advantages. I think the major advantage to a lodge hunt is the enjoyment of meeting other hunters, often people from all parts of the country. The lodge is going

Camping methods can sometimes be mixed. Here we have a pickup truck with a camper shell used in conjunction with tents in desert mule deer country. The tents can be used for beds and visiting areas. The shell is being used here as a place for the camp stove and to safeguard hunting gear in transit.

to be warm and dry and comfortable. Some hunters might even point out that they like these lodges because they give them more time to hunt. They would rather hunt than camp, they say. I won't argue with that. But let's just say there is room for both types of deer hunts—the do-it-yourself camp-out and the lodge.

The Trailer

Another good camp for deer hunters is some form of trailer. The trailer can be pulled into an area and set up as a home away from home. Some trailers have everything which can be found in the average home to include the TV set. Others are more of the "camp trailer" variety and offer shelter without indoor plumbing and maid service. While we enjoy the tent hunt, we also have a small travel trailer. It was originally used by General Grant, I think, and has seen service also in World War I, but it certainly offers a lot of almost shameful comfort.

The big item which makes camping trailers enjoyable is the fact that once you unhook from them, they are all ready to go, all set up. Even the plain units, such as ours, offers heat controlled by a thermostat, pump-it-yourself running water in a sink, and a number of other niceties. A deer hunter who has a decent trailer is in tall cotton, as they say. He can return to his camp to find warmth, a place to cook, a table to sit at, and most of the amenities of home. At the same time, the deer hunter who uses a trailer for camp shelter also has the option to enjoy those parts of the outdoors he wishes to enjoy. He may set up a safe fireplace and he may cook over coals and he certainly can enjoy sitting outside. He need not use the trailer at all times. But it is there when he wants it or needs it.

The Camper Shell

Another popular camping mode for the modern deer hunter is the camper shell. Here is a light "covered wagon" type enclosure for a pickup truck. The truck can still maneuver over backcountry roads with the shell in place. Yet the shell can offer a good deal of shelter. I have used a camper shell, though not for deer hunting, and it was pretty good camping. I do not find the shell warm unless the hunter sleeps with the pickup truck bed covered with a pretty good pad.

The Truck Camper

Another unit for the deer hunter to consider is the pickup truck camper. Many hunters use them today. They are, essentially, a small trailer attached to the bed of the pickup truck. They can be exactly what some hunters want and need as a shelter. They come as fancy as a person could want. The pickup is generally not as maneuverable as it was without the camper in place, but this is not always a handicap.

There are certainly many other ways for a deer hunter to experience the great outdoors in some semblance of comfort, and it is not our aim to explore all of these, such as the fifth-wheel trailer or the motor home. Eventually, every hunter finds his own way when it comes to the camping method best for him. I only offer the suggestion that a serious deer hunter explore many ways of living in the outdoors when he hunts deer away from home, as most of us do. Even ranchers and farmers who have deer in their backyards often prefer to get out and hunt from a camp. So there is a decided lure in adding camping to deer hunting.

chapter 25

Deer Hunting Gear

SOMETIMES I think we get too carried away with our hunting gear. I have known archers who spent more time trying to perfect their tackle than they spent shooting their bows. I have known deer hunters who spent more time seeking the "perfect deer rifle" than they spent hunting deer. On the other hand, man is the animal who uses tools. In fact, he is the only animal who uses a great variety of perfected tools.

Deer hunters are successful because of tools. Sad would be the hunter who tried to bag a deer by running it down and wrestling the buck to earth bare-handed. Not only how we use our tools as hunters, but also what tools we have to use will make a big difference in our "successful deer hunting" story.

The Sling

I borrowed a rifle one season because I was out of state, had just learned that some permits were left over and could be purchased for deer hunting, and the season happened to still be open. When my chance came, I took a sitting shot. Through my own fault I had not tried to "get into the sling" before that moment, and I soon found that the sling was cinched up so tightly that it could not be used for shooting at all. I could not get my arm through it. My friend later explained that he hunted with the sling in that position and then loosened the sling if he got a deer, so he could strap the rifle over his back.

Slings are for shooting. Slings are not solely for carrying.

The hasty sling, which is merely the act of slipping the elbow through the strap so that there is tension on it, can make for quite accurate shooting. Even off-hand shooting can become quite accurate when the sling is put into play.

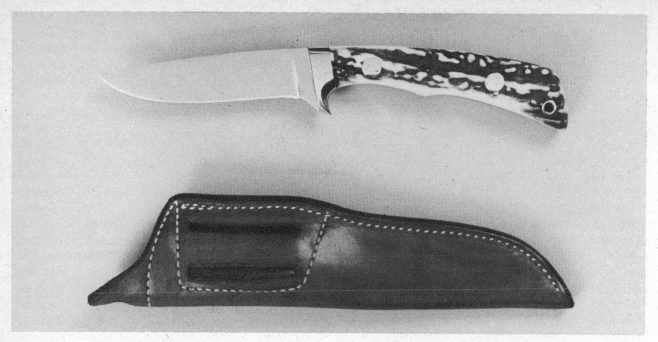

This is a Jimmy Lile knife, a custom-crafted model of good design for deer hunters.

(Right) A useful camp item is a hand axe or tomahawk such as the Hawken Shop tomahawk. It will perform small camp chores nicely, while being a handsome piece of gear at the same time. The 'hawk or hand axe should be carried in some form of holster.

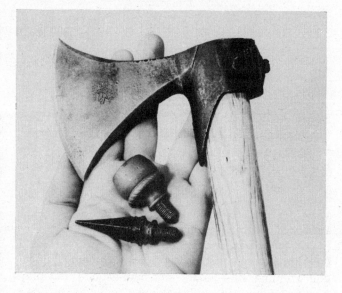

I believe that just about any shooter can prove this to himself if he will try. I suggest setting up a target at 100 to 200 yards and taking the sitting or even standing position, first without the aid of the sling and second with the sling. I firmly believe that most hunters will do better in terms of more shots in the bull's-eye with the sling. The sling can be used in the so-called "hasty" setup. I am not suggesting that the hunter take time to use a true full military sling or target approach. By simply slipping the arm through the loop of the sling one time, the slack taken up will steady the rifle, and that is what we are after. For a fast running shot at close range, forget the sling. But for that steady shot, use it.

The Knife

The deer hunter's knife has been the subject of many articles, and trends have come and gone over the years. Hunters, for a long period of time in this country, wore big knives in sheaths often attached to the belt. By a certain point in time, there was a backlash in this, and the hunter who had a sheath knife was often called a dude or "drugstore cowboy." The idea was to do the work of the deer hunter with a pocketknife and some of my friends moved from the absurd to the ridiculous with smaller and smaller knives.

I am not sure of today's trend. I suppose the large folding knife is one of the more popular models. But for me, I am back to the knife so often associated with the dude hunter. I want a blade of 4 or 5 inches or even a bit more, and I much prefer a plain style with a sharp point. Since I have started my own family of hunters plus several friends and their families, I have spent seasons where I can field dress and skin certainly over 50 head of game, and I am delighted that I went back to the bigger knife.

This is not to dissuade anyone from a pocketknife if that is what he wants. A tiny pocketknife can field dress a moose and skin it, too. But it is not for me. My own special hunting knife was given to me by Melville "Chuck" French of De Pere, Wisconsin, and it is very plain in style. The blade on this knife is 5 inches long. It is not a drop-point. The point of the knife is very sharp and prominent. I like this for field work, because the sharp point is useful in starting the incision which will remove the reproductive organ in the male deer, and the same sharp point is again useful in slitting open the abdominal cavity. Also, with a small knife of the pocket type the hunter is back to splitting the aitch bone (cinch bone) which allows the back legs to flop around and dirt to invade the nice meat of the haunch area. The longer blade with the sharp point makes "coring out" a rather easy task.

As for construction, I would like to be able to sharpen my knives without having to be a blacksmith or a knife-maker. I am in awe of super hard steel. It's wonderful stuff, and yes, if ever you can get such a blade sharp, it will remain sharp for a very long time. But I want tempering and blade hardness which will allow me to touch up the edge with a steel (a steel is not for sharpening a knife in the sense of metal removal as much as it is for straightening an edge). I'd like to be able to sharpen my knife with a set of ceramics or a stone.

Heavens, if a hunter has his favorite knife and is getting along well with it, be it a big-bladed Bowie or a little pen knife with a fingernail clipper built into it, he should stay

reading my compass and then taking the reverse of that line and fairly well end up where I started out. In some of the thick rain forests, such as found on the West Coast, I would want to faithfully pack along a compass and use it.

My own compass is very simple because my ability as a compass reader is very simple-minded. I have an old Marble's compass from many years ago, and it is very small, and has been pointing to magnetic north for as long as I have owned it. I suppose that the more intricate compasses have the ability to shoot a line on a particular bearing and all that. In fact, there is an interesting book called *Finding Your Way in the Outdoors* by Robert L. Moorers, Jr., and published in 1972 by Popular Science Publishing Company, an Outdoor Life book.

In my opinion, the deer hunter who studies the compass and relative points is gaining valuable knowledge and making himself a better and safer hunter. In my own plans for becoming a better hunter, there is at least a good session or two in compass reading in order. Anyone can get lost. Even the one and only Ben Lilly admitted to being a mite confused one time in the outback.

The Safety-Sharp is a useful knife sharpening device offered by the Case Company. A hunter's knife must be sharp, and the ceramic tool is very useful in keeping the blade fit for service.

with that knife. But I think if most hunters would try a good solid simple knife of top construction, with a plain straight blade and a sharp point, they would like these knives very much. The knife with a 4- or 5-inch blade need not always be carried on the hip.

I generally carry my hunting knife in a sheath, but the sheath also houses both my saw and my diamond sharpener, and then I tuck the sheath into my daypack or the packsack which rests on my packframe. Many hunters do not carry a packframe, which is fine, and they may wish to use the sheath on the belt.

Compass

A deer hunter does not always need a compass along. In a known area, it might be pointless to pack a compass. But I find that in the thick stuff I can "take a line" by

Maps

I have carried a topographical map with me and used it to much benefit in some terrain, but in certain areas where landmarks are few, the map would have done me much less good. I cannot, then, recommend a map for all deer hunting locales. If there is a series of hills to go by, or a stream or river, or lakes or changes in vegetation or landscape terrain itself, the map can be a very helpful tool in keeping found. It can also be a helpful tool more directly in successful deer hunting.

We have used topo maps in scouting and have marked each spot in which we have located deer or big bucks at least, and we have also marked the same maps as to our exact harvesting sites. I can't say that this has produced deer after deer for us, but it has been of some help. Especially, we have been able to pinpoint certain areas which are, for a time at least, "hot" for deer.

One season, we scouted a rough section of country for whitetails and found some dandy heads. We kept a clear and faithful record of our findings and after a few times in the area we noticed a pattern. The deer were seen primarily on a long ridge that began in a lower area and continued into a hilly part of the country. That coming season, we took four good bucks on that long ridge. Going back, we always found deer in that area.

A topographical map, then, can be a boon in finding our way and in remaining on the right trail in country that is not totally familiar to us. A hunter might get a

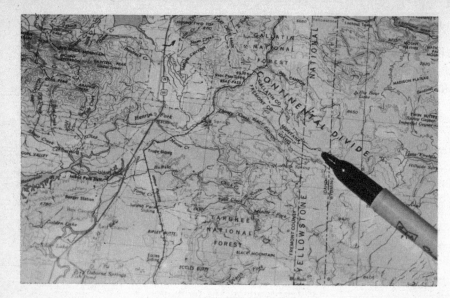

Roads, mountains and land status are clarified for the deer hunter who employs a map.

great deal of enjoyment as well as learning a lot if he will use a map to clearly mark his deer sightings and harvests. If for no other reason, the map can be used as a history of our own deer hunting.

Flashlight

Mentioned in our list of items for the packframe and/or daypack or packsack, the flashlight is an invaluable tool for the deer hunter. The hunter may find as I have that late afternoon is a golden time of the day to spot a feeding buck, and if he does bag his deer later in the day, he may next find himself in the dark. The flashlight can help him make it out of the area and back to camp, and it can also serve as a signaling device if necessary. There are many very good flashlights designed for sportsmen, and there are many good flashlights at the local hardware store. The only thing about a flashlight is that it needs batteries, fresh ones. The on-his-toes hunter will have fresh batteries in his unit at the beginning of each deer season.

First Aid Kit

My own first aid kit rests inside of a small plastic case which used to be a cartridge holder. The contents are simple, but I think useful. First, I have a large gauze sterile pad in my kit which might be useful for covering a camp burn. I have an extra tube of firestarter in this small kit. As one can tell, I do not trust my ability as a starter of fires with wet wood. There is also a roll of adhesive tape and Band-Aid plastic strips. There are some aspirins and some Alka-Seltzer tabs, the latter to calm the effects of certain camp meals when one of my partners takes his turn as the cook (he knows who he is).

We should check our gear at least at the beginning of the season. I see that it has been a couple seasons since I updated my little first-aid kit, and I pledge to do that before next season rolls around. Also in the kit is a small section of Mole Skin for foot care and a burn ointment.

Obviously, a hunter does not carry all possible gear with him at once. He learns what is available to him, and he then selects what works best for him, the selection often made through trial and error. A scouting trip may serve to help a hunter decide if he does want to keep a particular item as part of his personal hunting gear, in fact. Here, the author poses with the items which he placed in his daypack, few but important tools, including a water canteen, a small first aid kit, a little food, a cutlery set and so forth. The binoculars were carried, of course, around the neck for constant use. Each outing may demand slightly different gear, depending upon the time of year and the area hunted.

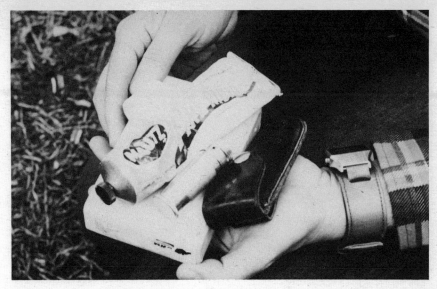

Carrying a fire starting agent is a wise move. It is definitely a safety measure. Even if the hunter does find shelter from a storm, he may need a fire, and wet wood is not easily ignited. If a hunter does become lost, with firestarter along he has a better chance of starting a blaze under trying circumstances.

I do recommend a small first-aid kit for the deer hunter, and think he should update that kit often.

Rain Gear

From a backpack shop I have purchased a nylon rain outfit which folds up to smaller outside dimensions than a box of big game rifle ammo. This is one item which can be very useful when rain comes down unexpectedly.

Marking Tape

I hesitate to mention this item for fear of its abuse, but anyone interested enough to read this far would not be the type of hunter to cover the outdoors with orange or pink tape anyway. I carry a roll of such tape with which to mark a deer after it is down or mark a trail when I am sure I can retrace my steps and pick up the tape. The marking tape can be a lifesaver. It can be used as a signal

A useful item for the deer hunter is a surgical sponge filled with soap. He can wash up nicely after the field dressing chore.

in the snow or on clear ground, and a hunter should carry it, using it only when he feels he must and then picking up the tape after its function is no longer needed.

Space Blanket

A space age type blanket can be carried. I have one in my pack, but it is an emergency item only and I have never had occasion to open the blanket and use it. It could give that small measure of added comfort that would be very welcome if a hunter had to bed down when he did not expect to stay out all night.

Hospital Sponge

I always carry a hospital sponge with me. These are small sponges with a rough exterior, and I load mine with liquid soap. In fact, I located a fine minty liquid soap which is very special. After a job of field dressing a deer, the sponge is perfect for clean-up. If near a source of water, or if water is being carried by the hunter, a little on the sponge will work up a good lather and the hunter can clean his hands with the sponge very neatly. I have always read about using plastic gloves for deer-dressing and I am sure this is all right and I, too, can suggest such gloves, but for those who do not use plastic gloves, the sponge clean-up is nice to have. These sponges can often be purchased at medical supply houses or at the pharmacy.

Skinner/Dragger

Recently, I tested an item called the Buckskinner Products Skinner/Dragger from the company of the same name, Buckskinner Products, 7250 Blue Hill Drive, Suite 105, San Jose, CA 95129. I used this item twice during the past deer season, both times in snow, and it seemed to work out well. While it might be true that one could use a hunk of rope and a pad of some sort in place of this item, I submit that we could use more basic tools in many cases, but this product was well-made, light, and handy and it worked not only for me, but for others I loaned it to.

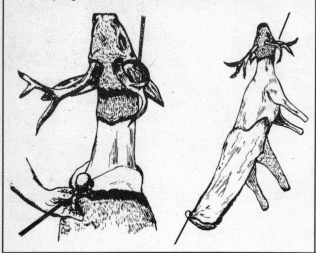

This is the Buckskinner Products Skinner/Dragger model. It will aid the deer hunter in dragging his buck back to camp or, as shown here, can be used in helping in the removal of a deer hide.

The tool is used for skinning as well as for dragging, but I did not personally test this application and therefore can only comment on the dragging aspect of it. With the tough cable and good handle, the dragger did make the task easier. The cable did not slip and the handle did not cut into the hand. As can be seen in the illustrations, the cable slips over the antler and the deer is dragged. As for skinning, the hide is slit all the way around the neck and the skinner/dragger is attached to a lump of hide right at the backbone area of the deer. Then, the hide is pulled off of the deer with the unit.

The Hoist

I have only tried one hoist in my hunting and I can therefore report on only that hoist. The model I have is a very light and small affair; its actual weight is 1.75 pounds. I do not recommend that a deer hunter carry such a hoist with him in the field unless he has practical application for it. When I hunt with someone, I won't pack mine. When I hunt alone, I am likely to pack it. When I am hunting game larger than deer, even with someone else, I'm likely to carry the hoist.

The hoist is very handy, however, back in camp. My boys and I, mainly, have managed to hand-lift and tug deer in order to hang them for proper skinning and draining. But the hoist makes this chore a very easy one for a lone man to perform. The hoist will aid in lifting to a great extent. The model I have is a Haltrac from England. I am sure that there are many other good ones on the market today.

Rope

The deer hunter is well-advised to carry along some rope. Rope is light and a lot of it coils up into a very small area. I have lately gone to, mostly, ¼-inch nylon rope for it tangles less and is easier to manage. Rope serves to tie on our carcasses when we use the packframe, but is also of value in holding up a rain tarp or poncho. For the hunter who does not have a dragging device, rope can aid here, too. Rope can also be used to hang a buck in the field, or to help hold back a leg as a lone hunter field dresses his buck.

The Deer Hunter's Pistol

I am going to classify the deer hunter's personal sidearm as a piece of gear here because I am not referring to the deer hunting big game handgun, but rather the incidental handgun. I do not pack a sidearm with me every time I go deer hunting. There are many times when I find no value in such a unit. But there are many times when a little handgun can be very nice to have along. Where I live, mountain grouse may be taken by sidearm, and I do now have a sidearm with which I can add such good food to my camp. This happens to be a Ruger Mark II .22 semi-auto pistol in the Target model. I chose the heavy-barreled target model because I can hit well with it.

I can bag a cottontail at close range, and I can put other edibles into the pot with the little Ruger. Others will have their own preferences for a deer hunting sidearm, to include no sidearm at all, to be sure, and I respect this.

The .22 handgun, as shown here in the fine Ruger Mark II semi-automatic pistol, can be welcomed by the deer hunter. For gathering small game (and sometimes birds) on the trail, the little .22 is hard to beat, especially in an accurate model such as this one. It should be coupled with a safe holster, such as this Uncle Mike's model, water resistant and rugged, while available at modest cost.

Certain gear is both decorative and useful. This powder horn, made by Vince Poulin, is a handcrafted item which will serve the black powder deer hunter. But it is also a collecting piece as well.

But on several occasions my camp food rating went up several points on the gourmet scale because of a little sidearm. The obligation of the hunter is to take only that game which is open for such a sidearm, of course, and it almost goes without saying that safety measures be observed.

The first safety item I think we should consider for the smaller incidental sidearm as well as for the big game handgun is how we carry the piece. For me, a good sound holster which is designed to contain the handgun is the right way to go, and I consider this factor far above any fast-drawing qualities a holster might have. Secondly, I think a holster should protect the handgun from the ravages of twigs and other obstacles in the deer hunter's path, at least to some degree.

Finally, I believe in the little sidearm for the purpose explained here, for gathering some legal food, and I suppose in the rare case that a hunter needs to signal for help or some other reason and he does not wish to fire the ammo in his deer rifle. What I do not care for is plinking in a deer camp. There are camps so remote that others would not hear the shots, but I look at deer hunting as a restful and purposeful endeavor, a quiet time but for the necessary and occasional boom of a firearm used in the process of harvesting a deer. In my opinion, camp plinking is, for the most part, out of place when the camp has been set up for deer hunters during a deer season.

Special Gear for Special Hunts

The black powder hunter has to consider a few items as necessary to his all around success in the deer field, and while he knows what these are as well as I, we might glaze over a few of them just as a reminder. The contents

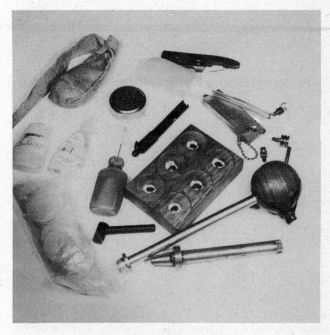

The black powder deer hunter requires some special items. He may have a ball bag, flush bottle, utility tool, capper, patches, short starter, powder measure, and many other little items among his muzzleloader accoutrements.

of the shooting bag (the bag which is often called the "possibles bag") has been mentioned elsewhere. We should remind the hunter that if he has a shooting bag all ready to go in a given caliber, he's most of the way home because when he grabs that bag, he has the essential items necessary for shooting.

In the bag he has his tools, and he has percussion caps and nipple picks, or flintlock priming tool and touchhole pick, readyloader, Kap Kover, and other gear. We might make just a few other suggestions. First, it might be nice

An item which may at first seem very out of place is this fishing kit. Actually, many deer hunters end up coursing through or camping in some fine fishing country, and such a little outfit can be packed easily and with little trouble. This is the Daiwa Minispin II and the entire kit is not much larger than a big holster.

if the hunter took with him a loading/cleaning rod. There are several good ones around. There is the fine rod made by the RIG Company and called the RIG Rod and the very good N&W rod, both having the muzzle protector, both being strong, both being very useful for the intended purpose of loading that first one downbore in the deer rifle and also for good cleanup of that firearm back in camp. If the hunter prefers a more primitive approach, he can use the "wiping stick" in place of the modern cleaning rod. A wiping stick is like a long ramrod, made of wood, with a threaded tip for jags and worms and screws and other accessories. It is more primitive in nature of course than the loading/cleaning rod. But I like the latter.

The archer also has special gear to worry about, the arrow case, maybe a camp target, extra bowstring, stringer, bow square, nocks and so forth. In both black powder and archery hunting, I suggest a special box of special tools. I have a black powder box which contains all of the essentials I could possible use in camp. Also, and this goes for any deer hunt anywhere, it is very nice to pack along an extra firearm, if not for every hunter, at least one for the camp. Deer arms are very reliable and the chance of one going haywire is remote. But anything can

happen, as they say, and that extra shooting iron or bow can save the day.

Fishing Gear

Fishing gear? Yes, fishing gear. A deer hunter can, at times, find himself in some very decent fishing holes, along mountain streams, on private ponds where permission to fish has been granted, even in rivers and lakes. The only problem is that while we may want to catch some panfish for supper and the enjoyment of the fishing itself, we do not particularly want to be burdened with a lot of fishing tackle. Yes, we could go primitive, but sometimes the romance of the primitive type fishing attempt outruns the number of fish in the creel.

However, there is a way that a deer hunter can have along some darn good fishing tackle without putting up with a lot of bulk, and this is the mini-system approach. The outfit I happen to have access to is a Daiwa Minispin II system. The entire fishing pole and reel are contained in a plastic "holster." The Daiwa 700C reel holds plenty of line, and the pole is ample for fish of the trout/bass class, especially the panfish size of the species.

Deer hunting is an experience, an often many-faceted experience at that, and a little bit of fishing tackle can add a lot to a deer hunting trip. The Daiwa Minispin II is held in a kit only 15 inches long and 5 inches wide at the widest point. It is no problem to pack it into a little corner somewhere and no problem at all to fit into a packsack. This, or a system like it, can add much to a deer hunter's experience.

The Gun Case

While it may seem a small item, consider this—the hunter arrives in deer camp. Everything is in order. He has practiced with his rifle. He knows there are deer in the area. The very next morning he gets his chance. It's not a difficult shot, but he misses, not only once, but a couple of times. He chalks it up as his own fault and continues to hunt. Later, he gets another shot. He misses again. This time he decides that something is wrong. Though he is not fond of shooting at camp, he knows he has to. Setting up a safe target, he takes a few shots and his rifle is nowhere near the mark. What went wrong?

In at least one real-life case that I can think of, I know what went wrong. The rifle's sights got banged around. In my opinion, any type of travel from airplane to mule can knock off a gun's sights, be they scope, peep or open type, front sight or back sight. This past season my son missed a shot with a muzzleloader, and he blamed himself. Then he missed again, and he blamed himself. Later, this time in a high country camp out of state, I happened to look at his rifle and discovered his front sight was bent.

The best way to keep a rifle sighted in is a good gun case. There are many good gun cases, of course, and I have no objection to the better soft models, but the shooter must recognize that the soft model protects from scratches but not necessarily from bumps and bangs. The hard gun case is a deer hunter's investment worthy of every cent spent on it. I have a decent plastic gun case which will withstand a pretty heavy blow, but I finally got into a hard gun case of the metal type, being a Treadlok model and now I feel confident that my deer arms will reach camp sighted in. The hard case, plastic, metal or homemade of wood, is a bit of insurance that no hunter can afford to be without unless he has a very foolproof means of getting his deer arms to camp and back with no chance of a bump or a bang.

Gear for deer hunters—it is a very long topic if all items are included. For now, we will close on the subject of gear and leave it up to the hunter to create his own personal list for the coming season. One good way of locating hunting gear is through magazines, books and catalogs. All of these have plenty of things deer hunters can use.

In Conclusion

Obviously, the hunter does not pack every conceivable piece of gear with him on every trek. The key here is appropriateness, and it is wise to check the contents of the daypack, pack or even pockets before a hunt begins. Still-hunters may wish to "go light," leaving behind anything which is not essential to the day's outing. If in totally familiar terrain in good weather, the hunter may pack no more than a sandwich and a few hunting essentials.

The hunter on stand, of course, can afford to have with him some extra gear and goodies, if he so chooses. After all, he will not have to pack these with him, unless he is walking long distances between stands. A vacuum bottle of hot drink, an extra coat, a hoist, and many other attending items may be on hand for the hunter who is going to sit instead of walk.

When hunting from a camp, certain gear may be provided by the outfitter himself. I have seen an outfitter loan personal gear to a hunter who has forgotten something behind. However, it is up to the hunter to decide on what he will carry in the field, and it is also his responsiblity to have the important items with him. What to carry and how to use it? The hunter carries what fits the situation, a packframe with life-saving gear for wild country prone to flash storms, for example, while leaving this gear out the scene when he is hunting familiar terrain during a nice time of the year. As to how to use the gear, there are two ways to learn: First, there are actual schools all over this country which teach many outdoor arts. Local colleges have classes in backpacking, for example, and hiking and camping. Hunter safety programs include information on how to use gear. It is not the scope of this book to instruct in compass-reading and backwoods camping; however, if the hunter is going to enter terrain which calls for these, then it is his definite responsibility to acquire the necessary knowledge which will make him safe and comfortable.

One of the most important single items any deer hunter can invest in is protection for his rifle. He may sight his rifle with utmost care, but if the firearm reaches the field having been banged out of whack, a missed or wounded deer could be the result. This is the strongly-constructed aluminum gun case with egg crate style padding from Treadlok Company.

chapter 26
The Well-Dressed Deer Hunter

A DEER HUNTER is sometimes no better than his clothing and his gear. Give me a totally miserable hunter, cold and uncomfortable, and I will give you a deer hunter who is not giving his all to the harvest of his game. So I think we have to take the question of hunter clothing very seriously. In the end, I believe that what is perfect for one hunter may be all wrong for another. I certainly do know that what is perfect for one area and one time of year can be totally wrong for another area and another season. That should go without saying. But we sometimes forget to prepare ourselves for change. I have certainly started a hunt during late fall only to find that it was, for all practical purposes, wintertime a day later. Agree, disagree, but be aware of clothing.

Getting down to the basics, clothes can only do a few small but terribly vital things. Clothes insulate and in very rare cases generate heat (electric socks). Clothing protects the body from the natural surroundings, such as boots warding off rock bruises and "man-eating" plants, cacti and the like. Certain clothing can also keep the body dry. When we look into outdoor clothing for hunting we also have to consider activity. Will the apparel allow us to move? The goal is to be warm and comfortable, and at the same time mobile. In the end, the hunter, I think, is going to have to make some mistakes. He's going to have to try different boots and socks and coats and other wearing apparel until he discovers what is just right *for him,* for his area and for his time of the year.

Boots

Over the past few years I have noticed that some of my friends, including those who make a living in the outdoors, such as John Kane, a Colorado guide, have turned to soft-soled and soft-sided shoes for hunting, especially for archery hunting. I have always had a problem with the "tennis shoe" in the outdoors, mainly with rock bruises, penetration of thorny plants and lack of support in general. So I quickly decided that the only thing for me was a tough leather boot. Most of the time, I still think so, but not all of the time.

I have found that in the woods, with a carpet of leaves, duff and softer earth, I not only get by well with softer hunting shoes, but I am much more quiet than I ever could be in hard boots. The first reason for such quietness is of course the soft soles of these shoes. But there is a strong second reason—you just don't go banging through the woods with soft shoes on. The fallen limbs and the rocks you might encounter even in the woods, will take a toll on your feet if you do. So, the hunter with soft shoes on is more quiet for at least those two reasons.

Due to a helicopter jump a long time ago which cost me at this point in time better than 1.5 inches of my used-to-be height, I can't wear lowtops out hunting. I suspect that many other hunters cannot either. So are soft-soled hunting shoes out with us? I don't think so. I have been using the L.L. Bean Maine Guide Shoe for 2 years with

The Lightfoot boot by Red Ball is one of the several modern boots of high insulation quality and light weight. With wool socks, author and sons have enjoyed reasonable foot warmth during cold hunting weather.

Having the correct clothing and footgear is only a part of the problem. The clothing and boot must remain in good shape and this is especially true of a boot used in snow or wet weather. Sno-Seal will aid the hunter in maintaining water resistant boots.

almost total success. The only problem that I had with the shoe was once when I set out for an area which I know to be devoid of cacti, but ended up hunting a different spot that day which had sharp cacti plants, and I managed to run a few of those through the side of the shoe.

The Maine Guide Shoe and other softer footgear of the same type may not offer quite the ankle support that some hunters require, but I found that my simple elastic ankle-wrapping was sufficient to put all of the support that I needed back into such a soft shoe. Still, I like the high-top soft shoe, with at least ankle height, and the Maine Guide Shoe has this. I have also seen lately a few of the so-called tennis or running shoes which appear to be tough, have higher tops and may be well worth looking into.

For hunting in rugged terrain, where rocks and "man-eating plants" abound, I'm still in favor of the leather hunting boot with good soles. I'm not yet convinced that the hard sole which "lasts forever" is the best, but for economy they certainly seem to be. I find the hard sole noisy and tough on the legs. My next pair of deer hunting leather boots will again have the soft sole I used to like so much. I know it is terribly expensive to have these boots "re-shod," but a hunter may consider that expense well worth it.

I am not trying to go overboard on the idea of being quiet. I realize that no hunter can make it through a jungle of downed limbs and leaves without a sound, and

a deer certainly can hear. But I also consider a hunter as harming his chances when he goes clackety-clack over the ground.

Waterproof boots are good. I have worn them for many years and am well satisfied with them. But the hunter has to take pains to keep his boots waterproof with the proper application of those substances recommended by the boot company. Also, I consider a very old pair of waterproof boots less than waterproof. I take my old waterproof boots and grease them heavily with the proper agents, warming the boots first, and in this way they are fairly good in wet weather for about a day, sometimes 2 days.

If the hunter needs waterproof boots, he is probably going to have to buy the rubber-type footgear and be done with it. My sons and I used the Lightfoot boots for a number of years with success. There is also the famous and popular boot with the rubber bottom and leather top. In one hunting camp, when I questioned about 20 hunters concerning footgear for snow and cold, all 20 preferred the latter type of boot.

While there are far too many different types of shoes or boots to mention here, I think the deer hunter should consider where he hunts, soft ground or hard, and when he hunts, snowtime or not, and then decide for himself which boot is best. I have found that the smart deer hunter never leaves home without extra boots, not for a long trip anyway. He also brings along a cold weather/

damp weather boot no matter what the normal or average conditions are where he is going hunting.

Socks

I like a pair of medium-heavy tube socks. Other hunters prefer a thin cotton sock and then a 100 percent wool sock over that. I have tried this in cold country, and it seemed to work very well for me in a rubber boot. There are many kinds of hunting socks, and there is no way to cover each type here. All I can suggest is that my feet seem to do better in terms of warmth and comfort when I do *not* use socks which take up all of the space inside of the boot. There should not be much room left in the boot, so much that the foot slips around, but an overly tight fit of sock in boot seems to defeat the warming or insulating ability of the sock.

As for the electric sock, my friend Bud Sprenger, a Michigan hunter before he moved West, made an informal study of the electric sock this past season during the elk hunt, since that constituted much colder weather in November than his deer hunt had to offer in October. He concluded that on a stand of any type, the sock was excellent. In walking, he was not as exuberant about electric socks, but found that they did not bother his feet. He simply felt that with good boots and regular socks a hunter who kept pacing was going to have fairly warm feet anyway. But on the stand, that is, staying still and studying the countryside with binoculars, the electric sock was a good investment.

Underwear

The long underwear of dual construction, a softer fabric on the skin and a very warm fabric bound to that on the outside, is what we have worn for a long time and we are satisfied with this. I suppose if a fellow got used to the all-wool "itchy-scratchy" type underwear it would be a true factor for warmth. Wool is certainly one of the most remarkable cold weather cloths, and everyone seems to agree with this, at least everyone I spoke with who does cold weather work or play.

All I can say about long underwear is that it works well, but everyone already knows that. I have carried a pair of long underwear in my pack on longer on-the-trail type hunts, just in case the weather got colder and also for sleepwear. As for the latter, long underwear seems, from my point of view, to increase my own personal feeling of warmth in a sleeping bag. I am told that sleeping totally naked is better in terms of warmth, and I hear this from experts, so I can't deny their point of view, but I think I am warmer with longjohns worn in the sleeping bag.

Sweaters

I learned about sweaters on the desert. In the cold air of first light, a deer hunter would shake like a hula dancer if he did not have warm clothing on. But about 2 hours after the sun was up in the sky, he'd roast if he were still wearing his warm clothing. So, the idea was to have warm

Here is the Wooly Pully sweater from Brigade Quartermasters Ltd., a sweater made especially for hunters. It is warm and comfortable and is reinforced at the shoulder and the elbow.

but light apparel which could be shed easily and packed the rest of the day. Glassing for deer when the hunter is cold is no good. The hunter must be comfortable in order to sit still and concentrate.

Sweaters helped a great deal in this situation. With a good quality sweater, preferably of wool or high wool content, we were warm in the early and late part of the day, but these sweaters could be quickly stripped off and stuffed into a daypack when not needed. A good wool sweater proved of great value to us on the desert, and I have also continued using such sweaters in the north country.

Scarf

I often use a large bandana as a scarf. At first, it seemed a bit silly to wear the scarf, since I looked like a B western film character with the scarf around my neck. But nobody laughed when they tried the scarf, and I have continued to use the scarf under certain weather conditions. The scarf keeps some of the dust out of the neck area, and it does add comfort in warmth, too. Just as important to me, I can slip the scarf off of my neck and wear it over my head. Now that really looks funny, but if a hunter ties the scarf over the top of his head and then down under his chin, with his hat on over the scarf, he gets pretty good windbreaking protection for his ears, but he can still hear through the scarf fairly well.

Shirts

Hunting shirts are of many types, and I like to wear the chamois type or the flannel shirt for most of my deer hunting. I think a wool shirt is better for colder weather, but most deer hunting that I do is not under conditions where I need a wool shirt *plus* all of the rest of my hunting clothing to boot. On a late season deer hunt in the mountains, however, one may wish to look into the wool hunting shirt.

The shirt is important because on many hunts a person simply has to strip down and get out of his jacket during the midday. If his shirt is all wrong, then he has a problem. I like to think of a hunting shirt as a garment which I can enjoy wearing on the outside, so to speak, and not simply as a garment that will always be covered by a coat or jacket. This is why the wool, chamois or straight flannel type hunting shirt is a good one.

Pants

In the West, we wear the denim type pants, most often, with long underwear when needed. I think that denim pants are OK for deer hunting, but they are certainly not the best type of leg covering for cold weather. The wool

We must dress according to the conditions and when the cold demands a good coat, the parka is often the answer.

Hunting clothing depends upon the weather, of course. A hunter may be able to get by very comfortably with no more than boots, pants and wool shirt, or as in this case, a flannel shirt. The hunter should try to be comfortable as well as prepared for anything the weather may try to deal him.

pant is far better. In my opinion, the eastern hunters who come West are generally better dressed for our western weather than we westerners are. In the brush, the so-called brush pants are nice, but the only pair I ever tried seemed a little more noisy than the wool pants. All in all, a wool pant is probably a good one for cooler weather deer hunting. I have seen the L.L. Bean Canada Gray Trousers, made of 85 percent wool and 15 percent nylon, and they seem to be nice.

The hunter should consider several points when he buys a pair of pants, not the least being comfort. He should also think about noise factor. Finally, a pair of wet denim pants is a pair of wet denim pants, but a pair of wet wool pants is not quite so bad. A hunter can stay warmer in wet wool pants, in other words, than he can in many other type of trousers.

Jacket/Coat

A good down coat, or similar type coat filled with any acceptable lofty material, is welcome on the hunt. One fellow hunter said he prefers the Orvis Gore-Tex™ 3-in-1 Coat. He liked the fact that the coat was waterproof and filled with down. His particular coat was the camouflage style, more for duck hunters than deer hunters, but with a blaze orange vest over the coat there would be no problem with the camouflage pattern.

In Alaska, I wore a parka, and I have since found that Alaska is not the only place suited for parkas. With an insulated set of coveralls and a parka, a hunter is prepared for cold weather. So dressed, with warm footgear, I managed to walk out in very cold weather. In 1970 I spent a winter in Fairbanks, Alaska, and managed to get out

The Browning Kodofil Reversible Trail Coat is an example of hunting wear made for hunters. It is a warm garment, yet it is light in weight. The reversible feature makes it extra handy for hunters who partake of the archery season as well as the regular deer season.

on foot when it was as cold as 65 degrees below zero. The wind, during that 70-71 winter, was nil when it was that cold, and I found that as long as I remained tucked into the parka, with the wolverine "tunnel" in effect, I could get around. Since that time, I have retained the parka as an emergency cold weather garment, to include the face mask. Most hunters will not find themselves in a situation where such a parka is of any value to them, but there are times and places when a truly warm coat or parka is needed. The idea is to match the jacket/coat with the conditions, perhaps keeping a backup coat for emergency use.

Windbreakers

I do have a windbreaker which is built in parka form with a hood. It is called a mountain parka, in fact, but it is primarily a windbreaker and when zipped up fully, it does keep the wind out. This type of hunting gear is useful in the high mountains and I have used it with great success at timberline. Wind is not a great factor in most of my own hunting, but when it is, wind can simply ruin a good day of hunting. I have never had much success hunting deer in a bad wind anyway, but when a hunter has limited time, he often feels that he has to hunt while he can, no matter the conditions, up to a point. If I hunt in the wind again, and no doubt I will, I will again wear my mountain parka windbreaker.

The garment worn by Bill Fadala, right, is warm in part because of its windbreaking ability. The hunter should consider the outer fabric of his jacket and his pants in terms of quietness and also in terms of ability to withstand the elements.

Snowmobile Suit

The snowmobile suit, known by other titles to be sure, is a good garment for cold weather. This insulated coverall is what I wore in Alaska, along with a full dress of clothing underneath, good footgear of the mukluk type, and my parka. I especially like this type of coverall because it is insulated and because it does what its name implies—it does cover the body pretty well, except for the hands and feet and face of course, and some even have a hood to take care of the head.

The Hat

The hat is extremely important to the deer hunter. The hat not only protects the head from loss of heat (and an occasional scrape with a tree limb) but it also shades the eyes, very important to glassing for deer and very important for shooting. If a hat will not shade my eyes properly, I do not want that hat for hunting. I like wool caps and will wear them on cloudy days when the sun is no problem, but that is the only time I will wear them out hunting, except as a night cap, when they can be very useful.

The western type hat is good as an instrument to ward off the direct rays of the sun. But I found that a truly widebrimmed western hat hit the top struts of my packframe. As a result I bought myself a western hat with a short brim which does not whack against the packframe

struts when I am walking. This hat has been a good one. The sun remains out of my eyes for glassing and yet the brim of the hat is not too large. I have fitted this hat with a leather chin strap, as it were, for that occasionally windy day. It's just right for most of my deer hunting, but not for all of my deer hunting.

Another hat I have found high favor with is a war surplus insulated cap with ear flaps. There are simply dozens of similar designs around today, and I hardly have to tell the reader where to find them. These hats are in all of the shops which carry outdoor wear, or most of them at least. A hunter might want to look for his hat at a sporting goods shop because he will most likely find a blaze orange one there. But I have seen blaze orange caps, insulated and with ear protection, in the standard department store as well.

Another type of hat I like very much is, I believe, called the Jones type. The hat has a small but excellent visor to keep light out of a hunter's eyes so he can shoot and glass, but it has no actual brim to get in the way. At the same time, a roll of material which is generally in the "up" position around the hat can be pulled down to form a brim if it rains or if the hunter wants more brim around his neck. Also, a flap on the inside of his hat folds downward to cover the ears of the hunter if he needs that protection. It is a very smartly styled hat and a very useful one. The model I have is insulated and I have had good

Kenn Oberrecht wears a bright orange pullover hat with a windbreaker. The windbreaker also has a built-in hood which can be pulled up if the weather changes.

(Right) The hunter wears an orange vest in accord with the law. He has a scarf in the form of a bandana, which may be tied about the ears if the wind takes up. His hat is small-brimmed so he can wear a packframe without the hat making contact with the frame.

service from this hat from Arizona to Alaska.

If the hunter will select his hat based upon a few criteria, he will be all right. First, he has to consider some shading effect for the eyes. Second, he must have a hat suited for the climate. Third, the hat has to be comfortable or it is no good for the hunter. It must suit his hunting style. Fortunately, there are hats for every head and for every use.

Belts

While it may seem overly picky to get into belts, I have seen some absolutely bad belts for hunting pants, and I think a hunter should be aware that the belt is a part of his outfit. I have a plain black belt with a plain buckle which fits the loops of my hunting pants, period. The belt is wide enough to slide a holster strap on it if I wish, but not so wide that a holster won't fit.

Mainly, I think that a hunter should be careful of the belt buckle. A buckle which is nice and fancy for city wear may cut into a hunter who is hiking where he must have a lot of body movement. Also, and worst of all, I have had buckles which cut into me when I was sitting back for a binocular glassing session or when I tried the sitting position for a shot. Such a buckle has no place holding up a set of deer hunter's pants.

The hunting belt should be simple and strong with a good plain buckle that will not cut into a hunter either when he is walking or sitting. I have seen some hunters use suspenders in place of a belt, and perhaps this is a good way to go. Either way, suspenders or belt, the pants should be held up high enough not to bind the legs. I have experienced trying to pack a deer out via a packframe when my pants were not cinched up high enough and my legs were not free to enjoy a full stride. This is annoying. The belt does a pretty important job in the field. It is a small item of hunter clothing, but one deserving of consideration.

Gloves

Miserable is the hunter with cold hands. It is easy to forget gloves, but it is hard to forget the discomfort caused by leaving the gloves home when they are needed. I have a set of gloves perpetually in my daypack, which is almost always fitted to my packframe on deer hunts. I always forget that they are there, and in fact have not mentioned them as part of my daypack contents in this very work. But they are there, and they are going to stay with me.

Even in the warmer deer climes I have enjoyed a pair of gloves, such as the buckskin gloves which we wear. They are generally enough protection against the cold of early morning and later afternoon hunts and for the evening walk back to camp. They are also protection against some of the thornier elements of that terrain. So, gloves are handy even in the not-so-cold deer hunting areas.

Without a doubt, they are useful where it is cold. A

Rain pants can be a very welcomed item of clothing, and we now have these from Browning in the ladies' sizes. The lady hunter can be dressed comfortably for the hunt, too, as she should be.

hunter may often have to choose between mitts or gloves when he is in the really colder areas. Generally, the mitten is warmer than the glove, and there are mittens which allow the forefinger access to the trigger. Not long ago, I tried a pair of gloves belonging to my nephew Mont Rydalch and found them to be extra warm. They were his ski gloves, and I'm probably going to invest in a pair. These are the Grandoe Gore-Tex[R] Film model.

There are all kinds of gloves on the market for all kinds of applications, from the soft deerskin glove to the extra-protection down-filled or similarly filled handwear models. The hunter must select what is right for him, for his area, for his needs.

Raingear

Once again we have a wide range of selection for the deer hunter to consider. My own raingear consists of a roll-up type nylon outfit, and it fits into my daypack nicely. On a very rainy hunt, where I will have to get out in the wet a lot, I'd prefer a full-fledged suit, and there are dozens of good ones to pick from. About the only consideration which truly means a lot to the hunter is a combination of high quality in a suit that has maneuverability. Being bound up in a rainsuit so that getting off a shot is difficult is no way to go. It's bad enough having to hunt in the rain without having to hunt in the rain and then miss a shot because the hunter can't move quickly within the confines of his rainsuit.

I much prefer avoiding the rain when I can, and I have been known to wait it out instead of wading it out, but

(Left) Camouflage clothing may be worn on various hunts. The idea of camouflage, obviously, is to break up the outline of the hunter, allowing his form to blend into the background. Andy Lightbody, left, and Ray Lightbody, right, use the coveralls here mainly for warmth and the convenience of the hunting pockets. Drab outfit of hunter in the background, Bill Fadala, will also tend to blend into the foliage. Movement of the hunter, however, remains more important than his clothing. No matter the clothing, movement will be picked up by a deer's keen and alert eyes.

there are times when a hunter must decide to stay dry and forget his deer trip or get wet and take a chance on locating a buck. When the choice boils down to a hunt or no-hunt deal, then out comes the rainsuit.

Blaze Orange

In the past, red was the hunter's special color. We were told to wear red because it was safer than other colors. That this was true or not, I'm unsure. Red seemed to go brown in the shade and did not seem to stand out as well as one would think. Then yellow was the craze. I recall watching a rifle walk across a meadow from one side to the other. It was, for all intent and purpose, a rifle without anyone holding it. I put up my binoculars and then could see the hunter outfitted from head to ankles in an all-yellow affair. I doubt that yellow was ever the answer. It seemed to fade out in some light, though it was probably very good in other light.

There was also a school of thought which established camouflage as the safest "color" for a deer hunter to wear. The idea was this: If they can't see you, they won't shoot you. "What do they wear in the war?," some hunters asked, and the answer was camouflage. "When you are deliberately trying *not* to get shot, you wear camouflage." That was the idea. I have no comment on it today, except that it is my opinion that the logic of not being shot by not being seen might be faulty. This is not a situation where staying unseen is necessarily the idea. Rather, we are supposed to be recognized for what we are, a fellow hunter.

Blaze orange seemed to be the answer for deer hunters and in many areas this color became a law. Here was a color that looked like it should. It did not fade into brown in the shade. It did not disappear in direct open sunlight. So blaze orange was accepted as *the* hunter color. Where I do much of my hunting, the wearing of orange, so many square inches of it per hunter, is the law. To be caught without your blaze orange is to invite a fine.

The Bowhunter

The bowhunter often enjoys an early hunt, or an isolated hunt in which only bowhunters can participate. This makes for a different story in the blaze orange department. The idea is that archers will have to get so close to their quarry that they will surely be able to tell man from deer no matter what the hunter is wearing. While it is, as I said above, the law to wear blaze orange where I hunt deer, this law does not apply to archers hunting during an archery-only deer season.

The clothing for the archer takes on a different set of

Clothing for a deer hunter is more than warmth and protection, though these factors are most important. The deer hunter must also consider what type of clothing he needs to fit his conditions. This bowhunter wears full camouflage clothing including a face mask.

goals. It should be soft, silent and dull. Camouflage is often the rule here. The archer must be able to move in his clothes. There is more motion in putting a bow into action, drawing it and releasing an arrow than there is in putting a rifle up and getting a shot off. At least it seems that way to me. Therefore, the clothing for the archer must fit his special needs of motion. Generally, a light coverall seems to work out well for the serious archer, though I believe that in some of the early season hunts, a camouflage shirt, camo pants, light footgear and maybe some camo paint might not be a bad wardrobe for the bowhunter, with a nice short-billed camouflage cap for headgear.

The Black Powder Hunter

Some black powder hunters enjoy dressing the part, that is, putting themselves into the time period they enjoy most, which is usually that of the Fur Trade era of the Far West, something like the early to middle 1800s. When the mountain man trapped beaver out West, he did the same thing that his eastern forebearers had done before him. He adopted some of the ways and some of the dress of the native American. Some historians feel that the

The deer hunter who wishes to enjoy the old-style clothing of an era gone by should remember that his buckskin clothing may not stand out, but in fact may end up looking like a deer. In this case, a blaze orange vest might be considered for the field.

Jerry Hill, well-known deer hunter and archer, clothes himself in soft buckskin apparel for deer stalking. With mocassins for footgear, the total clothing package is quiet. Soft-tanned deer hide (or other similar hide) will not make noise as the clothing rubs on itself or against certain obstacles in the woods.

white man on the Eastern Seaboard my have failed in settling in if he had not imitated the successful ways of the Indian people there.

Be that as it may, the black powder hunter must remember to remain within the limits of the law in his dress. When a shooter dons a fur cap and a buckskin shirt, or a buffalo robe in the colder regions, he tends to resemble other than a deer hunter. Also, the devoted black powder hunter wishing to dress up for the hunt must keep in mind that his gear should be top drawer in quality.

Certainly all of the gear worn by the mountain man of the 1800s served him well. There are a good many mountain men of modern times who have excellent old-time styled clothing and who know how to use it. They are comfortable on the trail and they enjoy their emulation of days gone by. They have every right to continue enjoying these methods of hunter dress, though where blaze orange is the law, they may have to spoil the overall looks of the outfit with a blaze orange vest or other legal garment. But back in camp they are again men reaching back into time for a touch with history.

Clothes may not make the man and they may not make the good deer hunter, either, but they are certainly important to him. A well-dressed deer hunter is just that much more able to move through the elements of the outdoors successfully. A well-dressed deer hunter is more comfortable. He can enjoy his sport with a greater chance for maintaining his concentration on the deer hunt instead of on his personal outdoor welfare in terms of the weather. Every deer hunter should consider his outfit very seriously, selecting the clothing which fits his personal needs best.

chapter 27

Trophy Hunting

THE WHITETAIL would just make the bottom of the record book. If I'd not been completely sure of that, I'd have held my fire. The buck was spotted with binoculars and studied for awhile, and its rack size was obvious. But there was a problem. It'd make the book, which was not that high at the time, but the buck lacked something. He lacked something I could not have seen when I'd spotted it bedded down with only the rack partially above and blending in with the brush. The buck lacked a tine. He was, by eastern count, a 9-pointer instead of a 10-pointer. No, there would not be an actual reduction because of the "odd" tine. On the other hand, the buck would only go as an 8-point buck. The fifth tine on the one side would be added in and then deducted in the Boone & Crockett measuring system.

I was very unhappy. Max Wilson, long-time friend, was standing right beside me and beside him was his young son, a beginning deer hunter. He was now allowed to go along on hunts and would be a "gun-toting" deer hunter the very next season. The beautiful buck was mine, but I had little appreciation for it. "He'd go up in the book pretty well if he had that other tine," I complained. Max Wilson looked at me and then at his son. "If I could have seen the bad side," I continued, "I probably wouldn't have shot." I continued to examine the rack as if the other tine might suddenly grow in place. "All I could see was the good side," I went on, feeling sorry for myself.

The boy looked confused. He had been bubbling with enthusiasm as we walked up the hill to look at my buck. But now he was glancing from me, to the buck, and then to his dad. "Well, it's just one of those things," I went on. "I should have waited to see the other side of the rack before getting trigger-happy." I slipped my pack-frame off and picked around in the daypack to find my sheathed knife/saw kit. Max and the boy began to help me each holding a leg as I began field dressing.

Then Max looked at me. "I've known you since you were only 14 years old," he said, "and this is the first time I've ever been ashamed of you." Boy, the words hit hard. I put the knife down and looked into my friend's eyes. He did not need to say another word. It was all there. I could hear my own words echoing in my ears. Here was a beautiful buck deer, my deer, a gift in that it was there for me to find, and I was complaining about it because a hunk of antler that might have been there wasn't there.

That was enough for me. I didn't have to be run over by a diesel truck in order to see where I had gone with my "head hunting." I'd still look for trophies, all right. But I'd start putting things back in perspective, things that had gotten way out of whack. I sat for a moment. I picked up my knife. "Beautiful deer, isn't it," I said with no question mark in my voice inflection, and I stuck to it. I still love a nice buck, you bet, and I still pass up the small ones, too. But I don't ever want to get totally "horn happy" again.

Once again, the hunter is confronted with a choice. Does he shoot? This is not a trophy buck, unless it is that hunter's personal trophy buck. If so, he should harvest this deer. If not, he should keep on looking for his big buck.

(Left) Should I shoot? Most hunters would say yes! But a dedicated trophy hunter might just have to say no. He might pass up a shot at this buck. A hunter has to make up his mind as to what he really wants, and if he wants a big buck, he'd best not shoot a little one, 'cause that is the end of his tag!

Your Trophy, My Trophy

The word "trophy" may have a very different connotation for various hunters. For me, there are only two kinds of trophies. First, a trophy is any deer which holds a special significance for a hunter. The significance of the animal may lie in the fact that it was a very heavy specimen, or the hunt was very special, or the deer may have been taken with a more basic type of hunting tool, bow and arrow or black powder firearm. The deer may be a trophy because the hunter had to look long and hard for the buck he ended up with. Or it may be a trophy simply because the hunter *likes* that particular animal.

I was visiting a friend in Arvada, Wyoming, during the turkey hunting season when I was ushered into a room which I knew housed a couple of huge mule deer mounts. I thought my friend was going to show me those heads again, which was all right with me. Instead, he produced an antelope mount, fresh from the taxidermist. The horns were no more than 13-inches long, certainly not a "trophy," but the head was a trophy to my friend. "Look at how those prongs curve inward and almost touch. Aren't they beautiful?," he asked me. They were beautiful. That head was a trophy.

My second category of trophy is more simply defined, and this is the "record head." Here, by reason of a scoring chart and method, a head is given a specific number of points, and if it manages to earn a certain minimum score, then it is "one for the book," the Boone & Crockett book of course. Local taxidermy shops generally have the latest scoring sheets for deer, along with the current minimum score required for each category of deer, Virginia whitetail, Coues, Sitka and so forth. The minimums have changed in an upward trend over the years because more and more heads have been entered and have qualified for recognition in "the book."

Values of Trophy Hunting

Looking for, and harvesting, the big buck is an honorable thing to do. When the venison-chase becomes nothing more than a search for antlers, however, I think the hunter is missing out on some deeply rewarding aspects of the hunt. But there is a lot of value in trophy hunting, and there is nothing wrong with "going for the big one." I can think of a good many reasons to hunt for trophies.

First, the trophy hunter gets a real deer season out of it. Instead of cropping the first deer he sees, which will most likely *not* be that big buck, our hunter continues to look. He continues to hunt. He, in fact, assures himself more time in the outdoors by hunting trophies. Because of this added time in the habitat of the deer, he gains much more experience. In fact, the hunter who passes up bucks has, in a way, mentally harvested a rather great number of deer. Many is the time he could have easily taken a buck, but he passed it up instead. However, he still had an experience, a harvest without pulling the trigger, you might say.

I think, then, that the trophy hunter gains much more experience than the non-trophy hunter. He has, if you will, a great number of "make believe" harvests. He does have much more experience in actually hunting deer under in-season conditions. He has the joy of seeing bucks under hunting conditions, sometimes over and over again in a season. He also has the great advantage of learning more about deer hunting, much more than he would have learned by taking the first buck that came his way.

Second, I believe that trophy hunting is a viable way of harvesting the mature animal. This is not always beneficial from the game management point of view, but generally it is. A big buck is most generally a mature buck. For a while there was some confusion on this score, because biologists recognized that a buck grew a good set of antlers because of conditions and family background more than because of age. However, it is also true that few 2- and 3-year-old deer are going to be big boys.

So, the trophy hunter is much more likely to harvest a mature buck, a buck that darn well would be off the land in a short time anyway due to natural attrition. As I admit, in some areas this is not good, for the herd needs a thinning effect created by taking more of the younger breeding stock. But all in all, there is nothing wrong with

taking a big buck from the biological standpoint. Furthermore, for those concerned that the big bucks will disappear if trophy hunters do too well in their quest for larger antlers, this is unlikely. The "genes" that trend toward big bucks are still carried in the stock at large. We can also be sure that not all of the big bucks will be harvested out of a given area.

Third, trophy hunting is very interesting. It is truly interesting to get out and try to find a big buck instead of just any buck. Dedicated trophy hunters learn a lot about their game, and they also learn a lot about the habitat of the game. While a perpetually successful hunter may lose a bit of the edge from his deer hunting, that edge is generally honed back to razor sharpness when he takes up the trophy chase. As stated earlier, the trophy hunter is more likely to see a great many more bucks than is the hunter who bags his deer first day out. "You don't get the big buck by shooting the little buck," trophy hunters say, and what they mean is that you don't spend your tag on the first buck that comes your way. You wait. You wait until that big boy is found. Sometimes you wait too long, and you go home with that tag in your pocket, uncancelled. But that is the chance a trophy hunter takes.

Fourth, I have come to find that a big buck in the rack is generally mature in the body as well. Not always is this the case, to be sure. But it holds up fairly well. In other words, the rack-chaser who gets his trophy is very likely

Here is the late Ed Stockwell, superb hunter, bighorn sheep guide and holder of the world record Coues deer, pictured here with Ed. The author was privileged to hunt with this master outdoorsman.

Oftentimes, the trophy is located, but not harvested. A hunter has to be able to make the shot after he has found his game. This buck will bolt in two heart-beats, and when he does, there will be a ridge between him and the hunter. A practiced hunter, however, is going to harvest this buck.

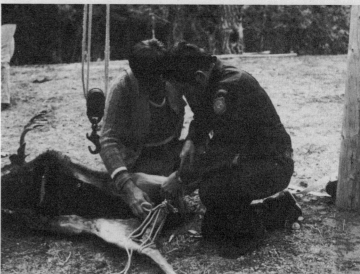

A careful check of the weight of bucks taken in a given area provide useful information for game biologists.

(Left) Game management has meant a lot to deer hunting in general and to trophy hunting because the game manager's goal is to maintain healthy herds of deer. The Wyoming Game Department personnel are dedicated to the study of all wildlife and an effort to keep wildlife thriving.

to have a good hunk of meat to show for his efforts as well as a nice rack. As I say, this is not a perfect correlation by any means, but it holds up in general. A mature buck is going to be mature in its body development as well as its rack development most of the time.

Fifth, there is the challenge. This could be rated along with the interest factors, but I think there is some difference here. There is, no doubt about it, a greater challenge in consistently bringing out a big buck than there is in taking a so-called "meat buck" every year, though I do not like that term when it means small buck. I still think a trophy buck is the better "meat buck." Be that as it may, the trophy hunter is accepting a definite challenge. With the challenge comes a special reward. The reward is not always that of taking home a big rack, either. Sometimes the reward comes in the form of pure hunting delight, being out there, looking at bucks which you will not harvest, and spending a great deal of time at a loved activity.

Sixth, a trophy can be a much more lasting memory than a smaller buck. I remember my biggest whitetail harvest best. But I remember it more for the situation and the men with me than I do the actual antlers, and that is for certain.

We had hunted for a very long time, and we had hunted hard. Furthermore, we had passed up some bucks that maybe we should have taken. I had a super day from first light, and pre-scouting had paid off better than ever before for us. Thirteen bucks had been in my vision that day and now the day was done. There was one more pocket of oaks to look at. That pocket of oaks gave me my big whitetail buck. I can't ever forget the rack of that buck as it seemed to weave in and out among the trees and I remember forcing myself to hold fire, to get ready, to be professional about the whole thing, waiting for the buck to zip through a small clearing. But most of all, I remember the event because my two hunting partners were as happy for me as I was happy for myself.

Competition

Competition can be a very degrading aspect of hunting or a very uplifting aspect. It all depends. When a hunter competes with his friends for a buck, he's missing the point, I think. Oh, sure, some friendly wager on the "big one" is all right, but I have seen the competition turn to envy and relationships ruined all for a rack. It isn't worth it. The "I got mine" syndrome is often a degradation of the hunt. I don't care for that type of competition.

But a deer hunter competing with himself is something else again. When partners go out hoping as much for the other guy to get the big buck as for themselves to get it, then you have a truly fine competition going, because the hunters are competing mainly with themselves but not against each other. They are in competition with the outdoors, with the instincts of animals with instincts far more keen than their own. When a successful hunter beats his chest like a gorilla because he has harvested good antlers, he's missing the point. He ought to be more humble, more grateful, and he might as well keep two things in mind. First, there is no doubt a bigger buck is out there running still. Second, the biggest bucks of the season generally go to a fellow who is *not* a trophy hunter. A few seasons ago, a 14-year-old boy took a big record head. It was the first deer he had ever fired at in his life. That might not happen very often, but neither will the dedicated trophy hunter bag the biggest buck taken in the state that year, at least not very often.

In short, I think a hunter is best off competing with himself rather than his hunting partner. Then the competition remains healthy. A hard-working hunter should be proud when he takes a big buck after passing up smaller ones. But he does not want to let pride spoil the more important aspects of the harvest.

The Advanced Deer Hunter

I believe we can safely say that most trophy hunters are advanced deer hunters or they are at least seeking that goal. An advanced deer hunter is simply one who has put more time and possibly more effort into his activity. He takes deer hunting seriously, but we hope not so seriously that he ends up seeking the wrong rewards from his interest. What does the advanced deer hunter do differently from a "regular" deer hunter?

I think the first thing an advanced deer hunter does is study his hunting. He probably has a library of books on the subject. He might even keep notes from season to season. He probably scouts for deer, if only to learn areas better and to gain more experience in the outdoors. He is always a student of deer. He does not stop deer hunting just because he cannot shoot a deer. He hunts deer vicariously all year long, even when the hunting is no more than an armchair adventure in talking over deer hunting with fellow enthusiasts.

The advanced deer hunter probably looks into game department studies. He might subscribe to the game department's monthly publication. He may even read into the unpublished data available in the form of master's degree thesis and doctoral dissertations. The advanced deer hunter is, in the main, pretty serious about it all.

The advanced deer hunter continues to learn about his equipment, too. If he's a modern arms hunter, he learns all he can about the best ammunition, and he tunes his firearms to a fine degree. He practices, too, and this goes double for the bowhunter. The black powder hunter learns his equipment, too, and though he has forsaken the aspect of high technology in his hunting tools, he does insist upon reliability.

The advanced deer hunter, in the main, thinks about deer hunting all year. He spends a lot of time between seasons in his study of deer, and he also knows his tools as a fine craftsman knows his tools. This hunter maintains his interest on a year-around basis.

Trophy Hunting Tactics

Good hunters do not need to be trophy hunters, and I daresay that there are countless excellent hunters who do not pursue antlers as their major objective. They most likely love getting a big buck, but they do not necessarily head into the field with trophies in mind. On the other hand, the trophy hunter who wants to consistently bag the big buck had better refine his methods. He may not use methods which differ much from those of his brother deer hunters, but he should have a plan. He should be prepared each season, knowing what he is going to attempt to do, where is going to attempt to do it, and how he is going to get the job done. Here are some considerations. There are no doubt many more, and the ones presented are hardly a last word.

Hunting Alone

Some of the best trophy hunters I know hunt alone. They cannot, it seems, fulfill their own plans when others

Wyoming Game & Fish Department official checks a hunter's harvest in order to aid in compiling useful records on a given area.

Trophy hunting can mean looking into areas not always hunted because the areas may, in fact, be less populated with deer than other locales. Trophy hunters are always looking for that "one special spot."

are along. In fact, a couple of trophy hunters in my list of acquaintances even camp alone. They prefer it that way. They scout an area by themselves and return to hunt later on by themselves. They do not want company. I might add that these fellows are not necessarily loners on an everyday basis. They bowl with friends. They have families they share their lives with. They like to chat on coffee breaks at work. But they darn well do not like hunting with others when it is trophy-chasing time.

As for me, and this is an opinion only, I do not see where hunting absolutely alone makes for a better chance for a trophy. In fact, I think four eyes are better than two. I think that two hunters can work together in many ways, in mini-drives and on stands separated by, perhaps, only a short distance. I like the idea of sharing a camp with a good friend and I have hunted trophy deer success-

fully with my family, too.

But I can understand the other fellow's point of view, too. Sometimes it is nice to be alone, to have the concentration that a hunter feels he might need. I'm not against hunting alone and I have hunted alone. But I do not believe it to be the only way to bag big bucks. The compromise, of course, available to any hunter, is camping with a partner or partners, but heading into the field alone, and then returning at the close of the day to share experiences. Probably, most hunters of the trophy ilk hunt in this way, sharing a camp, but not necessarily sharing the field on a step-by-step basis.

Partners

A lot of good trophy hunting can be done on the buddy system. Partners, to me, means year-around involvement,

Author poses with a whitetail buck trophy that he harvested while hunting with two friends, John Doyle and Ed Stockwell. The deer is a trophy, but the memory of a great hunt is a bigger trophy.

though I have had hunting partners whom I saw mainly during the season and not very often otherwise. But if the trophy hunter operates under a plan, then I think the plan is all the stronger when two or more serious outdoorsmen get together and share ideas. It is also nice to share skills.

I have learned a lot from hunting partners who understood deer hunting far better than I did. I hope these same men perhaps learned something from me about firearms and similar areas. So, the point is to share expertise from one man to the next. Two trophy hunters who share ideas are, in my opinion at least, much more knowledgeable in the long run than hunters who stay totally to themselves. Again, I am not knocking the solitary outdoorsmen. Some of the great hunters have been solitary hunters, such as Nessmuk and Ben Lilly. But partners is not a bad idea either for trophy chasers.

The Backpack

A couple hunters who take to the backtrails with temporary homes on their backs have, I think, a bit better chance of finding big deer on a regular basis. I do not mean that you have to backpack in order to be a trophy hunter! I use this statement for one reason only, and that is to point out that a backpacker can actually stay in the domain of the deer much longer than the hunter who spends a good deal of his time "going back to camp." The dedicated trophy hunter might consider the backpack method, then, for reasons of more time in the deer habitat, but also for more quality time in the habitat. When most hunters are heading back to the camp, the lodge or the house, this hunter is in deer country when the deer are more likely to be up and about.

Packing In

The idea that the big buck lives only in the outback away from civilization is not quite in line with the facts. Many a big buck has been taken right on the farm grounds or the ranchlands, or near popular camping sites or for that matter right on the outskirts of a big city. Two hunting friends of mine both bagged big trophy bucks a few seasons ago only 20 miles from a rather large city, in fact.

On the other hand, the reverse is not true either. Just because there are big bucks on farmlands and ranchlands and near cities and camping areas does not mean that there are few big ones way back in. As a matter of fact, the pack-in type of hunt can put an outdoorsman into some pretty interesting terrain. Mainly, this hunt is a western effort, but there are still places near population centers that "turn wild" in a hurry. Packing in can mean paying an outfitter to haul hunters and gear to a special spot, or it can mean backpacking in for a stay of more than a weekend usually. Packing in is one way of getting to a place not normally frequented by deer hunters. It is no guarantee of a big buck, but it can be worthwhile and interesting for the trophy hunter.

Here is Jeffrey Anderson of Anderson Designs, Inc., with a trophy whitetail buck which Jeff took with his own Anderson Magnum 245 broadhead. Total points are 14. The Pope & Young non-typical score is 151 ⅝ points. Most important for Jeff is the fact that the buck was harvested quickly, running 28 yards and piling up defunct.

The Time Factor

I think trophy hunters need to adjust their priorities in terms of time. Sure, a guy can bag a nice one the first few minutes out of camp. It happens. But on a year after year basis, I can tell the hunter with all truth that he will not harvest a big trophy buck the first hour out of camp all the time, and if he does, he'd best keep that little spot to himself! No, the trophy hunter may have to adjust his time situation so that he uses vacation or other blocks of scheduled time for his hunts.

I suppose I am saying this—trophy hunting takes time. The hunter who has a weekend instead of a week had best adjust his desires away from the big rack. At best, he may be able to trophy hunt one day, but he certainly better take what comes his way the second day if he has to go home that afternoon or evening. Also, I have seen trophy-hunting situations where it took a few days just to locate that special place within the special place. In short, that little patch of woods or brush or that one canyon which might have special feed attracting the deer

This archer uses his pit blind in hopes of bagging a trophy buck out of it. Patience is often the key to success for the trophy hunter.

in. Also, it can take time to learn an area thoroughly unless pre-scouting has been intense.

The Guide

Some hunters feel that it is like "buying a deer," but as we discuss in our chapter on guides and guiding, that is not necessarily so. On the other hand, let us look the situation squarely in the eye and call it for what it is—he who can afford professional help is all that much better off in locating and harvesting a trophy. If a guide is good, he knows where the game is, and this means he might know where some of the big boys are running. He might also know how to hunt them.

Today, with time pressing upon us from all sides, it seems, the hunter who truly wants a big trophy buck may indeed be well off to look into a guided hunt. It is definitely not the only only way to get a big buck, but the guided trip is a friend helping a friend get a deer. Either way, there is no shame in seeking help.

Trophy hunting can be the most interesting aspect of deer hunting that an ourdoorsman can participate in. When the idea of trophy antlers begins to overcome all of the other reasons for going hunting, then a problem could be in the making. Balance is the answer, as usual, a balance between the desire to harvest that big trophy and the desire to enjoy all of the aspects of the hunt. Trophy hunting is special hunting, and it holds special rewards for those who maintain a good attitude about it.

chapter 28

The Guided Hunt

SINCE WE are talking about successful deer hunting, we must include the guided deer hunt. In many ways, a guided hunt is the most successful hunt of all for those who are going into unfamiliar ground, and also for those who, to be very honest about it, may not have the hunting skill and know-how of a professional big game guide. For certain, a guide is interested in seeing his client harvest a deer, and he wants him to harvest a big one, too.

I think it is too bad that we place the harvest above all else, but we go deer hunting to get deer and the other joys of the hunt are incidental to this goal. We can talk about "smelling the roses" and "how wonderful it is to be out in nature;" I have heard this a hundred times. When a hunter tells me that he is really out there to experience the joys of nature, I ask him why he is packing a deer rifle. When a hunter tells me that it does not matter to him whether he actually gets a deer or not, I ask him how many deer he has taken. When he has bagged a few dozen bucks, then I believe him.

Usually, we go forth into the land of the deer to harvest a deer during the deer season, and that is exactly how it should be. The game department has set limits and issued tags for a reason. The reason is a harvest. The hunter who comes home without a deer has not necessarily aided in the preservation of the game at all. In some cases, he has done just the opposite. So we go deer hunting to get a deer, and a guide sure can help the hunter out.

How Do You Find a Guide?

Guides advertise, so it is no problem in locating a guide. All one need do is check into magazines for ads. As an example, I was just looking into *The Buckskin Report*, a magazine dedicated to black powder shooting, and I saw an advertisement offering guiding services for hunters interested in taking big game with the smokepole. This guide specializes in black powder hunting, and that is nice to know. His reputation is sterling. If a hunter wanted a black powder guide, he might consider a look into black powder publications.

Also, the state game department may have a listing of registered guides. In Alaska, just to mention one state, a guide must be approved. Also, aside from the registration factor, we find the name "Master Guide" attached to those who qualify in that specific level of guiding. If I were looking for a guide, I would check into various publications for ads, but I would also take a moment to write the game department of the state in which I intended to hunt. The department can offer a list of guides and guide services.

There are many other ways to find guides. One may read of a guide as he enjoys an outdoor article in one of the hunting periodicals. Oftentimes, a writer will state the name of a guide who took him into the country in pursuit of game. Local hunting clubs are another source of information pertaining to guides. The merits (or demerits) of a guide quickly spread around a hunting club. Furthermore, a hunter may speak directly with another hunter concerning a guide. Friends and acquaintances may also help us pick a guide. At any rate, there are ways to locate big game guides. And the above are only a few of the possibilities.

Credentials

There is nothing wrong with a hunter asking for credentials where a guide is concerned. In short, the guide should be registered with the state and/or some agency, and the hunter has a right to ask for these credentials. A license for guiding is the very basic credential, of course. But there are credentials beyond the license, including membership in professional organizations and various agencies.

References

The hunter also has the right to request references. Without a doubt, no guide in the world can please every hunter, and in my opinion the hunter looking into a guide's credentials should get at least two opinions from former clients. I entered a hunting camp to see a friend of mine who makes a living as a guide and is a very successful guide. He was guiding for deer. Every single member of that camp had a deer. You would suspect that the hunters were quite happy. Well, all of them were with the exception of one man. He was madder than a bear with a bee up its nose.

In fact, the man and his wife were packing to get out of there. He stopped me and began to tell his sad story. "You gonna be guided by this guy?" he asked. I said no, but I was going to hunt in the area. "Well don't let this guy take you out," he went on. I inquired whether the man had gotten his buck or not. Yes, he said, he'd gotten his buck all right, but it was hardly the one he had "paid all that money to get." In fact, I saw the buck. It was a good one, a mature 4-pointer western count, 10-point eastern count, with pretty good beams. Not a record buck by any means, but the head was certainly mature. It was a trophy.

After he left I asked the guide, my friend, what he had done to make the hunter so mad. "Did you make him eat cactus for breakfast?" I asked. Well, it turned out that the fellow's wife had shot a buck a bit bigger than that of her husband and it also turned out that the fellow wanted to "make the book" and nothing less would do. "Did you tell him to shoot that buck that he got?" I asked. My guide friend told me that when the hunter asked what he thought about the buck, he simply said it was a "good one." The fellow fired and that was that. A "good one" to John was a mature buck. A "good one" to this hunter was a record book buck only.

If a hunter asked the above gentleman for a reference concerning the above guide, he would have gotten a tirade of rather abusive adjectives describing this very good guide's ability. Therefore, I think that a hunter should

There is one aspect of guiding which stands out above all. A guide has to know his game. He has to be, first of all, a hunter himself. He must know his gear, too, and how to get the most from that gear. Tink Nathan (left) has taken a number of deer as a hunter and has helped many others bag a buck.

look at credentials with an open mind. But he should look at them all the same before he plunks down the greenbacks. I do suggest that a hunter seek references, however. The only problems with references I can see are two: First, you can have a situation where a person suggests you call John Q. Hunter for a reference, and when you call John Q. Hunter you find out that he's mad at the guide and considers him a fool. Therefore, more than one reference is necessary to get an accurate picture. The second thing wrong with references is that if you ask a guide for a list of past hunters, it's not terribly likely that he will give the names of the unhappy ones who have been in his camp. Nonetheless, references are important, though they are not foolproof.

What Does a Guide Owe a Client?

What is the guide being paid for? I think there is some confusion along these lines. And I think there is also some grave misunderstanding here, too, at times. Here are a few of my ideas on what a guide owes a hunter and what he does not owe a client.

First, it is my opinion that a guide should know his territory like the hunter knows his backyard. I do not think there is any excuse for a guide to have trouble just getting around the territory in terms of knowing where he is. Unfortunately, a guide may have to look into a brand new place at the last minute when things go sour for him. In one case, I heard of a guide having to abandon his well-known area for a new area at the beginning of the season because the place he wanted to hunt underwent an emergency closure. These things can happen. However, I'd be very displeased if I were with a guide who admitted that he was experiencing the locale for the first time. If I knew as much about the area as the guide knew about the area, I would be very disheartened about the services rendered by the guide.

Second, I think a guide should have some idea of where the game roams in his area. I do not believe that any hunter or guide can tell just where a deer is going to be on a certain day at a certain time, but I'd like to think that the guide has prior knowledge of the game in the area and that he knows where to start looking for that game. I also feel that a guide should know about the *current* situation on the game in the area. In other words, I feel a guide should scout prior to the season, even though he may have hunted that area in the past. Things can change. A hunter should not have to tramp around an area which the guide has not investigated recently.

Third, I think a guide should have hunting expertise. It is not enough to know the terrain and know that there is game in it. A guide should have a method for finding game, too. Most guides are guides because they love to hunt. So this criterion should not be a problem. However, it must be mentioned. In summary, on this one, I believe that a guide should be a good hunter. He should have

The guide will know how and when to use certain tips and tricks which lead to success in terms of bagged game. This hunter used Tink's Doe-in-Rut lure in Virginia with success.

One of the major plus factors a guide can offer is getting the hunter into "where the game is." If a guide can do that for a hunter, he has provided a good service. Of course, there are many more points of obligation. However, if a guide puts the hunter and the game on the same grounds, he has done the client a very good service.

The guide's job does not end when the game is sighted and it does not end when the hunter has scored a hit. It is up to the guide to locate any game which has been encountered, even when it is only a matter of following up on an archery harvested deer such as this one. (Photo courtesy J. Wayne Fears)

a very good idea of how to go about locating game in his given locale. I am not talking about guarantees here. That is another story.

Fourth, I think the guide should be willing to work. If he is not, then he should look for a new vocation. By work, I mean active pre-season scouting, setting up a good camp with a decent wood supply, getting the game out, hunting hard for the game in the first place and so forth. Guiding is beastly hard work at times and a guide has to accept the fact. One of my guide friends scarcely gets 4 hours of sleep a night throughout the entire season. But he knows that he has to put out the effort if he wants his clients to have a good hunt.

Fifth, the guide should have some decent gear. It is almost unfair to ask this of him in some cases, considering what some gear costs. But nonetheless, a guide should have the necessary hardware for a good camp and a good hunt. If horses are in the deal, then the horses are going

to have to be decent well-trained ones. Tents should not leak. Beds should be reasonably comfortable. All of the tools of the guided hunt should be in decent repair.

Sixth, a guide should have good food on hand. Sure, some evenings it is pretty tough to toss a meal together when game has been taken and has had to be dressed and brought into the camp. Hunters have to be reasonable and they must understand that every meal in camp cannot be a culinary experience on par with a good restaurant. But the guide should be able to offer one tasty meal a day at least, with an edible lunch.

Seventh, a guide should be able to dress the game professionally. He should be able to cape the head. He should know what to do to preserve the meat and the cape. He must be responsible for getting the game back to the camp. It's nice if he can help the hunter with at least information as to meat processing houses in the area. He does not owe the hunter a butchering job, but he does owe the hunter a dressed deer and a useable cape if the hunter does indeed want the cape for a mount.

Eighth, the guide should have sound transportation. We have already mentioned horses, but transportation means good vehicles as well. A known mechanical problem should have been fixed before the season. Once again, hunters have to be reasonable. Vehicles do break down. But in general, the guide must have some form of transportation for the hunter and that transportation should be in good shape. Also, the guide is going to have to either have some backup transportation or know where to get it if he does need it.

What a Guide Does Not Owe a Client

I do not believe that a guide owes a hunter any game. He only owes him an opportunity. There are so-called guaranteed hunts, and I have certainly been in areas where I would feel very confident in giving the hunter a guarantee that he would see some deer. But I would hate to have to guarantee the hunter that he would get a deer. I do not think it is the responsibility of the guide to sight in a client's rifle. I do not think it is the fault of the guide if the client misses a shot.

In my opinion, if the hunter goes out with the guide and they see game, then the guide has fulfilled his obligation. In fact, if the guide takes the hunter into good territory in good faith and it is obviously the right place to hunt, but for some reason the hunter does not get a shot, I consider that a part of the chance we take when we go hunting. The guide is not a miracle worker. He cannot control the weather. If it rains for the entire contracted hunting time, that is not the fault of the guide. If conditions of weather spoil a hunt, in other words, that is not the fault of the guide. The hunter has to be mature enough to accept the lack of success without blaming the guide for things out of the guide's control.

A guide is not a servant. He does not owe the hunter personal service other than the camp/food situation and the obvious factors we already discussed. The hunter does

The packtrip can be an ultimate hunt, and in some areas of the West, a hunter can go for deer and elk on the same trip, as well as other game, to include mountain grouse and even bear, depending upon the area. Some outfitters and guides offer excellent packtrip hunts.

not have any personal claim on the guide as a lacky. The best guided situation I know of are those in which the hunters and guides "hunt together" and "camp together" in the sense that they are both hunters and both campers. It won't hurt a hunter to do a camp chore that needs to be done. On the other hand, a hunter should be free from heavy camp chores (cutting the wood supply) that were supposed to be provided for him.

The Drop Camp

Another type of "guiding service" is the drop camp. This particular service is a good one and a practical one.

However, it means that there is no direct claim upon the time of the guide above and beyond what is contracted for. If a hunter has a problem, the guide should try to help out, but all in all, a hunter is on his own in a drop camp. For example, a skill of the guide not mentioned above is first aid. In a drop camp, the guide will not be there to render first aid. He will not be there to cook. He will not be there to advise. He will not be there, most of the time, period.

A drop camp is a very worthwhile way to hunt. But it is a camp which must be agreed upon in advance right down to the water supply. A hunter should know exactly

It is the obligation of the guide to set up a good camp. This high mountain camp was put up by John Kane, the professional bear/lion hunter and guide, and it provided all of the needs of the hunter.

what he is going to get before he takes on a drop camp, and he should expect no more than what was promised, unless he is willing to pay for the added service. In my opinion, here are the major tenets of a good drop camp:

1. The hunter is brought into a very good area for game. The guide has current knowledge of the area, and he knows it to be a worthwhile place to hunt.

2. The guide has provided a camp which is sound and safe. He has cut the wood supply or had it cut. There is a supply of water in camp or nearby, though the guide may not always be responsible for replenishing the supply of water in the camp, depending upon prior arrangement and agreement.

3. The guide should be able to direct the hunter in terms of telling him where to hunt. A topo map may be used, or the guide can drive the hunter around the immediate area and show the hunter where he might stand a chance of locating game.

4. The guide is responsible for getting the hunter and his personal gear into camp and back out to the headquarters.

5. He may or may not be responsible for food, usually not.

In short, the drop camp is simply a way for hunters to end up in a good game area for a fraction of the cost normally paid for a guided hunt. The hunter still gets some important services. He may have his game brought in for him, and he certainly has his camp prepared for him. While he does not have personnel working for him, the hunter who pays for a drop camp does have the expertise of the guide working for him. The whole idea of a drop camp is the convenience of having a hunting camp waiting for the hunter, but more than that, the camp is located where it should be and the guide does give the hunter some good tips on the area, where to hunt and where not to hunt. He should also be able to fill him in on all particulars about the area, including boundaries as to private property and game management units.

I repeat that the drop camp is a good idea. The hunter is on his own, which is not all bad. He can hunt with his companions, and he has been taken into an area pre-scouted by the guide. He does have some very important services coming to him, too, and he must communicate beforehand in order to establish what he is buying with his drop camp fee. He should also know exactly how often the camp will be visited by the guide, and he should know if it is his responsibility or the responsibility of the guide to pack the game back to camp.

The Guaranteed Hunt

Almost the opposite of the drop camp is the guaranteed hunt. The guarantee, of course, may be established in one of many ways and the hunter had best have a very clear understanding of the exact facets of the guarantee. A hunter should understand perfectly what the guarantee constitutes. Usually, about the only guarantee a guide can give is that the hunter will be shown a piece of game. I don't know how any guide can do more.

Generally, the client will pay more for a guaranteed hunt. He might want to ask the guide, however, what is expected of him, the hunter, under this guarantee. One guide told me that he will guarantee a hunt. He will

A guide may often make some of his own gear, such as this packing box which contains camp essentials. Guiding and outfitting are involved areas and the good guide or outfitter puts in plenty of long working hours if he intends to do a good job.

In some terrain, the use of horses can mean a lot to a deer hunter, mainly in helping him get into deer country quickly, range farther than he could on foot, and of course as a means of getting the deer back to camp. But good horse hunting requires good horse handling. These well-trained horses were expertly managed by Don Gustavo, a foreman on a ranch in Sonora, Mexico.

guarantee that if the hunter stays on his heels the whole way he will not only get a look at a buck, but he will get a look at a big buck. However, this guide qualifies his guarantee in the following way: The hunter has to sign with him for the duration of the season, more than 10 days, and he must be in physical condition which allows him to keep up with the guide. He must also recognize the fact that if he is shown one "big deer," the guarantee has been fulfilled. He has to live out of a backpack for part of the time, and he has to accept the fact that if he, the hunter, decides to turn back at any time, the fee is still paid the guide in full.

A guaranteed hunt is all right, I suppose. I have a problem with any situation in which something as tenuous as hunting is guaranteed, though. I can't imagine how a guide guarantees the weather, for example, but I guess that is a matter of taking a chance. If his client never sees game due to storms, the guide is out of luck as he must return the client's fee. All in all, I do not see a guarantee as being necessary. The guide should have a good camp set up in a good area which he knows better than the back of his hand, and he should be a good hunter willing to work hard for his client. I see that as offering a lot of service and I would personally ask for no more of any guide.

The Lodge

The hunting lodge can be one of many things. Essentially, I look at a hunting lodge as a motel situated in deer country. However, some lodges offer much more. Aside from good food and accommodations, a hunter may have a guide. He may be guided on a personal basis or there

may be one guide for several men. He may also be guided in the sense of having a knowledgeable person place the hunter on a well-used pass or perhaps a drive will be set up by the "management."

The hunting lodge has a lot to offer. However, the individual hunter has to make up his own mind as to what he wishes to experience on a hunt. If a hunter wishes to camp alone, or with one close friend, the lodge is not for him. If the hunter does not care to share experiences with other hunters, most of whom he may not even know, then the lodge is not for him. There are some lodges which do, however, often more private accommodations, such as individual cabins. The client must know the specific disposition of a lodge before he decides to hunt out of one.

I look at hunting lodges as I look at guides. The hunter who understands beforehand exactly what he is getting for his money should have no complaint later on as long as the promises are delivered. Also, a hunter should understand lodge life and accept it or look for another way to hunt. The big advantage of a lodge is having good accommodations, generally well-prepared food and a lot of get-together with fellow hunters.

A lodge can be a vacation and a hunt combined, and lodges should be able to deliver up a list of references just as a guide is expected to do. Lodges are often in very picturesque settings. If the outdoorsman is basically interested in getting into a good deer area, having a nice place to stay, talking with other hunters who may be from several states away, even foreign countries at time, then he should look into a lodge. Of course, we are talking about a professional hunting lodge here, and I noted in my research that there were some lodges which were in effect rented cabins, places hunters could stay in for a fee, but they had to do their own cooking and their own hunting, to include packing the game back to the cabin site.

The Outfitter

Sometimes there is a little confusion between the definition of outfitter and guide. I do not claim to have the perfect dictionary definition on hand, but I think of an outfitter as a manger of a hunting camp or hunting camps. He may or may not do any guiding at all. In fact, he usually has hired a band of guides to take care of the actual hunter contact. The outfitter may set up the hunt, making all arrangements for the hunter, but he will most likely *not* accompany the hunters afield. There are exceptions. I found one small outfitter who did have several hired guides, but who also acted as a guide himself, especially if his guides were having trouble putting a client onto some game.

The only thing that could bother me about this situation is contracting with an outfitter only to learn that the actual guiding was going to be accomplished by hired hands who may or may not have worlds of experience

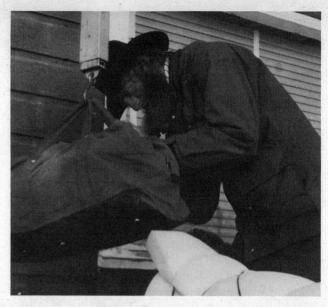

An outfitter weighs a hunter's duffel carefully so that he will be able to balance the load which the horse will carry and also he wants to insure that a horse will not be overloaded. A professional outfitter or guide is master of many trades.

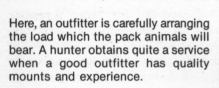

Here, an outfitter is carefully arranging the load which the pack animals will bear. A hunter obtains quite a service when a good outfitter has quality mounts and experience.

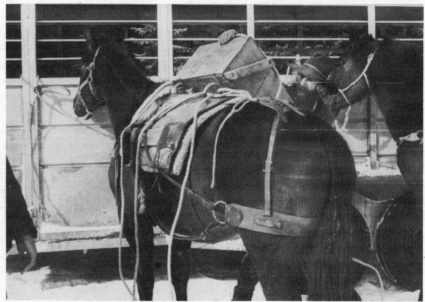

A guide or outfitter often has considerable investment in his gear. Here, we see a horse trailer owned by outfitter Keith Rush of Montana. Such equipment is expensive, but often essential to a successful pack trip.

Handling horses is just one of the many abilities a good guide or outfitter out West must possess. A hunter should expect reasonably good mounts, well trained and able to get a hunter into the country and game back out.

in the area. In my research, I spoke with an outfitter and learned that if I bought a hunt, I would be out with a fellow who had come from 2,000 miles away and had been in the area of the hunt for two seasons only. I do not for a moment suggest that this young man, for he was 21 years of age, would be less than a masterful guide. However, I would have to question paying a rather handsome fee to be shown the lay of the land by a gentleman who had been in the locale two times, actually only one time in the past, this season's hunt being his second experience in the hunting area.

Communication

I suppose it all boils down to communication. I like the idea of everything being in writing beforehand. I like the idea of having solid communication with my outfitter/guide before I plunk down my dollars. I would want to know, especially, who is going to actually guide me and how much experience he has as a hunter, and how much of that experience is in the area where I am to be hunting.

Provided that the hunter knows what he is paying for and the guide is willing to deliver on those specific points, I see no problem with the guided hunt. Others disagree with me, and they have a right to if they so choose. One fellow hunter suggested to me that if he had a guide show him a deer, it would be the same as the guide getting the deer. "Hunting means looking for and finding your own game," he told me, "and just because some guy has a bunch of money doesn't mean he's a hunter. All it means is that the guide did all but shoot the deer for him."

I reminded this particular hunter that two seasons earlier I had spotted a buck I did not want and he ended up harvesting that deer. Was that guiding? No, he said. That was just two buddies hunting deer together. I suppose the point here is that a hunter might consider the guide a fellow hunter, one who may know more about hunting and more about the area to be hunted.

I like to think that a polished deer hunter is capable of locating his own game, capable of making a good shot, and capable of dressing and getting that deer back to camp. At the same time, I don't think a hunter has to do it all for himself all of the time. Certainly, I have been guided by friends who knew the area better than I, and I have guided friends when I felt I knew the area better. There is no hunter code of ethics violated here that I know of, and neither is there any real problem inherent in the hunter/guide relationship. Prior agreement and communication can cement a very rewarding hunt for both guide and client.

chapter 29
Deer Taxidermy

THE SUCCESSFUL deer hunter may wish to have his trophy mounted, and by trophy, I mean that buck which is special to the individual hunter, and not only those deer with large racks. Why have a buck mounted? In the first place, good taxidermy is art. A mounted animal is a representation, just as a painting is a representation. In the second place, the preserving of a buck through a mount is in a sense the perpetuation of the animal. In the real world, the outdoor world of Mother Nature, deer do not live on and on and on. They perish at a rather rapid rate. They do not "go to waste" when they die in the field, for they are recycled, as it were, in the Conservation of Matter.

However, a special deer becomes even more special when it is preserved in a mount. A mount should be in honor of the game more than in honor of the hunter. That is, the buck is shown for itself, not as a badge for the hunter. When a hunter sees a beautiful mount, he usually comments first on the deer and maybe then on the guy or lady who shot the deer. "That is a beautiful buck," he might say, and ask only later, "Did you get him?"

Being very interested in good taxidermy, I have made it a point to seek out examples of the trade from Mexico to the Arctic. While others might be craning necks to see ancient statues or peering at oils on a wall, I am likely to be scrutinizing the art of the taxidermist in mounts of deer, boar, elk, bear and the like. I have praised the labors of masters and balked at the miscarriages of a few who

produce elk that resemble braying jackasses, deer which jut out of the wall like stuffed stockings, as well as fish that could pass for plastic-coated wall plaques and birds which would serve better on a badminton court than on a fireside mantle. The good examples are lifetime treasures, tangibles representing intangible memories of the outdoors. The bad ones are dust-catchers.

While taxidermy may have begun with cavemen who filled skins with straw, today the trade is an accepted art form. Being an art, it can be judged, as all art is. We may not have special taxidermy critics, as we do art critics, but all of us can learn to tell the difference between a "good" mount and a "bad" one. In fact, it behooves the serious hunter to think about judging taxidermy before buying any of it, as he will not only spend his money more wisely, but he will have much more long-lasting enjoyment from a mount well-prepared than from a sloppy work.

Symmetry

Reasonable symmetry in a deer mount is a must. A friend invited me over to look at his beautiful buck mount which he had just retrieved from the taxidermy shop. You simply can't hurt the feelings of a fellow, and besides, if a man likes the mount that he has received, then it is a good mount! This would solve the whole problem of good *vs* bad taxidermy but for one thing—as hunters grow more sophisticated in what they will accept as a

One of the true tests of a skilled taxidermist is a full body mount. Here, John Doyle, Tucson, Arizona taxidermist, poses by one of his mounts. You almost expect the deer to get up and walk away.

mount, they sometimes feel very unhappy about the old mount that now looks all wrong to them.

I looked at my friend's deer mount and praised it all I could bring myself to praise it. Actually, it was not all that bad, but one thing bothered me a great deal. The symmetry in the set of eyes was all goofed up. In fact, I later placed a straightedge across the bridge of the nose and one eye was a good half inch lower than the other eye. I don't know how the taxidermist accomplished this because all he had to do was mount the glass eye on the orbit on the form, but he had actually found a way to off-set the eyes somehow.

Lifelike

That same mount had ears that seemed to be made out of plaster of paris. They were stiff, as well an ear should be, but they had been gummed down somehow so that they were totally unnatural. Also, the ears were thrust forward at such an angle that it would have been impossible for a live deer to do that with its ears.

The good mount is not a corpse. It is not "stuffed." It has life. Part of the life comes from the taxidermist studying deer, and one taxidermist I know spends a lot of time at the zoos photographing animals in as many different poses as possible and studies them. He also studies good professional wildlife photography. He wants to see just how an animal does move its body and what expressions he can attain, as well as what poses he can-

not accomplish.

Life-like taxidermy takes these poses into account. The entire mount is positioned realistically. It is angled so that it looks natural. That symmetry we spoke of earlier is observed. Ears match in their position on the head, for example. The eyes are set into the orbit of the form correctly, not overly deep, but realistically deep. Deer mounts with bug eyes are the most glaring examples of poor taxidermy that one will find as he tours places that have mounts.

Naturally, good component parts are essential, too. The eyes should look real, for example. Those little touches are very important. The flare of a nostril must be just right. I have seen nostrils flared out on mounts to the point of looking ridiculous. The nose should be fitted cleanly to the form, too. I've seen noses that looked like they had been bitten by a rattlesnake. The paint job has to be good. Those tiny places which require a touch of paint, such as the corner of the eye, must be executed with good taste and accuracy. Noses are painted, too, to look wet. The taxidermist who does not handle the paint job correctly stands to lose some of the lifelike qualities of his mount.

A form should be altered according to the cape demands. It is rather pointless to stretch a cape onto a form too large for the cape, or to try making a cape which is too large fit a smaller form. A few millimeters of form cut away here or a bit of added plaster there can make

Here is another full-size mount. Take note especially of the eye. Due to its correct depth in the mount and correct angle, the deer seems to be looking at something. See also the front legs and the angle of the ears. A taxidermist must be familiar with wildlife.

all of the difference in the world. I was in a taxidermy shop one time looking at some pretty darn good deer mounts, except for one thing. They all looked just the same. Deer don't all look just the same. This fellow had maybe two different-sized forms and that was it, plus he did not add any musculature or trim the form anywhere. He was turning out carbon copies of bucks.

The real custom taxidermist can actually work from a photograph of the deer, a simple "hunter with buck" picture, and he can file parts of the deer form down and build other parts up so that each mount is a bit special, a little more like the actual deer which was harvested. That is, to me, a custom mount as opposed to a factory-like mount. The mount which is special has the lips tucked in correctly on the close-mouthed form, which most deer by far are. The tear duct is equally correct in being tucked in. I have seen lips which actually protruded and I have seen tear ducts which did the same.

Most taxidermists have a real gift in their hands and in their "eye" and all it takes is for them to look at live animals and observe how the anatomical structure really is. Then they will no longer produce mounts with bulging lips and eyes and tear ducts that push out. They will also attend to the little things, such as adding "ripples" to the back of the deer's neck. When an animal bends, the skin may crease somewhere. I have often seen deer which are turned abruptly to one side, but the turned side of the deer is smooth as glass. How could this be on a real live animal? If we turn our necks sharply to one side, there will be wrinkles. If a deer turns its neck sharply to one side, there will be wrinkles. The careful taxidermist puts the wrinkles in. A big deal? No, it's not a big deal. But why not have a piece of artwork in a mount instead of a factory assembly line product?

The Final Product

When details are strictly adhered to, then all of the parts come together in a life-like whole. When each part borders on perfection in realistic form, the entire mount is believable. Too often, a deer mount seems to be a conglomeration of pieces, eyes stuck into the face, ears attached to the side of the head, a nose glued on in front, all pasted to a rigid form. The hunter should look for the type of taxidermy which will give him a longtime work of art.

What a Mount Is

Essentially, a mount is the cape of the deer, the antlers of the deer, some commercial parts, such as the glass eye, all put together on a form. First, the form. The form is the hollow structure which is shaped like a deer's head. The form is the foundation of the deer. One can buy forms ready-made and they can be purchased in at least a couple of materials. The forms I am familiar with are actually custom constructed using a plaster cast. Strips of glue-soaked heavy paper are placed one after another into the form's cast until two halves are made and then the two halves are glued together to make the hollow form, the "foundation" which will hold the cape of the deer.

The mount's form is very important because it represents the *shape* and the *stance*. But it also represents that musculature we spoke of a moment ago. The custom taxidermist can make a form special. He can file it down and build it up so that the end product is *your* deer, not just any deer. When he adds the eyes into the sockets on the form, he does so with the right amount of clay so that the eyes neither bulge out nor sink in too far.

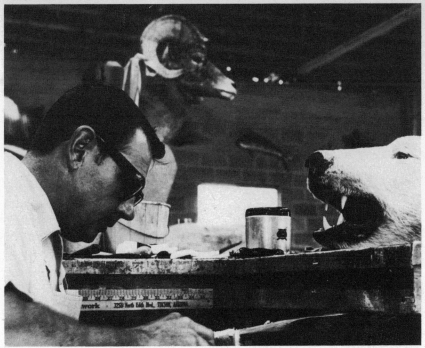

Jim Russell, accomplished taxidermist, patiently removes extra thickness from the cape so that the cape will flow with the lines of the form.

The ears have rigid materials to hold them out, but they are natural in that they are angled just right. So, we have a form with the eyes in it and then we build the ears up with a false "cartilage," and then the entire cape, generally in a wet state, is pulled over the form and then sewed in the back to hold it in place. Also, the form is coated with glue so that the cape is glued on as well. This is not a complete description, nor is it intended to be, but the hunter gets a crude idea of what makes a deer mount.

Cost

Comparative shopping for a mount is fine. But I would rather pay more and have art than pay less and have an assembly line product. Obviously, if two taxidermists do essentially identical work in terms of quality, then the one who prices his mounts for less is the one to go with. But this is not likely. As with most things in life, "better" costs more. It is up to the hunter to decide for himself how much he is willing to pay for excellence. He should look at the mount, however, as in investment. Mounts last a long time.

When the Mount is Home

Ideally, a mount should be placed upon the wall so that it is in a natural setting. By that, we do not mean bushes around it. By natural we refer to the natural way a deer would look in the woods or mountain. Many hunters place their mounts too high on the wall. If the hunter thinks of the mount as a painting, he will do all right. The mount should be visible in the room, not hidden. But it must not intrude either. Bumping into a mount does not enhance its artistic qualities. I like a deer mount high

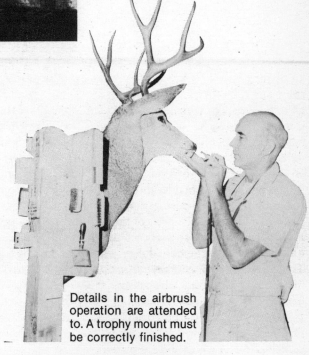

Details in the airbrush operation are attended to. A trophy mount must be correctly finished.

enough on the wall that I do not have to observe the chin as a prominent feature, but rather we look more into the eyes. I like the eyes of the deer to be mounted just about eye-level to a six-foot man. That is my prejudice, of course, and the hunter has every right to place his mount where he so desires.

The mount should be cleaned maybe once a week. A little damp rag will shine the nose up and a feather duster will liven up the coat. We can also use a gentle attachment for the vacuum cleaner and pull out some of the dust which might be hiding in a mount. Bugs can eat mounts. It is well to get a good look at a mount from time to time to insure that bugs are not making a home there. One can sometimes see the bugs right on the hairs themselves. A very mild and very light spray of certain

Take note of the deer in the foreground. The mule deer looks like a mule deer. The whitetail looks like a whitetail. This is custom taxidermy.

insect repellents won't hurt the hide, but do not use any insect repellent without first checking with *your* taxidermist. He knows what is best for his own mounts.

A good mount, that is a mount well-prepared with top grade glues and such, should last many years. I have been told that a properly constructed mount will last 20 years before it looks raggedy. But I have a mount here which is now 18 years old and it looks as good as new. I have always had the mount in a rather dry location in the home, never exposed to too much heat, such as a heater vent blowing on it.

Maybe this is why the mount still looks fine. I have moved a few times since that mount was prepared for me, and it has never been damaged in moving. So I think a mount can be treated with respect and made to last a very long time. From the looks of the mounts I have, I

can say that if a mount is cared for at all and kept free of excessive dust and bugs it will probably last a lifetime. Looked at from this angle, a deer mount is not very expensive after all.

In the Field

When a hunter knows that he is in the market for a mount, he should consider several factors. First, I do think that if he can shoot a deer behind the shoulder, he should. That is, he should avoid the neck shot. Of course a neck shot can be sewn up, even a rather big hole. A friend of my brother shot a deer and anchored it, but the buck showed signs of life when the hunter approached, so from about 10 yards out he shot the deer in the neck with a hot load (139-grain bullet) out of a 7mm Rem. Mag. The hole was immense. But the taxidermist sewed the cape so well that nobody noticed that hole after the mount was prepared. Nonetheless, when a hunter wants that deer for a mount, I see no reason to shoot a deer in the neck unless that is the only shot. It just makes more work for the taxidermist, and if the hole is just wrong, so to speak, it could be real trouble.

Furthermore, I like to hit a deer in the upper chest area just below, but not in, the spine. This is a deadly shot, and a buck so hit with a good ballistic force will drop immediately in most cases. There are always exceptions, of course. Also, the loss here is lung tissue. Remember, we are not talking about a spine shot which could destroy backstrap meat. Lungs are lost and that is about it.

Slitting the throat on a deer which has been struck by a bullet, even a round ball from a well-loaded muzzleloader, is usually of no consequence. The bullet itself has disrupted sufficient tissue to cause very extensive emptying of the vascular system. The deer is merely dressed out and drained, and it is fine. I mention this because I would hope that a hunter who desires a deer mount will not charge up to his buck and slit the throat.

The Cape

Remember that it is the cape of the buck which will be used in the mount. The cape is that hide and fur which covers the face and goes back to a point behind both shoulders. If a hunter is with a guide, the guide should know how to cape a deer. If a guide does not know how to cape a deer, he might consider spending some time with a taxidermist. It is not a terribly difficult trick, but there are two points that can bring disaster. At least, I still find these two places delicate to work with, but others may not at all. First, there is that area around the nose and this includes the upper lip. I always fear cutting back toward the nasal area of the buck in removing the nose itself. Also, the lips, in the trimming out process, are delicate, but not too bad. I really fear turning the ears.

Turning the ears means actually exposing the inner part of the pinna. I feel shaky on that part of the caping job. As I say, others may find this easy. If I were going to be on a long hunt, I would surely avail myself of some lessons with some sort of arrangement at the local taxidermy shop. Caping a deer is generally not the work of the deer hunter anyway. But it is a nice skill to have if one keeps in practice.

The hunter is advised to get the cape off of his deer as soon as possible. If a hunter is out of state, he can sometimes pay the local taxidermist for removing the cape. The cape is then heavily salted and/or frozen for its trip back to the hunter's home area and the hunter's own taxidermist who will create the mount. If the carcass is allowed to get too warm, the hair can "slip," which is the term used to describe patches of hair falling out of the hide. This is indicative of spoiling and of course the cape can then be ruined if too much hair slips before caping and salting. If a cape is ruined, however, a hunter can generally buy another cape from the taxidermist. Of course, this means a cape from another deer, but the antlers, will still be "original" of course.

The hunter can avoid a ruined cape by getting the head to a taxidermist soon. He can also freeze the head by wrapping it in a couple of thick plastic layers, placing the entire head in a freezer. About the only time this makes sense is when the hunter is far from home, but wants his own taxidermist to do all the work. So he freezes the head in a local locker, and then he takes it home frozen. Otherwise, I look at it this way—if he could get to a freezer, he could get to a taxidermist to have the cape removed, provided the taxidermist is not too busy during the hunting season.

What can a hunter do in dressing his deer in order to salvage the cape? First, he should not cut up through the brisket. He must leave the brisket and all of the cape intact to behind the shoulders. He might want to do this:

1. Slice from directly between the antlers on the very top of the head all the way down the center of the cape, that is, right along the top of the backbone.

2. Make a circle around the deer behind the shoulders so that the entire cape with brisket can be removed *forward*.

3. When all of the cape is removed up to the point of the deer's neck where the neck joins the head, then the neck meat is cut totally through, leaving a long trailing

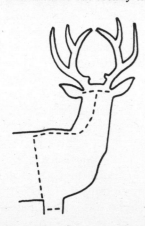

Make initial cut along back of neck and a second cut forming a "T" running to the base of the horns. Cut carefully around the horns or antlers, and cut the skin away from the base. On antlered game a heavy screwdriver is useful in prying skin loose around the antlers. (Courtesy Jonas Brothers, Inc.)

Cape is cut long enough for the type of mount desired. Shoulder mounts show more of the true form and character of the animal. Capes for these mounts should be cut at the forelegs in order to include enough of the brisket for a full shoulder mount. It is not necessary to clean the skull. The top of the skull with horns or antlers attached is all that is needed. Merely saw off the top of the skull through center of eyes after skinning is completed.

A good job of taxidermy can withstand scrutiny from any angle. This mount looks good from underneath, where the chin is seen as regular and the shoulder area defined properly. The jaw is especially well defined without jutting.

cape attached to the head, but not slit at the throat at all, only from the top of the head down the spine and around the shoulders (behind the shoulders, remember).

Now the cape with head attached can be carried to the taxidermist. Or, as suggested above, the head can be frozen solid in a locker plant. The dedicated taxidermist has a goal. He wants to create the illusion of suspended animation. He does not want a stuffed skin. The hunter must help the taxidermist by bringing him a cared-for deer in the first place. At the taxidermist shop, the cape is removed and salted totally and the antlers are cut off.

If a deer is caped in camp, the cape should be kept in a dry spot, and it must be heavily salted. Table salt will do, but one can buy a large bag of salt which is meant for applying to hides and similar work. The hunter who knows he is going to have a head mounted if he gets the buck he wants should have a 10-pound bag of such salt in the deer camp for the cape.

Cutting off the antlers is only a problem if one cannot saw straight. The cut should be made so that the orbit of the eye is centered as exactly as possible. This leaves the antlers intact on the skull and that little "cap" of skull is then screwed into a wooden base which is attached to the uppermost part of the deer form which we mentioned earlier.

The deer hunter who wants a good mount should consider ahead of time who is going to be his taxidermist. He can check shops in the area to see who is doing custom work. Of course, as we admitted earlier, if the hunter is happy with the mount that is all that matters. But the hunter might want to take a good long look at the work a taxidermist does. He may want to compare the work of different taxidermists. He should remember that a good mount will last a long time. It is an investment, and the investment should be made wisely.

A close-up view of a mount can show a hunter if there are flaws in the work. Are the tear ducts protruding or bumpy? Or do they rest well into the face as they should? Are the ears at an unnatural pose? Is the nose bulbous or smooth? Is the neck musculature visible? Is the jaw defined or rounded off?

chapter 30

Safety

THE JOYS of the hunt soon fade into unhappy memories when an accident mars the adventure. There is only one way to truly enjoy any outdoor experience and that is safely. Accidents, of course, can occur, and hunting is far safer by statistical fact than are many other activities. Of course, there is always an "act of nature" that we cannot avoid, true accidents, we might say, and these are a part of life. If we spent every moment worrying about the natural disasters that could fall on us, we would be a bundle of perpetually dancing nerves.

Here are a few points on safety for the deer hunter. There are no doubt many others which could be included, and we realize that the individual hunter will have specifics he wants to add to this list. But these are a start.

Shooting

The tenets of safe shooting are many. We have lists of commandments regarding shooting, and they are wisely suggested now and have been for a very long time. We would like to quote a list of firearms safety laws set down in 1879 and credited to a member of the New York State Sportsmen's Association. The listing is found in the *Sportsman's Gazetteer* by Charles Hallock, dated 1879. It reads as follows:

1st—Never in excitement nor in fun point it [the gun] towards any human being.

2d—Never carry it so that if accidentally discharged it would endanger the life of a dog even.

3d—Always think, when walking, which way your gun is pointed, and if a companion is in the field with you, no matter how near and how temptingly the game appears, do not shoot until you know just where he is, and that a stray shot may not possibly strike him . . .

4th—Never get into a wagon [or a vehicle] without taking the cartridges from the gun.

5th—Never get over a fence without either taking the cartridges out, or placing the gun through the fence on the ground, so that if you fall or the fence breaks it cannot be discharged.

6th—Always carry the gun at half-cock [on safety].

7th—Never let the hammers rest on the "plungers" or pieces which strike the cap. [We would say do not allow a hammer to rest forward.]

8th—Never try to close it when the hammers are down. [We might say, "Never manipulate the firearm without the safety on or the hammer at half-cock.]

9th—Never get in front of it yourself . . .

10th—After firing one barrel, take the cartridge from the other and examine the wad over the shot to see that it is not loosened by the concussion as it very frequently is, which would produce a heavy recoil, and if it gets up the barrel, will burst the gun and likely take a hand off besides.

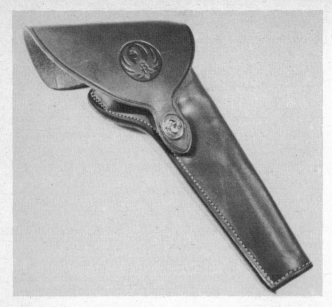

A good holster like this one from the Ruger Company spells a big measure in safety. A holster should keep the firearm protected, to be sure, but it should also retain the handgun as well.

[This one seems so 19th century as to be useless to us, but no, it is not at all useless to us. The modern black powder hunter should take care that the projectile of his rifle remains down upon the powder charge, for it may creep up the bore as he walks the deer fields. The modern user of a double barrel black powder shotgun or rifle should pay attention to this rule just as stated above.]

11th—Never take hold of the muzzle to draw it toward you, nor set it up, when, if falling its muzzle would be toward you.

Finally, follow all these suggestions and be self-possessed, and the fields will afford you sport without danger, and I hope without temptation.

Some of the advice from this old tome seems almost archaic, but as I read each one I had to agree with it. While accidents are a part of the deer hunt we may wish not to discuss, the successful deer hunter certainly must adhere to the rules of safety and we strongly offer the same advice today that was printed in this 1879 publication.

Be Sure of Your Target

Some things take on weird and misleading forms in the shadows of the woods and bush. We should all act as trophy hunters when we pursue deer, making certain that we can definitely distinguish the rack or the entire form of the deer as a deer before firing. Sure, some deer will get away while we are trying to establish beyond a doubt that we have a legal buck, but there is no other way to hunt. The loss of a chance at a deer is soon forgotten, but should someone get hurt, that certainly would not soon be forgotten.

The Safety

When I was a beginning shooter, I found myself at the range one day and one of the older hands was on the firing line. When he finished, he walked over to my bench, and seeing that I was a youngster, began with a bit of advice. Nothing wrong with that, but the advice was all wrong. He went on with a philosophy concerning the use of a safety. He said something like, ''I never put a safety on. In that way, I know darn good and well that my gun is ready to fire and that makes me twice as careful. When a man gets used to putting his safety on, then he gets careless because he figures his gun is safe.''

The man was well-meaning, but all wrong. Safeties are to be employed by all deer hunters at all times. Keep that safety on until ready to fire. The truth is, we need to have the safety in position, and we, at the same time, must observe all good handling points of the firearm. In short, carry your hunting gun with the safety on, but treat the gun as if the safety were off.

Finally, I believe I am right when I say that a half-cock setting is not a true safety. However, with some rifles the half-cock setting is the only safety we have. I suggest that at the beginning of each season or more often, the hunter try his rifle's half-cock setting, be it a muzzleloader or a modern rifle, by taking the *empty* rifle, still aimed in a safe direction though empty, and setting it on half-cock. Then with thumb pressure, the shooter should try to push the hammer forward off of its half-cock position. The same test is good on full-cock, for the hammer should remain on full-cock until the trigger is pulled. It should not fly forward from thumb pressure. I recently brought a new muzzleloader to my local gunshop, for when I pushed on the fully cocked hammer, it flew forward.

Buck Fever

I believe this is a good term, colorful to be sure, but accurate. I am not certain that there is one definition of buck fever which would truly explain the phenomenon. I think that the first point mentioned above in our quoting of the 1879 rules contains the key word to buck fever and that word is ''excitement.'' Hunting is a great thrill. Few activities are more exciting than hunting, especially when a buck breaks cover and scampers off into the bush or over the open spaces.

When the hunter becomes so excited that he is not in full control of his actions, I suppose that is buck fever. Getting excited is certainly not the problem. It is ''lack of control'' coupled with that excitement that can bring the problem. Usually, buck fever is not a problem. The hunter gets the ''shakes'' and the buck gets away, generally, and that is that. Sometimes, however, a hunter might do something uncalled for, such as firing in his excitement when the background is not clear. I do not know how to cure buck fever. However, it is my opinion that the hunter can stay under control as long as he sticks with a plan when he's afield.

He might act out in his mind just what he's going to

do if he sees a buck. He might remind himself that if a buck comes out of a canyon, where he will be able to see the deer for a long while, that he is going to take a quick look through his field glasses first, then slip into a hasty sling, after having planted his seatpants on the ground, and only then remove the safety, firing with a clear sight picture and a controlled trigger squeeze. In close cover he can also remember a plan, mainly that he will identify his target clearly and fire for open patches in the vegetation rather than trying to drive a bullet through the brush.

Broadheads

The bowhunter has to be careful, too, even though his tool is quite short-range in effect. He must identify his targets just as the gun hunter must identify his. But the bowhunter has to treat one aspect of his tackle with the utmost respect and that is the broadhead. A broadhead is razor sharp for a reason, and it can slice into the hunter and do much damage. In carrying any broadhead-tipped arrow, that arrow must be safe in that the broadhead is guarded by a bowquiver or backquiver. If the hunter carries an arrow strung on the bowstring, then he should certainly watch out where he is going with it. He should treat it as a loaded gun, to include care in crossing a fence.

Dead Deer

Another safety point is the approach we make on a downed deer, buck or doe. Either can kick a hunter into next Christmas. Generally, a deer will be in deep shock if not totally defunct by the time a hunter reaches it. But there are occasions when the deer will have the ability to level a hunter. This has happened more than once.

The hunter is advised to approach the deer carefully with the firearm somewhat ready for use, on safety but certainly not totally unloaded. If there are visual signs

This Amacker treestand has a safety retainer and that retainer should be used faithfully by the hunter. Falling out of a tree stand, especially when broadheads are being held, is very dangerous.

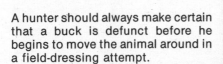

A hunter should always make certain that a buck is defunct before he begins to move the animal around in a field-dressing attempt.

Handloading is as safe as the person doing the handloading. A shooter who puts his own loads together for deer hunting should follow his loading manual every step of the way with no detours.

of life, then a hunter can elect to take a careful second shot, aiming where head and neck join if the deer is not to be mounted. If the deer is going to be mounted, then a shot behind the shoulder is probably wiser. At any rate, the hunter will have to figure the angle of the bullet's path as closely as possible in order to avoid spoiling a lot of meat from a close-range high velocity strike.

If the deer seems finished, but there is any question, it is wise for the hunter to pick up a long limb and touch the eye of the deer with it. If there is any movement, then the deer is still vital. This sounds like a punishing thing to do, but we are talking about a deer which has been

dropped by a great deal of energy and the systems are definitely not going to be acute. Furthermore, the hunter's harvest is decidedly the quickest way a deer will finish its time, for a winter kill or a kill by some predators can be much less quick.

Loads

While both handloads and factory loads have a wonderfully high level of reliability and safety, it is up to the hunter to use proper ammunition in his deer firearm. If he buys ammo across the counter, he should pay attention to what he is purchasing. I listened once as a salesperson almost sold a shooter a box of 7mm Remington Magnum cartridges for a 7mm Mauser. There would have been no real problem, since the big 7mm Magnum rounds would not have chambered in the 7mm Mauser, but it does serve as an example of what can happen.

If the hunter is going to use handloads, then all proper care is essential. Loading manuals will give good sound instructions as to methods of handloading as well as loads. No max load should ever be exceeded. What a hunter may gain in a few feet per second could be lost totally in terms of load safety. All handloads must be prepared exactly as the manual instructs. Juggling components at will is dangerous.

Travel

A part of the modern deer hunt is travel in one form or another. It is a safety precaution to put vehicles in good shape so that breakdowns will be less likely in the outback and also it goes almost without saying that we should be aware of our driving and the road conditions. Since deer hunting can take us into some rough terrain, sometimes very bad roads, sometimes roads which wind along dropoffs that will turn our tin horse into so much scrap iron if we slip from the road, then we must be careful. The

Vehicle safety for hunting is a must. John Kane, professional bear and lion hunter as well as guide, tries to maintain his vehicles for backroad use and he also respects the conditions of backwoods roads. An accident in a vehicle poses potential danger anywhere, including the backwoods.

The little camp is weather-tight, and the hunter can make himself a hot drink in the pot he has along. If he can't easily start a fire, or if he does not wish to, there is the small backpack stove to consider, and the Peak 1 backpacker's lantern will provide light for the darkness.

worst roads I have been on to date are in the Southwest, though bad roads can exist almost anywhere. I learned from these roads and some close calls that sometimes it is wise to make camp ½-mile away from your intended destination. One can make up the distance with a little bit of hiking. There are usually deer in the area anyway and walking that extra ½-mile may show the hunter a buck.

Another point worth considering is the use of the 4-wheel drive vehicle in a safe and reasonable manner. I have seen and I guess I have to admit I have also been a part of attempts to make it over bad road almost as if that were the challenge of the day. I have had my own vehicle teetering dangerously when I failed to pay attention to its high center of gravity. Safe driving is a part of the deer hunt.

The Camp

A deer camp can be a safe place or a dangerous place depending upon many factors. Something as seemingly simple as an axe which is in the wrong spot can ruin a good time in a hurry, and while speaking of axes, the safe and proper use of that tool in camp is absolutely vital. There are many points concerning camp life which we can make when talking safety. We need to handle fuel properly, keeping cans of the stuff well away from our tent and out of the way. We must also handle camp lanterns and stoves with respect.

Where a camp is pitched is vital. In the Southwest one time I saw a camp pitched right in the bottom of a dry sandy wash in December during a bowhunt. When I was

a city fireman I helped pull people from flash floods and my own brother was caught in one, the vehicle a total loss. Flash floods are deadly. One should never pitch a camp in any area which could be flooded if he can possibly foresee the danger. Again, this may seem far afield for a book dedicated to deer hunting, but the deer hunter is involved in a total activity, a rather complex one when considered from all sides. Each little facet must be handled with safety if the hunter is to enjoy true success.

Snakes

In quite a number of deer hunting haunts there are deadly snakes. I have been conscious of snakes from the beginning of my own deer hunting because I spent so much time in the deserts and desert mountains along the Mexican border. The first line of defense for the hunter is *awareness*. The hunter who is in snake country has to be aware of the fact. He does not reach into bushes without probing around first with a stick.

He does not sit down next to a shady bush without taking a look first. He might probe a grassy spot before rushing through it. These seem like time-wasters, but they only take seconds out of a day, and those seconds can save a great deal of time and trouble for the hunter.

The point here is that a deer hunter who frequents areas known to be inhabited by poisonous snakes should be aware of the fact, should take precautions on the matter and should also learn sound up-to-the-minute snakebite techniques from an expert in the area. Very few people are bitten by snakes. But that fact is of small comfort to the individual who *is* bitten.

On a private ranch, and in the days when the hunters were fewer in number, packing a deer in this manner was commonplace. Today, we strongly advise a hunter to cover the rack with abundant bright orange material.

(Right) Here, Bill Fadala puts a bright orange vest over the antlers of a deer he is about to pack out of the woods. While this will not totally guarantee that another hunter will not mistake the carcass for a live and moving deer, it certainly will help.

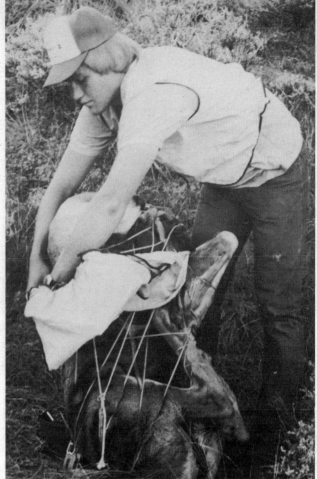

Insects

While a horde of mosquitos may not kill a deer hunter, it can surely make life miserable for him. Insect repellents can work well. I suggest that a hunter buy and try insect repellent before going into an area known to be heavily infested with any of the flying fellows that can make our lives so grim. Some areas do have heavy insect populations during a deer season, and I have been in the high mountains for early hunts and have found many insects on hand to greet me.

Also, there are a few dangerous insects to be found in deer country. I can speak from experience when I say that scorpions and similar fellows like to hide under firewood. The hunter and the scorpion often seem to like the same type of wood, one for burning in a campfire and the other for shelter. A hunter in areas which contain harmful insects should first be aware of the fact and second watch for these little charmers when pitching a tent, setting up camp in general and grabbing up wood. I have used the term "insect" to cover a range of little fellows, and I have not tried to be scientific about it. The scorpion, mentioned above, is an arachnid, as is a black widow spider. The classifications are not important to the deer hunter. Staying away from these fellows is.

Streams

Crossing bodies of water can be dangerous at times. Falling into an icy late fall or early winter stream can bring about the demise of a person. We should be very careful crossing any waterway at any time of the year. Even a nice friendly stream can bring disaster if a hunter trips on a slippery rock and cracks his head on another rock in the water. While on the subject, let's remember that for those who go by boat or canoe for a deer, all safety precautions pertaining thereto are well advised.

Hiking

One dark afternoon a friend of mine was helping a friend of his make his way into deer country. They were both anxious to pitch a backpacker's camp right in the heart of the deer country and I think both were hurrying a bit too much. The newcomer stumbled on a rock, fell forward, split his glasses to pieces on another rock and cut his face up, all in one fell swoop. He had no extra eyeglasses, and he could not see well enough to hunt without them. That hunt was over before it started.

We simply have to observe some basic hiking rules, which are to watch where we are going, keep a pace we can manage and watch the places we can fall off of.

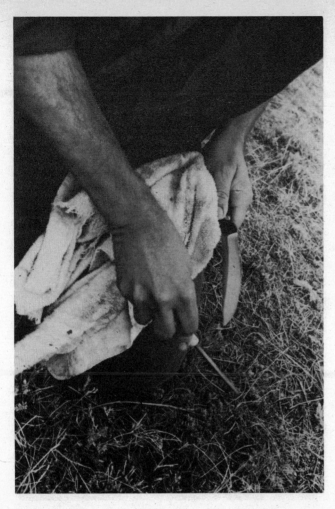

In getting a deer back to camp, the hunter should remember that he can be injured by straining himself or he may stumble and get hurt. Safety in getting a deer out of the woods is an absolute must.

(Left) A knife should be sharp in order for it to function properly, but the hunter must remember that any knife, even a dull one, is capable of inflicting a severe and dangerous wound.

Hiking in most deer terrain is no trick, though I have found myself on ledges a few times wondering how I got there and why I had gotten there. But even though most deer country is quite negotiable on foot, it's a good idea to hike with safety in mind.

First Aid

First aid classes are available for anyone willing to sign up for them. Deer hunters are certainly wise to learn at least some of the life-saving basics taught in these classes. Knowing how to stop bleeding, for example, or what to do for someone who has been in a fall, or for that matter, knowing how to help a person who is choking on food, can all be very worthwhile bits of knowledge on a deer hunt. Also, it is wise to keep up on the latest techniques.

Carrying a Deer

One must not tote a deer out of the woods in such a manner as to be mistaken for a deer. In a nutshell, that is it. Even when dragging a deer, it seems wise to me to have hunters talk and make sounds which mark them as hunters and not deer. Is this fair to other hunters? Won't the boys bringing the buck in spoil the hunting for others in the area? I do not think they will. After all, a deer can certainly hear a hunter or two dragging a carcass along.

Besides, think of it as a mini-drive. Maybe the noisy hunter will push a buck toward, rather than away from another hunter.

Knives

Safety in knife-handling is a must. I sometimes think a dull knife is an enemy of the hunter. Instead of slicing with the knife, he starts to push and saw and pretty soon he's cut himself. There is no special trick here. Be careful. That is all we need to say about knife handling. Knives are tools and nothing more than tools. And as with any tool, be it a rake, a hoe or a can opener, used improperly, danger can present itself.

Have a Plan

I think it is safest to have a plan and try to stick with the plan. Also, I like the idea of leaving word with someone when we go on our deer hunts. We need to draw a map and give our stay-at-home friend an itinerary which fairly well pinpoints our time plan as well as location. Haphazardness is not the safest way to do anything, including a deer hunt. Carefully planned, hunts are safer, I think, for we have planned for emergencies and we have the gear and method to use the gear well prepared in advance.

chapter 31
The Deer Hunting Tradition

SO FAR, we have been fairly businesslike in our approach to successful deer hunting. Perhaps this chapter is businesslike in a way, because we are going to offer information again; however, I prefer to look at this part of our effort as both concrete and abstract. North American deer hunters have been dedicated to the harvesting of their game for much longer than written history records. However, we do have some recorded information from the past which should offer a great deal of interesting reading for a modern dedicated deer hunter. Here is a little bit of it in paraphrased form, with all proper annotations, of course, so the reader can go back and take a look at the original if he wishes to.

Nessmuk

Nessmuk was the pen name of George W. Sears. Though Mr. Sears died in the 19th century, he was still alive when the cartridge appeared, and yet he remained faithful to the muzzleloader for his deer hunting. He lived in the East at a time when deer hunting was less restricted than it must naturally be now, but he did not care to harvest more than he could use. He was a thinking and a caring deer hunter and his opinions of game seemed to differ from the opinions we read from other hunters. In the main, however, Nessmuk was known for his camping love, his thrill in heading into the outback with what he could carry, "living off the land" in part, and also from what foods and gear he could pack with him. A Nessmuk

book I have enjoyed very much and which I believe would be enjoyed by campers and hunters is *Woodcraft and Camping,* which is a reprint of *Woodcraft.* The original book, *Woodcraft,* was published, according to my data, by Forest & Stream Publishing Company in 1920. I do not fully understand the facts surrounding the publishing date listed as 1920, for Nessmuk was dead at that time. However, 1920 is the publishing date that I have. The reprint, *Woodcraft and Camping,* is published by Dover Publications, Inc., of New York, and I imagine can still be ordered through a bookstore. My own copy was purchased from The Sitting Fox Company, 23529 Beverly, St. Clair Shores, Michigan 48082.

In *Hunting Big Game,* a good book by the famous Colonel Townsend Whelen, and printed by the NRA in 1946, we learn something of Nessmuk. We are told that, "He was born about 1823 'in a sterile part of sterile Massachusetts, on the border of Douglas Woods, within half a mile of Nepmug Pond, and within three miles of Junkamaug Lake.' " (p.125) Whelen goes on to say that "One of these old Indians [from a nearby reservation], named Nessmuk, 'a fine woodsman, a trusty friend, and as good as gold' was his teacher, and in after life he adopted his name as his pen name. He states that he ran away from school to study the great book of Nature, and well did he learn it." (p. 125)

Colonel Whelen met Nessmuk when Whelen was but a young boy, and he recalled that the hunter ". . . had a diminutive canoe, and his whole outfit including the canoe, tent, bedding, etc., did not weigh fifty pounds. He let me lift the canoe, and little kid that I was, I could do so with one hand.'' (p. 125) I think the modern hunter might enjoy reading Nessmuk. Today, we would not likely use his tools or methods very much, though a Nessmuk type banked fire and a Baker tent make a fine camp for a deer hunter. But, he is enjoyable to read and we can learn something from him.

Nessmuk tells us of his rifle, and we find that it was made by one of the masters of 19th century firearms building. In the Dover edition we read, on page 82, ''My rifle was a neat, hairtriggered Billinghurst, carrying sixty round balls to the pound a muzzle-loader, of course, and a nail-driver. I made just three shots in ten days [on one of his hunts], and each shot stood for a plump young deer in the 'short blue.' ''

He writes of one of his cross-country treks, and I think his commentary is interesting for the modern deer hunter, not from the standpoint of how-to knowledge so much as the enjoyment of hearing about the adventure. At one place he says:

And again, on the morning of the sixth day out, I blundered on to such an aggregation of deer as a man sees but once in a lifetime. I had camped over night on low land, among heavy timber, but soon after striking camp, came to a place where the timber was scattering, and the land had a gentle rise to the westward. Scarcely had I left the low land behind, when a few deer got out of their beds and commenced lazily bounding away. They were soon joined by others; on the right flank, on the left, and ahead, they continued to rise and canter off leisurely, stopping at a distance of one or two hundred yards to look back. It struck me finally that I had started something rather unusual, and I began counting the deer in sight. It was useless to attempt it; their white flags were flying in front and on both flanks, as far as one could see, and new ones seemed constantly joining the procession. Among them were several very large bucks with superb antlers, and these seemed very little afraid of the small, quiet biped in leaf-colored rig. [Nessmuk himself] They often paused to gaze back with bold, fearless front, as though inclined to call a halt and face the music; but when within a hundred yards, would turn and canter leisurely away. As the herd neared the summit of the low-lying ridge, I tried to make a reasonable guess at their numbers, by counting a part and estimating the rest, but could come to no satisfactory conclusion. As they passed the summit and loped down the gentle decline toward heavy timber, they began to scatter, and soon not a flag was in sight. It was a magnificent cervine army with white banners, and I shall never look upon its like again. The largest drove of deer I have ever seen in twenty years consisted of seven only. (p. 84-85)

So much for this grand old hunter. He was an interesting person and a dedicated outdoorsman. We can note above that he did not take a shot at his ''cervine army,'' preferring to observe in this case. We can also note with interest that Nessmuk was dressed in a sort of camouflage pattern. Remember that in those days his chances of running across so much as one hunter on such a backpack trip would be small at best, so he could get by with this outfit.

Osborne Russell

Osborne Russell was a trapper, and his manuscript entitled *Journal of a Trapper* is currently available as edited by Aubrey L. Haines and published by the University of Nebraska Press, a ''Bison Book.'' Russell was in the Far West in the period which is note as 1834-1843, and he saw some of the deer hunting lands which we now hunt in the West. On page 99 of his book, he says, ''Vast numbers of Black Tailed Deer are found in the vicinity of these springs and seem to be very familiar with hot waters and steam. [Russell was in the area of the geyser basins of Shoshone Lake and the Firehole River probably not too far from Old Faithful according to Haines.] The noise of which seems not to disturb their slumbers for a Buck may be found carelessly sleeping where the noise will exceed that of 3 or 4 engines in operation.''

I think it is interesting that Russell observed the mule deer as caring not about the noise of the ''boiling waters,'' for we note here a trait of game, which is to become used to both natural and man-made conditions. Not all game in all circumstances acts in this fashion, but I once watched a mule deer buck which was bedded no more than 100 yards or so from a crew which was cutting timber. I have seen deer within sight of paved highways and the deer seemed perfectly contented. We have to be aware that deer will often inhabit areas which we would not consider them in because of our own ideas about deer temperament and not really based upon deer traits as such.

We will leave Osborne Russell, but first here are some of his remarks on mule deer, which he called Black Tailed Deer. From page 135 we read:

This animal is somewhat larger than the common Deer of the US; its ears are very long from which it has derived the appellation of Mule Deer: its color in summer is red but in the latter part of Aug. its hair turns to a deep blue ground with about half an inch of white on each hair one fourth of an inch from the outer ends which presents a beautiful grey color: it lives among the mountains and seldom descends among the plains: its flesh is similar in every respect to the common Deer. The tail is about 6 inches long and the hair's upon it smooth excep (sic) upon the end where there is a small tuft of black.

Vilhjalmur Stefansson

From the above mentioned Whelen book, we hear about this noted hunter. Colonel Whelen extracted the data from *The Friendly Arctic* by Vilhjalmur Stefansson from the 1921 edition published by The Macmillan Company of New York. Whelen chose to include Mr. Stefansson's comments on binoculars for use in open country, and in my opinion Whelen was using this data to help the hunter realize the importance of the glass. We quote from page 71 of the Whelen book for the same reason.

In hunting on the grassy plains of the Arctic, a good pair of glasses and a knowledge of their use are about as important as the quality of your rifle and the pair of legs that carry you. I have found it as difficult to teach a new man the proper use of field glasses as to teach the use of the rifle or the understanding of any of the principles of hunting in the open country. The green man stands erect with his heels together, lifts the glass jauntily to his eyes and spins slowly around on one heel, taking from half a minute to a minute to make a complete survey of the horizon. Then he announces that there is no game in sight. The experienced hunter will take some pains to find the best place to sit down, will bring out from somewhere a piece of flannel that is clean no matter how dirty he himself and every other item of his outfit may be, and wipe every exposed lens till he is sure there isn't a speck of smudge anywhere. If the landscape is well within the power of his glasses he will probably rest his elbows on his knees, but if the distance is great or if the wind is blowing, he will lie down flat with elbows on the ground, or will build up out of stones or any available material a rest for the glasses that cannot be shaken by wind . . .

I think that the entire "tone" of the above is so well executed that the modern deer hunter is wise to listen to it. I am not particularly fond of cleaning binoculars in the field, preferring to carefully clean the lenses at home only when necessary and then keeping them clean. But it is obvious that Mr. Stefansson, admired by Colonel Whelen, "lets his glasses do the walking" for him at times. We can certainly go on record with plenty of witnesses to support the fact that binoculars can do a world of good for the open country deer hunter and often a great deal of good for the brush hunter or woods hunter. This is why we have included the words of Stefansson as quoted by Colonel Whelen.

The Big Game of North America

This book is edited by G. O. Shields, and it is a Rand, McNally & Co. printing from 1890. It covers, as the title suggests, big game on our continent, and it's an interesting book. A few of the entries are, in this one person's opinion, somewhat far afield in parts, but in the main it reveals an American hunting tradition. One of the entries is entitled "The Columbia Black-Tailed Deer," and it is concerned with the coastal deer, speaking mainly of Oregon's blacktail range. One interesting part of this entry is a report of a deer hunter injured by a deer. The author, Thomas G. Farrell, says "We had to carry the wounded man sixty miles on a stretcher, and he never fully recovered from the terrible experience." (p.132) While the distance on the stretcher sounds a bit like a Mark Twain "stretcher" in itself, we must remember that the writer is not talking about our time period, but instead of a late 19th century time period.

Mr. Farrell calls the .44 (I believe he meant the .44-40) the best caliber for the blacktail deer. In this same text, another entry is offered from Reverend Joshua Cooke and his colorful writing is on the subject of mule deer. His description of camp life is interesting, I think, and his evening meal was a real hummer designed to keep a hunter going. They had deer liver when available, coffee, potatoes, bread, onions with the liver, and bacon. Sounds good enough to eat. The reverend also mentions his deer rifle. "I was shooting, in those days, a 100-grain Sharps shell, 405 of lead, and I do not remember ever finding the ball [bullet] in a Deer's body." (p. 153) Then the reverend goes back to eating pleasures when he describes an ordinary or "regular meal," as he calls it. "Reed was an adept at flap-jacks; I undertook the coffee, the tongue, the liver, the tenderloin, the Saratoga chips—and, above all, onions, for Reed said: 'I can eat onions till I can't see.' " (p. 160)

Another entry in this old book is entitled "The Mule Deer of Southern California," by T. S. Van Dyke. Although I had to wonder if the gentleman meant black-tail instead of mule deer, I was surprised to hear a piece of hunting advice from him which suggested that a hunter show himself at times on a ridge or hill, sitting there in view of a parcel of real estate in order to finally make a buck nervous enough to show himself. In the Southwest, we have used this tactic with mild success.

Yet another entry in this book is by Walter M. Wolfe on "The Virginia Deer," in which the author describes a rather unusual means of deer hunting in which, "The negroes of the South frequently erect scythes or sharp stakes in their runways, knowing that the Deer, in leaping over some log or fence, will be so mutilated that he will drop within a half mile. Thus many a cabin, without labor on the part of its occupants, is kept supplied with venison." (p. 189) We would not think of nabbing a venison roast in such a fashion, but the methods of deer hunting and deer hunting tradition have changed greatly as the tools of the hunt have changed and as man's convictions have altered.

The Foxfire Book

The *Foxfire* series, of which we will report briefly from the first book in the line, is dedicated mainly to preserving some of the old traditions and ideas from America's people. I enjoy this series of books very much, and I think a deer hunter would find parts of some of the books worthwhile. In the first book we find, on pages 270 to 272, some commentary on deer, mainly dressing and cooking ideas. As part of the deer hunting tradition, I think we might take a look at a couple of these suggestions.

On "Skinning and Dressing," we read, "After killing, remove the scent glands (on the hind legs at the inside of the knee joint), the testes, and cut the jugular vein immediately. Then hang the carcass up by its hind legs, and ring each of the back legs below the knee. Cut down the inside of the back legs to the crotch, cut down the belly to the center of the chest, and ring the front legs in a manner similar to the back. Cut down the inside of the front legs to meet the cut in the chest. Peel the hide off the back legs, down the body, and off the front legs up the neck to the ears. Cut off the head right behind the ears with an axe."

There is more than one way to skin a cat, they say, and we might add that there is more than one way to skin a deer, and to dress it, too. While most modern hunters who have studied the deer feel that removing the metatarsal glands is of no use, others feel that it is a good idea, especially if the buck is in the rut. I have no facts to report from. We never touch the gland at all, preferring to remove it intact with the hide. But when a buck is in the rut, maybe the removal of the gland is a good measure. I sure would watch out for getting the scent on the knife and on the hands of the hunter, however, for this might be far worse in the end than simply removing the gland during the dressing and butchering process.

The advice continues under the heading of "Cooking," and we read that, "Before cooking meat from the smoke-house, soak the pieces overnight in clear water. If you kept them in brine, simply cook without adding salt." The advice continues that, "For steaks from the smoke-house or brine, slice into pieces a half inch thick, four inches long, and three inches wide. In a skillet, brown in butter and simmer until tender depending on the tough-ness of the meat." More advice interested us because we had been shaping our meat with a meat hammer for years and *Foxfire* stated that, "One woman told us to pound the steak, and soak it for an hour in a mixture of a half cup vinegar, one cup water, and a teaspoon of salt (for two pounds of steak). Remove from the liquid, dry, and roll in about a cup of flour. Season with salt, pepper, and garlic salt, and brown in shortening at a high heat. Cover, and simmer at a low heat for forty-five to sixty minutes."

Hunting the Hard Way

I believe that just about every bowhunter will want to read something by Howard Hill or something about Howard Hill, and there are a number of writings which we can turn to. *Hunting the Hard Way* is one such book. I feel that Howard Hill is a great part of the American deer hunting tradition, and this particular book is quite clear on the subject of hunting deer with the bow. In fact, Chapter 10 is devoted to the subject and Chapter 11 is Part Two on the same subject.

Hill begins Chapter 10 by saying, "Of all the American animals the deer is the most beautiful as well as one of the most useful. Deer have been of great help to mankind down through the ages. Their meat sustained the lives of millions long before domestic animals were raised for food." (p. 131 of the Jerry Hill edition) Actually, every chapter of this book can help the deer hunter interested in bagging a buck with a bow, especially the longbow. But in chapters 10 and 11, Mr. Hill tells about his own deer hunting experience and he does so very clearly.

Howard Hill is a part of the American bowhunting tradition and his books, *Wild Adventure* and *Hunting the Hard Way* are well worth looking into. Sometimes the local library will carry copies of these books. Nephew Jerry Hill, a fine archer in his own right, has offered

Hunting the Hard Way in reprint form. At this time, many longbow enthusiasts are hoping Jerry Hill will think about offering *Wild Adventure* in reprint as well. As we have stated more than once, Howard Hill and his type of hunting are a very strong part of the American bowhunting tradition and there is tremendous reward in hunting his way.

The Thompsons

One is not likely to find much on the Thompsons, but both Maurice and Will were very instrumental in bringing about a rebirth of archery in this country. I believe that Maurice was more the writer, and I have been told that after the Civil War Maurice and Will entered into archery because they were not allowed hunting rifles where they wanted to hunt. I do not offer this last statement as hard fact. It is from an old document, based upon secondary sources and surely third-hand as information now, but nonetheless could be true.

I have found a long-out-of-print work of Maurice Thompson which I felt to be a strong part of our American hunting tradition. It is called "Bow-Shooting," and it includes the raw basics on handling the longbow. There are neat illustrations of arrows and tackle in general. The bow was, of course, the traditional longbow of English design (primarily). At the time Maurice Thompson wrote his long article, one could purchase some bow and arrow equipment, and Maurice gives advice on this subject. However, Maurice was mainly instructing the new archer in the making of his own equipment. Apparently, there was not much over-the-counter bowhunting gear available at the time.

If one can turn over some writing by the Thompsons, he will find that writing to be interesting. If one wants to make bows, he's probably interested in the old-time data all right, but had best look to Howard Hill's work for advice. In the main, I suggest buying a bow crafted by one of the better bowyers in the business if one should become interested in the English style longbow. These are not going to be self-bows. They will be laminated bows of sophisticated style and fine handling/shooting properties.

Fred Bear

Another tradition in archery is Fred Bear. Fred's *The Archer's Bible* has good basic information for the bowhunter. This is a Doubleday book and still generally available from the bookstore, I am told. Chapter 10 of this book speaks to big game hunting in general, and Fred talks about deer hunting here. He also mentions *The Witchery of Archery* as a good book. This book was written in 1877, and is a collection of Maurice Thompson's writing. In fact, as I re-read parts of this book, I came across a second documentation on Thompson's situation as to firearms ownership. Fred Bear says, on page 92, "The revival of bowhunting as a popular sport in America was due in a large part to four men. The first of these were Maurice and Will Thompson, brothers who fought for the South in the Civil War. At the war's end they returned to their plantation only to find it in ruins. Maurice had been severely wounded in the fighting and was advised by his doctor to live in the open air if possible. The brothers had no means of livelihood and, as ex-Confederates, firearms were denied them. They took to the woods, where they lived chiefly on game killed with bows and arrows which they had learned to make and use in their youth.''

Bear goes on to name Dr. Saxton Pope and Arthur Young as two more greats in the revival of bowhunting and in this we must also include Ishi, the last Yana Indian of California, who taught both Pope and Young about bows and about bowhunting. One may wish to locate and read Dr. Pope's book *Hunting with the Bow and Arrow,* which stimulated many archers of the day and still offers good advice to our modern archers.

But back to Fred Bear. Bear helped to popularize bowhunting to a great degree, and much of his advice, I think, will always hold up. In reading into the book mentioned above, Bear says, on page 95, "The second point is remembering to pick a certain spot on the animal at which to aim. Nine out of every ten deer shot at and missed by archers are missed simply because the hunter shot at the entire animal instead of concentrating on a tiny spot in the most vital area." I believe this is true of firearms deer hunting in some cases as well, and it is certainly good advice from a hunter who knows what he is talking about.

Charles Hallock in 1879

I enjoy thinking about deer hunting when I am not deer hunting and sometimes it is a great deal of fun to go back in time and look at the older viewpoints. Charles Hallock's book, *Sportman's Gazetteer,* dating back to 1879, is one such writing. Here is what Mr. Hallock had to say about mule deer:

When shot at in the forest, they retreat at a furious rate, often falling over prostrate tree trunks, and crashing through thickets, making the dead sticks crack and fly in every direction. They sometimes charge directly toward the hunter. The scent of the Mule Deer is very keen, and it is useless to hunt them to 'leeward,' as they will smell the approaching hunter, and bound away long before he is near enough to sight them. They are remarkably sharp sighted, and are constantly on the lookout for danger, particularly the does when they have their young with them. (p. 77)

Mr. Hallock also speaks briefly on the Black Tailed Deer, as well as the Virginia Deer, as he calls the two. Here are some remarks on the first.

The Black Tailed Deer is a Pacific Coast species which does not, apparently, extend its range much east of the Sierra Nevada Mountains. Its favorite haunts are among the dense forests of redwoods which clothe the sides of these mountains in Oregon and California. Further south it frequents the dense thickets of chapparal and manzanita which cover the hillsides, and through which it is quite impossible for a man to force his way. To these thickets the deer betake themselves when wounded, and in such cases are sure to be lost. (p. 78)

About the whitetail, Mr. Hallock says much, to include some commentary by a Scotch hunter. Hallock says "An eminent Scotch writer and hunter, whose kindred excel in deer-stalking, designates the qualities requisite for success in this method [still hunting] of hunting, as follows:"

It may readily be supposed, that for the pursuit of deer-stalking a hardy frame and plenty of pluck are required. These qualities are indispensably necessary; but in the other points he may carry as much as the average of men are seen to do. The model deer-stalker, however, should be of good proportions, moderately tall, narrow-hipped to give speed, and with powerful loins and well-developed chest for giving endurance and wind. No amount of fat should be allowed; indeed, the deer-stalker ought to be in as good training as the race-horse and greyhound. (p. 85)

Well, so much for me. I am happy that this 19th century writer did begin his discourse stating that a person *might* get by if he happened to be less well built than a race horse or a greyhound. One can see that a brief glance into the old-time tradition of the hunt is worth a little time and effort. There truly is a lot to learn from the traditions established by our deer hunters in this country of ours.